English Alive!

Nelson Thornes Caribbean English

for CSEC

Alan Etherton
Thelma Baker
Joyce Jonas
Judith Pereira

Nelson Thornes

Acknowledgements

The author and publishers are grateful to all the staff and students involved in sampling *English Alive!*, in particular Dianne Boyd at the Convent of Mercy Academy 'Alpha', Merlyn Taylor-Cox at Haile Selassie High School and Shawna Henry at St Hugh's High School, Kingston, Jamaica. Thanks also to Vishnu Gosine, Couva, Trinidad.

The author and publishers would like to thank the following for permission to reproduce copyright material:

Photos:

Corel 286 (NT) pp58, 116 and 179; Corel 448 p351; Cover image Tropical band by Leon Zernitsky/Images.com/Corbis; Sophie Kelly p217; Photodisc 10 (NT) p164; NT/Colin Babb pp41, 54, 72, 87, 102, 103, 164, 261, 290, 291.

Extracts and poems:

I Shall Return by Claude McKay. Courtesy of the Literary Representative for the Works of Claude McKay, Schomburg Center for Research in Black Culture, The New York Public Library, Astor, Lennox and Tilden Foundations; *The Land* by the Hon. Victoria Sackville-West; *Bajan Entertainment*. This extract is taken, with permission, from *The Rough Guide to Barbados*, published in 2001, by Rough Guide Ltd; *To Sir with Love* by E.R. Braithwaite; *The Chrysalids* by John Wyndham. Taken from the Penguin edition; *The Grapes of Wrath* by John Steinbeck. Copyright ©1939 by John Steinbeck. Reprinted with the permission of McIntosh and Otis, Inc; *The Woman Speaks to the Man Who Has Employed Her Son* from *Selected Poems*, by Lorna Goodison (Ann Arbor: The University of Michigan Press, 1993); *Rebecca* by Daphne Du Maurier. Reproduced with permission of Curtis Brown Ltd, London on behalf of The Chichester Partnership. Copyright Daphne Du Maurier Browning 1938; *Scarce Resource, How Could We?* and *I Ain't Turnin' Back* from *Still Standing* by Michael C. Pintard published by Congo Town Ltd 1995.

Every effort has been made to contact copyright holders and the publishers apologise to anyone whose rights have been inadvertently overlooked and will be happy to rectify any errors or omissions. We have been unable to trace the copyright holders of the following extracts and poems:

Husks by Anthony McNeill; *Carrion Crows* by A.J. Seymour; *Alvin Curling's Achievement* from *The Sunday Gleaner*; *Roman Holiday* by Frank Collymore; *Yussouf* by J.R. Lowell; *A Cure for Serpents* by Antonio Denti di Pirajno; *Day's End* by Frank Collymore; *Lost Trail* by F. Cunynghame; *Fuss-pot* by Ian McDonald; *Country* from *L'oubli* by E.McG. Keane; *Too Soon It Was My Allotted Task* by Edward Anthony Watson © BIM Magazine, Barbados; *From Pillar to Post* by Laurin Zilliacus; *The Conquest of Disease* by Cedric Dover in *The Scientist and You* edited by Maurice Goldsmith; *This is a Hymn* by Lorna Goodison; *Dives* by Edward Braithwaite; *The Woman Speaks to the Man Who Has Employed Her Son* by Lorna Goodison; *The Dragon Can't Dance* by Earl Lovelace; *The Castle* by Mervyn Morris; *The Fringe of the Sea* by A.L. Hendriks; *A Fairy Tale* by Anson Gonzalez; *The Despairing Lover* by William Walsh from *The Dragon Book of Verse*, Book II; *The Washerwoman* by Owen Campbell.

English Alive!

Contents

Introduction		xii

Unit 1 *Grandma* — page 1

1.1/3	Reading comprehension	1
1.4	Vocabulary: meaning in context	3
1.5	Handwriting	4
1.6	Answering multiple-choice vocabulary questions	6
1.7	The appreciation of poetry	9
1.8	Enjoying poetry: 'Husks'; 'Carrion Crows'	11
1.9	Writing: argumentative or factual topics	13

Unit 2 *They Have Done Well* — 14

2.1/3	Reading comprehension	14
2.4	Vocabulary: meaning in context	16
2.5	Paragraphing (review)	17
2.6	Making a summary	18
2.7	Punctuating dialogue	21
2.8	The Simple Present tense (active)	22
2.9	Asking questions	24
2.10	Enjoying poetry: 'Roman Holiday'	25
2.11	Writing: a story or giving advice	27

Unit 3 *Who Told the Truth?* — 28

3.1/3	Reading comprehension	28
3.4	Vocabulary: meaning in context	30
3.5	Antonyms	32
3.6	Making summaries	33
3.7	Problems of agreement	34
3.8	Spelling: a review of some basic guidelines	35
3.9	Enjoying poetry: 'Yussouf'	36
3.10	Writing about a picture of a person	38

Unit 4 *The Sting* — 42

4.1/3	Reading comprehension	42
4.4	Vocabulary: meaning in context	45
4.5	Writing: finding a plot	46
4.6	Writing: making a summary	47
4.7	Writing a story (review)	47
4.8	Writing: starting a story	49
4.9	Setting out dialogue	50
4.10	Two warnings	51
4.11	Enjoying poetry: sonnets 'Sonnet 71'; 'I Shall Return'	51
4.12	Writing: test – SSS and SAD	53
4.13	Writing a story: pictures and given words	54

Unit 5 *Tourism* — 55

5.1	Writing: straight and crooked thinking	55
5.2/3	Reading comprehension	57
5.4	Vocabulary: meaning in context	59
5.5	Writing: summary practice	60
5.6	Grammar: phrases and clauses (revision)	61
5.7	Spelling: prefixes	63
5.8	Making comparisons: using pie charts	64
5.9	Writing: the good and the bad	65
5.10	Enjoying poetry: 'The Seven Ages of Man'	68
5.11	Argumentative writing	70
5.12	Writing: stories or an argumentative topic	72

Unit 6 *Crossing the Line* — 73

6.1–3	Reading comprehension	73
6.4	Vocabulary: meaning in context	76
6.5	Comprehension: looking for clues to meaning	78
6.6	Topic vocabulary: a hospital	79
6.7	Writing skills: telling a story	81
6.8	Writing: setting out dialogue	83
6.9	Expressing sentences in a different way	83
6.10/11	Enjoying poetry: 'Day's End'	84
6.12	Writing: stories or an argumentative topic	87

Unit 7 *Drama* 88

7.1/3	Reading comprehension: acting	88
7.4	Vocabulary: meaning in context	92
7.5	Discussion: drama	93
7.6	Grammar: the Present Continuous tense (revision)	93
7.7	Punctuation (1): using a full stop	95
7.8	Punctuation (2): review exercises	96
7.9	Grammar: using the right possessive adjective	97
7.10	Grammar: using prepositions	98
7.11	A Short Story	99
7.12	Understanding and vocabulary	101
7.14	Writing stories or an argumentative topic	102

Unit 8 *Gold!* 104

8.1/4	Reading comprehension	104
8.5	Vocabulary: meaning in context	108
8.6	Say it another way	110
8.7/8	Grammar: using the Simple Past tense: active and passive	111
8.9	Enjoying poetry: 'Fuss-pot'	114
8.10	Writing: stories or a controversial topic	116

Unit 9 *City of the Future?* 117

9.1/3	Reading comprehension	117
9.4/5	Vocabulary: meaning in context	120
9.6	Writing: summary	122
9.7	Say it another way	124
9.8	Vocabulary: what's the difference?	125
9.9	Writing about proverbs	125
9.10	Writing: making up a plot for a story (review)	128
9.11	Writing: a story or argumentative topics	131

Unit 10 *Bajan Entertainment* 132

10.1/3	Reading comprehension	132
10.4	Vocabulary: meaning in context	134
10.5	Writing: straight and crooked thinking	136
10.6	Discussion	137

10.7	Grammar: common errors	138
10.8	Grammar: reflexive and emphatic pronouns (revision)	139
10.9/10	Writing a factual account	141
10.11	Writing: choice of factual topics	146
10.12	Enjoying poetry: 'Country'; 'The Death of Lancelot'	146

Unit 11 O'Hare 150

11.1/3	Reading comprehension	150
11.4	Vocabulary: meaning in context	152
11.5	Vocabulary	153
11.6	Grammar: relative pronouns (1)	154
11.7	Grammar: defining and non-defining clauses	155
11.8	Grammar: relative pronouns (2)	157
11.9	Punctuation and setting out dialogue	158
11.10/14	Speaking and listening: debating	159
11.15	Enjoying poetry: 'Too Soon It Was My Allotted Task'	163
11.16	Writing: stories or a speech	164

Unit 12 The Penny Post 165

12.1/3	Reading comprehension	165
12.4	Vocabulary: meaning in context	168
12.5	A cloze passage	169
12.6	Vocabulary: idioms	170
12.7	Grammar: inversion of subject and verb	170
12.8	Grammar: correcting errors	172
12.9/10	Grammar: relative pronouns (3), (4)	173
12.11	Grammar: synthesis	175
12.12	Writing: a simple report	176
12.13/14	Writing: starting and ending a composition	177
12.15	Writing: stories or an expository topic	179

Unit 13 Louis Pasteur 180

13.1/2	Reading comprehension	180
13.3	Vocabulary: meaning in context	185
13.4	Vocabulary practice	186
13.5	Writing: summaries – good and bad	187
13.6	Writing: rules and regulations	189

13.7	Grammar: prepositions	191
13.8	Grammar: using the Present Perfect tense (revision)	193
13.9	Enjoying poetry: 'This is a Hymn'	195
13.10	Writing: a variety of topics	197

Unit 14 *AIDS* — 198

14.1/3	Reading comprehension	198
14.4	Vocabulary: meaning in context	201
14.5	Vocabulary practice	202
14.6	Vocabulary: problem words	203
14.7	Writing a speech of thanks	204
14.8	Writing a letter	205
14.9	Equivalent (similar) sentences	205
14.10	Grammar: the Past Perfect tense	207
14.11	Punctuation: using an apostrophe (revision)	209
14.12	Enjoying poetry: 'Dives'	210
14.13	Writing: a variety of topics	212

Unit 15 *Moving On* — 213

15.1/3	Reading comprehension	213
15.4	Vocabulary: meaning in context	216
15.5	Writing: style	217
15.6	Vocabulary practice	218
15.7	Vocabulary: problem words	219
15.8	Grammar: reporting orders and requests (revision)	221
15.9	Grammar: reporting statements (revision)	222
15.10/11	Grammar: indirect questions	224
15.12	Writing: summary	226
15.13	Enjoying poetry: 'The Woman Speaks to the Man . . .'	227
15.14	Writing: a variety of topics	229

Unit 16 *People* — 230

16.1/2/4	Reading comprehension	230
16.3	Writing: starting a story	231
16.5	Vocabulary: meaning in context	233
16.6	Vocabulary practice	234
16.7	Vocabulary: problem words	235

Contents vii

16.8	Writing: composition length – a reminder	236
16.9	Writing: descriptions of people in a short story	236
16.10	Writing: different attitudes	237
16.11	Writing: what does 'describe' mean?	239
16.12	Writing: describing people – a checklist	240
16.13	Writing: significant detail	241
16.14	Enjoying poetry: 'Scarce Resource'	243
16.15	Writing: a variety of topics	245

Unit 17 *Rebecca* 246

17.1/3	Reading comprehension	246
17.4	A writer's skill (1)	249
17.5	Vocabulary: meaning in context	249
17.6	A writer's skill (2)	250
17.7	Writing: describing places	251
17.8	Writing: arranging ideas	253
17.9	Spelling	254
17.10	Punctuation: using a question mark (revision)	254
17.11	Grammar: giving advice	255
17.12	Grammar: asking questions	256
17.13	Is it similar?	258
17.14	Enjoying poetry: 'The Castle'	260
17.15	Writing: a variety of topics	261

Unit 18 *Letters to the Editor* 262

18.1/3	Reading comprehension	262
18.4	Vocabulary: meaning in context	264
18.5	Vocabulary practice	265
18.6	Vocabulary: problem words	267
18.7	Answering comprehension questions	268
18.8	Writing: making a summary	270
18.9	Slander and libel	271
18.10	Writing: making a complaint	271
18.11	Is it similar?	273
18.12	Enjoying poetry: 'The Fringe of the Sea'	275
18.13	Writing: a variety of topics	276

Unit 19 *In Court* — 277

19.1/3	Reading comprehension	277
19.4	Vocabulary: meaning in context	279
19.5	Vocabulary: proverbs and sayings (revision)	281
19.6	Grammar: conditional sentences (1)	282
19.7	Grammar: what's wrong?	285
19.8	A cloze passage	286
19.9	Grammar: conditional sentences (2)	287
19.10	Enjoying poetry: 'A Fairy Tale'	289
19.11	Writing: a variety of topics	290

Unit 20 *English in Business (1)* — 292

20.1/3	Reading comprehension	292
20.4	Vocabulary: meaning in context	295
20.5/6	Vocabulary: business expressions	296
20.7	Using the internet: email	297
20.8	Writing: making a summary	298
20.9	Using the internet: writing an email to a friend	298
20.10	Using the internet to obtain information	299
20.11	Writing business letters: basic points	299
20.12	Writing business letters: layout	300
20.13	Writing business letters: ordering goods	301
20.14	Writing business letters: asking for further information	302
20.15	Writing business letters: making an enquiry	304

Unit 21 *English in Business (2)* — 306

21.1	Memos	306
21.2/4	Reading comprehension	307
21.5	Vocabulary: meaning in context	311
21.6	Vocabulary: problem words	312
21.7	Writing reports	313
21.8	Punctuation practice	318
21.9	Enjoying poetry: 'The Despairing Lover'	320
21.10	Writing: a variety of topics	321

Unit 22 *History?* 322

22.1/3	Reading comprehension	322
22.4	Vocabulary: meaning in context	325
22.5	Vocabulary: what's the difference?	326
22.6	Vocabulary: definitions	327
22.7	Grammar: future actions (revision)	328
22.8	Public relations work	330
22.9	A cloze passage	332
22.10	Say it another way	333
22.11	Enjoying poetry: two poems by Michael C. Pintard	334
22.12	Writing: a variety of topics	336

Unit 23 *Reporting the News* 337

23.1/2	Reading comprehension	337
23.3	Vocabulary: meaning in context	340
23.4	Vocabulary: expressions using 'take'	341
23.5	Vocabulary: from the newspapers	343
23.6	Writing: making a summary	343
23.7	Writing	345
23.8	Say it another way	345
23.9	Grammar: 'a', 'an', 'the' (revision)	346
23.10	Grammar: using participles	347
23.11	Grammar: making comparisons	348
23.12	Enjoying poetry: 'The Washerwomen'	349
23.13	Writing: a variety of topics	350

Unit 24 *The Persuaders* 352

24.1/2	Reading comprehension	352
24.3	Vocabulary: meaning in context	356
24.4	Vocabulary: prefixes	357
24.5	Discussion: advertising	358
24.6	Understanding graphs	359
24.7/9	Meetings: convening, agenda and the Minutes	360
24.10	Discussion	365
24.11	Writing: a variety of topics	366
24.12	Grammar: using gerunds	366

Contents

Unit 25 *Offences* — 369

25.1/3	Reading comprehension	369
25.4	Vocabulary: meaning in context	372
25.5	Vocabulary practice	373
25.6	Grammar: infinitives (revision)	377
25.7	Writing: setting out dialogue (revision)	379
25.8	Writing: plotting practice (revision)	380
25.9	Writing: a variety of topics	381

Unit 26 *Applying for a Job* — 382

26.1	Preparing to apply for a job	382
26.2	Check these points	382
26.3	Preparing a curriculum vitae	383
26.4	Sending a covering letter with your CV	384
26.5	Discussion: work methods	386
26.6	Grammar: using perfect infinitives	386
26.7	Spelling	389
26.8/9	Grammar: prepositions	390
26.10	Say it another way	393

Appendix 1:	All About Verbs	395
Appendix 2:	The Main Uses of Tenses	399
Appendix 3:	Irregular Verbs – Principal Parts	404
Appendix 4:	Glossary of Language Words	409
Appendix 5:	Glossary of Literary Terms	415
Appendix 6:	Problem Words	421

Index — 434

Introduction

English Alive! for CSEC has been written with three main aims:

- to help students to do well in their school and CSEC examinations
- to help students to become increasingly accurate, perceptive and sensitive when they make or receive communications in English
- to present a moral purpose common to all major religions where that is possible.

The course is meant to be student-friendly and teacher-friendly. It has been developed as a pan-Caribbean series and supports English learning across the region, leading to the CSEC examinations. In this book the main emphases are on the following basic areas.

Reading comprehension

In addition to a variety of prose passages, this section includes the understanding and appreciation of poetry. The poems have been chosen to encourage students to develop a positive attitude to the appreciation of poetry and to illustrate a wide range of styles and topics. As in previous books in this series, the emphasis is firmly on enjoying poetry, but greater attention is paid to the various stylistic devices which poets can use.

Questions on reading passages include ones set in multiple-choice and free-response form and cover a number of reading skills listed in the various syllabuses. When possible, the skills of writers are studied to see how a particular effect is achieved by an author.

Vocabulary

The emphasis here is not only on understanding meaning in context but on the development of vocabulary and on the way in which individual words contribute to the enjoyment of the reader and/or to the fulfilment of the author's aim. In addition, there is considerable work on such areas as antonyms, synonyms, idioms, proverbs, affixes and words known to cause problems at this level.

Grammar

Teachers are free to decide how much formal grammar they feel is appropriate for their students and helpful to them. The aim throughout the series is to provide students with an understanding of the basics of grammar, e.g. the parts of speech, sentence construction and the correct use of tenses, pronouns, etc. These elements should provide a foundation for subsequent work on correct usage. A great deal of the work on grammar is based on error analysis at this level, i.e. in addition to providing a clear guide to usage, the grammar sections deal with problems which are known to exist at Form 5 (or Grade 11) level.

Writing

This area includes work on paragraphs, informal and formal summaries, reports, statements, spelling and punctuation. It also provides a wide range of composition topics (often related to a theme or passage in the unit) to give students practice in various types of written work. As far as possible, interesting topics have been chosen to act as a stimulus for the writer.

Throughout the book, students are introduced to specific writing skills and there is particular emphasis on the techniques involved in writing a short story.

A **Teacher's Guide** is available on the internet at www.nelsonthornes.com/international or in hard copy from your local agent. The Guide contains answers, helpful suggestions and scripts for use in listening practice work.

1 Grandma

1.1 Pre-reading

Read the passage in 1.2 and say whether you agree with Grandma's advice to Deena.

- Does any of her advice apply to you?

- How can what a person does in a year and a half decide how the person will live in the following 50 or 60 years?

1.2 Reading

Grandma

As I walked downstairs from my room, I was trying to decide what to do: stroll across the road to my friend's house and have a chat, watch one of my favourite programmes on television or start my English homework, which entailed writing about a picture of a boy. I had no idea what to say about the inoffensive boy, so I
5   was not keen to start my homework. I felt that if I could defer it for an hour or two inspiration might come somehow.

    I hesitated and walked towards the television set. Then I noticed Grandma. She was sitting in a corner in her favourite chair, apparently sewing peacefully. I should have known better. Grandma rarely did anything peacefully.

10   'Deena!' she said suddenly. 'It's time for us to have a little chat. Have a seat.'
    This was a summons I would not dare to ignore. I sat down, knowing that my trip to my friend's house had just been cancelled.

    'So now you're in Form 4,' Grandma started. 'That's good but there are one or two things I want to talk to you about.'

15   I wondered if I had done something wrong, so I kept quiet.

    'I'm old now,' Grandma continued, 'and sometimes when I look back over my life there are things I wish I'd done differently. My time at school is one of them. I had only one chance and I didn't make the most of it. I don't want you to make the same mistake. What you do during the next year and a half will decide how you live
20   for the next fifty or sixty years. Just think about that.'

    I thought for a moment and began to see that Grandma was probably right.

    'You just get this one chance,' she said, 'so make the most of it. I wish somebody had explained that to me. Put all your energy into your work for the next year and a half. Do the best you can – all the time. Don't dodge off. Don't find

25 excuses for slacking. Never mind gossiping, watching TV, going out with your friends – female or male. Concentrate on your work. Work hard. You'll get your reward later on. You'll be driving a car while others are riding a bicycle or pushing a cart in the rain. It's your choice. Do you understand?'

'Yes, Grannie. I understand,' I assured her.

30 'Do you agree with me: yes or no?' Grandma demanded, fixing me with a look which had kept my father under control for many years.

'I agree. I agree,' I said hastily. 'Thank you for thinking about me.'

I waited to see if Grandma had finished but she took a deep breath and continued.

35 'And there's another thing I want to tell you. You're pretty – a beautiful young lady in fact. All the boys will be chasing after you. Sooner or later, you'll fall in love …'

I felt slightly embarrassed and wondered if she was going to give me a lecture on the facts of life.

Grandma misinterpreted my silence. 'Ah!' she said. 'So you're in love already!'

40 'No! No! Not at all,' I said hurriedly. 'Definitely not. I want to have a successful career.'

Grandma smiled. 'Good girl,' she said. 'That's the way to think but I'll tell you anyway, just in case. Eventually, you'll fall in love but something may go wrong. You'll think your heart has been broken permanently. Don't worry. It will heal

45 within a few weeks. The second time you have boyfriend trouble, your heart will recover within a few days. The third time, it will heal in a few hours. So don't think a broken heart is anything very serious. And when you do find a possible boyfriend, go for strength of character – not for muscles or a pretty face. On the whole, men are about as trustworthy as snakes but there are a few good ones about. Watch out

50 for them but don't start looking for the next few years.'

I was too surprised by Grandma's lecture to make much of a reply.

'Do you understand me?' Grandma asked. 'Do you agree: yes or no?'

'Yes. Yes. I really do understand and I think I agree,' I said. 'Thank you again.'

I gave Grandma a kiss and then sat down to start my homework and digest what

55 she had said. I thought about it in bed later and decided that Grandma was right. I told her so the next day. That was the first time I had seen any sign of a tear in her eyes.

1.3
Understanding

A Choose the most appropriate answer each time.

1. When Deena left her room to go downstairs, she ____.
    A. had decided to do her homework
    B. had decided to watch television
    C. had not yet decided what to do
    D. wanted to speak to her grandmother

2. In line 5, 'it' refers to ____.
    A. the inspiration
    B. Deena's homework
    C. a television programme
    D. deciding what to do

3. What should Deena 'have known better'? (lines 8–9) She should have known that ____.
   A. Grandma was not really sewing at all
   B. her grandmother was not in a good mood
   C. Grandma was not really asleep
   D. her grandmother had not settled down peacefully

4. In line 11, 'summons' is used with the meaning '____'.
   A. command   B. request   C. invitation   D. suggestion

5. In lines 11 and 12, what made Deena think that she would not go and visit her friend that day?
   A. Her grandmother would stop her from going out.
   B. She preferred to stay at home and watch a film on television.
   C. She expected the conversation with her grandmother to last some time.
   D. She expected her grandmother to prevent her from watching television.

B Answer these questions about the passage.
   1. What was the 'same mistake' which Grandma mentioned in line 19?
   2. What can we infer about Grandma by the fact that she mentioned a mistake?
   3. In line 25, what is the meaning of 'Never mind'?
   4. What was Grandma's purpose in mentioning broken hearts to Deena?
   5. Suggest a reason why there was a tear in Grandma's eye (in line 56).

1.4
Vocabulary: meaning in context

Choose the word(s) which best show(s) the meaning of the underlined words as they are used in the passage in 1.2.

1. my English homework, which <u>entailed</u> writing about a picture of a boy (line 3)
   A. prevented   B. presented   C. involved   D. suggested

2. I had no idea what to say about the <u>inoffensive</u> boy (line 4)
   A. weak-looking   B. harmless   C. wretched   D. very poor

3. I could <u>defer</u> it for an hour or two (line 5)
   A. consider   B. study   C. cancel   D. postpone

4. <u>inspiration</u> might come somehow (line 6)
   A. an idea   B. relief   C. bravery   D. an escape

5. She was ... <u>apparently</u> sewing peacefully (line 8)
   A. obviously   B. happily   C. clearly   D. as far as one could tell

6. Don't <u>dodge off</u>. (line 24)
   A. allow your standard to decline
   B. copy from other students
   C. try to avoid doing whatever you should be doing
   D. pretend that the work is too difficult for you

7. Don't find excuses for <u>slacking</u>. (line 25)
   A. being lazy   B. copying   C. fighting   D. staying at home

8. <u>Concentrate on</u> your work. (line 26)
   A. settle down on
   B. pay a lot of attention to
   C. work more slowly but accurately on
   D. try not to forget to do

9. Grandma <u>misinterpreted</u> my silence. (line 39)
   A. misunderstood
   B. ignored
   C. paid no attention to
   D. showed no sympathy for

10. your heart has been broken <u>permanently</u> (line 44)
    A. seriously   B. for ever   C. fatally   D. unexpectedly

11. It will <u>heal</u> within a few weeks. (line 44)
    A. grow bigger
    B. fade away
    C. last
    D. become better

12. <u>digest</u> what she had said (line 54)
    A. think about and fully comprehend
    B. deal with in my stomach
    C. find fault with
    D. take out the good points

1.5 Handwriting

Imagine this situation: you are about to take part in a 100 metres race. All the competitors are on their marks and ready to start. Then somebody comes up behind you and fastens a 20 kg weight to your right ankle. The starter fires his gun. The race starts. You don't have a chance with a 20 kg weight on your ankle. You are last.

The previous paragraph is symbolic. The 'race' is an examination such as the CSEC examination. The 20 kg weight is bad handwriting. If *your* handwriting is difficult for an examiner to read, you have very little (or no) chance of doing well – in English or in other subjects. There are two reasons for this:

- An examiner cannot give high marks to *every* candidate. Some students will get low marks and some will fail. Bad handwriting suggests that a student is discourteous and/or lazy. This is the type of student who is most likely to fail.
- If a student's handwriting is difficult to read, an examiner will have to slow down when reading a composition, summary or report. By the time the examiner reaches line 4 or 5, he or she will probably have forgotten what the student wrote in lines 1–3. Then it is very difficult for an examiner to assess the value of the student's work. The result is a low mark.

Observe the following guidelines in your school work and in an examination.

Guidelines for handwriting

1. If possible, use black or dark blue ink. It is easier to read than light blue ink.

2. Don't write too quickly. Take your time and *form each letter correctly*:
   - Don't make 'd' look like 'cl'.
   - Don't make an 'e' look like an 'i'.
   - Check that your letters 'u', 'v', 'm' and 'n' are clearly different.
   - Cross the letter 't'.
   - Put a dot above a small letter 'i'.
   - Don't put long tails on letters such as 'g', 'f', 'p' and 'y'. They may interfere with words on the next line.
   - Make capital letters twice as big as small letters so that a reader can see where a new sentence starts.

3. Use clear and correct punctuation marks. Make your full stops clear but don't use tiny circles. Use dots.

4. Don't make your handwriting too small, like this. It is difficult to read and will annoy your reader. This is written in Mistral font. You can find it on your computer. Don't imitate it.

5. Don't squeeze the letters of each word up like this. If you look for Onyx font on your computer, this is what you will find. Leave more space between letters. Leave sufficient space between words.

Unit 1 · *Grandma*

Practice

1. Copy as much of the following passage as you can write in exactly *two minutes*. Use your normal handwriting.

   ```
   Polar bears are large white bears weighing as much as 750 kg.
   They live mainly on seals and walruses. During the summer
   months, many of the bears follow the seals southwards. When
   winter comes, they return to the north. They know that seals
   like to lie on floating ice floes, and that is where the bears
   find their food. A polar bear is a highly dangerous and
   unpredictable animal. When hungry, it can smash its way into a
   wooden house in seconds. One blow from a paw can crush a man's
   skull, and the bear can run much faster than any man.
   ```

2. At the end of two minutes, stop writing.
   a) Count the number of words you have written. Divide by two. Write down the number of words you have written in each minute. We need that number later on in this book.
   b) Show your writing to at least two other students. Ask them to write comments on it, e.g.
      Very good   Good   Not easy to read   Difficult to read.
      Ask them to circle letters which are *not* formed correctly.
   c) Do the same for at least two students in class.
   d) If your classmates have criticised your handwriting, try to improve it in future. Make sure that you don't have a 20 kg weight fastened to your ankle when you take the CSEC examination!

1.6 Answering multiple-choice vocabulary questions

In the CSEC examination, you may have to answer multiple-choice questions about vocabulary. Here is an example:

Choose the best word(s) to complete each sentence.
The Government grant will go a long way to _____ the hardship caused by severe flooding of the Western district of the capital.

A) enhance   C) mitigate
B) endure   D) elucidate

A◯   B◯   C◯   D◯

Guidelines for multiple-choice vocabulary questions in an examination

1. You need to take into the examination hall at least two 2B or 3B pencils and two erasers.

2. Look for clues within the question and in the answers. A Government will not want to *increase* hardship, so answer (A) is wrong because 'enhance' means 'make greater'. Answer (B) must be wrong because it is the people who will endure hardship, not the Government or its grant. Answer (D) means 'make clear' and is unsuitable because the hardship will already be clear if it is caused by flooding.

3. If three of the four answers are wrong, the answer must be the fourth one – even if you do not know that 'mitigate' means 'lessen' or 'make less severe'.

4. If you have to give an **antonym** (or a word most nearly opposite) do not choose an answer which is a *synonym* (a word of *similar* meaning).

5. Perhaps you do not know the meaning of 'mitigate' and 'elucidate', so you cannot decide whether (C) or (D) is the right word to use. Then you can use this technique:
   a) Put a small pencilled cross by the answers that seem *wrong*, i.e. (A) and (B) in this case.
   b) Go on to the next question. When you have answered all the questions you can, go back to unanswered ones. In this example, perhaps you think that the answer is either (C) or (D). Look at the sequence of answers to questions before and after this question. Let us say that this question is number 5. You may see that your answers to other questions give this sequence:

   1. B   2. A   3. D   4. D   5. ??   6. A   7. B   8. A
   Then the answer to question 5 is more likely to be C than D. We can blacken the space for C.

Remember: It is better to make a sensible guess than to leave the question unanswered.

No answer = no mark. Even a hurried guess is better than no answer.

Unit 1 · Grandma   7

Over to you!

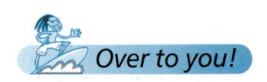

To answer this type of question, you usually have to blacken the space containing the letter of the best answer. In Exercises 1 and 2, find the best answer.

Exercise 1

Choose the best word(s) to complete each sentence.

1. The word 'homicide' is ____ from two Latin words.
   A. descended   B. deprived   C. derived   D. defied

2. An increase in bus ____ will ____ poor people.
   A. fees … effect
   B. fares … affect
   C. fees … affect
   D. fares … effect

3. One of the first things to do at a meeting is to check the ____ of the last meeting to see if they are an accurate record.
   A. results   B. items   C. seconds   D. minutes

4. The number of students in this school has ____ to over 2,000.
   A. raised   B. increased   C. grew   D. become

5. Quite a few people ____ rice to bread.
   A. prefer   B. like   C. love   D. eat

6. The security guards at the factory were very efficient and ____ the robber from escaping.
   A. retained   B. avoided   C. rejected   D. prevented

7. The detective was ____ for catching a man trying to deal in heroin.
   A. awarded   B. praised   C. prized   D. promote

8. Daljit was late in paying the third ____ on his car, so the firm sent him a ____.
   A. settlement … invoice
   B. debt … remainder
   C. premium … bill
   D. instalment … reminder

9. I don't know how Leela puts ____ with her brother. He is spoilt and selfish.
   A. up   B. down   C. away   D. off

10. The company has failed to make a profit in the past year, so there is a ____ in its accounts.
    A. whole   B. deficit   C. profit   D. lost

11. A major hurricane is approaching, but we have had plenty of warning and are all ____ for the onslaught.
    A. braced   B. prepare   C. hardened   D. equip

12. When our team scored the winning goal, there was chaos for a few moments, with spectators trying to rush onto the field but the stewards were very efficient and soon ____ order.
    A. made   B. did   C. restored   D. resisted

8 *English Alive!*

Exercise 2

Choose the best antonyms (words of opposite meaning) for the underlined words as they are used in the sentences.

1. I decided to stroll across the road to my friend's house.
   A. walk   B. hasten   C. go   D. stagger

2. Anna wanted to watch one of her favourite programmes on television.
   A. least liked   C. most preferred
   B. least disliked   D. most popular

3. I was not keen to start my homework.
   A. reluctant   B. eager   C. unwilling D. disinterested

4. Grandma rarely reads the paper peacefully.
   A. sometimes   B. frequently   C. always   D. occasionally

5. I began to see that Grandma was probably right.
   A. definitely   B. certainly   C. possibly   D. unlikely to be

6. Put all of your energy into your work for the next year and a half.
   A. part   B. some   C. none   D. most

7. Do the best you can – all the time.
   A. worse   B. badly   C. bad   D. worst

8. 'I agree. I agree,' I said hastily.
   A. readily   B. reluctantly   C. slowly   D. gladly

9. This part of the river is quite deep, so be careful.
   A. shallow   B. rough   C. fast-flowing D. slow

10. Anna felt slightly embarrassed when her grandmother spoke to her.
    A. extremely   B. not at all   C. a little   D. somewhat

11. Don't think that a broken heart is anything very serious.
    A. significant B. trivial   C. amused   D. rare

12. When you find a possible boyfriend, go for strength of character.
    A. absence   B. novelty   C. depth   D. weakness

1.7
The appreciation of poetry

If an experienced person is buying a used car, he or she knows exactly what to look for, e.g. the condition of the engine, bodywork, battery and tyres; the mileage, signs of rust or damage caused by accidents; the condition of the brakes, steering, upholstery, etc. In other words, he or she has a set of values by which to judge the car.

Similarly, when you come to find a wife or husband, you will have your own set of values, e.g. honesty, frankness, a sense of humour, appearance, health, personality – and perhaps wealth.

In the same way, there are definite standards by which you can appraise a poem. If you think about them, discuss them and then apply them to a number of poems, you will find that poetry is not too difficult to appreciate and evaluate.

We can divide these standards into two sections:

- those which concern the subject matter of the poem
- those which concern the techniques which the poet has used to set down his or her ideas.

We can then make up the following table:

Subject matter ATA	Techniques VVIRR
Aim What is the poet's **aim**? Is it to instruct, to delight or just to give vent to self-expression as a result of some strong emotion?	**Vocabulary** Consider the range of the poet's **vocabulary** and the aptness of words. Are there any archaisms (words from long ago that are no longer used) or invented words? If so, what do they achieve? What is the effect of particular words? Do you feel that the words are well chosen?
Theme What is the **theme** of the poem? Is the poet trying to describe an object, a scene or an emotion? Is there any moral?	**Variety** What **variety** of pace, emotion and structure is there? Is there any change in the normal order of words and, if so, what effect is achieved?
Attitude What is the poet's **attitude** to his topic? Is he prejudiced, unimaginative, sad, original, amused, critical, sympathetic, hostile or what? How does his attitude affect the presentation of his ideas or views?	**Imagery** Consider the sources, effectiveness and extent of the **imagery**, e.g. the similes and metaphors. What other figurative devices are used and are they effective?
	Rhythm What type of **rhythm** is used and why?
	Rhyme To what extent is **rhyme** used and does it help the poet or restrict him?

There are other aspects which can be considered, depending upon the type of poem you are studying, but the above headings are useful when you come to appraise a poem. If it will help, you can make up these acronyms:

- ATA:
  A – aim
  T – theme
  A – attitude

- RIV RIV (using I twice):
  R – rhyme   **R** – rhythm
       I – imagery
  V – vocabulary   **V** – variety

1.8
Enjoying poetry

Read these two poems and decide whether they are about the same or a similar topic.

Husks

Legs tucked, pressed
Into the strict undercarriage,
they circle the air
in full <u>cognisance</u> of its drifts and secrets.   awareness, knowledge
5 Each sneaks out a <u>loft</u>   an area of supporting warm air
and settles upon it,
straddling it till the wings laze wide and relax,
content with this slow, effortless round and descent.

Cunning, they all assume
10 a careless carnival spirit,
less vultures than children
spinning harmlessly round the under-sky's axis.

They are dangerous, nevertheless.
Their starved eyes, endlessly seeking,
15 relentlessly reconnoitre our steppes.
At the first proof of death
that charming balance disrupts,
and the crows, cropped into dread
fallen angels, crash down and rip
20 at our leavings till nothing is left.

Then they are off,
    flapping back, fat
    but still famished,
    in an ache for more servings from death

25 hungering home from the husks of the spirit.
Anthony McNeill

Carrion Crows

    Yes, I have seen them perched on paling posts –
    Brooding with evil eyes upon the road.
    Their black wings hooded – and they left these roosts

    When I had hissed at them. Away they strode
5 Clapping their wings in a man's stride, away
    Over the field. And I have seen them feast
    On swollen carrion in the broad eye of day,
    Pestered by flies, and yet they never ceased.

    But I have seen them emperors of the sky,
10 Balancing gracefully in the wind's drive
    With their broad sails just shifting, or again
    Throwing huge shadows from the sun's eye
    To brush so swiftly over the field's plain,
    And winnowing the air like beauty come alive.
A.J. Seymour

Questions

1. What attitude does each poet show to the crows? Is there any similarity? What are the reasons for your opinion?

2. One editor suggested that the first poem might *not* be about crows but might be a lengthy metaphor dealing with a different topic. Do you agree with him or disagree?

3. Look at lines 5–12 of 'Husks'. Which lines in 'Carrion Crows' deal with a similar quality which crows have?

4. Why do the 'starved eyes' ('Husks', line 14) 'reconnoitre our steppes'?

5. The last line of 'Husks' could mean: 'They fly off home, still hungry and leaving behind empty shells of creatures which are now dead but which once contained a living spirit'. Do you agree with this interpretation or do you think it has another meaning?

6. In line 8 of 'Carrion Crows', a suitable antonym for 'ceased' is

   A. worried   B. stopped   C. afraid   D. continued

7. In line 11 of 'Carrion Crows', the 'sails' are evidently

   A. cloth   B. sheets   C. wings   D. legs

1.9
Writing

Write 180–200 words on *one* of these topics. Do not spend more than 25 minutes on planning, writing and correcting.

1. Read 1.2 again. Then say why you do or do not agree with Grandma's advice.

2. Which subject(s) would you like to study at a university or at a post-secondary college if you have the chance?

3. What news and information can readers find in a newspaper in your country?

2 They Have Done Well

2.1
Pre-reading

Many emigrants from Caribbean countries have done extremely well overseas. In 2003, Lady Amos became the Leader of the House of Lords in the UK. Born in Guyana, she became the first black woman Cabinet minister and became a role model for other female emigrants from the Caribbean.

From Trinidad, Trevor McDonald went to the UK and joined the BBC World Service. In 1973, he moved to ITN and became the network's first black reporter. In 1999, he was knighted for his services to television. He now has his own chat show and presents a weekly investigative news programme.

Many other emigrants from the Caribbean have done well in their adopted country. In 2.2 we can read about Jamaica's Alvin Curling, who has just achieved the unique feat of being elected Speaker of the Ontario Legislature in Canada. The report comes from the *Sunday Gleaner* of Jamaica.

2.2
Reading

Alvin Curling

Once again there is cause for celebration of the achievement of a Jamaican son of the soil who has been elevated to a position of respect and influence in another land. The latest news of the election of Kingston-born Canadian resident Alvin Curling to be Speaker of the Ontario Legislature, thus becoming the first man of
5 colour to attain such a position of eminence in Canada, serves to underscore the commitment to excellence which has been demonstrated by many of our people when they become adopted citizens of another country.

Mr Curling is one of an exemplary band of Jamaican-born men and women who have not been content merely to take the opportunity for advancement offered in
10 the setting to which they migrated, but have found a way to give back to the community and in so doing have brought prestige and honour to the two societies which can lay claim to them.

Alvin Curling's story is one of persistence and perseverance, of sustained involvement in public service given through the political system. Having migrated
15 from Jamaica in the 1970s, he has represented the electorate in the Province of Ontario as a legislator for over 18 years, savouring victory and tasting defeat along the way, but never giving up. A member of the Liberal Party, he has served variously as Minister of Housing, Minister of Skills Development, as well as

Parliamentary Secretary to a former Premier, David Peterson. He also has the distinction of being the first to win a Provincial legislative seat six times and now comes the elevation to the chair of the Speaker.

While Canada has been a haven for people of many races and cultures, life in that country has not always been a triumphant experience for all immigrants. The success of an Alvin Curling is often overshadowed by the anti-social and even criminal behaviour of other Jamaican migrants who have not been able to seize the opportunity for development. In the minds of some, they are the ones with whom Jamaica's name is more readily associated. The victory of Alvin Curling and others, including Mary Anne Chambers, a Jamaican who rose to the post of senior vice-president in Scotiabank, Canada, and has gone on to become a first-time winner in representational politics, serves to remind the people of Canada and Jamaica that there is both good and bad among our people. We should not all be judged by the worst.

It has been noted that many Jamaicans abroad have failed to grasp the significance of becoming fully integrated into their host communities by getting involved in the political process, not necessarily through running for public office but by registering as voters. This goes with the acceptance of citizenship which provides protection through the law of the land but does not make provision otherwise for non-citizens.

Many of our people abroad still dream of coming back home to settle and thus seem to regard citizenship elsewhere as denying that dream. The fact that our Constitution allows for dual citizenship seems to escape them. The result is that, in times of difficulty, persons can be deported unceremoniously back to Jamaica, even though they had not had a presence here for most of their lives.

While citizenship should not be undertaken as a matter of expediency, it is to be hoped that the message will reach those of our family sojourning in Canada and elsewhere, that they can play a part in the life of their adopted community and still maintain loyalty to 'Jamaica Land We Love'. Alvin Curling and others who make up the list of successful Jamaicans abroad should provide inspiration.

2.3
Understanding

1. The writer distinguishes between two different types of Jamaicans who live in Canada.
   a) What are those two types?
   b) Why does the writer mention each group?

2. What is the connection between Lady Amos, Trevor McDonald and Alvin Curling?

3. What can we infer from the writer's use of 'again' in line 1 of the passage?

4. In line 11, what are the 'two societies' mentioned by the writer?

5. According to the writer, how can any emigrant from the Caribbean best become 'fully integrated' in the community to which he migrates?

6. What reason does the writer put forward to explain why many Caribbean migrants do not become citizens of the country to which they emigrate? What is his opinion of the reason?

7. For whom, according to the writer, should Alvin Curling 'provide inspiration' (line 48)?

2.4
Vocabulary: meaning in context

A Choose the word(s) which are closest in meaning to the underlined words as they are used in 2.1 and 2.2.

1. He now has his own <u>chat</u> show (2.1, line 7)
   A. news   B. commercial   C. conversation   D. investigative

2. who has just achieved the <u>unique</u> feat of being elected Speaker (line 10)
   A. unequalled   B. excellent   C. outstanding   D. praiseworthy

3. who has been <u>elevated</u> to a position of respect and influence (2.2, line 2)
   A. introduced   B. raised   C. moved   D. transferred

4. the first man of colour to <u>attain</u> such a position (line 5)
   A. seek   B. desire   C. want   D. reach

5. a position of <u>eminence</u> in Canada (line 5)
   A. prominence   B. power   C. high status   D. publicity

6. serves to <u>underscore</u> the commitment to excellence (line 5)
   A. stress   B. detract from   C. repeat   D. disclose

7. which has been <u>demonstrated</u> by many of our people (line 6)
   A. shown   B. repelled   C. advertised   D. sought

8. one of an <u>exemplary</u> band of Jamaican-born men and women (line 8)
   A. steadily increasing   C. determined and persistent
   B. setting a fine example   D. hoping to succeed

9. have brought <u>prestige</u> and honour to the two societies (line 11)
   A. popularity   B. wealth   C. affection   D. distinction

10. <u>sustained</u> involvement in public service (line 13)
    A. deeply appreciated   C. kept going
    B. with no thought of profit   D. not obvious to the public

11. <u>savouring</u> victory and tasting defeat (line 16)
    A. winning   B. enjoying   C. experiencing   D. claiming

12. he has served <u>variously</u> as Minister of Housing, Minister of Skills (line 18)
    A. in different posts   C. with different degrees of success
    B. now and again   D. with outstanding success

16 *English Alive!*

B Match the underlined words with the meanings which they have in the passage.

Words from the passage	Meanings
1. a haven for people (line 22)	a) people
2. is often overshadowed by (line 24)	b) can be used
3. they are the ones with whom (line 26)	c) accepted as a member of
4. serves to remind people (line 30)	d) convenience
5. becoming fully integrated into (line 34)	e) preventing (them) from fulfilling
6. running for public office (line 35)	f) staying
7. denying that dream (line 40)	g) swiftly and without formalities
8. deported unceremoniously (line 42)	h) a place of refuge
9. a matter of expediency (line 44)	i) taking part in an election
10. sojourning in Canada (line 45)	j) exceeded in importance

2.5
Paragraphing (review)

We met these points in earlier books in this series. We can review them here as a reminder.

- Short paragraphs are better than long ones. If a paragraph is longer than about 6–8 lines, the reader may become bored, so keep your paragraphs reasonably short, as in 2.2.

- Normally there should be a link of ideas between paragraphs. A new paragraph often shows one of these:
  – a change of time (a step forward or back)
  – a change of place, e.g. from Canada to Jamaica
  – a link of similarity or contrast, e.g. from immigrants who do well to those who bring Jamaica a bad reputation
  – an extension, expansion or modification of an idea already mentioned.

- When you use dialogue, each new speaker starts a new paragraph, as in 1.2. Use inverted commas to enclose the actual words of the speaker, e.g.
  'Have you come from the States?' Paul asked the group of tourists.
  'No,' one of them explained. 'We're all Canadians. Most of us live in Toronto but there are a few in our group from Montreal.'

- Sometimes there is a topic sentence at the start of a new paragraph. A topic sentence shows what the whole paragraph will be about. However, in many cases paragraphs do not start with a topic sentence.

Over to you!

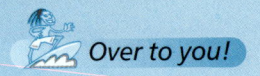

Exercise 1

1. Read section 2.2 again. There are seven paragraphs in it. Say whether each paragraph starts with a topic sentence.

2. Which two paragraphs (if any) in 2.2 could be joined to make a single paragraph?

3. Look at two more passages in this book. In each case, say:
   a) whether each paragraph starts with a topic sentence
   b) what link there is between successive paragraphs.

2.6
Writing: making a summary

There are three main types of summaries:

- Reduce the whole of a passage to a smaller size:

  ```
  An original passage          →    A summary
  or some data
  ```

  The original passage may be an article, a prose passage, two or more letters, graphs, pie charts or tables, some dialogue or a mixture of two or more of these. In this case, we have to summarise the main points and omit unimportant details. This type of summary is common in daily life (e.g. when we tell somebody about a film or an accident) but some examination questions are not as simple.

- Make a summary of *one part* of a passage:

  ```
  Not relevant
  The relevant part            →    A summary
  Not relevant
  ```

  Sometimes it may be necessary to read through long reports or sets of statistics to find and summarise information about one or two points which concern you. If you go to university or get an office job, you may often need to make this type of summary. It is not difficult if you know what you are looking for.

- Make a summary of *one aspect* of a passage:

  ```
  Not relevant
  Relevant
  Not relevant                 →    A summary
  Partly relevant
  Not relevant
  Relevant
  ```

English Alive!

The passage may deal with a number of different topics but you have to deal with only one of them.

> **Guidelines for writing summaries in an examination**
>
> 1. Study the question very carefully. See whether you have to make a summary of the whole of a passage or about one part or topic only.
> 2. Underline the relevant points in the passage. Make rough notes which summarise them. The total length of your notes should be not more than half the number of words you are allowed to use.
> 3. Omit details, illustrations/examples, negative information and repetition.
> 4. Arrange your points in a logical order. Do not add your own comments.
> 5. Try not to copy long expressions from the original. Use your own words whenever possible.
> 6. Use suitable connectives to link your points so that they read smoothly.
> 7. Use as many paragraphs as may be necessary (unless you are told to use one paragraph only). Keep strictly to the word limit.
> 8. Use the correct format, e.g. an article, a letter, a report, etc.

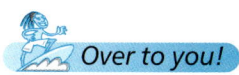

Over to you!

Exercise 2

1. In not more than 50 words, summarise the information given in 2.2 about Alvin Curling.
2. In not more than 50 words, summarise the advice which the writer (in 2.2) gives to Jamaicans who live overseas.

Exercise 3

The passage below tells a simple story:

- Deena ate some food and felt very ill.
- She went to a hospital but had to wait a long time, so she left.
- She went to a doctor who cured her.

Read the passage and then make the summaries required.

```
My friend, Deena, always seems to get into trouble. I am sure
that if she walked under a ladder it would immediately collapse
on her. But last week Deena was both unlucky and lucky. Last
Thursday Deena decided to have lunch at Horrible's Restaurant
in Food Street. She had plenty of money, so she ordered a
really good meal and thoroughly enjoyed it. She had already
decided to go on a diet in the following week, so she felt that
she could indulge herself until it was time to start her diet.
```

A few minutes after leaving the restaurant, she had a sharp pain in her stomach. She assumed that the pain would soon disappear but the opposite happened: it grew rapidly worse. Deena found a taxi and went off to Chopemup Hospital. She entered the Casualty Department and completed a form. Then she sat down and waited impatiently to see a doctor. Two hours later and still in great pain, she felt that she could not wait any longer. She felt so ill that she was sure that she was going to die.

Deena left the hospital and caught another taxi. This time, she went to her family doctor, Dr Helpful Chan, who examined her and said she probably had food poisoning. He gave her some medicine. Deena took some of the medicine at Dr Chan's clinic and began to feel better. When she arrived home, she told her mother what had happened and showed her the bottle of medicine. She took some more of the medicine and lay down to rest. Within an hour, she felt perfectly well again.

1. You are the owner of Horrible's Restaurant. You have read this report of Deena's case. Summarise the information given in it about Deena as far as it affects your restaurant.

2. You are an assistant to the Medical Superintendent of Chopemup Hospital. He wants a very brief account of the part which his hospital played in Deena's case. In two short sentences, summarise the information in the passage about Deena's visit to your hospital.

3. You are Dr Helpful Chan. In two short sentences, summarise the information in the passage about Deena's visit to your clinic. (These two sentences will be put in the file which you keep about Deena.)

4. Look at the last few lines of the passage. In not more than 50 words, summarise what Deena told her mother.

English Alive!

2.7
Writing: punctuating dialogue

Put direct speech inside inverted commas (quotation marks *or* speech marks), as follows:

- in printed matter, single or double inverted commas are used, e.g.
  'I'm going out but I'll be back in an hour,' my mother said.
  "I'm going out but I'll be back in an hour," my mother said.

- in handwriting, use double inverted commas (especially in an examination), as in the second example above.

Study these examples, taken from a story by a Grade 10 student:

wrong: One day a young girl said to her mother that I think I am getting smaller. Her mother's reply was that the idea was foolish. You are not getting smaller, you are getting bigger every day.

right: One day a young girl said to her mother, "I think I'm getting smaller." Her mother's reply was that the idea was foolish. "You're not getting smaller. You're getting bigger every day."

wrong: One night at the dinner table Nancy's father looked at her. Begin eating Nancy, and sit up when you are at the table. I cannot sit up and I cannot see you. I am getting smaller she said, don't be foolish you are getting bigger her father said, you are a growing girl and should behave properly.

right: One night at the dinner table, Nancy's father looked at her. "Begin eating, Nancy, and sit up when you're at the table."
"I can't sit up and I can't see you. I'm getting smaller," she said.
"Don't be foolish. You're getting bigger," her father said. "You're a growing girl and should behave properly."

Note: Double inverted commas are used in the correct examples because the student was using handwriting.

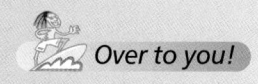

Over to you!

Exercise 4

Write out each of the following correctly. Put in inverted commas and other punctuation marks when necessary. Put in capital letters when they are needed. Remember that each new speaker starts a new paragraph. These examples come from the same source as the 'wrong' ones above.

1. On her way to class Nancy saw a girl who said, look at Nancy she is getting smaller, she looks almost like a baby.

2. In the class the teacher said Has anyone checked on Nancy, the students laughed, I am here miss Morris Nancy answered, I am right behind you, but Nancy was so small the teacher could not see her. Well miss I cannot see you too well, the teacher told Nancy you will have to go home until you are big again

3. Wake up, wake up, Nancy's mother said to her. Nancy opened her eyes oh she said, I was having a horrible dream, I dreamt that I was getting smaller, her mother laughed well you're not she said now it's time for you to get dressed and washed

Exercise 5

Follow the instructions for Exercise 4.

1. As soon as Deena entered the room we all began to sing happy birthday happy birthday dear Deena she was very surprised but very happy thank you thank you very much she said

2. Deena showed us a lovely gold bracelet, where did you get that Nataya asked her Deena said my mother gave me it, she bought it in Trinidad several months ago, its beautiful Natalie said, you are very lucky

3. I'm going to have a party on Saturday Deena told me I hope you can come Thank you very much I replied, what time will it be? It will start at 5 p.m. Deena said and finish at about 10 p.m. Thanks very much I said I'll be there

2.8

Grammar: the Simple Present tense (active)

Uses

This list shows the most common uses of the Simple Present tense. Try to give at least one example of each use:

- for habits, routine actions and universal truths

- in time expressions, e.g. with 'when', 'until' and 'before'

- in 'possible' conditions which refer to a specific situation, e.g.
    If she **arrives** this evening, please let us know.

- to express future planned action connected with travel, e.g.

    He **leaves** for Barbados next Saturday and **returns** on the following Thursday.

- in place of the Present Continuous tense with verbs which have no continuous form, e.g.
    Q: Who **has** the key to this door? A: I think Grandpa **has** it.

English Alive!

- to give a commentary on a sporting event
- to summarise the story of a film, book or television programme.

Problems

- Remember that the verb must agree with its subject. Use 'he walks' and not 'he walk'.

- We sometimes use two (or more) verbs with the same subject. Make sure that *both* verbs agree with the subject, e.g.
    He usually **leaves** for work at 8 a.m. and **returns** at about 6 p.m.
    We **study** with our friends and **play** with them.

Over to you!

Exercise 6

Make short sentences, using the Simple Present tense of the verbs in brackets.

1. The computer (work) well now.
2. Francine (appear) tired but happy.
3. The girls (seem) happier now.
4. Grandpa (speak) quite slowly.
5. Jolie (know) the way to the sea.
6. Our players (expect) to win.
7. Most of this furniture (look) new.
8. Leela always (try) her best.
9. This road (lead) to our village.
10. It often (rain) heavily at night.

Exercise 7

Use the correct form of the verb ('look' or 'looks') each time.

1. That cut ____ fine now.
2. Everything ____ much better now.
3. The weather ____ quite good now.
4. All of them ____ ready to start.
5. This one ____ the best of the lot.
6. That soup ____ very good.
7. Anna and Sue ____ very pretty.
8. This meat ____ OK to me.
9. Your plan ____ very sensible.
10. The soil here ____ very fertile.

2.9
Grammar: asking questions

Check that you can ask and answer questions like these:

Do I/you/we/they know him?	**Does** he/she/it sleep in the afternoon?

Exercise 8

Put in 'Do' or 'Does' to complete these questions.

1. ____ your brother still collect stamps?
2. ____ anybody want to come with us?
3. ____ sharks ever attack divers?
4. ____ that bus go to Georgetown?
5. ____ you know the way to the city?
6. ____ hurricanes ever come in March?
7. ____ the roof still leak?
8. ____ that shop sell batteries?
9. ____ everybody agree with the decision?
10. ____ any of your friends speak French?
11. ____ your teeth still hurt?
12. ____ everything here belong to your parents?
13. ____ 'tough' rhyme with 'cough'?
14. ____ those keys belong to you?

Exercise 9

Put in 'does' or 'do' to complete these questions.

1. How often ____ your friend in California write to you?

24 *English Alive!*

2. When ____ she graduate from high school?
3. Where ____ this road go?
4. Why ____ your brother look so miserable today?
5. Who ____ the man want to speak to? What ____ he want to talk about?
6. How fast ____ a helicopter usually go?
7. How much ____ your father pay to rent that field?
8. How far ____ you walk on an average day?
9. What time ____ the final start on Saturday?
10. How ____ tourists usually come to Antigua: by sea or by air?
11. What kind of bicycle ____ your friend want to buy?
12. When ____ men set fire to the cane fields?
13. Where ____ we have to change buses to get to Kingston?
14. Why ____ so many people emigrate from Jamaica every year?
15. How long ____ you want to borrow the bike for?

2.10
Enjoying poetry

The title of the poem below is 'Roman Holiday'. That gives us a clue concerning the tone of the poem and the likely aim of the poet. A 'Roman holiday' is a spectacular event, possibly riotous, and one which sometimes involves the suffering of others, e.g. gladiators, persecuted Christians, condemned criminals, wild animals, etc.
What is the tone of the poem? Is it gentle and mocking, or is it harsh and sarcastic?

Roman Holiday

O, it was a lovely funeral!
One hundred and thirty-two cars,
And three of them packed high with flowers
And the streets thronged with people –
5 It reminded me of the Coronation –
And then such a beautiful service;
Organ and full choir of course,
And hardly a dry eye in the chapel.
And there were so many people present that they couldn't all get in
10 And ever so many of them had to stand outside

  And during the service there was such a hard shower,
  And most of the gentlemen in morning coats and top hats too.
  And a well-dressed respectable-looking woman turned to me
  And asked me –
15 Poor creature, she could scarcely articulate the words –
  If it was true he'd really died from what we heard,
  And I told her it was only too true, poor man.
  And it wasn't until afterwards that I discovered
  It really wasn't *his* funeral at all.
20 Because there was another one that evening and they had
  both got mixed up in all the confusion;
  And I do think they ought to see to it
  That better arrangements should be made –
  I mean, it can put one out so;
25 And when I did manage to get outside and reach the grave
  It was all over.
  But it really was a lovely funeral,
  And I don't know when I've cried so much,
  And that reminds me, my dear:
30 Have you heard that his youngest daughter
  Has run away
  With the chauffeur?

Frank Collymore

Questions

1. What evidence can you find in the poem to suggest that the speaker might be a woman?

2. What effect do the first two lines of the poem have on you? What can we tell about the poem from the first two lines?

3. What is the poet referring to when he mentions 'the Coronation' in line 5? Suggest a reason why the speaker compares a funeral to a coronation.

4. In line 8, suggest two reasons why there was 'hardly a dry eye'.

5. Why does the speaker refer to a well-dressed woman as a 'poor creature' in line 15?

6. In line 24, what is the meaning of 'put one out so'? Why did the poet use this expression?

7. What is the attitude of the poet to the speaker he has created and the society she lives in?

8. What do you think the poet's aim was in writing this poem? How successful is he in achieving this aim?

2.11
Writing

Write about 400–450 words on *one* of the following topics:

1. Write a story which ends in *one* of these ways:

    … *Deena made up her mind to emigrate as soon as her chance came.*
    or
    … *Deena decided not to emigrate after all.*

2. Write a true or imaginary story about a Caribbean person who has emigrated and become successful in his or her new country.

3. Using email, you have become friendly with a teenager of your own age who lives in Africa, India, China or any other country and wants to know whether you would advise him/her to try to emigrate to your own country.
   Write an email giving whatever advice you think is most suitable. Give reasons in support of your opinions.

Unit 2 · *They Have Done Well*

3 Who Told the Truth?

3.1 Pre-reading

In 3.2 you can read two different news reports of the same incident.
- How is it possible for different newspapers to give two different accounts of one incident?
- Can we believe the news items in newspapers, on television and on the radio?
- If some of the reports are false, why is that?
- In what ways can a reporter or newspaper select incidents and language to give readers a dishonest or prejudiced account of an incident?

Read the two reports and then you may be able to answer some of these questions.

3.2 Reading

Report 1

POLICE KILL GIRL STUDENT

Mary Blank, aged twenty-eight, a student at the Institute of Higher Education, was gunned down this afternoon when masses of heavily-armed police attacked a small group of peaceful demonstrators in Market Street. The unarmed and defenceless students were protesting against the Government's decision to slash social welfare benefits.

The students had gathered to consider the evil effects on society of the Government's hasty action and were peacefully discussing the problem with shopkeepers when the police launched an unprovoked attack on them, using guns, clubs and other dangerous weapons.

Terrified by the vicious assault, the law-abiding students tried to shelter in nearby shops but they were relentlessly hunted down and beaten by groups of policemen, aided by savage dogs.

Mary Blank, one of several brilliant scholarship students in the Social Welfare Department of the IHE, became a martyr when a policeman shot her at close range. At the time, she was unselfishly helping a trader to move his goods to a safer place to protect them from damage or looting by the police raiders.

Mary's cousin, Peter Blank, is a disabled orphan in Newtown, and Mary was on a mission of mercy to him. She intended to take him a present and help him with his school work when she was brutally shot down in cold blood.

Thirty-two other students were beaten up by the police, attacked by dogs or seriously injured in the battle of Market Street.

So the innocent students were beaten up by gangs of bad policemen – or were they? Read on and learn about the other side of the story.

Report 2

HEAVY DAMAGE TO SHOPS

Organised looting led to losses of at least $4 million in Market Street today. Traders estimate that goods worth at least $3 million were stolen by gangs of hooligans, and that damage to premises will cost a further $1 million to repair.

25   According to reliable eye-witnesses, many of the looters had just come from the Institute of Higher Education's annual soccer match in which they lost to rivals from Middletown. Angered by a poster in a shop supporting Middletown, they smashed the windows and started to carry away goods on display. The owner of the shop, Mr Jack Williams, 43, explained that he had put up the poster because his
30   son plays for the Middletown team. When a group of half-drunk hooligans forced their way into his shop and threatened him with knives, he offered to take the poster down.

'The young thugs would not listen,' Mr Williams told our reporter from his hospital bed.

35   'While four of the men held me, a hysterical woman started to slash my chest and arms with a knife. Luckily for me, her friends pulled her away to help with the looting. I crawled to the back of the shop and phoned the police. Then I collapsed.'

The looters spread out along both sides of Market Street and numbered several hundred. When a squad of eight policemen arrived, most of the looters ran away.
40   Some were trapped with their stolen goods and were arrested by the police, who acted with great restraint. One policeman was attacked by a group of men and women armed with knives and iron pipes. In an attempt to scare them, he fired two shots in the air. A bullet glanced off a light fitting and hit a woman, who was later identified by Williams as one of his attackers. She was certified dead on arrival at
45   hospital.

Five policemen were injured in the incident. Eight people were arrested and will appear in court today.

3.3
Understanding

A   Choose the best words each time.

1. Which report is the more truthful?
   A. the first report
   B. the second report
   C. They are both truthful.
   D. We cannot say for sure.

2. Which report is the more likely to lead to further trouble in the streets?
   A. the first report
   B. the second report
   C. both of them
   D. neither of them

3. Which word is used figuratively in line 4 but literally in Report 2?
    A. protesting   B. decision   C. slash   D. benefits

4. In the first report, which of these words is *not* used in an attempt to portray the police in an unfavourable light?
    A. evil   B. unprovoked   C. vicious   D. relentlessly

5. Peter Blank is mentioned in the first report in order to ____.
    A. get sympathy for disabled people
    B. present Mary Blank in a more favourable light
    C. show that Mary did not take any goods from a shop
    D. show that he had no parents

6. Which word in the first paragraph of Report 2 creates the impression that the looting had been planned and was not spontaneous?
    A. organised   B. hooligans   C. premises   D. further

7. How did the writer of Report 1 explain the injuries to Mr Williams?
    A. He blamed them on a hysterical woman.
    B. He claimed that they were caused by the police.
    C. He said that the police launched an unprovoked attack.
    D. He did not even mention them.

8. According to Report 2, some of the looters were caught ____.
    A. with green fingers   C. in a blue moon
    B. red-handed   D. yellow-bellied

B Answer these questions about the two reports.

1. How do the reports differ in their treatment of police casualties?

2. Outline the steps you would take to investigate whether the death of Mary Blank was an accident or not.

3. How do the reports differ in their accounts of the cause of the trouble?

4. Which of the reports seems to you to be more truthful? Give reasons for your opinion.

3.4
Vocabulary: meaning in context

Choose the word(s) which best show(s) the meaning of the underlined words as they are used in the passage in 3.2.

1. the Government's decision to <u>slash</u> social welfare benefits (line 4)
    A. cancel   B. annul   C. drastically reduce   D. greatly increase

2. the Government's decision to slash social welfare <u>benefits</u> (line 5)
   A. payments
   B. numbers
   C. qualifications
   D. conditions

3. the police <u>launched</u> an unprovoked attack on them (line 8)
   A. prepared   B. unleashed   C. organised   D. foiled

4. the police launched an <u>unprovoked</u> attack on them (line 8)
   A. unexpected
   B. alarming
   C. not in response to anything
   D. not showing any kind of control

5. Terrified by the <u>vicious</u> assault (line 10)
   A. cruel and spiteful
   B. very boisterous
   C. sudden and unexpected
   D. not fully justified

6. they were <u>relentlessly</u> hunted down (line 11)
   A. in an unjustified manner
   B. with great enthusiasm
   C. in a determined and severe way
   D. showing considerable skill

7. became <u>a martyr</u> (line 14)
   A. a person who dies as a result of an unfortunate accident
   B. somebody who brings about his or her own death
   C. a person who dies bravely while fighting an enemy
   D. somebody who dies for a (worthy) cause.

8. a policeman shot her <u>at close range</u> (line 14)
   A. with unusual accuracy
   B. while touching her with a gun
   C. when he was very near her
   D. so that she could not escape

9. <u>Organised</u> looting led to losses (line 22)
   A. very serious
   B. violent and unrestrained
   C. systematic and planned
   D. unplanned, spontaneous

10. damage to <u>premises</u> will cost (line 24)
    A. homes   B. shops   C. public buildings   D. goods

11. many of the looters had <u>just</u> come from (line 25)
    A. scarcely   B. only   C. peacefully   D. very recently

12. a <u>hysterical</u> woman started to slash my chest (line 35)
    A. determined to achieve her goal
    B. who had lost control of her emotions
    C. shouting, fighting and aggressive
    D. acting under the influence of drugs

3.5 Vocabulary: antonyms

An **antonym** is a word which is opposite in meaning to another word. If you have to give antonyms in an examination, make sure that you understand the meaning of the words in a passage. Some words have more than one meaning. Consider the following example.

Which of the following is an antonym for 'put out' in this sentence?

Lisa did not like Jason, so she was not at all **put out** when he did not invite her to his birthday party.

   A. pleased   B. inflamed   C. annoyed   D. offended

Meanings of 'put out':

- Firemen can put out a fire. (= extinguish)
- A company can put out a report about its progress. (= produce, publish)
- Fishermen can put out to sea when the weather is suitable. (= go out to)
- A factory can put out more goods with improved machinery. (= manufacture)
- Somebody will probably be put out if you imply that he or she is dishonest. (= offended)

In the sentence about Lisa, 'put out' means 'annoyed, offended', so we need a word with an opposite meaning. The answer is A. Answers B, C and D are more like synonyms than antonyms.

Over to you!

Exercise 1

In each case, choose the word or expression which is an antonym for the underlined word as it is used in the reports in 3.2.

1. masses of <u>heavily</u>-armed police (line 2)
      A. thinly   B. well   C. bad   D. lightly

2. students were protesting <u>against</u> the Government's decision (line 4)
      A. towards   C. in accordance with
      B. not in favour of   D. in support of

3. the <u>evil</u> effects on society of the Government's hasty action (line 6)
      A. beneficial   B. well   C. harmful   D. benefit

4. tried to shelter in <u>nearby</u> shops (line 11)
      A. distance   B. local   C. open   D. distant

English Alive!

5. beaten by groups of policemen, <u>aided</u> by dogs (line 12)
   A. without   B. hindered   C. assisted   D. watched

6. move his goods to a safer place to <u>protect</u> them (line 16)
   A. expose   B. conceal   C. defence   D. blemish

7. attacked by dogs or <u>seriously</u> injured in the battle (line 21)
   A. fatally   B. shallowly   C. comically   D. slightly

8. According to <u>reliable</u> eye-witnesses (line 25)
   A. liable   B. not liable   C. innocent   D. untrustworthy

9. <u>Angered</u> by a poster in a shop (line 27)
   A. upset   B. enthralled   C. pleased   D. surprised

10. arrested by the police, who acted with great <u>restraint</u> (line 41)
    A. sense of justice   C. lack of rashness
    B. sense of vengeance   D. lack of self-control

3.6
Writing: making summaries

1. A friend asked you what Report 1 was about. Finish this summary of the report by adding up to 20 more words to this beginning:

   According to the report, some students were protesting against proposed cuts in social welfare benefits.

2. In not more than 80 words make a summary of Report 2. Include information about:

   - football supporters
   - started to loot shop
   - owner stabbed
   - goods stolen
   - police came
   - girl killed accidentally
   - policemen injured; people arrested.

Unit 3 · Who Told the Truth?

3.7

Grammar: problems of agreement

You already know that a verb must agree with its subject. Sometimes the verb is not near the subject. Then you must be careful because you may accidentally make the verb agree with the wrong word. These examples are correct. The subject is in bold type and the verb is underlined.

> The **cost** of machinery and spare parts for use in repairing various kinds of vehicles <u>has</u> increased steadily in recent years.
>
> The main **argument** for requiring people to wear seat-belts in a vehicle <u>is</u> that it reduces the risk of being injured in an accident.
>
> The **principles** on which this school was founded more than a century ago <u>are</u> just as valid today as they were in the nineteenth century and <u>present</u> all of us with a worthy challenge.
>
> **Some** of the more serious errors in this composition <u>are</u> probably the result of lack of care. Your **handwriting** strongly <u>suggests</u> to me that you were writing too quickly.

Over to you!

Exercise 2

These sentences show different types of common errors. Choose the correct words from the brackets.

1. One of my (classmate, classmates) (have, has) been chosen to attend the Shell Cricket Academy. He (hope, hopes) to play for the West Indies one day.

2. One of the most restful (room, rooms) in our school (is, are) the library. There (is, are) many interesting and useful books in it.

3. The teeth of an animal such as a dog, fox or wolf (is, are) sharper than (that, those) of a human being and (is, are) designed to enable the animal to hold and tear.

4. My parents (was, were) very excited when (he, she, they) heard the result of the lottery and discovered that (it, they) had won.

5. Coming down the road towards us (was, were) a big lorry laden with large pieces of timber.

6. Vimala's teeth (is, are) lovely and so (is, are) her long hair.

7. This pair of scissors (are, is) quite sharp. Those other scissors (is, are) blunt.

8. Approximately 10% of the desks in this room (need, needs) to be repaired. We notice that about 20% of the ceiling also (need, needs) attention to deal with leaks.

English Alive!

9. There (is, are) several small shops and a supermarket not far away. The former (is, are) useful for local fresh food and a few other items but the latter (is, are) very popular because people (like, likes) to buy many different things at one place. In addition, the prices of most items in a supermarket (is, are) lower than (that, those) in small shops.

10. Nearly everybody in our class (know, knows) how to use a computer. However, not every (student, students) (has, have) his or her own computer at home. One of the major reasons for this (is, are) the cost of buying a computer.

11. There (is, are) a lot of rice in this tin but there (is, are) not a lot of biscuits in that one.

12. There (is, are) a number of reasons why tourists (like, likes) to visit Caribbean countries. We can tell this because the number of visitors (increase, increases) every year.

13. Who (was, were) the opening batsmen at the game yesterday? Who (was, were) the opening bowler?

14. This type of (camera, cameras) is cheap but reliable. Most of the other kinds of (camera, cameras) (is, are) much more expensive but not necessarily as reliable.

15. (Is, Are) the agenda for tomorrow's meeting a lengthy one?

3.8

Spelling: a review of some basic guidelines

Check that you know the meaning of the words below and that you can spell them correctly:

- **final 'c'** Add 'k' when you add a suffix beginning with 'e', 'i' or 'y', e.g.
  picnic – picnicked   panic – panicky   traffic – trafficking

- **'ce' or 'se'** In these pairs of words, nouns have a 'c'; verbs have an 's', e.g.

nouns:	his advice	a licence	more practice	a prophecy	a device
verbs:	to advise	licensed	practising	to prophesy	to devise

- **doubling final consonants**
  – a short word of one syllable: when adding a vowel suffix, double the final consonant if the word ends with a short vowel and a single consonant, e.g.
  run – running   hit – hitting   beg – beggar   rob – robbery
  – a word with two syllables: when adding a vowel suffix, double the final consonant if the second syllable is stressed, has a short vowel and ends with a consonant, e.g.
  begin – beginning   omit – omitted   to rebel – rebelled

- **final 'e'**
  - In most cases, omit the final 'e' when you add a suffix beginning with a vowel or 'y', e.g.

    write – writing   fame – famous   serve – servant
    make – making   ease – easy   simple – simply

  - Keep the final 'e' when adding a suffix to a word ending in 'ee', 'oe' or 'ye', e.g.

    agree – agreeable   canoe – canoeing   eye – eyeing

  - Words ending with 'ce' or 'ge' keep their final 'e', e.g.

    change – changeable   courage – courageous   notice – noticeable

- **'ei' and 'ie'**
  - Remember the rule '**i** before **e** except after **c**', but notice that this rule applies *only* when 'ei' and 'ie' are spoken with the sound /ee/ as in 'see', e.g.

    cei: receive, deceive, conceive, ceiling, perceived, receipt, conceited
    ie: piece, believe, chief, brief, thieves, priest, relieved, grief, handkerchief

  - The letters 'ei' and 'ie' do *not* make the sound /ee/ in these words:

    ei: their, neighbour, foreign, leisure, weight, veil, reign, eighteen, weird
    cie: science, ancient, conscience, proficient, efficient, sufficient, glacier

Now your teacher can test you on some of the words above or you can have a competition between two halves of your class.

3.9
Enjoying poetry

This is a very serious poem. It is not easy to understand unless you know the background to it:

- The poem stresses the need for self-discipline (called 'self-conquest' in line 20). Amongst the Bedouin Arabs of North Africa and the Middle East, there is a long tradition of hospitality. The Bedouins are nomads who move across deserts, seeking food for their herds of animals. If a stranger arrived at a man's tent, he would receive food and shelter to help him on his way.

- Ibrahim killed Yussouf's eldest son but Yussouf did not know who had killed him. Later on, the two men met unexpectedly when Ibrahim sought food and shelter at Yussouf's tent. Yussouf's kindness led Ibrahim to confess what he had done. Instead of seeking revenge, Yussouf overcame his 'black thought' (the desire to get revenge) and sent Ibrahim on his way, thus accepting God's decrees, which are 'balanced and just'.

The theme of the poem is in line 18, 'nobleness enkindleth (= produces or leads to) nobleness'.

Yussouf

A stranger came one night to Yussouf's tent,
    Saying – 'Behold one outcast and in <u>dread</u>,   fear
Against whose life the bow of Power is bent,
    Who flies, and hath not where to lay his head.
5 I come to thee for shelter and for food:
To Yussouf, call'd through all our tribes the Good.'

'This tent is mine,' said Yussouf – 'but no more
    Than it is God's: come in and be at peace;
Freely shalt thou <u>partake of</u> all my store,   have things from
10   As I of His who buildeth over these
Our tents His glorious roof of night and day,
And at whose door none ever yet heard Nay.'

So Yussouf entertain'd his guest that night;
    And waking him <u>ere</u> day, said – 'Here is gold;   before
15 My swiftest horse is saddled for thy flight
    Depart before the prying day grow bold!'
As one lamp lights another, nor grows less,
So nobleness enkindleth nobleness.

That inward light the stranger's face made grand
20   Which shines from all self-conquest; kneeling low,
He bow'd his forehead upon Yussouf's hand,
    Sobbing – 'O Sheikh! I cannot leave thee so –
I will repay thee – all this thou hast done
Unto that Ibrahim who slew thy son!'

25 'Take thrice the gold!' said Yussouf – 'for with thee
　　　Into the desert, never to return,
　　My one black thought shall ride away from me.
　　　First-born, for whom by day and night I <u>yearn</u>   long (for); feel great
　　Balanced and just are all of God's decrees;   tenderness for
30 Thou art avenged, my First-born! Sleep in peace!'

　　　　　　　　　　　　　　　　J.R. Lowell

Questions

1. To whom does 'one' refer in line 2?

2. What kind of figure of speech is 'the bow of Power' in line 3?

3. In line 4, 'hath' is an old form of 'has'. Find three other old forms of verbs in the poem. Why does the poet use them?

4. Why did Yussouf wake Ibrahim before dawn?

5. What figure of speech does the poet use in line 17?

6. In line 18 to what act does each word 'nobleness' refer in this poem?

7. In line 19, what caused the 'inward light' within Ibrahim?

8. What do you think 'my one black thought' refers to in line 27?

9. In what way was Yussouf's son avenged? (lines 28–30) This is an extremely difficult question. More than one answer is possible.

10. What can an ordinary person learn from this poem?

3.10
Writing about a picture of a person

Catching a rabbit and catching a tiger are two different tasks. Similarly, writing a short story for publication is quite different from writing one in an examination. An author may spend two or three days and write 10 or more pages on a short story. In the CSEC examination you will have much less time and can write fewer words. In this section, we will concentrate on writing a story based on a picture in an examination.

Length

You will have to follow this length and time:
　　General Proficiency: 400–450 words in 45 minutes

On page 6, you worked out the number of words you write in 1 minute. If you have forgotten, copy the first paragraph above in your ordinary writing for 2 minutes. Then count the number of words you have written and divide by two. Let us say that you write, for example, 20 words in 1 minute. Then you can write 420 words in 20–25 minutes.

This means that you will have about 20 minutes left in which to study the question, plan your work and correct any mistakes.

Over to you!

Exercise 3

1. Find out how many words you normally write in 1 minute.

2. Work out how long it takes you to write a story of the length shown above.

Exercise 4

1. Find out how many words you write per line.

2. Find out how many lines you will have to write for the length above.

Don't count the number of words in an examination. That is a waste of time. Count the number of lines instead. For example, if you write about 9 words per line, you must write about 47 lines for the General Proficiency story. When you see the examination paper, write on it the number of **lines** you need to write. This will save time and be a useful guide.

The instructions

Study the instructions. They may ask you to do one of these things:

- Write a story based on (a given picture).
- Write a story suggested by (a picture).
- Write a story leading to the person/picture/scene in (a picture).
- Write a story which includes/involves the person (in the picture).

Notice that these instructions do *not* ask you to describe the person in the picture. Be prepared to give the person a name. You may need to make up his/her age as well as a place and date or time of the year.

The format

Think about the format you will use. It could be (a story told in) a letter, a report, in conversation or in an examination.

Who are you?

- Are you going to pretend to be the person in the picture (or a friend or relative)?

- Are you going to write a 1st or 3rd person narrative?

Don't worry about this. The question will answer itself when you work out your plot and plan.

Working out a plot

It is a good idea to work out some plots in your mind and carry them into the examination hall with you. Let us call the person in the picture X. These are some possible plots:

- X saved/rescued you or somebody else from a fire, a flood, drowning or another misfortune. That is why you like to keep a photo which X gave you.

- You saved X from some trouble such as a fire, flood, accident, drowning, etc. That is why X gave you his/her photo.

- X is missing from home. The photo was issued by the police. You help to search for him/her and find the person.

- X entered a competition and won. Everybody was happy.

- This photo of X was taken for an advertisement or tourist brochure. X was paid for it. (Look at X's face carefully. Work out why he/she looks sad or happy.)

- X hurt himself/herself. You helped him/her.

- You hurt yourself. X helped you.

- Why was this photo taken? Your answer will lead you to a simple plot.

Many other plots are possible. In the list above *either* X is in trouble and somebody helps him/her *or* X helps somebody who is in trouble. Other possible plots include:

- X forgot to do something. What happened as a result?

- X was seriously ill but is better now.

- (X is an adult.) You were very fond of X. The photo was taken a month ago. Six months previously, a doctor had told X that he/she had three months left before he/she died of cancer. He/she died last night.

- (X is a child.) X was your best friend when you were younger. He/She emigrated to the USA (or UK) and lost your address. You were looking at the photo when you unexpectedly received an email/letter inviting you to spend a holiday with your friend after an interval of several/many years.

English Alive!

Over to you!

Writing practice

Write a story of 400–450 words based on *one* of the people in the pictures below. Do not spend more than 45 minutes on the story (including planning time).

4 The Sting

4.1
Pre-reading

Amongst criminals, to 'sting' somebody is to cheat them. Recently, however, the police in several countries have found that one way of catching criminals is by using their own tricks against them. In 4.2, we can read about one very successful 'sting' in the USA.

Notice that the facts in this account are presented chronologically, i.e. in time order. We find out how the sting was planned, what happened when it was carried out, and what the final result was. We shall see later in this unit that there are other ways of starting the account, and other ways of arranging the facts.

4.2
Reading

The Sting

Police in America have hit upon a new method of catching wanted criminals – you send them an invitation to a party and then arrest them when they arrive. Of course, you have to make sure that the invitation looks irresistible and convincing.

One such successful 'sting' was organised recently by the Marshals Service in
5   Washington, DC. The marshals compiled a list of hardened and dangerous crooks who were a threat to society and sent them an invitation. Each invitation said that the recipient's name had been selected at random by a computer, using lists of local residents. They promised a lavish party with free drinks and free tickets to a popular football game between Washington Redskins and the Cincinnati Bengals,
10 with a good chance of winning an exclusive all-expenses-paid trip to watch the Super Bowl final in New Orleans. To about one hundred of the 'lucky' recipients, the invitation sounded too good to miss.

On the appointed day, these people turned up at the Washington Convention Centre, hoping that they would win a coveted ticket to the Super Bowl. Any
15 lingering doubts they may have had disappeared when they arrived and were surrounded by a deceptively warm and friendly atmosphere. A queue of gullible people lined up to have their invitations checked. While they waited, they were given free drinks and food by attractive hostesses. Soothing music filled the air and a giant video screen showed replays of the Washington Redskins' previous games.
20 To add to the fun, one man was dressed in the full costume of a Red Indian chief while another was pretending to be a chicken.

The invited guests were overjoyed. They laughed, shook hands and congratulated each other on their good fortune. They were completely relaxed as they waited their turn to go up to the check-in desk, where each was required to establish his or her identity by showing a driving licence or an ID card. A smiling host checked the name with his list, announced in delight: 'Another lucky winner!' and asked the person to go through into a waiting-room, where all winners would shortly receive their complimentary tickets for that afternoon's football game.

But the whole operation was an elaborate trick. All the staff – hosts, hostesses, and even the Red Indian chief and the chicken – were police officers, most of them armed. (The chicken packed a pistol under his left wing.) All the guests were crooks, and when they had proved their identity and had assembled in one room, their smiling host revealed some totally unexpected news.

'I'd like to welcome you here today,' he said, 'and I'd really like to thank you all for coming. Now we have a big surprise for you! You're all under arrest!'

The 'lucky' winners smiled and clapped at what they thought was an amusing joke but their smiles disappeared when dozens of uniformed police officers burst into the room and pointed shotguns at them. Some of the guests were so astonished that they were still laughing and smiling as the police put handcuffs on them and took them away. Some of them even imagined that the 'arrest' was simulated and part of their welcome. They soon discovered that they were sadly mistaken.

Police later announced that they had arrested 98 men and women who had been wanted for crimes which included murder, armed robbery, arson and assault.

4.3 Understanding

A Choose the best answer each time.

1. In line 1 of the passage, 'hit upon' is similar in meaning to ____.
   A. discovered   B. investigated   C. implemented   D. embraced

2. Which of these words, used later in the passage, best explains why 100 out of 3000 crooks attended the party?
   A. successful   B. lucky   C. friendly   D. gullible

3. For the majority of the crooks on the marshals' list, the invitation proved to be ____.
   A. convincing   B. resistible   C. fateful   D. disastrous

4. In line 11, the word 'lucky' is in inverted commas because ____.
   A. it is a quotation from the invitation sent to guests
   B. this is a way of emphasising the word
   C. the word is used in a way which is different from the normal use
   D. the names were selected at random by a computer

5. In line 14, 'coveted' tells us that a ticket to the Super Bowl was ____.
   A. highly desirable but hard to obtain
   B. available free to some of the lucky winners
   C. not really going to be given to any guest
   D. good for more than one year

6. The Red Indian chief and the chicken were intended to make the party seem ____.
   A. long   B. genuine   C. improvised   D. historical

7. The real purpose of the check-in desk was to ____.
   A. ensure that the guests were wanted crooks
   B. make the guests happy when they first arrived
   C. enable the guests to meet each other and have a chat
   D. stop the guests from leaving too early

8. The marshals probably felt that the happy atmosphere ____.
   A. contributed to the success of their scheme
   B. was a good way of persuading people to come to the party
   C. was a method of allowing the police officers to enjoy themselves
   D. kept a large number of people away from the event by making them suspicious

B Answer these questions about the passage.

1. Who probably paid for the free drinks and food?

2. What is a Convention Centre normally used for?

3. Suggest a reason why the majority of the crooks on the marshals' list did *not* accept the invitation.

4. Why were some of the guests not upset or angry when they were arrested?

English Alive!

4.4 Vocabulary: meaning in context

A Choose the word(s) which best show(s) the meaning of the underlined words as they are used in the passage.

1. the invitation looks irresistible (line 3)
   A. unacceptable
   B. unbelievable
   C. too attractive to decline
   D. beyond one's belief

2. the invitation looks irresistible and convincing (line 3)
   A. making one believe that it is genuine and attractive
   B. arranged in a suitable and attractive manner
   C. planned in a way which is profitable for the organisers
   D. sent only to people with a high reputation

3. The marshals compiled a list of dangerous wanted crooks (line 5)
   A. looked carefully through
   B. examined in detail
   C. put together
   D. used as their base

4. name had been selected at random (line 7)
   A. with great care
   B. on purpose
   C. using sound criteria
   D. by chance

5. They promised a lavish party (line 8)
   A. to which only carefully chosen guests were invited
   B. with a lot of good food (and perhaps entertainment)
   C. better than, and different from, normal parties
   D. from which each guest would gain something

6. a good chance of winning an exclusive all-expenses-paid trip (line 10)
   A. excellent and available only to certain people
   B. which does not omit anything reasonable
   C. which includes a visit to something good
   D. with travel in both directions paid for

7. the invitations sounded too good to miss (line 12)
   A. evade   B. deny   C. not decline   D. not accept

8. On the appointed day, these people turned up (line 13)
   A. designated   B. following   C. next available   D. awarded

9. Any lingering doubts they may have had (line 15)
   A. still remaining
   B. considerable
   C. even very small
   D. unjustified

10. the deceptively warm and friendly atmosphere (line 16)
    A. clearly   B. able to deceive   C. rather   D. pleasantly

Unit 4 · The Sting   45

B Match the underlined words with the meanings which they have in the passage.

Words in the passage	Meanings
1. <u>Soothing</u> music filled the air (line 18)	a) pretended, unreal
2. They were completely <u>relaxed</u> (line 23)	b) gathered together
3. their <u>complimentary</u> tickets (line 28)	c) deliberately setting fire to property
4. the whole <u>operation</u> (line 29)	d) extremely surprised or shocked
5. (it) was one <u>elaborate</u> trick (line 29)	e) provided free of charge
6. had <u>assembled</u> in one room (line 32)	f) disclosed
7. host <u>revealed</u> some … news (line 33)	g) calming and restful
8. guests were so <u>astonished</u> (line 39)	h) event
9. the 'arrest' was <u>simulated</u> (line 41)	i) at ease and without stress
10. <u>arson</u> and assault (line 44)	j) intricate

4.5
Writing: finding a plot

From a writer's point of view, there are three possible approaches to the 'sting' story in 4.2:

- Write from the point of view of a police officer (1st or 3rd person narrative).
- Write from the point of view of one of the victims (1st or 3rd person narrative).
- Write from the point of view of an observer or reporter (1st or 3rd person).

The account in 4.2 uses the third method above. This reminds us that when we write about a person shown in a photograph, we can make the person the 'saver' (fire, flood, drowning, etc.) *or* the rescued person *or* a witness or reporter.
As an aid to memory, we can use the expression 'Saver, saved, saw' to remind us of three approaches to writing about somebody shown in a picture:

S – saver: The person in the picture saved somebody.
S – saved: Somebody saved the person in the picture.
S – saw: The person in the picture was an eye-witness to an accident, rescue, etc.

Remember SSS. It may help you when you write any kind of story.

English Alive!

4.6
Writing: making a summary

Make a summary of the passage in 4.2.

- Do not use more than 100 words.

- Do not spend more than 30 minutes on this task.

- Use *one* of these two methods:
  a) Aim to write 10–15 words about each of the six main stages in the passage:
     wanted to catch
     invited
     checked ID
     assembled
     arrested
     98 charged.

    Check that each sentence or point follows smoothly and logically from the previous ones. Check for errors and that you have not written more than 100 words.
    or
  b) Make rough notes about every few lines of the passage. Keep your notes short. In total, your notes should be about half the length of your final summary, i.e. about 50 words. Join your notes up. Make sure that they read smoothly. Check for errors and length. Finish.

4.7
Writing a story (review)

In 3.10 we saw that 'Catching a rabbit and catching a tiger are two different things.' This was a reminder that writing 400–450 words in an examination is different from writing 4000–4500 words in a short story for publication. The ingredients and skills set out below apply to most novels, films, TV stories and published short stories, but you may not be able to include them all in a story written during an examination.

Setting or background

These are examples of some settings used for stories:

- **medicine/health/hospitals** Many stories deal with problems affecting doctors or patients in a hospital. There are several TV series set in hospitals.

- **crime/detectives/police work** Sherlock Holmes and modern detectives set out to catch criminals.

- **space/aliens/space wars** Can you name any films or books with this setting?

- **love/romance** Can you name any books or films dealing with this popular topic?

Unit 4 · The Sting

Other (less common) settings include:

- horse-racing
- the work of a vet (veterinary surgeon)
- life in a farming community
- ghosts and phantoms (*Scooby Doo*)
- a factory (*The Simpsons*).

If you can provide an interesting setting or background for a story, your reader will learn something at the same time as he or she is entertained by the plot.

Plot

The three main ways of working out a plot are by creating conflict:

- **between people**, e.g. two men hoping to marry the same girl, two people competing for the same job, a bully and a victim
- **within a person**, e.g. action arising because somebody is too ambitious, too mean, too trusting, too sensitive, too greedy
- **with some extraneous event**, e.g. fishermen trapped in a storm; a punctured tyre; flood victims; a traffic accident; fire victims.

Characters

If possible, the reader needs to sympathise or identify with one of the characters (the people in the story). When you are writing, you may be able to base your characters on people you know or have seen in a film or on television. We saw in Book 3, that you can develop some of your characters by using one or more of these methods:

- describing what the person looks like, e.g.
  He was a small man with the sharp features and beady eyes of a hungry rat.
- describing the person's clothes if they reveal character
- showing how the person moves and speaks
- showing what other people think of a character and how he or she reacts with them
- putting words into a character's mouth to reveal his or her character and motives
- letting the character's actions reveal his or her personality.

Language and dialogue

In the CSEC examination, you are allowed to use dialect for dialogue, but make sure that it suits the character.

4.8
Writing: starting a story

We can start a story in any of the following ways. We can apply them to the story of the 'sting'. Study the examples below and in each case give two more examples.

- Start with a **statement**, e.g.
  Police Chief Morris studied the crime figures for his district and frowned. Far too many of the reported crimes remained unsolved.
  or
  Police in America have hit upon a new method of catching wanted criminals.

- Start with **action**, e.g.
  Police Chief Morris jumped out of bed and hurried to his desk in his home. He was anxious to make notes before he forgot his new plan.
  or
  Tug Wilson opened the envelope and looked inside. He was surprised to find an invitation with a promise of free food, free drinks and a free ticket to watch his favourite football team tackle the Cincinnati Bengals. This was one chance he was not going to miss.

- Start with **dialogue**, e.g.
  'I've got it!' Police Chief Morris said to his wife. 'We'll invite them all to a party!'
  'Invite them to a party?' his wife said. 'What – a party for criminals! You must be joking. You'd better stay at home for a few days and have a rest.'
  or
  'Hey! Look at this!' Tug Wilson said to his wife. 'Look at this! I've got an invitation to a party and I'm going to get free tickets to the Redskins game. It's me lucky day!'
  Or so he thought.
  It is also possible to start a story with a quotation or proverb, but the three methods shown above are easier to use. Remember **SAD** – **s**tatement, **a**ction, **d**ialogue.

Over to you!

Exercise 1

Answer *one* of these questions. Write 2–5 lines only.

1. Look back at the way in which Jack Williams was wounded in 3.2. You are a reporter and have interviewed Williams in his hospital bed. Use SAD and write down three different ways of starting the story of how he was wounded.

or

2. You are a reporter and have decided to write an account of the way in which Mary Blank died in 3.2. Use SAD and write down three different ways of starting your account.

4.9
Writing: setting out dialogue

A few months ago, I joined the police force in Washington DC, USA. Last week, Sgt Paula Johnson stopped me in the police precinct.

'I've got a job for you,' she said.

'Yes, Sarge,' I said. 'What is it?'

'I want you to dress up as a chicken,' she said.

I thought she must be joking. I stared at her in total disbelief.

'As a chicken? What — that thing that lays eggs or goes "Cockadoodledo"?'

'That's right — a chicken with yellow feathers. You'll look really … er, striking!'

I had heard of police officers disguising themselves as taxi-drivers, labourers and even as beggars but as a chicken? Impossible, surely. However, I was a comparatively new recruit and did not want to lose my job or be rude.

'Could you explain, please?' I asked politely.

Sgt Johnson giggled at my discomfort. 'Certainly,' she said. 'We're planning to invite a whole load of crooks to a party. We need somebody to represent the Redskins. Your job will be to represent the Bengals. …'

Exercise 2

Study the passage above. Notice that each new speaker starts a new paragraph. Then imagine that you are a new recruit in the Washington police force. Sgt Johnson wants you to dress up as a Red Indian to represent the Washington Redskins football team. Write a dialogue between Sgt Johnson and yourself. Write at least 15 lines. You can leave the dialogue unfinished, as in the example above.

English Alive!

4.10
Two warnings

1. Notice that in the above situation, you could not use dialect because Washington police officers do not use Caribbean dialect.

2. If you had to write an account of the 'sting' in an examination, you would not have time to write 15 lines of dialogue because you still have to develop the plot: an invitation, checking-in, the arrest. If you start a story (in an examination) with dialogue, don't let it run away with you. Get to your plot as soon as possible. If you finish your plot earlier than expected, you can probably add some dialogue near the end to reach the required length.

4.11
Enjoying poetry: sonnets

A **sonnet** is a type of poem with 14 lines. It is usually about a single idea and is written with this rhyme scheme: *abab, cdcd, efef, gg*. The lines are usually written as **iambic pentameters** (an iamb is an unstressed syllable followed by a stressed syllable, 'pent' means 'five', so an iambic pentameter consists of five iambs). In the lines below, the stressed syllables are in bold and the first line has been split into iambs:

```
   1         2        3       4      5
```
No **lon**|ger **mourn**| for **me**| when **I**| am **dead**
Than **you** shall **hear** the **sur**ly **sul**len **bell**
Give **war**ning **to** the **world** that **I** am **fled**
From **this** vile **world** with **vil**est **worms** to **dwell**.

The gist of the following sonnet by Shakespeare is this: 'Don't mourn for me after I am dead because that might upset you. Just forget about me completely. I don't want my death or your love for me to cause you suffering, so forget about me.' The sonnet was written about 400 years ago.

Sonnet 71

No longer mourn for me when I am dead
Than you shall hear the surly sullen <u>bell</u>   in a church at a funeral
Give warning to the world that I <u>am fled</u>   have died
From this vile world with vilest worms to dwell.
5 Nay, if you read this line, remember not
The hand that writ it; for I love you so
That I in your sweet thoughts would be forgot
If thinking on me then should make you woe.
O, if, I say, you look upon this verse

10 When I perhaps <u>compounded am with clay</u>,	have died
Do not so much as my poor name <u>rehearse</u>,	repeat, say
But let your love even with my life decay,	
Lest the wise world should look into your <u>moan</u>	sorrow, distress
And mock you with me after I am gone.	

William Shakespeare

Note: In Shakespeare's time, 'moan' and 'gone' rhymed when they were spoken.

Questions

1. In line 2, the poet calls the bell 'surly' and 'sullen'. Is this an example of personification or a simile?

2. In line 5, which word can we omit without changing the meaning of the line?

3. In line 10, how is the normal order of words changed? Why is the word order changed?

4. In line 11, suggest a reason why the poet chose to use 'rehearse' instead of 'repeat' or 'say'.

5. What is the attitude of the poet to the person to whom the poem is addressed?

6. Which five syllables in the last line are stressed?

Now read this sonnet by Claude McKay, written in 1954:

I Shall Return

I shall return again; I shall return	
To laugh and love and watch with wonder-eyes	
At golden noon the forest fires burn,	
Wafting their blue-black smoke to sapphire skies.	
5 I shall return to loiter by the streams	
That bathe the brown blades of the bending grasses,	
And realize once more my thousand dreams	
Of waters rushing down the mountain passes.	
I shall return to hear the fiddle and fife	
10 Of village dances, dear delicious tunes	
That stir the hidden depths of native life,	
Stray melodies of dim-remembered <u>runes</u>.	ancient forms of writing
I shall return, I shall return again,	
To ease my mind of long, long years of pain.	

Claude McKay

Questions

1. Where do you think the poet was when he wrote this poem?

2. To which place did the poet want to return? Find any evidence in the poem to support your answer.

3. What alliterating sounds does the poet use in:
   a) line 2?
   b) line 6?
   c) line 10?

4. What does 'realize' mean in line 7?

5. Why does the poet mention 'my thousand dreams' and 'long, long years of pain'?

6. In what ways is the tone of this sonnet different from the tone of Shakespeare's sonnet?

4.12
Writing: test – SSS and SAD

1. The letters SSS show three quick ways of making up a plot when you write about a picture of a person. What do the letters SSS stand for?

2. The letters SAD show three ways of starting a story (or almost any form of composition). What do the letters **SAD** stand for?

Unit 4 · The Sting

4.13
Writing

Write about 400–450 words about *one* of the following topics. Allow yourself a maximum of 45 minutes for thinking, planning, writing and correcting.

1. Write a story based on the people in *one* of the pictures above.

2. Write a story which finishes with these words:
   …*When I finally went home, I felt quite pleased with myself.*

3. Write a story which begins with these words:
   There is a well-known saying: 'Too many cooks spoil the broth'. …

5 Tourism

5.1
Writing: straight and crooked thinking

Sometimes you may have to write about an argumentative topic, i.e. one in which you discuss a situation or have to consider both sides of a problem. When you write about this type of topic, be aware of these errors and try to avoid them:

- **unreasonable exaggeration**, including making wild and untruthful claims, e.g.
  Tourism has done more to harm this country than any other factor. Most tourists bring drugs with them and this has led to the widespread use of drugs amongst our people.

- **unfair generalisation** based on a single example, e.g.
  The trouble with foreigners is that they all drink too much and become abusive and violent. A couple of days ago, the police had to arrest one young man who had drunk so much that he could hardly walk.

- **presenting an opinion as if it is a fact**, e.g.
  Of course, it's well known that the vast majority of our people bitterly resent tourists coming here and ruining the place for local people. I reckon the Government doesn't care what the people think.

- **making a false comparison**: comparing the worst of one group to the best of another group, e.g.
  Tourists are a menace on the roads in their flashy rental cars. Yesterday I saw one of them run straight into the back of a bus. We've had a car for twenty years and have never had an accident. It just shows how dangerous tourists are on the roads.

- **selective arguing**: choosing only those points that suit your argument and ignoring those that do not, e.g.
  As far as I am concerned, all those tourist hotels should be pulled down. They spoil the view for local people and take up valuable land.

- **failing to argue objectively** (i.e. without personal bias; without looking fairly at the facts) **and becoming subjective** (i.e. allowing personal bias or feelings to affect your judgement), e.g.
  Just look at the way they throw their money around as if they own the place. They think money can buy anything. Most of the time, they're just showing off and treating other people like dirt. It really burns me up!

If you are interested in a topic, it is easy to get carried away and argue unfairly. Especially in an examination, try to be objective, fair and truthful. Remember that there are two sides to most arguments. Consider both sides fairly.

Over to you!

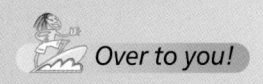

Exercise 1

Comment on the reasoning shown in these sentences.

1. Ice and butter melt in the sun. This strongly suggests that all things melt in the sun.
2. It is well known that women are the weaker sex. They don't make good professional wrestlers. Any male team can beat a women's team at football or cricket.
3. Most men adhere to a code of ethics which is non-existent.
4. It seems likely that the people who first settled in some parts of the country and from whom some of us are descended definitely consisted of women.
5. It is not suitable for our secondary schools to give rewards or to punish the pupils. As pupils are human beings, and human beings cannot avoid making mistakes, there should be no punishment in schools.
6. Is it right for a woman to rule a country when there are men, learned men, available for the task?
7. The position of adverbs is always before the verb.
8. Conditions on the main road leading into town have become worst as a result of heavy rain during the night.
9. In my opinion, it is wrong to allow women to vote in elections. We can compare the task of governing a country with the business of boxing or weight-lifting. Whoever heard of a female heavyweight boxing champion of the world?
10. The airport should not be extended. We have managed well enough with one runway in the past. Building a second runway would establish a precedent. Airlines might seek a further expansion in the future if this proposal is approved.
11. The population of Trinidad is greater than the area of Guyana.
12. British and American English have totally different forms of pronunciation, spelling and writing.

England and America are two countries separated by a common language.

5.2 Reading

Read this passage. See if you notice any illogical or unfair reasoning.

Talking about Tourism

Nadia Ramball backed her car out of her yard and set off to work. A few minutes later, she saw a former classmate waiting at a bus-stop. She stopped her car and shouted to her friend, 'Hi, Donna. Can I give you a lift? I'm going downtown.'

Donna was glad to get a lift. The two young women chatted as Nadia drove towards the town where she worked. Donna was in a talkative mood. A coach full of tourists passed the car.

'Tourists everywhere!' Donna exclaimed. 'Everywhere I go, I see them! And now there's going to be a new hotel at Devil's Bay! It'll spoil the view for everybody except a whole load of wealthy foreigners! The Government should stop it!'

'What's the matter with you today?' Nadia said. 'You should be glad to see a lot of tourists around. Nearly half of our income comes from tourism …'

'Well, none of it comes my way!' Donna retorted.

'Yes, but you can use all the new facilities built to make tourism possible,' Nadia said. 'There's the airport and …'

'You won't catch me flying,' Donna said, 'and I certainly shan't be going on one of those cruise ships.'

'Yes, but we've got better taxis and other facilities to cope with tourists,' Nadia said, beginning to get a little annoyed by Donna's negative tone.

'And we get more litter on the beaches in return, more traffic on our roads, and more noise as a result,' Donna commented.

'Don't forget that tourism provides thousands of jobs here,' Nadia said. 'In addition to hotels, taxis, guides and others, there are many small businesses that rely on tourism and employ local people as a result.'

Donna was quiet for a moment and Nadia hoped that she would change the subject but a few minutes later she suddenly said, 'What about drugs and alcohol? Tourists have brought those in.'

'Oh, come on,' Nadia replied. 'Do you mean to say there would be no drugs and alcohol if we had no tourists? You're not living in the same world as I am! Those things were here long before tourism developed. They might get ganja here but I very much doubt whether they bring it with them. Don't forget that hotels buy large quantities of local fruit and vegetables, which helps our farmers. In the popular tourist areas, the shops, restaurants and medical services have improved steadily. Even the dentists profit from tourists who develop toothache.'

'I guess you're right,' Donna said eventually. 'It's just that I don't like to see our land used for hotels and tourist resorts, but maybe you're right. How far into town are you going?'

'As far as the Lido Hotel,' Nadia said. 'I work there at the Reception desk. Where can I drop you off?'

'Oh, anywhere,' Donna said. 'I was only going into town to look for a job.
40 Nobody seems to want a newly qualified book-keeper. I've been hunting for a job for more than six months. Any chance of getting a job at your place?'

'As a matter of fact, I think there is – a good chance. I know we need two more members of staff to deal with accounts.'

'Really? Can I try for one of the jobs? Maybe this is going to be my lucky day,'
45 Donna said.

'OK. Come with me and we'll see Miss Kissoon. She's in charge of staff. You'll like her. She's very friendly but don't knock tourism when you're talking to her. You know what they say: don't bite the hand that feeds you!'

Donna laughed. 'Me bite? Never! I've always been in favour of tourism – well
50 ever since I heard about the jobs at the hotel.'

5.3
Understanding

A   Choose the best answer each time.

1. As far as we can tell from the passage, Donna lived ____.
   A. opposite Nadia
   B. a few yards from Nadia
   C. some distance from Nadia
   D. in the centre of the city

2. In line 9, Donna's use of 'wealthy' suggests a feeling of ____ on Donna's part.
   A. resentment   B. appreciation   C. joy   D. evil

3. In line 12, 'retorted' is used to show that ____.
   A. Nadia was not in a good mood
   B. Donna knew that her friend was partly deaf
   C. Nadia's remarks did not get a very sympathetic response
   D. Donna was anxious not to upset her friend and be ungrateful

English Alive!

4. In lines 13 and 17, Nadia uses 'Yes' with the meaning '____'.
   A. You're quite right
   C. I'm inclined to agree with you
   B. That may be so
   D. Despite what I say

5. A major reason why Nadia began to get 'a little annoyed' (line 18) may well have been the fact that ____.
   A. Donna had bullied her when they were both at school
   B. Donna had not yet found a job
   C. the traffic did not really bother her
   D. her job depended upon the arrival of tourists

6. The most likely words which Nadia omitted after 'Oh, come on' in line 27 are ____.
   A. hurry up
   C. don't delay
   B. I agree with you
   D. be realistic

7. In line 31, 'which' refers to ____.
   A. buying local produce
   C. large quantities
   B. fruit
   D. vegetables

B Answer these questions about the passage.

1. Why did Nadia stop to offer Donna a lift?

2. In what way did Nadia and Donna differ in their attitude towards tourism?

3. In line 12, Donna said, 'Well, none of it comes my way!' What does this tell us about her attitude towards tourism?

4. What is the meaning of the expression 'negative tone' in line 18?

5. What did Donna mean when she said, 'Me bite?' in line 49?

5.4

Vocabulary: meaning in context

Choose the word(s) which best show(s) the meaning of the underlined words as they are used in sections 5.1 and 5.2.

1. people bitterly resent tourists coming here (5.1, line 13)
   A. prevent   B. are opposed to   C. criticise   D. complain

2. I reckon the Government doesn't care what people think (line 14)
   A. consider   B. know   C. am certain   D. wonder if

3. Tourists are a menace on the roads in their flashy rental cars. (line 18)
   A. nuisance   B. risk   C. common sight   D. threat

4. It'll spoil the view for everybody (5.2, line 8)
   A. destroy   B. detract from   C. obliterate   D. change

Unit 5 · Tourism 59

5. 'Well, none of it comes my way!' Donna <u>retorted</u>. (line 12)
   A. quickly denied
   B. claimed somewhat sadly
   C. said sharply
   D. interrupted

6. you can use all the new <u>facilities</u> built to make tourism possible (line 13)
   A. hotels and restaurants
   B. things of use to people
   C. airport and docks
   D. amusement centres

7. I certainly shan't be going on one of those <u>cruise</u> ships (line 16)
   A. taking people sightseeing on holiday
   B. offering special prices to emigrants
   C. very modern and large
   D. luxurious and expensive

8. we've got better taxis and other facilities to <u>cope with</u> tourists (line 17)
   A. welcome   B. deal with   C. move   D. please

9. there are many small businesses that <u>rely</u> on tourism (line 23)
   A. grow   B. expand   C. support   D. depend

10. 'I guess you're right,' Donna said <u>eventually</u>. (line 34)
    A. reluctantly   B. at last   C. slowly   D. suddenly

11. Nobody seems to want a newly <u>qualified</u> book-keeper (line 40)
    A. trained and found to be proficient
    B. with a university degree
    C. experienced and eager to work
    D. with the right age and background

12. but don't <u>knock</u> tourism when you're talking to her (line 47)
    A. mention   B. speak badly about   C. discuss   D. avoid

5.5
Writing: summary practice

Read through the passage in 5.2 again. Imagine that you are Donna and have managed to get a job in the hotel where Nadia works. As a result of your new job, you are now very much in favour of tourism (because if no tourists come you will lose your job).

In no more than 70 words, make a summary of the advantages and/or good aspects of tourism, using material in the passage. Work in this way:

1. Read the passage, make relevant notes and write down (in rough form) the five major advantages or good points of tourism. Use 1–4 words for each note.

2. Then link up your notes to make a draft summary of no more than 70 words.

3. If possible, ask a classmate to check your draft summary for errors.

4. Then write out your final summary.

5.6

Grammar: phrases and clauses (revision)

There are several reasons why you need to know the following points. You may meet some of these grammatical terms in the CSEC examination, so you should understand what they mean. For example, you must know the difference between the words 'phrase' and 'clause'.

- A **phrase** is a group of words which does **not** contain a finite verb and its subject. Many phrases start with a preposition or with a participle. We can have noun phrases, adjectival phrases and adverbial phrases, e.g.

    noun phrases: **To log on to the internet** does not take very long.
    Many tourists like **scrambling up Dunn's River Falls**.
    adjectival phrases: The girl **with long hair** is Teerath's sister.
    A truck towed away the car **damaged in the accident**.
    adverbial phrases: We can leave our bikes **under that tree**.
    Nadia left her car **in the hotel car park**.

- A **clause** is a group of words which contains a finite verb and its subject.
    – A **main clause** makes complete sense and can stand by itself. Two main clauses *must* usually be separated by a full stop, question mark, semicolon or (more rarely) by a colon *or* they must be linked by a connective such as 'and' or 'but'. All the six sentences above are main clauses.
    – A **subordinate clause** can do the work of a noun, an adjective or an adverb. Notice that a subordinate clause is *not* a sentence. It must be joined to a main clause. Then it forms *part* of a sentence. We can say that a subordinate clause is like a baby in its mother's arms. The baby cannot survive without its mother. Similarly, a subordinate clause cannot be used without its 'mother', i.e. a main clause, e.g.

    noun clauses: Do you know **when Uncle's plane arrives**?
    How the men escaped from prison is still a mystery.
    adjectival clauses: Anybody **who lives in Ocho Rios** knows Dolphin Cove.
    This is the costume **which I intend to wear at the Carnival**.
    adverbial clauses: Several roads will be closed **when the Carnival starts**.
    If we get up at 2 a.m., we will hear the start of the Carnival.

Over to you!

Exercise 2

Say whether the words in bold type below are phrases or clauses.

1. There's plenty of room **in the back of the car.**

2. Any motorist **caught exceeding the speed limit** will be fined.

3. **Whatever you do**, don't forget to water the plants **while we are away**.

4. Tourists like to travel on cruise ships **because they can visit several different places**.

5. Any bags **left lying around at the airport** will be regarded **with suspicion** and are liable to be destroyed.

6. The book **you asked me to try to get** is out of print at the moment.

7. **Although tropical storms sweep through the Caribbean every year**, it is rare for a hurricane to affect us.

8. The referee took the name of the player **who kicked the goalkeeper deliberately** and then sent him **off the field**.

9. The house **Mr Harris has just bought** is much nearer to the town **in which he and his wife both work**. It is also more convenient **for both of his children**.

10. **To get to the beach from here** takes about five minutes.

Exercise 3

Correct any mistakes of punctuation in the following:

1. Although tourism is extremely important to the economy of our country. It is not the only source of revenue for the Government.

2. In the opinion of one expert, tourism is the driver of economic activity across all sectors of the economy. Agriculture, manufacturing, transportation and entertainment, as well as other important areas of Jamaican life.

3. The Tourism Minister, Aloun Assamba, stressed the importance of tourism. 'We are not doing well simply because others are doing badly,' she said, 'we are reaping the benefits of the hard work done by people involved in the industry.'

4. At the moment, seven to eight vessels visit Ocho Rios every week, this figure will be increased by three more ships in January. Making this cruise shipping season one of the best seen in years.

5. Barbados and Antigua are already well-established tourist resorts, Guyana is likely to increase in popularity within the next year or two, it has a wide diversity of natural attractions to offer visitors.

6. Tourism is a phenomenon which has developed immensely since the Second World War. Largely because of the development of large planes which can carry passengers thousands of miles. Faster and more cheaply than ships can do.

7. Every European country is anxious to encourage and develop tourism. Now it is quite common for students to take a year off (known as a 'gap' year) between leaving school and entering a university, they save up the money for the first stage of their journey, then they work at each stage to get the money for the next stage.

8. One result of a 'gap' year is that students learn more about how people live in other countries, the experience also tends to make students more mature, as a result, they work harder when they enter a university.

5.7
Spelling: prefixes

When we add the letters below to a word, we do not have a double letter unless the last letter of the prefix is the same as the first letter of the word or root to which we add the prefix.

Check that you know the meaning of the following words and how to use them.

Prefix	Examples
un-	unhappy, unknown, uneasy, unaltered, unsophisticated, unfortunately, uneven
unn-	unnecessary, unnatural, unnamed, unnumbered, unnoticed, unneeded
mis-	misfire, misconduct, mistake, miscount, misguided, misunderstand, mistreat
miss-	misspell, misstate, misstep, misspeak
dis-	disappear, disagree, disappointed, disadvantage, disinterested, disorganised
diss-	dissolve, dissatisfied, dissimilar, disservice, dissuade, dissect
ill-	illegal, illicit, illegible, illegitimate, illiberal, illiterate, illogical, illusion
in-	insincere, inconvenient, ineligible, insignificant, inflexible, inexperienced
inn-	innocent, innocuous, innovation, innumerable
aqu- acqu-	The Latin word for 'water' is 'aqua', so English words derived from 'aqua' start with 'aqu'. Some other words start with 'acqu'. aquarium, aquanaut, aquatic, aqueduct, aqueous acquainted, acquaintance, acquiesce, acquire, acquitted, acquisitive

Now a partner can test you on some of the above words or you can have a competition between two halves of the class.

5.8
Making comparisons: using pie charts

Look at the pie charts. They show the comparative importance of sections of the economy in three countries: A, B and C.

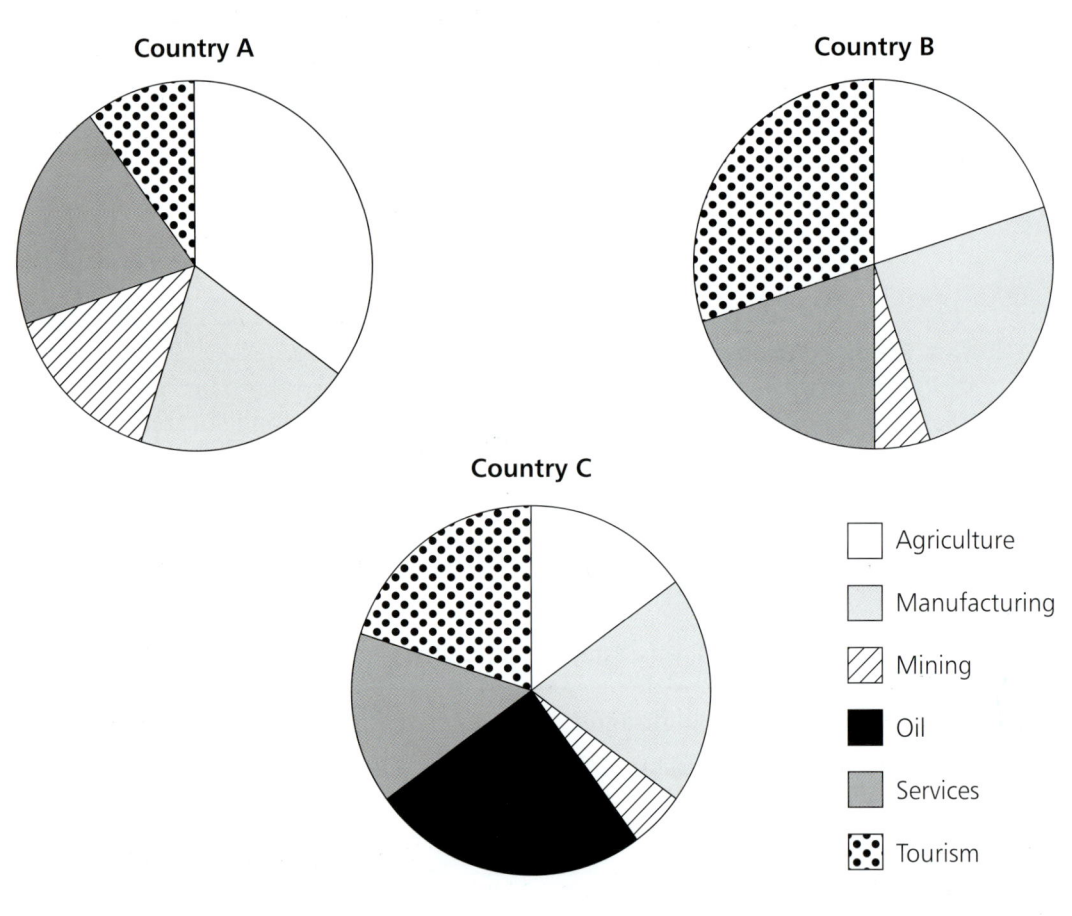

Country A

Country B

Country C

- Agriculture
- Manufacturing
- Mining
- Oil
- Services
- Tourism

Over to you!

Exercise 4

Study the charts and answer the following questions.

1. Say whether each of these sentences is: O an opinion, F a fact, U untrue.
   a) Agriculture appears to be more important in Country A than in either of the other two countries.
   b) At the moment, oil is not particularly important in two of the countries but this could change if oil is found in or near either of the countries.
   c) Country A ought to make a greater effort to attract tourists.
   d) If Country B tries to attract more tourists, the importance of agriculture may decline.
   e) There is no land suitable for growing crops or keeping cattle in Country C.
   f) If more tourists go to Country B, it is certain that fewer will go to Country C.
   g) Tourism is more important than the services sector in all three countries.

English Alive!

h) In Country B, manufacturing relies mainly on mining and oil in the country.
i) Country C is probably less reliant on imported fuel than Country B is.
j) The Government of Country B is not very interested in developing mining because agriculture is more important.

2. Answer these questions about the charts.
   a) In which country is tourism the least important at the moment?
   b) If tourism is developed in the country in question 2(a), which sector may become less important? What is your reason for your opinion?
   c) If you were the prime minister of Country B, would you try to reduce the number of tourists or not? What is the reason for your answer?
   d) Give three examples of occupations in the 'services' sector.
   e) Which two sectors are the most important in Country B?

5.9
Writing: the good and the bad

This is topic 2 from 4.13:

> Write a story of about 400–450 words which finishes with these words:
>
> … When I finally went home, I felt quite pleased with myself.

Read these two stories written in response to the topic.

Story 1

A student remembered SSS (save, saved, saw) and decided to write about a rescue at sea. This what he wrote:

> Last week my friend ask me if I want to go fishing with he, so I said yes, lets go. On Saturday, my friend borrowed his Uncles boat and we went fishing in the sea near Kraken Point, that is about two miles from me home. At first we do not catch anything, then my friend, Mark, shouted because he hook a really big fish. It was too strong for he to land by hisself, so he want me to help him.
>
> I held on my friend so that he will not fall out off the boat. The fish was very strong and pulled us a long way out to sea. In the end, we had to cut the line and let the fish to go. We went on fishing for more than a hour and we catch quiet a few fish. Then we see a very fast motor-boat coming towards us. We tried to row away from motor-boat but the currant was very strong, so we could not get out of the weigh. Suddenly the motor-boat raced passed us. It made a big wave. The wave hit our boat and

made it turn over. Me and my friend were thrown into the sea.
The boat hit the side of my head and I blacked out.

When I wake up, I see that I was in hospital. My friend was
there too. She said that I could not swim, so he holding on to
me and the boat. Some fishmen rescued us, then my friend took
me to hospital. I had a cut on my head, it was not a deep one.
After a hour, I was better, so I left the hospital. I was very
thankful to my friend for saving me, When I finally went home,
I felt quite please with myself.

This composition would not get even 30 per cent of the marks. It is full of mistakes, e.g.

- The writer could not even copy the last sentence from the question paper correctly. This type of carelessness annoys examiners.

- The story is weak. The writer was pleased with himself but he did not do anything to help his friend when their boat overturned.

- There are mistakes of spelling, punctuation, grammar and vocabulary.

Correct and discuss the mistakes in this composition. Then read Story 2 which deals with the same topic.

Story 2

Another student remembered SSS (save, saved, saw) and decided to write about a rescue at sea. This what she wrote:

Last week my friend, Nadia, asked me if I would like to go
fishing with her and her brother. I was delighted to go, so
Nadia's brother borrowed his uncle's boat and we set off from

Kraken Point. What we did not realise is that there is a strong off-shore current in the area. By the time we had discovered it, we had drifted nearly a mile away from the shore. At the time, we did not think this was important.

After we had been fishing about an hour, Nadia pointed and said, 'Hey, Selva, look at that speedboat! It's heading straight for us!'

Nadia was right. A large speedboat was racing towards us from the south-east. We shouted and waved but the speedboat came nearer and nearer. Then, almost at the last minute, it swerved away but created a big wave which smashed into our dinghy, hurling us into the water.

Our boat overturned and hit Nadia on her head and shoulder. Selva disappeared under the overturned boat. I managed to grab Nadia by her left arm and pulled her to the boat, where I struggled to keep her head above water. Then Selva appeared from under the boat and helped me to hold Nadia, who was still unconscious.

Quietly I prayed that God would help us because I could see that Nadia needed medical help and I began to feel worn out holding onto the overturned boat with one hand while holding Nadia up with the other. Within a few minutes, my prayer was answered. A tourist yacht appeared and the men managed to pull us onto it. Then they turned and headed back to the harbour. One of the men used his mobile phone and we were relieved to see an ambulance waiting for us when we reached the jetty.

The ambulance took us all to hospital. By this time, Nadia had recovered slightly. A doctor examined her carefully and said she needed to rest but was not in any danger. She was grateful when her brother told her how I had saved her. When I finally went home, I felt quite pleased with myself but deeply grateful to God for answering my prayers and for giving me the strength to help my friend.

Notice:

- There are no mistakes in the story, so the writer must get full marks for accuracy of language.

- The writer gives a better reason for feeling pleased with herself but then – to avoid being thought proud – she subordinates herself to God.

- The vocabulary is not difficult. If you study the writing of John Steinbeck or Ernest Hemingway, you will see that they use a comparatively simple style. Don't be tempted to put difficult, long or unusual words in your compositions. You may use them wrongly and they will probably seem odd to the examiner.

- The composition is slightly too short but we can easily add two sentences to the last paragraph to make it over 400 words.

5.10
Enjoying poetry

The following lines are taken from Shakespeare's play *As You Like It*. Jaques, a character in the play, describes the seven ages (or stages) through which a man passes from birth to death. Which age are you in now?

The Seven Ages of Man

    All the world's a stage,
    And all the men and women merely players.
    They have their exits and their entrances,
    And one man in his time plays many parts,
5 His acts being seven ages. At, first the infant,
    <u>Mewling</u> and <u>puking</u> in the nurse's arms.   **crying; being sick**
    And then the whining schoolboy, with his satchel
    And shining morning face, creeping like snail
    Unwillingly to school. And then the lover,
10 Sighing like furnace, with a woeful ballad
    Made to his mistress' eyebrow. Then the soldier,
    Full of strange oaths, and bearded like the <u>pard</u>,   **leopard**
    Jealous in honour, sudden and quick in quarrel,
    Seeking the bubble reputation
15 Even in the cannon's mouth. And then the justice,
    In fair round belly with good <u>capon</u> lined,   **chicken (eaten)**
    With eyes severe, and beard of formal cut,
    Full of wise <u>saws</u> and modern instances;   **sayings**
    And so he plays his part. The sixth age shifts
20 Into the lean and slippered <u>pantaloon</u>   **foolish old man**
    With spectacles on nose and pouch on side,
    His youthful <u>hose</u>, well saved, a world too wide   **stockings, long socks**
    For his shrunk <u>shank</u>; and his big manly voice,   **lower part of the leg**
    Turning again toward childish treble, pipes
25 And whistles in his sound. Last scene of all,
    That ends this strange eventful history,

Is second childishness and mere <u>oblivion</u>,
<u>Sans</u> teeth, sans eyes, sans taste, sans everything.
As You Like It, Act 2, Scene 7

being unaware of everything
without, not having

Questions

A Choose the best answer each time.

1. In line 2, Jaques' use of 'merely' presents ____ point of view.
   A. an optimistic
   B. a unique
   C. a fatalistic
   D. a cheerful

2. The first simile in this extract is in line ____.
   A. 2
   B. 6
   C. 8
   D. 10

3. In line 8, Jaques uses 'creeping' in order to ____.
   A. show how a snail moves
   B. contrast it with 'shining'
   C. intensify his description of the boy
   D. suggest that the boy is not typical

4. In line 14, 'bubble' is used to suggest that a person's reputation ____.
   A. may not last long
   B. is difficult to achieve
   C. is something very valuable
   D. is related to washing and cleanliness

5. In line 15, 'in the cannon's mouth' is a reference to ____.
   A. a church dignitary
   B. a battle of some kind
   C. warships fighting
   D. listening to a sermon in church

6. The 'modern instances' in line 18 would apparently be used ____.
   A. to praise somebody
   B. to obtain money
   C. as a form of punishment
   D. to give advice

B Answer these questions about the extract.

1. In line 4, Jaques says: 'And one man in his time plays many parts'. What does he mean by this?

Unit 5 · Tourism 69

2. What evidence can you find to suggest that Jaques' description was written many years ago?

3. What mood should an actor portray when speaking the extract on stage as part of the play *As You Like It*? What is your reason for your answer?

4. To what extent would you say that Jaques has accurately described the life of an ordinary person?

5.11
Argumentative writing

Great care is needed in writing about topics such as these:

- Discuss the view that a woman's place is in the home.

- What value, if any, do you think a study of literature has for science students?

- Do you think that the money now being spent on exploration of the moon, Mars and outer space is justified?

Follow these guidelines.

> **Guidelines for argumentative writing**
> - **Make sure that you can provide *quantity* as well as *quality*.** It is often difficult to find enough information to write calmly and fairly about this type of topic. Remember that you may have to write 30–40 lines. To reach a high standard, practise so that you can exceed this target.
>
> - Don't lose your temper or be arrogant or prejudiced. Stay cool! Look at this table. Discuss each item. Make sure you understand it.

Don't be …	Try to be …
Irrelevant and vague	Relevant and specific
Ignorant, omitting facts	Well informed and shrewd
Muddled and unable to develop your points logically	Logical, a good planner and an orderly person
Deliberately unfair	Honest and fair
Angry or bitter; quick to criticise or find fault	Self-controlled, generous and understanding
Inaccurate and exaggerated	Accurate, modest and fair to both sides
A domineering bully	Modest and tolerant

- **In an examination, study the question carefully** and find out whether you have to prove that a statement is true, disagree with it or consider both sides. If you fail to understand the question, the whole of your composition may be irrelevant.

Over to you!

Exercise 5

Comment briefly on each of these statements.

1. There is no racial prejudice in my country. It occurs only in other countries.
2. Children should be seen (rarely) and not heard.
3. Old people rarely understand the younger generation.
4. Television has a bad effect on both children and adults today.
5. Foreign influences are usually bad.
6. Today most young people have long hair and take drugs.
7. Without scientists, the world would collapse entirely.
8. The world would be a safer and cleaner place without science.

Exercise 6

In an examination question, what does the word 'discuss' mean? Does it mean 'agree', 'disagree', 'give your own opinion', 'consider both sides', or what?

Exercise 7

Look at these topics. In each case, say whether you have to (a) consider one side of the case only or (b) consider both sides.

1. Explain why Science students are more useful to the community than Arts students.
2. 'Science students are more useful to the community than Arts students.' Discuss.
3. Consider the claim that Geography is a more useful subject than History is.
4. 'Obedience at all times is the most important aspect of family life.' Discuss.
5. Show that too little homework may have a harmful effect on students.
6. 'A patriotic and loyal citizen supports his country whether it is in the wrong or right.' Consider this statement.

Exercise 8

Choose one of these topics. State your theme and make a detailed plan in not more than 15 minutes. Do *not* write the composition.

1. Which is better: coeducation or separate schools for boys and girls?

2. Discuss the view that, in matters of trade, no country is really independent, since all countries rely to some extent on external trade.

3. Consider the opinion that it is better and more convenient to live in an urban area than in a rural area.

4. 'Television and computers are slowly changing the traditional patterns of family life.'

5. What is your view of the suggestion that before a couple can produce a child they must obtain a certificate of physical and moral fitness from a special government unit set up to investigate the physique and character of the potential father and mother.

5.12
Writing

Either: Write 400–450 words on topic (1) or (2) in about 45 minutes.
or: Write 250–300 words on topic (3) in about 30 minutes.

1. Write a story based on *one* of the pictures above.

2. Write a story with the title 'A Happy Surprise' or 'An Unpleasant Surprise'.

3. In your country, which groups of people are most likely to want to encourage tourism? Which groups are most likely to discourage or oppose it? To which groups should the Government pay more attention?

English Alive!

6 *Crossing the Line*

6.1
Pre-reading

The passage in 6.2 explains how a doctor solved a rather tricky problem. One day a patient complained to him that he had a snake in his stomach. The patient, Colonel O'Reilly, was an important and very influential leader in the community. The doctor, who is the narrator in this extract, was certain that there was *not* a snake in Colonel O'Reilly's stomach but the Colonel was firmly convinced that there *was* one inside him. The Colonel continued to pester the doctor until the time came when a decision had to be made.

6.2
Reading

Crossing the Line

I came to the conclusion that something must be done about Colonel O'Reilly's snake or I would inevitably be placed in a padded cell. It was then that I decided to cross the narrow line that separates the physician from the charlatan.

One evening, Colonel O'Reilly was waiting for me at the corner of the street as I
5   left the dispensary. I reluctantly agreed that there was only one infallible way of confirming whether or not the snake was living inside the Colonel: I would have to open his stomach and do it in such a way as to convince my patient one way or the other.

'If there's no snake,' I explained, 'I'll close the stomach and say to you, "My
10 friend, I was right." On the other hand, if I find a snake, I'll drag it out and you can crush it or even retain it as a gruesome souvenir.'

I realised that I would have to take my dispensary assistant into my confidence. He was happy to play his part and solemnly swore to carry the secret to his grave. It could all be done in the evening, he proposed, when the dispensary would be
15 empty and the city preparing for sleep.

My assistant had worked for three years in the operating theatre of an overseas hospital and had administered chloroform before. He also undertook to provide the element which was absolutely indispensable for the success of our plan: a large snake. Gleefully, he promised me snakes of such a size that I was obliged to curb
20 his enthusiasm and to remind him that a human stomach could not contain a mature python.

The Colonel arrived punctually with the servants who were to carry him home after the operation. He climbed onto the operating table, and my assistant fixed

the chloroform mask on the patient's face. The pious man was praying; his voice
became muffled under the mask and very soon the words faded away and he was
breathing deeply and regularly. I took up a lancet and made a lengthy incision
which seemed sufficient for the extraction of even a young crocodile. I stopped the
bleeding and sewed up the superficial wound in the Colonel's abdomen.

The Colonel was still sleeping peacefully. His men carried him away on a
stretcher. With a feeling of great relief, I watched them go, followed by my
assistant. Under his arm, he carried a cardboard box, carefully closed and tied with
string, containing an unfortunate and furiously struggling snake. For a fleeting
moment, I wondered what the Animal Rights activists would make of the situation.
On the following day, I went to see the Colonel at his home. I found him
extremely well. He was, of course, resigned to remaining in bed for a fortnight or
so, since it would be unwise to take risks after such a serious operation. But he was
radiant and sought with great magnanimity to comfort me.

'We all make mistakes, doctor. You see, there *was* a snake – a very active one. God
has spared my life, so I have set the snake free.'

Deeply moved, he embraced me. He did not wish me to take my mistake to
heart, he said. It saddened him to see me confused and mortified.

'But you have saved me, my friend!' He embraced me again, patting me on the
back to encourage me.

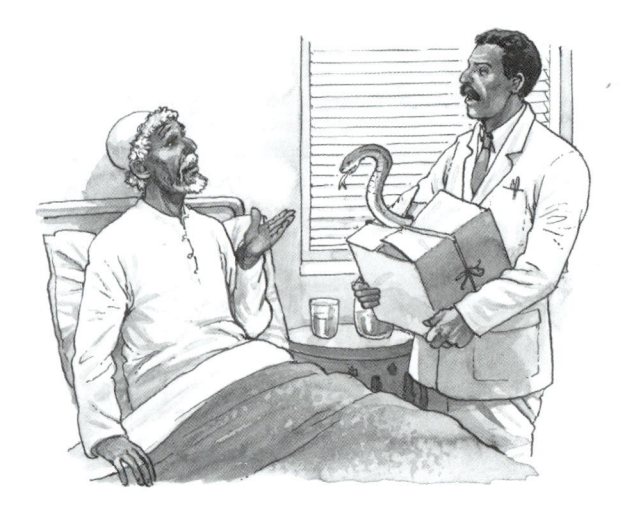

6.3
Understanding

A Choose the best answer each time.

1. In the mind of the narrator, the 'decision' (mentioned at the end of 6.1) involved answering this question:
   A. Shall I have the Colonel put in a padded cell?
   B. Shall I carry out an operation to satisfy the Colonel and myself?
   C. Will it be illegal to operate on the Colonel?
   D. How soon will it be before I am placed in a padded cell?

2. The doctor apparently felt that he would become a charlatan if ____.
   A. he refused to help the Colonel
   B. he cured his patient by means of a trick
   C. the operation showed that there was no snake in his patient
   D. it turned out that there *was* a snake in the man's stomach

3. In line 3, the 'narrow line' was something which involved the doctor's
   A. code of honour
   B. code of conduct
   C. financial standing
   D. ambitions

4. Which word in section 6.1 best shows why the doctor was probably not surprised to find Colonel O'Reilly waiting for him?
   A. solved   B. tricky   C. pester   D. decision

5. As far as we can judge, the Colonel was ____ to have an operation.
   A. anxious   B. reluctant   C. unwilling   D. unprepared

6. Which of the following expressions can best be inferred after 'right' in line 10?
   A. to carry out an operation
   B. to take out the snake
   C. to close the stomach
   D. in my earlier diagnosis

7. The dispensary assistant was necessary to act as ____.
   A. a nurse
   B. a laboratory assistant
   C. an anaesthetist
   D. an assistant surgeon

8. The incision in line 26 was long because ____.
   A. the Colonel had a large stomach
   B. it had to be big to extract a snake or young crocodile
   C. it had to be very deep so that the surgeon could see inside the patient
   D. this would convince the patient that the job had been done properly

B Answer these questions about the passage:

1. In your opinion, what was the *main* reason why the doctor carried out the operation?

2. What was the attitude of the doctor's assistant to the operation? Quote a word or expression in support of your answer.

3. What does the word 'superficial' (in line 28) tell us about the way in which the doctor carried out the operation?

4. In what two ways had the doctor deceived his patient?

Unit 6 · *Crossing the Line*

6.4 Vocabulary: meaning in context

A Choose the word(s) which best show(s) the meaning of the underlined words as they are used in 6.1 and 6.2.

1. an important and very <u>influential</u> leader in the community (6.1, line 3)
   - A. extremely wealthy
   - B. able to get people to do what he wants
   - C. highly respected for his honesty
   - D. having many friends

2. the Colonel was firmly <u>convinced</u> that there *was* one inside him (line 5)
   - A. of the opinion
   - B. very worried
   - C. making a claim
   - D. scared

3. The Colonel continued to <u>pester</u> the doctor (line 6)
   - A. bother persistently
   - B. make formal visits to
   - C. earnestly request
   - D. challenge the doctor's opinion

4. I would inevitably be placed in <u>a padded cell</u>. (6.2, line 2)
   - A. a special prison for medical staff
   - B. a room in a place for people with mental problems
   - C. a situation where he had a problem which could not be solved
   - D. a room in a military prison where potential suicides are kept and watched

5. the narrow line that separates the physician from the <u>charlatan</u> (line 3)
   - A. a person who intends to defraud and deceive by making false claims
   - B. somebody who attempts a task which is beyond his skills
   - C. a boastful person who promises more than he can deliver
   - D. somebody who lacks a serious purpose and is irresponsible

6. there was only one <u>infallible</u> way of confirming (line 5)
   - A. which can be done quickly
   - B. which can be done simply
   - C. which is inexpensive
   - D. which is bound to succeed

7. retain it as a <u>gruesome</u> souvenir (line 11)
   - A. long-lasting
   - B. horrible to look at
   - C. highly unusual
   - D. obtained through much pain

8. I would have to <u>take</u> my dispensary assistant <u>into my confidence</u> (line 12)
   - A. conform to
   - B. confide in
   - C. confirm with
   - D. comply with

9. He <u>solemnly</u> swore to carry the secret to his grave. (line 13)
   - A. of his own free will
   - B. causing somebody great relief
   - C. in a very serious way
   - D. not very often

10. he had <u>administered</u> chloroform before (line 17)
    - A. heard of
    - B. given (to a patient)
    - C. purchased
    - D. studied about

B Match the underlined words with the meanings which they have in the passage.

Words from the passage	Meanings
1. which was absolutely <u>indispensable</u> (line 18) 2. <u>Gleefully</u>, he promised me (line 19) 3. to <u>curb</u> his enthusiasm (line 19) 4. contain a <u>mature</u> python (line 21) 5. The Colonel arrived <u>punctually</u> (line 22) 6. The <u>pious</u> man was praying (line 24) 7. his voice became <u>muffled</u> (line 25) 8. I took up a <u>lancet</u> (line 26) 9. made a lengthy <u>incision</u> (line 26) 10. seemed sufficient for the <u>extraction</u> (line 27)	a) restrict b) devoted to his religion c) obscured d) cut e) taking out f) adult g) surgical knife h) essential i) on time j) very joyfully
11. the <u>superficial</u> wound (line 28) 12. in the Colonel's <u>abdomen</u> (line 28) 13. For a <u>fleeting</u> moment (line 32) 14. Animal Rights <u>activists</u> (line 33) 15. <u>resigned</u> to remaining in bed (line 35) 16. for a fortnight or <u>so</u> (line 36) 17. he was <u>radiant</u> (line 37) 18. with great <u>magnanimity</u> (line 37) 19. <u>take</u> my mistake <u>to heart</u> (lines 40–41) 20. to see me confused and <u>mortified</u> (line 41)	k) people who try to get something done l) thereabouts m) generosity of spirit n) be upset by o) happy and smiling p) humiliated q) stomach r) passing very quickly s) slight, not deep t) having agreed to do something he knew he would not enjoy

6.5
Comprehension: looking for clues to meaning

If you have to give the meaning of a word in an examination, (a) look for clues in the passage and (b) if you know Latin, see what the Latin roots of the word mean, e.g.

- **incision:** 'I took up a lancet and made a lengthy **incision** which seemed sufficient for the extraction of even a young crocodile.'
  We learn these things from the passage:
  – line 26: The doctor is going to open his patient's stomach.
  – line 27: The opening is large enough for him to pull out a young crocodile.
  – line 28: The doctor made a wound and there was blood.
  If we put all the clues together, we can see that the meaning of 'incision' must be 'cut'. It cannot be 'hole' because we learn from line 28 that the wound was superficial.

- **magnanimity:** 'But he was radiant and sought with great **magnanimity** to comfort me.'

The context tells us that the Colonel was trying to comfort the doctor for (so he thought) having made a mistake. Lines 38–43 reinforce this impression. If you know Latin, you will see that 'magnanimity' comes from two Latin words: *magna* = great, and *animus* = spirit. So the word means 'with a great/generous spirit'.

Over to you!

Exercise 1

Study these sentences and work out the meaning of the words in bold type.

1. Study this table. It shows **how** many traffic accidents happened in Trinidad last month. In each case, the cause of the accident is shown.

2. More than 1200 companies **belong** to the Georgetown Chamber of Commerce. Its membership is now nearly double what it was last year.

3. Most of the hotels along this strip of coast **belong** to a large American company which plans to build several more in the coming year.

4. To ordinary people, some of the words and expressions used by IT specialists are simply **jargon** and mean nothing unless you are an IT expert yourself.

5. When we asked the Police Inspector about the cause of the fire, his reply was deliberately **ambiguous,** so we still don't know whether it was caused by arson or not.

6. The **penultimate** clause of this agreement is not clear but all the others, including the last one, number 8, seem sensible. However, we need clarification of number 7 before we can decide whether to sign the agreement or not.

7. Mr X has a terminal heart condition and is not expected to live more than another month or two, so he has been admitted to a **hospice,** where he will probably spend his last few weeks receiving dedicated care.

8. A large travel company has chartered a liner for six months. If the company detains the ship beyond the agreed term, it will have to pay a fine called **demurrage** and this will prove to be very expensive for the company.

9. Cows are **herbivorous** animals, so they will not be interested in eating the carcase of a dead sheep.

10. The National Heritage Society is doing its best to persuade the **philistines** amongst us to take an interest in the traditional culture of the country but they are not having a great deal of success at the moment.

11. One problem with eating **succulent** fruit such as pineapples, papaws and mangoes is that the juice gets on your clothes if you are not careful.

12. Our new neighbour is a very **loquacious** man, so be prepared to spend most of your time listening (rather than talking) when he comes this evening.

6.6
Topic vocabulary: a hospital

Study the words in the following lists.
1. Decide which words will belong only to your passive (recognition) vocabulary, i.e. you must know their meaning but need not know how to use them.
2. Decide which words will belong to your active vocabulary, i.e. you must know what they mean and how to use them.

Unit 6 · Crossing the Line   79

People

a receptionist	a laboratory technician	an intern
a ward sister	an anaesthetist	a psychiatrist
a staff nurse	a radiologist	a midwife
a ward orderly	a physiotherapist	a dispenser
a physician	a surgeon	a paediatrician

Diseases and ailments

influenza	diphtheria	rheumatism	a cardiac condition
bronchitis	measles	tuberculosis	venereal disease
dysentery	cancer	tonsillitis	a heart attack
cholera	mumps	ringworm	poliomyelitis
epilepsy	AIDS	pneumonia	whooping cough
appendicitis	hernia	anorexia	diabetes

Places and things

a ward	an ambulance	an oxygen cylinder
a maternity ward	a stretcher	an oxygen mask
a labour ward	a gurney (US)	an antibiotic
the casualty department	a stethoscope	a dressing
the out-patients department	a thermometer	a dispensary
the reception desk	a syringe	a bandage
the emergency ward	crutches	medicine

Miscellaneous

sterilised	septic	dementia	DOA (dead on arrival)
antenatal	to faint	in a coma	in intensive care
postnatal	infectious	in isolation	in a critical condition
antiseptic	contagious	an epidemic	a terminal illness
to diagnose	to immunise	to recuperate	to be discharged from
a diagnosis	convalescent	a sanatorium	an endemic disease
inoculation	rehabilitation	in quarantine	under observation
vaccination	a drug addict	a post-mortem	on the danger list

English Alive!

If you are interested in what happens inside a hospital, you might like to read *The Final Diagnosis* by Arthur Hailey or you can watch one of the series about hospitals on television.

6.7
Writing skills: telling a story

In this section we will study some of the skills involved in writing a story. You may be able to use them when you write your own stories.

Who is telling the story?

The story in 6.2 was written by the doctor himself. Four other people could have written it:

- **An author** (who did not take part in the action) could start:
  Dr Harris studied Colonel O'Reilly's medical history and made a fateful decision. 'Either I operate on him,' he thought, 'or he drives me mad, coming here every day with a ridiculous story about a snake in his stomach.' …

- **The patient** (Colonel O'Reilly) could start:
  I knew I was right all the time but it took me weeks to persuade that stubborn doctor to operate. But I'm not angry with him. After all, he did save my life, even if he took his time about it. I remember how it all started …

- **The dispensary assistant** could start:
  Dear Diary,
  Today I'm going to let you into a secret which nobody else (except Dr Harris) will ever know.
    It all started about five weeks ago when a patient complained that he had a snake in his stomach! Impossible! Well, that's what the boss told him as politely as possible but the patient, Colonel O'Reilly, wouldn't take 'No' for an answer.
    Nearly every day …

- **One of the Colonel's men** could start the story – see Exercise 2.

Over to you!

Exercise 2

Imagine that one of the Colonel's men is writing the story. Write the first lines of his story.

Where (= at what point) shall we start the story?

Here is a timeline for the story:

A	B	C	D	E	F
Colonel complains and complains	Doctor decides to operate	Doctor plans		Operation	Visiting the happy patient in bed

In 6.2, Dr Harris started his story at B and then moved through C, D and E to the end, F. He could have started it at any of the other points, using flashback when necessary, e.g.

- **starting at D:**
    'Come in and sit down,' Dr Harris said to Winston Dosman, his dispensary assistant. 'I've made up my mind. I'm going to operate on the Colonel before he drives us all insane. I shall need your help. You've administered chloroform before, haven't you?'
    'Yes, many times,' Winston said. 'I'll be glad to help.' …

- **starting at E:**
    Dr Harris made sure that his patient was comfortable. He nodded at his assistant, who picked up the oxygen mask and switched on the oxygen. …

Over to you!

Exercise 3

Start the story at the point where the doctor visits Colonel O'Reilly in his home after the operation. Write the first few lines.

How shall we start the story?

Do you remember SAD?

S – Start with a **statement**, as in 6.2 and E above.

A – Start with **action**, e.g.

```
Dr Harris put the file down and rang for his assistant.
```
or
```
Winston Dosman pushed the snake into a cardboard box and tied
it up firmly.
```
or
```
Colonel O'Reilly climbed onto the operating table and began
to pray.
```

D – Start with **dialogue**, as the patient did in the example on page 81 and when starting at D above.

Over to you!

Exercise 4

Retell part of the story in 6.2.
a) Decide *who* will tell the story.
b) Decide *at what point* on the timeline you will start.
c) Decide *how* you will start (SAD).
d) Write the first 10–15 lines of the story. Enjoy yourself.

6.8
Writing: setting out dialogue

Read again lines 13–21 of the story in 6.2. Then set out the conversation between Dr Harris and his assistant, Winston Dosman.

- Use inverted commas for direct speech.

- Remember that each new speaker starts a new paragraph.

- If you need help, look at 'starting at D' on page 82 but don't copy it. You can add as many extra details as you like. Try to do a better job than the example on page 82.

- If it will help you, exchange your draft answer with a classmate and see if you can learn from your classmate.

6.9
Expressing sentences in a different way

Exercise 5

1. In each case below, complete the second sentence but retain the meaning of the first sentence as far as possible.
    a) There was no way to satisfy Colonel O'Reilly except by cheating.
       The only way of …
    b) It was difficult for us to understand him because of his strange accent.
       His strange accent …
    c) Yvonne was delayed for two hours by a traffic jam but not even that made her angry.
       Not even …
    d) My friend and I don't like to swim in the river near our house.
       My friend and I dislike …

e) It looks as if bad weather has delayed Uncle's plane.
　　　　Uncle's plane must …
　　　f) 1200 people were prosecuted for driving offences last year.
　　　　There …
　　　g) My sister and I went shopping with my mother.
　　　　My mother took …
　　　h) Peter is not such a good swimmer as Marlon.
　　　　Marlon …

2. Make up new sentences as similar as possible to the original sentences but using the words given in brackets.
　　　a) If John won't go with you, Peter will. (either)
　　　b) Francine can't swim well and her sister can't either. (neither)
　　　c) Deena prefers listening to the radio to doing housework. (likes)
　　　d) It's not necessary for Natoya to go shopping now. (need)
　　　e) We do not intend to visit Mike until late this month. (intention)
　　　f) The police officer refused us permission to enter the building. (allow)
　　　g) The man told us that we had to pay a hundred dollars each month for the television set or he would take it back again. (unless)

6.10
Enjoying poetry: pre-reading

What do poets write about?

West Indian poets often write about these three things:

- **nature** – trees, flowers, the sea, rivers, hills, the forest

- **people**, especially ones who are very young, very old or beloved in some way. For many years, life has been difficult for most people and this is reflected in the works of some poets. We see respect for the hardships which people have endured – and, in some cases, still have to suffer.

- **death** – seen more as a bringer of eternal peace than as something to be feared.

In 6.11, Frank Collymore combines all three of the above topics in one poem.

How do poets write?

In her poem 'The Land', Victoria Sackville-West compares the poet to a craftsman (or artisan) such as a carpenter who knows how to use his tools skilfully.

The poet like the artisan
Works lonely with his tools; picks up each one,
Blunt mallet knowing, and the quick thin blade,
And plane that travels when the hewing's done;
5   Rejects and chooses; scores a fresh faint line;
Sharpens, intent upon his chiselling;
Bends lower to examine his design,
If it be truly made,
And brings perfection to so slight a thing.

In 6.11 we can see what one poet-craftsman made.

6.11
Enjoying poetry

Day's End

Here in this remote corner,
This neglected fringe of a fishing-village,
Bare with the sea-blast, where only
Cactus flaunt their flagpoles in the sun
5   And the scorched grass seeks precarious tenure
Of the sharp-toothed cliffs of clay,
I saw her one evening, an old woman,
An old peasant woman, barefooted,
Clad in a faded gown, her head

10 Wrapped in a dingy cloth. She walked
    Slowly up the hill: her face
    Shrivelled with age, skin and bone
    Only, the dark living skin
    Drawn taut upon the bone that soon
15 Would claim identity with clay and rock.
    She walked with regal dignity,
    With stark unconscious pride that well
    A player-queen might envy,
    The dignity that springs from toil and age.
20 Her face, moulded by poverty and resignation,
    Hoping for nothing, desiring nothing,
    A symbol of this bare and rocky fringe
    Carved in a human face, beyond
    Either the cares or fears of time.
25 Yet deep within the budding skull
    Lingered the tenderness of eyes,
    Eyes to reflect the setting sun,
    To gaze across the darkening sea
    Beyond the memories of her womanhood
30 To spy another lover, death;
    The meeting sure. But unafraid,
    And proud; proud and regal, unafraid,
    A queen waiting to greet her king,
    To grasp his hand and go with him
35 Down to her marriage-bed within the earth
    Where bone shall bloom to everlastingness.

Frank Collymore

Questions

1. a) What example(s) of alliteration can you find in the first four lines?
    b) What is the meaning of 'seeks precarious tenure' in line 5?
    c) Most of the poem is about an old woman.
       i) Why does the poet start by describing the scene where he saw the woman?
       ii) Which two lines later in the poem perhaps show why he described the landscape?
    d) What feature of the woman particularly impressed the poet and perhaps inspired him to write a poem about her?
    e) What is the meaning of 'the bone that soon would claim identity with clay and rock'? In which later line is this idea repeated?
    f) In line 31, why is 'the meeting sure'?

2. Now see if you can work like the poet described in 6.10.
   a) Find line 10 in the poem. Start a new line with 'She walked' and write four lines, using the words in the poem but setting them out slightly differently. Stop writing at 'living skin' (line 13).
   b) Compare your version with the way Frank Collymore set out his lines. Do you think your method is better or worse than Collymore's?

6.12
Writing

Either: Write 400–450 words about topic (1) or (2) in about 45 minutes.
or: Write 250–300 words about topic (3) in about 30 minutes.

1. Write a story based on *one* of the pictures above.

2. Write a story in which a doctor or a nurse plays an important part.

3. Do you think Dr Harris crossed the 'narrow line that separates the physician from the charlatan' by operating on Colonel O'Reilly in 6.2? Try to present the main points of both sides of the argument.

Unit 6 · *Crossing the Line* 87

7 Drama

7.1
Pre-reading

In 7.2 we can read the opening lines of Act 1 of a play called 'An Echo in the Bone' by Dennis Scott. The play was first performed in 1974 in Jamaica. (You can read the whole play in 'Plays for Today', edited by Errol Hill and published by Longman Caribbean Writers in 1985.)

Many years ago, a farmer called Crew murdered a white estate owner, Mr Charles, who refused to allow Crew access to water for his farm. Crew then committed suicide or was killed. The play starts with a Ninth-Night Ceremony held to honour and comfort Crew's spirit. During the lengthy ceremony, many truths are revealed.

We meet these characters:

Rachel: Crew's widow, who has arranged for the ceremony 9 days after her husband died.

Sonson: Rachel's eldest son: 25 and tough.

Brigit: In her 20s, Rachel's daughter-in-law married to Jacko, Rachel's younger son.

Seven other characters appear in the play but not in our extract.

7.2
Reading (an extract from the play 'An Echo in the Bone')

Act One

[*Blackness*]

RACHEL [*off, sings*]: Me alone, me alone, in de wilderness.

[*Repeat*]

Forty days and forty nights in de wilderness. [*Repeat*]

[*Lights up. RACHEL enters. A pretty woman. Strong. Tired. Proud. She carries a hurricane lantern. Places it on the table in silence. She stands beside the table, gripping the old clothes tightly. Rock a little.*] Aiee, Crew. [*Replaces the clothes softly, turns the lamp down, moves to the window. The moonlight silhouettes her.*]

BRIGIT [*off*]: Ma!

RACHEL [*to herself*]: Don't call me tonight, child. I have business. If you want me, find me. Tonight I belong to the dead.

BRIGIT [*off*]: Ma Rachel!

[*SONSON A violent man of 25. Brooding. Seeing RACHEL stops*]

RACHEL: You late.

SONSON: I had was to go all the way to the corner for the cheese and de money you give me wasn't enough. Why you didn't send to Madam?

RACHEL: I shame to ask her. She is a guest in the house tonight. You find food on the table.

SONSON: I not hungry.

RACHEL: I tell the girl to leave for you. Wash yourself and go eat. The moon rise already. Night getting old.

SONSON: Wash? Is a dance I going to?

RACHEL: Is respect you must show. You not no dutty old nigger that don't know better. Where's you pride?

SONSON: There. [*Puts cheese on the table*] The chinawoman say I could credit 'll month-end. Them say tell you don't forget this time.

RACHEL: Feisty, them couldn't say it to me face though.

SONSON: If you poor, dog eat you name.

RACHEL: I should send Jacko for things like that. You so bitter.

SONSON: Is me madda I learn it from. And – and him.

[*Nods towards the table.*]

RACHEL: Run to clean yourself up. Change your shirt and call the others.

[*He turns to go. BRIGIT is at the door.*]

BRIGIT: Oh! you come back? You food on the coal stove. Ma, ah cyan find the bag with the candle.

RACHEL: Ah have to do everything meself?

SONSON: You better find dem or you gwine have to go shop dis time.

RACHEL: Sonson hush you mouth! Don't interfere wid what is not your business.

SONSON: Is my business, Ma. I is de man of the house now. You better know that Miss Brigit.

BRIGIT: I do you anything? Ma, I don't say a word to the man. Him come here wid him striking self and bad talk me. Whey you want eh?

SONSON: Whay you do all day? Who clear up this old shack and get the place ready, scrub de table when I should be cooling me head, before I go back to clearing the field? Who build the benches and patch the roof so good? Don't blow out all the candles while I praying. All a dat who responsible? Me and she!

BRIGIT: But wait!

SONSON: All you want to do is fix you face and laugh wid the man down de village.

BRIGIT: Damn liar!

SONSON: I don't know how Jacko stand you.

BRIGIT: Is him a married to, not you.

SONSON: You cyan find nothing in de house. You don't know where nothing is. All you do is chat, chat, and leave de work to you mother-in-law.

BRIGIT: You don't own me mouth.

SONSON: You damn right. Thank God I don't own no part of you.

BRIGIT: Das the trouble –

RACHEL: Sonson, Brigit?

BRIGIT: Das what bun you!

RACHEL: Hush! You hear me? One likkle question cause that? You run you mouth too much, de two of you. I see the candlestick on top of the dresser in the kitchen. Go bring dem come. No you Brigit …

[*SONSON stands angrily for a moment, then goes. Pause.*]

When I am old woman, what you going to do eeh? The three of you …

[*BRIGIT starts to cry, RACHEL goes to comfort her.*]

This is a hard time for him. Him did look to his father. Hush, hush now, don't make Jacko see you crying. It's bad for him, child. Besides we have worse things to cry about. If you eye going shed water, make it rain down for the dead man.

BRIGIT: I do like you say, Ma. I stay far from him. I keep myself quiet when he around. And still I can't do nothing to please him. Is like somebody curse him.

RACHEL: A family must be able to live in de same house and don't fight people so all the time. I will talk to Jacko in the morning.

BRIGIT: Don't do that, Ma Rachel. Him will say I only make trouble me in de house and blame me.

RACHEL: Well then, don't fret. Bide your time. Is the child getting heavy in you belly that make things hard to bear. Don't fret. Go call Jacko before people start to come.

BRIGIT: Ma, what you doing this for? Why don't you make the dead stay dead? Is best the village forget him now, and forget how how he spill the blood of another man.

RACHEL: And I am to forget him too! Is my man. I going satisfy his ghost with whatever respect I have to give him. You think you can wipe out thirty years of him together just so?

7.3 Understanding

A Choose the best answer each time.

1. We learn from the Pre-reading section that Sonson's father died …
   A. because he declined to share an irrigation source with an estate owner
   B. in a way which was not entirely clear
   C. when he made up his mind that the best thing for him to do was to kill himself
   D. because Mr Charles' workers wanted revenge for the death of their employer

2. Who had apparently decided to hold a Ninth-Night ceremony?
   A. Rachel   B. Crew   C. Jacko   D. Brigit

3. Who was supposed to gain most from the Ninth-Night ceremony?
   A. Sonson   B. Rachel   C. Brigit   D. Crew's sprit

4. When Rachel said, 'Aiee, Crew' at the start of Act 1, she showed her
   A. anguish   B. optimism   C. satisfaction   D. anger

5. In the stage directions at the start of Act 1, the 'old clothes' which Rachel gripped tightly were most probably.
   A. her husband's
   B. a table-cloth
   C. the only clothes she had
   D. bed clothes

6. Near the start of Act 1, Rachel said, 'I have business.' The business was
   A. getting food for her family
   B. trying to get money to pay off her debts
   C. attending to her husband's funeral later on
   D. holding a Ninth-Night ceremony

7. Sonson said, 'The chinawoman said I could credit it…' Here, 'credit' means
   A. easily believe
   B. trust completely
   C. obtain without paying at the time
   D. obtain only by paying cash at the time

8. The words 'madda', 'dis' and 'de' all show …
   A. difficulty or unwillingness to pronounce the sound of 'th'
   B. a lack of respect by the speaker
   C. that the speaker's ancestors had come from Ghana
   D. that the speaker was very religious

9. When Brigit said 'I do you anything?' to Sonson, she probably felt
   A. rather puzzled
   B. anxious to help
   C. the need to show love
   D. quite indignant

10. 'You don't know where nothing is' is an example of
    A. an implied comparison
    B. a double negative
    C. a metaphor
    D. a missing question tag

B Answer these questions about pages 88–90.

1. What did Crew want Mr Charles to do?

2. Why was Rachel more in favour of a Ninth-Night ceremony than Brigit was?

3. What did Brigit imply when she said to Sonson 'Das the trouble…' and 'Das what bun you!'?

4. Pretend that you were watching Scott's play. A friend arrived late – just after Rachel said 'You think you can wipe out thirty years of him together just so?' Briefly explain to the friend what has happened.

5. If you were a member of the audience watching this play being performed, what do you think may happen next?

7.4 Vocabulary: meaning in context

Match the underlined words with the meanings which they have on pages 88–90.

Words from pages 88–90	Meanings
1. first performed in 1974 2. the whole play 3. published by 4. access to water 5. committed suicide 6. many truths are revealed 7. (it) silhouettes her 8. Him will … blame me 9. don't fret 10. Bide your time	a) say it is (my) fault b) made known c) wait d) shows her outline e) printed and sold f) being able to obtain g) worry; be upset h) killing (him)self i) entire j) acted

7.5 Discussion: drama

1. In Dennis Scott's play there are ten characters. How many additional people are needed to produce a play in a theatre? What does each person have to do?

2. How can the author of a play try to make his or her play interesting as early as possible in the play?

3. Which of these methods of showing drama is most popular in your district?

   a) on the stage of a theatre   d) at a cinema
   b) in the open air   e) on television
   c) on the radio

4. Pretend that you have just written a play. A company has offered to produce your play on one of (a) to (e) in question 3. Which would you choose and why?

5. Can you think of any examples of these types of plays?

   a) comedies   c) histories   e) romances
   b) tragedies   d) crime/detection   f) daily life activities ('soaps')

   Which types do you prefer?

92 *English Alive!*

7.6

Grammar: the Present Continuous tense (revision)

Active forms

		Short speech form	
I am (not)	writing a letter now.	I'm not	
He/She/It is (not)	hiding from us.	He's not	He isn't
We/You/They are (not)	making a mistake.	We're not	We aren't

Uses

The main uses of the Present Continuous (*or* Progressive) tense are:

- **for temporary actions** which are happening now but may stop soon, e.g.
  Hurry up! A bus **is coming**.
  Are you **waiting** for Carla?

- **for planned future actions** (often about travel or movement), e.g.
  Auntie **is coming** to see us next Saturday morning.
  Are you **going** to Sting in Portmore on Boxing Day?

- **with 'always' to express an action which is repeated frequently.** This often suggests that the speaker is annoyed or irritated by the action or thinks it is unreasonable, e.g.
  Why **are** you *always* **complaining** about the neighbours?

Over to you!

Exercise 1

Complete these questions by putting in 'Am', 'Is' or 'Are'.

1. ____ anybody going to Barbados with you?
2. ____ everyone here waiting for the same bus?
3. ____ your sister taking part in the carnival this year?
4. ____ all this luggage waiting to be checked?
5. ____ Nickesha and her sister still working in Georgetown?
6. ____ any of the players travelling by coach?
7. ____ I sitting in the right place?
8. ____ the hurricane heading in our direction?
9. ____ we going with Pa or with Uncle?
10. ____ this arrow pointing the right way?

Passive forms

We use the passive form of this tense when the action is being done *to* the subject and not *by* it.

```
            I am (not)      being transferred to another hospital after all.
        He/She is (not)     being asked to make a speech at the wedding.
            It is (not)     being reopened until the end of July.
    We/You/They are (not)   being informed of the result until next Saturday.
```

Over to you!

Exercise 2

Put in the passive form of the Present Continuous tense of the verbs in brackets.

1. Look at those two men. They ____ (take) away for questioning in connection with the attempted robbery. They ____ (escort) by armed police.

2. Nobody lives in those old houses. They ____ (pull) down later this month. Somebody told me that a big block of flats ____ (build) on this site later in the year.

3. We'll have to catch a bus today. Mother's car ____ (service) at the moment. The windscreen ____ (replace) as well. There were two cracks in it.

4. Can I use your computer while mine ____ (repair), please? The tower ____ (check) and some of the hardware ____ (update).

5. There's a big traffic jam in Harbour Road. Part of the road ____ (resurface) and the road ____ (widen) in two places.

6. Our new television set ____ (deliver) tomorrow morning. The old one still works well but it is smaller. I think it ____ (give) to a home for elderly people.

7. My brother is not at work today. He ____ (interview) for a Government job.

8. This wall needs to be repaired. It ____ gradually ____ (wear) away by the river.

9. We're not sure what is wrong with Grandpa. He ____ (admit) to hospital tomorrow for tests and observation.

10. (Store assistant to a customer) Can I help you? ____ you ____ (serve) right now?

7.7
Punctuation (1): using a full stop

These are reminders of points in earlier books in this series:

- Use a full stop to separate two main clauses *or* join them with a conjunction, e.g.
    - *wrong:* This is not my pen, it must be yours.
    - *right:* This is not my pen. It must be yours.
    - *right:* This is not my pen, so it must be yours.

- Don't punctuate a subordinate clause as if it is a main clause, e.g.
    - *wrong:* When the old woman had studied the address on the envelope and had understood the message shown by it. She returned the letter to the postman.
    - *right:* When the old woman had studied the address on the envelope and had understood the message shown by it, she returned the letter to the postman.

- Be careful when you use 'then', 'therefore' and 'thus'. Use a conjunction before these words *or* start a new sentence, e.g.
    - *wrong:* The old woman looked at the envelope, then she gave it back to the postman.
    - *right:* The old woman looked at the envelope. Then she gave it back to the postman.
    - **right:* The old woman looked at the envelope and then she gave it back to the postman.

*A comma is possible before 'and' in this sentence.

Over to you!

Exercise 3

Correct the punctuation mistakes in the following sentences, most of which have been taken from newspapers or books.

1. Ethanol is an important chemical compound, it is useful in many ways.

2. Since it was first diagnosed in the 1980s, AIDS has spread across the world, killing an increasing number of people each year, it has become the main danger to health in many countries, there is no cure for it at present.

3. The prisoners alleged that they were treated badly, they suffered from hunger and the cold climate, therefore their health began to deteriorate and their human rights were abused.

4. When the police first entered the house and commenced their search. It appeared that there was nobody on the ground floor or upstairs, then a detective discovered a trapdoor, it led down to a cellar.

5. This tyre is not the same as the other one, that was a Dunlop tyre, as far as I remember, therefore this tyre did not come from the suspect's truck.

6. The survivor's expression told us nothing, her voice revealed a lot. Showing that she was still under a lot of stress from being buried by the earthquake.

7. Yes, you'll have to stop him from leaving the country, I suppose, fix it with the stations, ports and airports, then let me know if there is any trace of him.

8. The key witness has disappeared. Leaving the prosecution uncertain whether or not to proceed with the case, therefore the suspect has not yet been formally charged.

9. In these two triangles, two sides and an included angle are equal, therefore the triangles are congruent, this is what we set out to prove in the beginning.

10. In modern times, a new topic has appeared in Geography, it is called Urban Geography, it involves studying how towns and cities have developed and how the land is used in them

7.8
Punctuation (2): review exercises

Exercise 4

The aim of this exercise is to enable you to check that you know how to use the words and punctuation marks concerned.

1. When does 'its' have an apostrophe? When does it *never* have an apostrophe?

2. Which of these words *never* have an apostrophe?
   a) hers
   b) ours
   c) yours
   d) theirs
   e) womens
   f) boys
   g) theres
   h) his
   i) ones

3. Which punctuation mark (other than a question mark or an exclamation mark) can sometimes replace a full stop at the end of a statement?

4. Which two of these punctuation marks are most similar in the way they can be used?
   A. a colon (:)   B. a semicolon (;)   C. an apostrophe   D. a full stop

5. Put in a colon when necessary.
   a) Vimala collects stamps, coins, leaves and postcards.
   b) Donna collects several things stamps, coins, postcards and leaves.
   c) Daljit entered for four events the shot put, throwing the hammer, the 10,000 metres, and the long jump.
   d) Tourists visit many countries in the Caribbean including Barbados, Jamaica, Trinidad and Tobago, Guyana and St Lucia.
   e) Suresh is interested in several possible careers medicine, the law, accountancy, engineering and scientific research.

6. Which punctuation mark will you usually see at the end of an indirect question?

7. Which of the following should be enclosed in inverted commas in written work?
    a) the title of a book
    b) the author's name
    c) a girl's name
    d) a day of the week
    e) direct speech
    f) the name of a magazine
    g) the name of a newspaper
    h) a word from another language

8. Punctuate these statements correctly:
    a) she watched the door it opened suddenly her father came in carrying a large parcel and looking very pleased with himself
    b) she watched the door it opened suddenly and her father entered he was carrying a large parcel and looked very pleased about something
    c) he was exhausted he would not surrender help would arrive eventually
    d) he was exhausted but he would not surrender help would arrive eventually then he would be a free man again

Exercise 5

Punctuate the following passages correctly.

1. father shook his head sadly as his son paul left the room for the third successive month his report card showing nothing but ds im finally convinced he told his wife that paul must have a sixth sense what makes you think that she replied in a puzzled tone well said her husband his report cards show no signs of the other five

2. a panda walked into a restaurant had a good meal and then stood up it took out a gun fired a shot into the ceiling and started to walk to the door hey said the waiter whats wrong with you the panda stopped and took a book about animals out of a bag the punctuation in this book isnt much good look me up and see what you get the waiter looked in the book and saw this entry panda large black and white animal like a bear eats shoots and leaves do you understand now the panda said it picked up the book and walked out

7.9

Grammar: using the right possessive adjective

Check that you can use the words in bold type correctly:

I hurt **my** left foot yesterday.

Can you spell **your** name?

Carla has sold **her** bicycle.

The man shook **his** bald head.

We have lost **our** cat.

They are going to sell **their** house.

The cat has eaten all **its** food.

One must protect **one's** reputation.

Unit 7 · Drama   97

Exercise 6

Put in the right possessive adjective each time.

1. We have a new boy in our class. I'm not sure what ____ name is.
2. When Cassandra opened ____ eyes in the morning, she was surprised to see ____ mother standing by the bed.
3. We always know whenever a stranger comes to ____ village. Then we try to find out ____ or ____ name and what the person wants.
4. Part of that tree had to be cut off because two of ____ branches were overhanging the road in a dangerous way.
5. This is where I live. As you can see, ____ house is at the junction of two roads.
6. Our country is well known for ____ fruit and vegetables.
7. The path to the waterfall is narrow, so tourists have to leave ____ car or van at the bottom of the hill and follow ____ guide until they reach the waterfall.
8. Grandma is over 80 but ____ memory is still excellent.
9. Mark, I'll help you to repair ____ bicycle when I've finished ____ homework.
10. One must defend ____ life and property if burglars come.
11. Don't leave ____ shoes there, Delroy. Somebody may trip over them.
12. At the end of the game, the players got in ____ coach and drove back to Kingston.

7.10
Grammar: using prepositions

Preposition	Example
'at' + the exact time	He came at half past six and left at nine o'clock.
'in' + a period of time	Jaimi was born in June. He was born in 1988. It is cooler in the evening.
'on' + a day	Kedeshia had a party on her birthday. Uncle leaves for New York on Saturday morning.
'for' + a length of time	We played football for nearly two hours.
'since' + a point of time	We haven't seen Leela since last Saturday.

In most cases, we do not put a preposition (except 'since') before 'last', 'next', 'this day' and 'that day'.

Over to you!

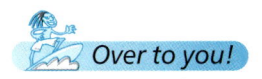

Exercise 7

Choose the best word(s) to complete these sentences. – means that no word is needed.

1. We could not go out ____ last Friday because of the storm.
   A. on   B. –   C. at   D. in

2. We must leave here ____ exactly five o'clock and not a minute later.
   A. –   B. in   C. at   D. on

3. The new term will begin ____ September.
   A. to   B. –   C. on   D. in

4. The semi-final will be ____ September the fifth.
   A. on   B. at   C. in   D. –

5. His plane leaves ____ 9 a.m. ____ next Saturday.
   A. – ... –   C. at ... –
   B. at ... on   D. in ... on

6. The new law will come ____ force ____ 1 January, according to this paper.
   A. to ... –   C. by ... –
   B. into ... on   D. of ... in

7. ____ Sunday we went for a picnic with some friends. *(British English)*
   A. At   B. In   C. –   D. On

8. The first meeting of the committee will be ____ Monday evening. *(British English)*
   A. on   B. –   C. in   D. at

9. The new regulation will come ____ force ____ effect ____ 2 January.
   A. into ... have ... –   C. into ... with ... from
   B. of ... and ... on   D. with ... and ... at

10. We expect to be in Florida ____ the sixth ____ the fifteenth ____ August.
    A. on ... to ... in   C. from ... through ... at
    B. from ... to ... of   D. at ... to ... of

7.1.1
A Short Story

Question: In about 45 minutes, write a short story of 400–450 words in which somebody learns a lesson.

Answer: A few days ago, Mary went to her local store to do some shopping for her mother. She laughed and joked with the son of the owner who served her. John was in her class at school.

Unit 7 · Drama   99

'Father's busy stock-taking,' he told Mary, 'so I have to deal with the customers.'

When Mary returned home, she found that her mother had gone to visit a sick relative. She unpacked the goods and put them away neatly. She hid her soft drink at the back of the refrigerator where her greedy brother, Mark, would not see it. Then she went to tidy her bedroom and start her homework.

For the next two hours, Mary worked quietly in her bedroom. She wrestled with some Maths problems and wondered whether to ask Mark to help her.

'No, I won't,' she thought. 'I know him. He'll demand something in return.'

At about noon, her mother returned and started to prepare lunch. After lunch, Mary washed the dishes. Then she remembered her soft drink hiding in the fridge. She took it out and noticed that the top was easy to unscrew.

'That's odd,' she though. 'How come the top came off so easily?'

She looked at the bottle suspiciously but did not discover anything wrong. The bottle looked somewhat old but there was nothing definite to confirm her suspicions. She poured the drink into a glass and took a preliminary sip. Then she stopped and stared at the glass and the bottle.

'There's no taste! It's just plain water!' she said to herself. 'Wait until I see John again. The label says, "Lemon and sparkling spring water" but I reckon this came straight from a tap. I'm surprised at you, John, trying to cheat your customers!'

Then Mark came into the kitchen. Mary saw him grinning at her. Immediately she guessed what had happened. Mark had drunk the contents of the bottle and had filled it up with tap-water! She was about to accuse him when there was a loud knocking on the door of their home.

Mary opened the door and saw John standing there, looking agitated and holding out a bottle.

'That bottle of spring water I sold you,' he blurted out. 'Can I have it back? I hope you haven't drunk anything from it. Here,' he said as he handed a new bottle to Mary, 'take this one. I'm very, very sorry but I gave you Grandpa's medicine by mistake. It has no particular taste but it's a very strong laxative. Can I have it back, please?'

In a daze, Mary exchanged the bottles and closed the door. Then she saw Mark rush out of the room.

'That will teach him a lesson,' she thought.

(About 460 words. It is easy to delete 10 words but this is not necessary.)

7.12 Understanding

Choose the best answer each time.

1. John was working in the store because
   A. he was Mary's class-mate
   B. his mother had gone to visit a relative
   C. his father had other things to do
   D. he liked to help the customers

2. The word 'wrestled' tells us that Mary found her Maths homework
   A. easy   B. enjoyable   C. difficult   D. fascinating

3. Mary decided not to ask Mark to help her with her homework because
   A. she knew that it was nearly time for lunch
   B. she preferred to help her mother prepare lunch
   C. she feared that he could not solve the problems
   D. she thought that his help would not be given freely

4. The fact that Mary took a preliminary sip suggests that she
   A. was not sure what was in the bottle
   B. was not really thirsty
   C. did not really trust John
   D. knew that John had changed the bottles

5. Mary's expression 'Wait until I see John again' amounts to
   A. an order
   B. an apology
   C. a threat
   D. a request

6. Mary saw her brother 'grinning at her'. Here the word 'grinning' can convey a sense of … which 'smiling' does not.
   A. mockery
   B. friendship
   C. sympathy
   D. hatred

7. John was most probably agitated because
   A. he was worried about the possible consequences of his mistake
   B. he thought he had charged Mary too much for the drink
   C. he knew that Mark was a greedy boy
   D. he was worried that Mary might think he had tried to cheat her

8. We are told that Mary was 'in a daze', so we know that she felt … by what had happened.
   A. amused
   B. annoyed
   C. pleased
   D. confused

7.13 Vocabulary

Match the underlined words with the meanings which they have in the story.

Words from the story	Meanings
1. She <u>wrestled</u> with some problems	a) to some extent
2. 'That's <u>odd</u>,' she thought.	b) prove they were correct
3. it looked <u>somewhat</u> old	c) (tentative) first
4. to <u>confirm</u> her suspicions	d) believe
5. a <u>preliminary</u> sip	e) a medicine to relieve constipation
6. a preliminary <u>sip</u>	f) on the point of doing something
7. I <u>reckon</u> this came	g) tried very hard to solve
8. She was <u>about to</u> accuse him	h) said suddenly on impulse
9. he <u>blurted out</u>	i) strange; unusual
10. a strong <u>laxative</u>	j) very small drink; a taste

7.14 Writing

Either: Write 400–450 words on topic (1) or (2) in about 45 minutes.
or: Write 250–300 words on topic (3) in about 30 minutes.

1. Write a story in which *one* of the characters shown in the pictures below plays a significant part.

2. Write a story in which an unexpected *or* a mislaid letter plays a part.

3. 'This country would probably be a better place if it were governed by women and not by men.' To what extent do you agree with this view?

> (*Remember:* Stay cool. No exaggeration. Don't lose your temper. Be polite. Show that you can tackle this type of topic in a calm, mature way.)

8 Gold!

8.1 Pre-reading

Throughout history, people have valued gold as a 'store of value'. In India and other parts of Asia, in particular, gold is regarded as more valuable than money. Currencies can rise and fall but gold retains its value because demand outstrips supply.

The passage in 8.2 shows the hardships which men will face in their search for gold. In the twenty-first century, the search continues in several parts of the world.

8.2 Reading

Gold!

In 1896 gold was discovered in Alaska and there was a desperate rush to stake claims. The target of the rush was an isolated area known as Eldorado Creek, where men reported that they had obtained US $100, then $200 and then $800 from a single pan. Some of the men became so intoxicated with their good fortune that
5 they could not settle down to steady work. Unaccustomed to wealth, they drifted from one claim to another, showing everybody what they had found, and speculating on what they might do with their sudden riches. The gold was so abundant that when a miner went down into his prospecting hole with a lighted candle, the bystanders could see the gold glittering in the gravel as the light fell on
10 it.

There was only one major drawback, one great worry in all this atmosphere of fantastic wealth. There was a great scarcity of provisions in an area where the approach involved a long trek by river or across mountains, where the land was one vast frozen swamp and where the ground had to be thawed before it could be
15 dug. Flour was $12 to $16 a hundredweight, blankets were $25 each and at times it was impossible to buy anything at all.

In Dawson City, hungry millionaires paraded the streets and tried to forget their unappeased appetites by improving their crude shacks or by going to the saloons and dance-halls which had quickly sprung up. There was no real poverty but no
20 one knew when or where he was going to get his next meal. They just had to sit with empty stomachs and wait patiently for a steamer to come up with food.

News was scarce too. When an enterprising man arrived with a newspaper, he stood on a wagon and read part of the news to a crowd of eager listeners. Then he stopped abruptly and announced that he would read out the rest in a hall nearby –

25 admittance one dollar. In fifteen minutes the place was thronged at that price with five hundred men who stood patiently for over an hour. The shrewd owner then read every item in the newspaper, including accidents, suicides, advertisements and the smallest details.

Throughout this period there were extraordinary instances of fortunes being
30 made and lost. On one occasion two men were talking and drinking whisky in a cabin. One of them had just staked a claim on Eldorado Creek. At the time, his part of the creek was entirely unprospected, and he was doubtful whether his claim would eventually prove to be of any value. He accordingly persuaded his drunken companion to buy his claim for $300. The next morning, his companion became
35 sober and realised what he had done. He wished he had not bought the claim, and wanted his money returned. The other man was adamant that the sale had been made in good faith and was perfectly legal. He refused to refund the money, insisting that the bargain must be kept. Later on, when the creek became more thoroughly prospected, the property proved to be worth about a quarter of a
40 million dollars.

8.3
Understanding (1)

In each case, choose the most suitable answer. The questions have been arranged to show you some of the *different types* of comprehension questions you can expect to meet in an examination.

Information contained in a passage

1. Why did some men find it difficult to work steadily at Eldorado Creek?
   A. They soon became too drunk to work properly.
   B. There was no steady work for them to do.
   C. The unexpected wealth unsettled them.
   D. They worked first at one claim and then at another.

2. Food was short in Dawson City because ____.
   A. prices were extremely high
   B. the city was remote and comparatively inaccessible
   C. it was winter time, when there is always a shortage of food
   D. the miners were too busy digging up gold to worry about food

Inferences and implications

3. We are told that 500 men paid a dollar each to listen to a man reading a newspaper. From this incident we may infer that ____.
   A. most of the men were uneducated and thus could not read
   B. the news items which they were listening to must have been sensational
   C. the men were too busy prospecting for gold to read the paper themselves
   D. this was the only way in which the men could obtain news of the outside world

4. In line 13, the use of 'trek' instead of 'journey' implies that ____.
   A. horses were used on the route
   B. the route was long and difficult
   C. the writer is fond of old-fashioned words
   D. people were forced to travel on foot most of the time

The attitude of the author

5. In line 22, what does the word 'enterprising' tell us about the author's attitude to the incident with the newspaper?
   A. It shows that he disapproved of the man who read out the news items.
   B. It suggests that he approved of the man's initiative.
   C. It proves that he was unsympathetic towards the miners.
   D. It is evidence that he regarded the man as an unscrupulous profiteer.

6. Taken as a whole, this passage was most probably written to:
   I. inform   II. entertain   III. criticise   IV. seek reform
   A. I only   C. III only
   B. I and II   D. I, II, III and IV

The development of ideas

7. In line 33, 'accordingly' is logical because ____.
   A. we would expect a drunken man to behave in this manner
   B. both of the men were dishonest
   C. the two men were good friends
   D. the seller thought the claim was not of great value

8. In the fourth paragraph, the writer describes the miners' interest in news. In the next paragraph, he describes an attempt by one man to cheat another. What expression does he use to link these two paragraphs?
   A. 'Throughout this period'   C. 'the smallest details'
   B. 'extraordinary instances'   D. 'fortunes being made and lost'

English Alive!

The meaning and use of words

9. In line 18, 'unappeased' is similar in meaning to ____.
   A. unsatisfied
   B. unsatisfactory
   C. dissatisfied
   D. dissuaded

10. In line 5, 'drifted' is used instead of 'went' because it ____.
    A. is a more literary word
    B. reminds us that the area was a vast frozen swamp
    C. gives a more precise account of what happened
    D. stresses the determination with which the men worked

References within a passage

11. To what does 'it' refer in line 10?
    A. the light
    B. the gravel
    C. the gold
    D. the hole

12. The 'period' mentioned in line 29 was evidently at the ____.
    A. end of the eighteenth century
    B. beginning of the nineteenth century
    C. end of the nineteenth century
    D. beginning of the eighteenth century

Punctuation (including the use of italics)

13. In line 12, the full stop after 'wealth' could most reasonably be replaced by a ____.
    A. colon
    B. comma
    C. hyphen
    D. question mark

14. In line 31, the full stop after 'cabin' could most reasonably be replaced by a ____.
    A. semicolon
    B. comma
    C. colon
    D. hyphen

Summary

15. Which of these sentences best summarises the ideas contained in the second and third paragraphs of the passage?
    A. In winter, the price of food was very high.
    B. Nobody in this area knew how to obtain food, so many of the men amused themselves with various odd jobs.
    C. Because of its remoteness, food was difficult to obtain in this area at that time.
    D. Millionaires were prepared to pay high prices for their food, thus depriving others of necessary food.

8.4 Understanding (2)

1. Imagine that we are living in the year 1896. A man in California is thinking of going north to Eldorado Creek to prospect for gold. Tell him about *three* obstacles which he will have to face.
2. In line 23, why did the man read out only part of the news?
3. In what way was 'justice' done in the final paragraph?

8.5 Vocabulary: meaning in context

A Choose the word(s) which best show(s) the meaning of the underlined words as they are used in 8.1 or 8.2.

1. demand outstrips supply (8.1, line 3)
   A. replaces   B. follows   C. exceeds   D. creates

2. The target of the rush was an isolated area (8.2, line 2)
   A. very cold   B. remote   C. barren   D. unpleasant

3. Some of the men became so intoxicated with their good fortune (line 4)
   A. affected by alcohol
   B. emotionally affected
   C. under the influence of alcohol
   D. aggressive and uncontrolled

4. Unaccustomed to wealth, they drifted from one claim to another (line 5)
   A. having failed to get
   B. not expecting to get
   C. still very keen to get
   D. not used

5. they drifted from one claim to another (line 5)
   A. moved aimlessly
   B. changed places
   C. went
   D. moved on

6. speculating on what they might do with their sudden riches (line 7)
   A. buying and selling shares
   B. making promises
   C. considering possible actions
   D. preparing to deal with

7. The gold was so abundant (line 8)
   A. difficult to reach
   B. beautiful and shining
   C. easy to see
   D. plentiful

8. the bystanders could see the gold glittering in the gravel (line 9)
   A. labourers who moved the dirt
   B. men who strengthened the holes
   C. people who stood and watched
   D. people holding a lighted candle

B Match the underlined words with the meanings which they have in the passage.

Words in the passage	Meanings
1. There was only one major <u>drawback</u> (line 11)	a) entailed
2. There was a great <u>scarcity</u> (line 12)	b) walked up and down
3. a great scarcity of <u>provisions</u> (line 12)	c) roughly built
4. <u>involved</u> a long trek (line 13)	d) unfrozen
5. the ground had to be <u>thawed</u> (line 14)	e) food
6. millionaires <u>paraded</u> the streets (line 17)	f) lack
7. their <u>crude</u> shacks (line 18)	g) keen, enthusiastic
8. an <u>enterprising</u> man (line 22)	h) suddenly, without warning
9. a crowd of <u>eager</u> listeners (line 23)	i) disadvantage
10. Then he stopped <u>abruptly</u> (line 24)	j) willing to attempt new projects
11. <u>admittance</u> one dollar (line 25)	k) examples
12. the place was <u>thronged</u> (line 25)	l) unyielding
13. <u>instances</u> of fortunes being made (line 29)	m) registered in his name
14. One of them had just <u>staked</u> a claim (line 31)	n) crowded
15. He <u>accordingly</u> persuaded (line 33)	o) with both sides acting fairly
16. his companion became <u>sober</u> (line 35)	p) intensively
17. The other man was <u>adamant</u> (line 36)	q) entrance, admission
18. the sale had been made <u>in good faith</u> (line 37)	r) pay back
19. He refused to <u>refund</u> the money (line 37)	s) therefore, thus
20. more <u>thoroughly</u> prospected (line 39)	t) not under the influence of alcohol

Unit 8 · Gold!

8.6
Say it another way

Exercise 1

Make up new sentences as similar as possible in meaning to the original sentences but using the words given in brackets.

1. Gold was abundant in the area. (abundance)

2. Food was scarce in Dawson City. (scarcity)

3. The men became very excited and could not settle down to work. (so … that)

4. Dawson City was very remote and thus food was very expensive. (so … that)

5. The men drifted from one claim to another, and showed everybody what they had found. (showing)

6. It was necessary to thaw the ground before it could be dug. (had to be)

7. It was necessary to bring food by river or across the mountains. (had to be)

8. The shelf was very high, so Anne could not reach it. (too)

9. The ground was very hard, so we could not dig it. (too)

10. I am not sure that he is telling the truth. (doubt whether)

8.7

Grammar: using the Simple Past tense (1) (revision)

Active forms

	Statements	Negatives	Questions
*Regular	showed looked waited	did not show did not look did not wait	Did … show …? Did … look …? Did … wait …?
Irregular	went found wrote	did not go did not find did not write	Did … go …? Did … find …? Did … write …?

*Check that you know how to pronounce the '-ed' at the end of regular verbs. Say these words. The final sound is in bold type:
- /d/ showed, turned, moved, rained, followed, borrowed
- /t/ looked, helped, walked, pushed, reduced, approached
- /id/ waited, married, wanted, decided, provided, expected

Over to you!

Exercise 2

All these actions happened some time in the past. Put in the Simple Past form of the verbs in brackets.

1. Some years ago, Mark and Dave ____ (be) in the same class at school. Dave ____ (not work) hard because he ____ (prefer) to go out with his friends in the evenings. At one time, he ____ (want) to become a musician. He ____ (join) a band but ____ (be) not good enough, so he ____ (leave) and ____ (become) a member of a local gang.

2. The gang leader ____ (make) Dave sell drugs and twice the police nearly ____ (catch) him. Dave ____ (steal) from shops and ____ (find) a girl-friend. Then one day, a member of a rival gang ____ (shoot) him and nearly ____ (kill) him. The police ____ (take) him to a hospital, where he ____ (need) an urgent operation to save his life.

3. Meanwhile, Mark ____ (work) hard at school and ____ (have) good results. He ____ (go) to a university in Jamaica and then ____ (emigrate) to the USA, where he ____ (enter) medical school. When he ____ (graduate) as a doctor, Mark ____ (decide) not to stay in the USA. He ____ (want) to return to Jamaica and help people there.

4. Mark ____ (become) a surgeon and ____ (start) work at a well-known hospital in Jamaica. He ____ (like) to help people and always ____ (do) his best to save lives. Then one day he ____ (have) a surprise when the police ____ (bring) in a man who had been shot in a gang fight. Mark ____ (recognise) the wounded man. It was Dave, who had been at school with him.

5. Mark ____ (operate) on Dave and ____ (save) his life but he ____ (know) that Dave would never walk or work again. He ____ (feel) sorry for Dave but he ____ (think) to himself, 'Well, you ____ (make) your choice. You ____ (bring) this trouble on yourself.'

Exercise 3

Make new sentences. Take out the words in bold type. Put in 'not' and the words in brackets, e.g.
   Mark worked hard at school. (Dave)
   Dave did not work hard at school.
   We played **football** yesterday. (cricket)
   We did not play cricket yesterday.

1. **Bavita** wanted to become a nurse. (Carlotta)

2. **Kerry** went to Trinidad with her parents. (Janet)

3. **The crowd at the game** agreed with the referee. (One of the players)

4. **Mark** lived a long time after the operation. (Dave)

5. **Dave's brother** became a successful businessman. (Dave)

6. **Dave** wasted the early part of his life. (Mark)

7. My **sister** saw the accident happen. (brother)

8. The policemen stopped the **white** car. (red)

9. Nadia bought pair of **shoes** at the market. (jeans)

10. The Government increased the price of a **taxi** licence. (driving)

11. The storm affected the **north** coast of the island. (south)

12. The fire destroyed **two shops** near our school. (any homes)

Exercise 4

Complete the following by putting in the question form (Simple Past tense) of the verbs in brackets.

1. ____ you ____ (remember) to get some stamps at the Post Office?

2. Where ____ you ____ (get) that mobile phone?

3. What ____ Natoya ____ (say) when you showed her the letter?

112 *English Alive!*

4. ____ anybody ____ (phone) while we were out?

5. ____ it ____ (rain) heavily during the night?

6. ____ the taxi ____ (stop) at the red light?

7. Which of the committee members ____ not ____ (agree) with the proposal?

8. How much ____ your brother ____ (pay) for his bicycle?

9. Why ____ you ____ (not tell) us about the meeting?

10. ____ you ____ (not lock) the door last night?

11. ____ anybody ____ (not tell) you about the game?

12. Why ____ Deena ____ (not come) to the concert?

8.8
Grammar: using the Simple Past tense (2) (revision)

Passive forms

The passive form of this tense is made with 'was' or 'were' + a past participle.

	Statements	Questions
I, he, she, it we, you, they	He was (not) arrested. They were (not) caught.	Was he arrested? Were they caught?

We use the passive form of the Simple Past tense when we:

- do not know who did something, e.g.
  My bicycle **was stolen** last night.

- want to emphasise what happened and not who did it, e.g.
  Several homes **were destroyed** last night when the hurricane came.

Using 'get'/'got'

In speech, people sometimes use 'got' or 'get' in sentences like these:
A spectator got killed at the Portmore Sting.
Did any of the crowd get injured?

Unit 8 · Gold! 113

It is better to use 'was' or 'were' and *not* 'get' or 'got' for two reasons:

- When used in this way, 'get' and 'got' are colloquial forms and should not be used in formal writing or speaking.

- In many cases, we cannot use 'get/got' instead of 'was/were', especially when giving an account of a science experiment or a similar action, e.g.
   The compound was weighed. Then it was heated.
   The battery was replaced and the tyres were checked.
   That pipe was repaired several months ago.

Over to you!

Exercise 5

Put in the passive Simple Past form of the verbs in brackets.

1. When silt threatened to prevent large ships from entering the harbour, a dredge ____ (use) and thousands of tons of mud ____ (remove). The work took nearly a month but in this way the harbour ____ (make) safe for cruise ships to use. As a result, hotels ____ (not force) to close down and jobs ____ (not put) at risk.

2. Last week two men ____ (rescue) when they were cleaning out a tank on a ship. They ____ (nearly overcome) by fumes but one of them managed to call for help. His shouts ____ (heard) by other workmen who carried the men to safety. The two men ____ (admit) to hospital and ____ (give) emergency treatment.

3. Primitive airplanes ____ (build) early in the twentieth century, and the first flight ____ (make) by the Wright brothers in 1903. In the next ten years, improved planes ____ (build), and planes ____ (use) during the Second World War. Subsequently, designers set to work and it was not long before large passenger planes ____ (develop).

4. ____ anything ____ (steal) in the robbery? ____ anybody ____ (arrest)?

5. ____ you ____ (invite) to the party? ____ your brothers ____ (ask) to provide the music?

8.9
Enjoying poetry

Fuss-pot

The old woman never stopped complaining:
It seemed her sign of life, her signature.
The food was bad or salt or made her sick,
Water had the bitter taste of aloes in her mouth,

5   Bed was hard or full of lumps or flea-infested,
The light was bad, mosquitoes stung her toes,
The place was hot or cold, whichever was most trouble,
And she never got the right amount of good attention.
And whenever the children visited, she let them have her tongue.

10 She deserved the <u>suck-teeth</u> she all the time received.   *insults, scorn*
Strange, then, at the end, when agony came on,
She was calm and quiet as the day is long.
Lay back and never made a single petty call
And seemed to try and find a deepening peace within.
15 And when the children came you noted, with surprise,
How close they clung to her with many signs of love.

Who can <u>delve</u> into all the years gone by?   *dig, enquire*
All one can tell is in behaviour now.
She takes on strength and certainty and love,
20 She summons seriousness in place of spite.
Death for her is drama worth her while
Too big, it seems, to make a fuss about.

Ian McDonald

Questions

Note that in some cases there is no definite 'right or wrong' answer to a question. The answer may be a matter of personal opinion.

1. Is the woman dead or not? What evidence can you find to support your answer?

2. What do you understand by 'her signature' in line 2?

3. In line 7, does 'whichever was most trouble' refer to the woman or to other people in the house with her?

4. In line 9, what is the meaning of 'she let them have her tongue'? Is the expression meant literally or figuratively?

5. If the poem is divided into two parts, at what point does the first part end?

6. Why do you think the children 'clung to her' closely? (line 16)

7. Explain the meaning of the last two lines.

8. What was the poet's purpose in writing this poem?

8.10
Writing

Either: Write 400–450 words on topic (1) or (2) in about 45 minutes.
or: Write 250–300 words on topic (3) in about 30 minutes.

1. Write a story in which the scene shown in the picture below plays a part.

2. Write a story with the title 'A good excuse'.

3. On the whole, do you feel that television programmes have a good or bad influence on *you*?

116 *English Alive!*

9 City of the Future?

9.1
Pre-reading

In *The Waste Makers*, Vance Packard writes of a problem faced by manufacturers throughout the world. Unless people can be persuaded to change their cars, houses, mobile phones and television sets periodically, production will exceed demand. If there is insufficient demand for manufactured goods, there will be massive unemployment.

In the extract from his book in 9.2, Packard describes an imaginary city, a paradise for salesmen and manufacturers. It may seem far-fetched but, the author asks, is it really so imaginary?

9.2
Reading

City of the Future

What will the world of tomorrow be like? Marketing people already dream of a utopia called Happy City, where selling is easy because the citizens are encouraged to get rid of old or surplus products and buy new ones all the time.

In Happy City all the buildings will be made of a special reinforced papier-mâché. These houses can be torn down and rebuilt every Spring at house-cleaning time. The motor-cars will be made of a light-weight plastic that develops fatigue and begins to melt if driven more than six thousand kilometres. Owners who turn in their old motor-cars at the regular turn-in dates – New Year, Independence Day and Labour Day – will be rewarded with a bond, and a special additional reward will be given to families able to surrender four or more cars at each disposal date.

A quarter of the factories of Happy City will be located on the edge of a cliff, and the ends of their assembly lines can be swung to the front or rear doors, depending upon the public demand. When demand is slack, the output of refrigerators or other products will go straight over the cliff and drop out of sight without first overwhelming the consumer market.

Every Monday, the people of Happy City will stage a gala launching of a space rocket. Components for the rockets will have been made by eighteen sub-contractors in the area. This is another contribution to national prosperity. One objective of the space probe will be to report to Earth what the back side of Neptune's moon looks like.

Wednesday will be Navy Day. The Navy will send a surplus warship to the citydock. It will be filled with surplus clothes, food, vacuum cleaners and television sets that have been stock-piled at the local Department of Commerce complex of warehouses for surplus products. The ship will go fifty kilometres out to sea,

25 where the crew will sink it from a safe distance.

As we peek into this Happy City of the future, we learn the heartening news that the Guild of Appliance Repair Artists has passed a resolution declaring it unpatriotic for any member even to look inside an ailing appliance that is more than two years old.

30 The heart of Happy City will be occupied by a titanic push-button supermarket built to simulate a fairyland. This is where all the people will spend many happy hours a week strolling and buying to their heart's content. In this paradise of buying and selling, there are no jangling cash registers to disrupt the holiday mood. Instead, the shopping couples – with their five children trailing behind, each
35 pushing his own shopping cart – gaily wave their lifetime electronic cards in front of a recording eye. Each child has his own card, which was issued to him at birth. Conveniently located throughout the mart are receptacles where the people can dispose of the old-fashioned products they bought on a previous shopping trip. In the jewellery section, for example, a playfully designed sign by a bin reads:
40 'Throw your old watches here!' Happy City's marvellous market is open around the clock, Sundays included. For Sunday shoppers who have developed a church-going habit in earlier years, there is a little chapel available for meditation in one of the side alcoves.

Is Happy City a feverish dream or perhaps a prototype for the City of Tomorrow?
45 In the next twenty years the broad outlines of Happy City will seem less and less fanciful, if current trends continue. Already a chapel has been built in a shopping centre outside Miami. A lifetime electronic credit card is under development. Already watches are being sold as fashion accessory items. Already paper houses are being marketed. Already the life expectancy of cars has shown a notable drop.
50 Already supermarkets are staying open around the clock in many areas. Already the stock-piling and disposing of subsidised but unwanted agricultural products have become world-wide scandals. Already some home furnishings are being built to break down within a few years, and product makers have been showing a growing fascination with the idea of setting 'death dates' for products.

9.3 Understanding

A Choose the best answer each time.

1. What seems to be the primary aim of the author?
    A. to warn his readers against an undesirable trend
    B. to urge them to be more careful when buying
    C. to persuade them to buy more goods
    D. to enable his readers to adjust to improved conditions

2. Happy City is referred to as a utopia (line 2) because ___.
    A. it is only a vision and not likely to happen
    B. people living in it would be able to dispose of unwanted goods easily
    C. it would be perfect from a salesman's point of view
    D. there would be no discontented people living in it

3. At the end of the passage, the author says that manufacturers are becoming interested in setting 'death dates' for their products. This idea is referred to earlier in the passage when the author mentions ___.
    A. the use of lifetime electronic credit cards
    B. cars built of light-weight plastic
    C. the launching of a space rocket
    D. surplus agricultural produce in warehouses

4. The author suggests that surplus manufactured goods could be destroyed to ___.
    A. maintain retail prices
    B. give the Navy something to do
    C. hide mistakes made in manufacturing them
    D. create unemployment and thus lower prices

5. How would the regular launching of a space rocket be a 'contribution to national prosperity'?
    A. It would keep the nation in the forefront of space research.
    B. It would bring essential scientific information back to Earth.
    C. Equipment used in each rocket would be destroyed and have to be replaced; this would benefit manufacturers and workers.
    D. It would provide good entertainment after a boring weekend.

6. If Happy City comes into existence, the author believes that Navy Day (line 21) will become ___.
    A. an accepted part of the new scheme
    B. a world-wide scandal
    C. only a rare necessity and one to be avoided
    D. an intolerable financial burden for the nation

7. The author's use of 'heartening' in line 26 is probably ___.
    A. sincere
    B. satirical
    C. hypocritical
    D. envious

Unit 9 · City of the Future?

8. What reason is implied by declaring that it will be unpatriotic for a mechanic to look inside an appliance more than two years old?
   A. This would make the task of the mechanics easier.
   B. Such an appliance would not need to be repaired.
   C. To create employment, appliances should be thrown away before they are two years old and should not be repaired.
   D. In Happy City no worker is expected to work hard.

9. Why is it appropriate to put the supermarket in the 'heart of Happy City'?
   A. It would be built like a fairyland and would entertain people.
   B. Everybody would be happy at the supermarket.
   C. Nobody would have to travel very far to reach it.
   D. The city would depend upon constant selling and buying.

10. After line 44, the author's attitude to Happy City becomes more ____.
    A. apprehensive   C. prophetic
    B. trivial   D. comprehensive

B Answer these questions about the passage.

1. For whom would Happy City be a utopia? (line 2)

2. Give two reasons why motorists in Happy City might be glad to change their cars frequently.

3. Why would the crew of a ship wish to sink it?

4. For what reason would the supermarket be built so as to 'simulate a fairyland' (line 31)?

5. What seems to be the author's attitude to setting 'death dates' for products? How is this attitude shown in the title of his book?

9.4 Vocabulary

Give oral answers to these questions. The words in bold are taken from the passage.

1. What are (a) a **paradise** (line 32), (b) a fool's paradise, (c) a **utopia** (line 2)? In which one would you prefer to be?

2. What happens if the metal wing of an aeroplane **develops fatigue** (line 6)?

3. What happens on the **assembly lines** (line 12) of a factory? (If you want to know all the details, read *Wheels* by Arthur Hailey.)

4. Explain how a **consumer market** can be **overwhelmed** (line 15) by goods.

5. Name any **component** (line 17) of a car.

6. Who employs a **sub-contractor**? (line 17) If a new hotel is being built, what work might be done by sub-contractors?

7. The USA has a **stock-pile** (line 23) of petrol, rubber and other raw materials. What is a stock-pile? Why do some countries have stock-piles?

8. What work might a man do in your country if he is a member of the **Guild of Appliance Repair Artists**? (line 27)

9. Make up an example of an **unpatriotic** act (line 28) in modern times.

10. If an appliance is **ailing** (line 28), what will you do about it?

11. What does **titanic** (line 30) mean?

12. What would you expect to see in a **mart**? (line 37)

13. If a person is **meditating** (line 42), what is he or she doing?

14. At a motor show, Mr Harris saw a **prototype** (line 44) of a new car. What does 'prototype' mean here?

15. Name two **fashion accessories** which people sometimes buy.

16. If a country **subsidises** (line 51) agricultural products, what does it do? Why do some other countries complain if a country subsidises any of its products?

9.5

Vocabulary: meaning in context

Choose the word(s) which best show(s) the meaning of the underlined words as they are used in sections 9.1 and 9.2.

1. It may seem far-fetched but, the author asks, is it really so imaginary? (9.1, line 7)
   A. rather exaggerated
   B. unimaginative
   C. not very pleasant to consider
   D. rather improbable

2. the buildings will be made of a special reinforced papier-mâché (9.2, line 4)
   A. indestructible
   B. strengthened
   C. used again and again
   D. extremely thin but durable

3. When demand is slack, the output of refrigerators (line 13) is
   A. non-existent
   B. weak
   C. at its highest
   D. lazy

4. This is another contribution to national prosperity (line 18)
   A. economic success
   B. self-esteem
   C. global recognition
   D. high reputation

5. stock-piled at the local Department of Commerce complex of warehouses (line 23)
   A. large group
   B. economic reserve
   C. complication
   D. compound

Unit 9 · *City of the Future?*

6. As we <u>peek</u> into this Happy City of the future (line 26)
   A. make sensible guesses about
   B. take a quick look
   C. study the possibilities of
   D. investigate thoughtfully

7. a titanic push-button supermarket built to <u>simulate</u> a fairyland (line 31)
   A. rival
   B. include
   C. appear like
   D. outshine

8. there are no <u>jangling</u> cash registers to disrupt the holiday mood (line 33)
   A. irritating
   B. constantly in use
   C. fixed, not portable
   D. noisy

9. <u>Conveniently</u> located throughout the mart are receptacles (line 37)
   A. much to everybody's relief
   B. recently installed
   C. done in a generous spirit
   D. in suitable positions

10. the broad outlines of Happy City will seem less and less <u>fanciful</u> (line 46)
    A. unrealistic
    B. practical
    C. attainable
    D. unimaginative

9.6
Writing: summary

Look at the following summary question. Then study the summaries which follow.

Question

Make a summary of the main methods which, in section 9.2, the author thinks may be used in the city of the future to sustain an adequate demand for goods. Use only the material in lines 1–43. Your summary must not contain more than 120 words. Use your own expressions as far as possible and do not copy sentences or long expressions from the passage.

Summary 1

The main methods which the author thinks may be used in the city of the future to sustane an adequate demand for goods will be called Happy City, where selling is easy. Because the citizens are encourage to get rid of surplus product and buy new ones.

Buildings will be made of papier-mache and will be changed every year, factories will tip there rubbish into the sea or it will be sent up into space to find out about the moon. Every week, men will sink a ship in the sea. It won't have an army or air force.

All the supermarket will be happy places to stimulate a fairyland, and each family will have five children so that they can buy more of things. People will spend many happy hours strolling around the place and if they like they can easily throw away any goods they don't want, and they can go to the chapel in the supermarket, then they will be happy all the time.

Comments

Mark: probably 0. Cover the rest of this page and make a list of the types of mistakes in the Summary 1. *No cheating, please!*

These are the main mistakes in the summary:

- The summary should not contain more than 120 words but it contains about 170 words. The writer will lose many marks for this.

- The summary starts with an unnecessary introductory sentence, most of which is copied from the question.

- The punctuation is seriously wrong.

- There are spelling mistakes, including mistakes in words copied from the passage.

- The summary contains long expressions copied from the passage.

- The writer has inserted information (about an army or air force) not given in the original passage.

- Unnecessary details are included (about papier-mache, children and the chapel).

- The 'summary' is not a summary at all. The writer has made no real attempt to express the main points in his/her own words. Some points have been omitted.

How many of these mistakes did you find? Did you notice any other mistakes?

Summary 2

First we must find the main methods of sustaining demand in the future. We can make rough notes. They do not have to be in sentences or even in good English. They will be crossed out later on. We can use up to 120 words, so we aim to write notes containing about a third to a half of this figure. (That allows for putting in good English and linking words when we make the summary.) Target: 40–60 words.

Notes:

products not last long – buy new
people encouraged to get rid of old things – buy replacements
dump surplus in sea – sustain demand
don't repair if 2+ yrs old
v. attractive marts with disposal bins

Number of words: 34. We are below the target of 40 words but that does not matter. It is easier to add words than to eliminate some.

Draft summary:

The author thinks that manufacturers will reduce the life of their goods so that people will need to replace them. There will be various ways of encouraging people to get rid of old goods. It will

Unit 9 · *City of the Future?*

not be possible to get somebody to repair an appliance more than two years old. This will necessitate buying replacements frequently.
Surplus factory goods will be dumped in the sea.

Stop and count words or lines. I have used about 70 words so far. I can afford to use up to 50 words for the final point(s). It is *vital* to stop and make a rough check of your number of words *before* you finish your summary. Then you can make adjustments more easily.

At the centre of the city of the future, there may be a huge supermarket which is made very attractive and in which <u>whole</u> families can enjoy themselves using lifetime electronic cards <u>to buy whatever they like</u>. They can even bring unwanted goods and throw them into disposal bins <u>provided for them</u>.

I have added about 52 words, making the total length about 122 words, which is slightly too long. Delete the nine underlined words. The final length is about 110–15 words. The amended draft summary is now my final summary.

There are other ways of making a summary but the principles remain the same:

1. Study and understand the question. Underline the main points in the question.

2. Make notes of the relevant material in the passage. Your notes should not be more than a third to half of the final number of words.

3. Link up your notes to make a draft summary.

4. Check for length before you finish your summary.

5. Add or delete words to reach the right length.

9.7
Writing: say it another way

Express these sentences in a different way. Use the word in brackets but retain the meaning of the original sentence as far as possible.

1. Very few people want to buy wigs now. (demand)

2. We told her it would be a good idea if she applied for the job. (encouraged)

3. It is easy to rebuild wooden houses. (rebuilt)

4. They will be rewarded if they work hard. (provided)

5. The accused man had to hand his passport to the police. (surrendered)

6. You ought to have asked me before you borrowed my bicycle. (without first)

7. Jangling cash registers cannot disrupt the holiday mood. (There are)

8. It took the electrician nearly an hour to repair the faulty switch. (spent)

9. Each child is given a name when it is born or soon afterwards. (birth)

10. That shop is open all the time and even on Sundays. (including)

9.8 Vocabulary: what's the difference?

Briefly explain the difference between the words in each pair below. Use each word correctly in a separate sentence.

1. personal, personnel
2. human, humane
3. lose, loose
4. award, reward
5. past, passed
6. wounded, injured
7. alternately, alternatively
8. beside, besides
9. morale, morals
10. unqualified, disqualified

Lose or loose?

9.9 Writing about proverbs

Be careful if you have to write about a proverb in an examination. Most proverbs have a literal and a figurative or metaphorical meaning. Here are some examples:

- **You can't tell a book by its cover.**
  literal meaning: The cover of a book may not be a good guide to the quality of the story or contents of the book.
  metaphorical meaning: Don't judge a person or thing by its appearance.

- **He who rides on a tiger can never get off.**
  literal meaning: If you go for a ride on a tiger, you can't get off because then the tiger will eat you.
  metaphorical meaning: If you get involved in something dangerous (like drug-dealing), you won't be able to stop (and will eventually be destroyed or get into serious trouble).

- **He who pays the piper calls the tune.**
  literal meaning: If you are paying a musician, you can tell him what tune to play.
  metaphorical meaning: If you are financing an undertaking, you have the right to say how it will be carried out.

- **Don't put all your eggs in one basket.**
  literal meaning: When you are gathering eggs laid by hens, don't put them all in one basket (because you may drop the basket and smash all of them).
  metaphorical meaning: Don't rely on one source only. Don't put all your money or effort into a single project.

- **The burnt child fears the fire.**
  literal meaning: If a child has been burnt by a fire, he will be afraid of fire.
  metaphorical meaning: If somebody has been hurt (physically or mentally) by something, he will be afraid or very cautious in dealing with the same thing again.

Over to you!

Look at the following proverbs. Say whether the meanings below them are literal or metaphorical.

1. Make hay while the sun shines.
   a) Cut the grass to make hay when the weather is good and the grass is dry.
   b) When the opportunity comes, make the most of it.
   c) Enjoy yourself when you get a good chance to do so.

2. Let sleeping dogs lie.
   a) Don't stir up trouble.
   b) Don't start investigations which may lead to trouble.
   c) If you see a dog is sleeping, don't wake it up (because it may bite you).

3. You will reap what you sow.
   a) The crop you get will depend upon the seeds you plant.
   b) Your future will depend upon the actions you take now.
   c) What happens to you in the future depends on how you behave now.

4. Don't skate on thin ice.
   a) Don't take dangerous risks.
   b) Be sensible and keep away from very risky activities.
   c) When the ice on a pond or river is thin, don't try to skate on it (or you may fall through the ice and be drowned).

5. People in glass houses shouldn't throw stones.
   a) If you are vulnerable to criticism, don't criticise other people.
   b) If you have done something which makes it possible for people to attack you, it is foolish to attack other people.
   c) If your house is made of glass, don't throw stones at people (because if you do, they may throw stones at you and smash your house).

When you write about a proverb in an examination, deal with the figurative meaning of the proverb and not with its literal meaning. Sometimes, you *may* be able to consider the literal meaning of a proverb but your main focus should be on the metaphorical meaning. Look at the following examples.

Example 1

Write a story based on the saying 'You can't tell a book from its cover'.

Theme:

I will write a story showing that the given saying can be correct.

Plan:

four friends out fishing at sea

wave from motor-boat; their boat rocks

one boy/girl thrown into water

two macho boys/girls won't jump in to the rescue – can swim but scared

timid fourth person jumps in and saves boy/girl

although everybody had always thought he/she was timid and weak, he proves to be the bravest of the three teenagers – which shows that you can't judge people by appearances, i.e. we can't judge a book by looking at its cover

Notice that the proposed answer has nothing to do with covers and books.

Example 2

Write a story based on the saying 'Nothing ventured, nothing gained'.

Theme:

I will write a story showing that if you want to be successful or make a profit, you sometimes have to take a (sensible) risk.

Plan:

in the early days of computers in X's country

X took a risk and went to Miami to take a course in computers

returned to own country; set up company as an IT specialist

computers became available – great demand for them
X much in demand to help businesses and individuals set up computers
had to employ others; became leading IT company in his/her country

Over to you!

Write out a theme and plan for a story based on one of these proverbs.

1. Still waters run deep.
2. Faint heart never won fair lady.
3. More haste, less speed.
4. A leopard doesn't change its spots.
5. Cockroach no business in a fowlyard.
6. Look before you leap.

9.10
Writing: making up a plot for a story (review)

In Unit 4, we saw that most plots involve conflict and derive from one of these situations:

- **Somebody is in conflict with another person or with several people**, e.g.
  - A boy or girl is in conflict with a bully at school or outside school.
  - Two men are rivals for the same girl or job.
  - A thief or robber is in conflict with his brother, who is a police officer.
  - A modern girl is in conflict with her old-fashioned grandmother.
  - Somebody is in conflict with a neighbour or an employer.

  *Make up at least **two** more examples of this type of conflict.*

- **Somebody is in conflict with external circumstances**, e.g.
  - A seriously ill person is being rushed to hospital in an ambulance when a wheel of the ambulance comes off or collapses.
  - An important crop is ready to be harvested when it is destroyed by fire or a storm.
  - Fishermen are caught at sea or on a wide river by bad weather.
  - At an airport, a young woman claims the wrong luggage at a carousel (where luggage is put when it comes off a plane). When she goes through Customs, concealed drugs are found in the case.
  - The driver of a taxi is suddenly stung by a bee.

  *Make up at least **two** more examples of this type of conflict.*

- **Somebody is in conflict with himself**, i.e. there is some physical or mental quality (good or bad) which causes the person to become involved in a problem, e.g.
  - A young man is weak, so he joins a gang, commits crimes and is killed when he is 20.
  - Mr X is greedy and will do anything for money. This leads him into trouble.

- Miss X is extremely trusting. She trusts somebody after having been warned. She is nearly cheated out of her savings.
- Abiose is full of curiosity about almost everything in life. One day she discovers a secret which could lead her to her death.
- Paul is addicted to gambling. One day, luck is with him.

*Make up at least **two** more examples of this type of conflict.*

The structure of a plot

Look at the diagram below. It shows the structure of a plot. The horizontal axis measures time. The vertical axis shows the degree of excitement.

- The story starts on a point of interest, revealing the conflict and problem.

- The plot develops through a series of peaks, each of which is more exciting or interesting than the previous one. The problem may get worse before it gets better.

- The climax comes near the end. Once it has been reached, the story is finished as quickly as possible.

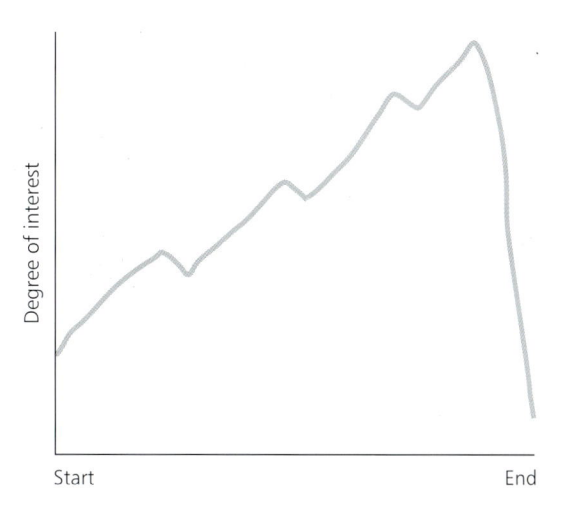

Over to you!

Exercise 1

Make up the outline of a plot for *one* of these stories. You can use notes (extending to about 5–8 lines). Your plot must be original.

1. Write a short story with the title 'The Mysterious Old Man/Woman'.

2. Write a story with the title 'A Narrow Escape'.

3. Write a story having as its main theme the problems of a newcomer to a village, town or city.

4. Write a story in which a river plays a major role.

5. Write a story which starts with these words:
   It all happened so quickly that at first the danger was not obvious. ...

6. Write a story which ends with these words:
   ... One day I hope to go back there again.

Exercise 2

Make up the outline of a plot for *one* of these stories. You can use notes (extending to about 5-8 lines). Your plot must be original.

1. Write a story concerned with the unexpected landing of an aeroplane or a helicopter.

2. Write a story based on *one* of these titles:
   a) More haste, less speed.
   b) The monkey knows which tree to climb.
   c) Every cloud has a silver lining.

3. Write a story by continuing the following:
   I had heard that she was a strange woman but now, as she approached me for the first time, ...

4. Write a story which starts in this way:
   Donna listened to the radio and then checked the guest list at the hotel where she worked on the Reception Desk ...

5. Write a story which ends with these words:
   ... For several weeks after the incident, Sonia wondered whether she had made the right decision or not.

6. Write a story based on the picture below.

9.11
Writing

Either: Write 400–450 words on topic (1) in about 45 minutes.
or: Write 250–300 words on topic (2) or (3) in about 30 mintues

1. Take your plot outline from Exercise 1 or 2 and develop it into a short story.

2. Is it better to live in a town or in the countryside? What is *your* personal choice and why?

3. Read again Vance Packard's article about the City of the Future in 9.2. Then say whether you think you would like to live in Happy City or not. Do you think the majority of people would like to live there? Why or why not?

10 Bajan Entertainment

10.1 Pre-reading

In 10.2 we can read about two aspects of entertainment in Barbados: music and festival. Both of these topics involve expository writing but they show different methods. To deal with the first topic, 'Music', the writer uses a **chronological** (time) approach. In the second, 'Crop Over Festival', the writer is more concerned with **describing** what the festival is and what happens during it.

Notice that we could change these approaches and use a descriptive account for 'Music', and a chronological approach for 'Crop Over Festival'.

Later in this unit, we will consider other ways of writing about factual and expository topics.

10.2 Reading

Music

For centuries, the folk music of Barbados has preserved musical traditions – particularly traditional African drumming – imported by the slaves who came to work on the island's sugar plantations. The plantation owners tried to kill off this musical heritage, banning and burning drums and other instruments, but the music
5 remained underground, surfacing only after the freeing of the slaves in 1834.

Its most distinctive form was the 'tuk' band, so named for the rhythmic beating sound of their main instrument, the big log drum, with a banjo or tin flute providing the melody. On public holidays, tuk bands went from village to village with their simple but lively songs, normally accompanied by a dancing cast of
10 characters that included a stilt-man and a shaggy bear.

By the early twentieth century, the influence of Trinidadian calypso music had reached Barbados, and calypsonians took on the tuk band's role as wandering minstrels, spreading their songs of political satire and social comment around the island. However, the music remained frowned upon officially. Ironically, it was a
15 white band, **The Merrymen**, which popularised calypso in the 1960s, with traditional songs like *Sly Mongoose* and *Brudda Neddy*. Their success helped to spawn a new group of performers who emerged after independence in 1966, including the grandly named **Mighty Viper, Lord Summers** and **Mighty Gabby**.

The 1970s saw the explosion of reggae from the ghettos of Jamaica and, though
20 the music never took off in the same way in comparatively well-off Barbados, its success in the dancehalls did trigger two new musical forms. The first was *spouge*, a

132   English Alive!

sort of reggae/calypso hybrid that was briefly popularised by singer Jackie Opel in the early 1970s; the second, rather more enduring, was soul calypso or *soca*, which offered a more lively and danceable version of traditional calypso.

Today, the best-known performers in Barbados are its calypsonians, particularly Antony Carter, better known as the Mighty Gabby. Gabby's radical calypsos often provide a focus for issues of national concern.

Crop Over Festival

The Crop Over festival, held every summer, traditionally celebrated the completion of the sugar harvest and the end of months of exhausting work for the field labourers on the sugar estates. As in many other countries, the festival immediately precedes a period of fasting. Crop Over carried a frenzied sense of 'enjoy-yourself-while-you-may', as workers knew that earnings would now be minimal until the next crop. Alongside the flags, dances and rum-drinking, the symbol of the festival was 'Mr Harding' – a scarecrow-like figure stuffed with the dried leaves of the sugar cane – who was paraded around and introduced to the manager of the sugar plantation.

Though Crop Over has lost some of its significance since the 1960s, with sugar replaced by tourism as the country's main industry, it's still the island's main festival and an excuse for an extended party. Things start slowly in early July, with craft exhibitions and band rehearsals, heating up in late July and early August with street parades, concerts and competitions between the tuk bands, steel bands and – most importantly – the battle for the title of calypso monarch, dominated in recent decades by the Mighty Gabby and Red Plastic Bag who, between them, have won nine times in the last thirty years.

10.3
Understanding

A Choose the best answer for each of the following.

1. In line 1 of the passage, 'folk' is used with the meaning ____.
   - A. crude
   - B. rarely heard
   - C. of ordinary people
   - D. best

2. The attempts to kill off folk music in Barbados proved to be ____.
   - A. largely successful
   - B. eventually in vain
   - C. expensive to plantation owners
   - D. motivated by envy

3. One of the early functions of tuk bands was to ____.
   - A. lead a revolt against plantation owners
   - B. criticise the colonial government
   - C. start the Crop Over festival
   - D. provide entertainment

4. The social comment of the Trinidadian calypso music was evidently ____.
   - A. unpopular with colonial officials
   - B. welcomed by the colonial government
   - C. frowned upon by ordinary people
   - D. disliked because it came from Jamaica

5. What was ironic about the success of The Merrymen?
   A. They were white men.
   B. They enjoyed their work.
   C. They were not paid to perform.
   D. They were never really merry.

6. By using 'spawn' in line 16, the writer implies that ____.
   A. the new performers were not much good
   B. the new performers changed their music when they grew older
   C. the Merrymen had many imitators
   D. the Merrymen did not help other performers

7. In the fourth paragraph, the words 'comparatively well-off' form a contrast with ____.
   A. 'the explosion of reggae'
   B. 'the ghettos of Jamaica'
   C. 'took off in the same way'
   D. 'rather more enduring'

8. In line 27, 'provide a focus for' is somewhat similar in meaning to ____.
   A. 'throw a spotlight on'
   B. 'take pains to avoid'
   C. 'pretend they have not noticed'
   D. 'have caused major changes to'

B Answer these questions about the passage in 10.2.
1. What period of years is covered by the account of Bajan music?
2. Why was calypso music not popular with officials?
3. Why did reggae not prove as successful in Barbados as in Jamaica?
4. What was the reaction of people to *soca* when it appeared in Barbados?

C Make up three more questions (similar to those in B1–4) about the Crop Over festival. Make up the answers to them. Ask the questions in class. Say whether the answers are acceptable or not. If you reject any answers, say why you think that they are unacceptable.

10.4
Vocabulary: meaning in context

A Choose the word(s) which best show(s) the meaning of the underlined words as they are used in the passage in 10.2.

1. the folk music of Barbados has <u>preserved</u> musical traditions (line 1)
   A. influenced
   B. retained
   C. modified
   D. improved

2. The plantation owners tried to kill off this musical <u>heritage</u> (line 4)
   A. inheritance
   B. ancestry
   C. skill
   D. descendant

134 English Alive!

3. <u>banning</u> and burning drums and other instruments (line 4)
   A. confiscating
   B. destroying
   C. objecting to
   D. prohibiting

4. the music remained underground, <u>surfacing</u> only after the freeing of the slaves (lines 4–5)
   A. living on
   B. improving
   C. reappearing
   D. continuing

5. a dancing cast that included a stilt-man and a <u>shaggy</u> bear (lines 9–10)
   A. rough-coated
   B. lively and dancing
   C. able to sing
   D. strange-looking

6. Calypsonians took on the tuk band's role as wandering <u>minstrels</u> (line 13)
   A. singers and musicians
   B. political activists
   C. entertainers
   D. critics of the government

7. spreading their songs of political <u>satire</u> and social comment (line 13)
   A. opposition
   B. attempts to get change
   C. disagreement
   D. mocking scorn and ridicule

8. Ironically, it was a white band, **The Merrymen**, which popularised calypso (lines 14–15)
   A. as we might expect
   B. much to our disgust
   C. contrary to what one might expect
   D. in an amusing turn of fate

B Match the underlined words with the meanings which they have in the passage.

Words in the passage	Meanings
1. the music never <u>took off</u> (line 20)	a) lasting
2. did <u>trigger</u> new musical forms (line 21)	b) tens of years
3. rather more <u>enduring</u> (line 23)	c) at their lowest
4. months of <u>exhausting</u> work (line 29)	d) reason given to justify
5. immediately <u>precedes</u> … fasting (line 31)	e) almost maddened
6. carried a <u>frenzied</u> sense (line 31)	f) importance
7. earnings would be <u>minimal</u> (line 32)	g) very tiring
8. lost some of its <u>significance</u> (line 37)	h) comes before
9. an <u>excuse</u> for an extended party (line 39)	i) became very popular
10. in recent <u>decades</u> (line 43)	j) produce or lead to

10.5
Writing: straight and crooked thinking

In Unit 5, we considered some of the tricks which people use in arguments and to try to persuade other people. Here are four more tricks. In each case, give further examples from your personal experience, if you can.

Playing on the prejudices and tastes of the audience

The speaker appeals to the religious beliefs, customs, patriotism or other (irrelevant) beliefs of the audience in an attempt to obtain support for his (or her) policy. He may try to persuade his listeners (or readers) that a certain course of action (which he opposes) is unsporting, unsocial, unpatriotic, irreligious or contrary to the wishes of a particular group of people. Something may be said to be good or bad because it is/was done by white (or black) people.

The dangers of this trick in a multi-racial society are obvious. Sometimes people use racist expressions when their case has no real merits and the only thing they can do is to try to stir up racial feelings.

Making wild claims without evidence

Look at these examples:

Guzzlo is the largest-selling soft drink and ideal for your health. Live longer and better with Guzzlo – the life-giving drink! *(Where? On St Helena?)*

More people use Nippy petrol than any other kind of petrol. *(Any proof?)*

Modern research has proved that women prefer our new green washing powder with essence of ripe durian in it.

'Stinko' beer: the most popular brand on the market.

The idea behind these and similar claims is that if most people prefer brand X it must be the best, so we should buy it. If we don't buy it, people may think we are odd in some way. Don't let wild claims fool you.

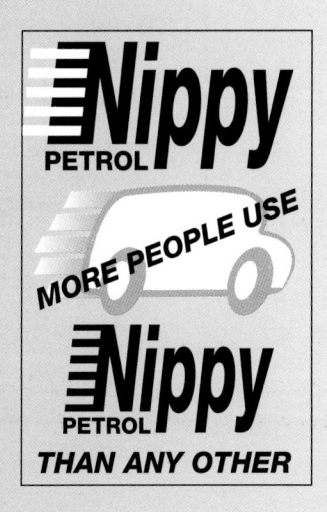

Mixing truthful and untruthful statements

The speaker deliberately makes one or two truthful statements which make an unsuspicious listener assume that *all* his statements are truthful, as in the advertisement of Guzzlo. Amongst them will be the particular lie which the speaker (or writer) wants you to accept unthinkingly. This is common in advertisements and not unknown in politics.

Using words which have an emotive effect

A Minister for Housing said, 'It would be a good idea to demolish eight old houses in Market Street. We can build an apartment block for 60 families on that site.'

- A newspaper which *supports* the Minister's party can report this as 'Minister suggests housing expansion' or 'More homes for working families!'

- A newspaper which is *opposed* to the Minister's party can say, 'Minister demands demolition of workers' homes!' Another newspaper may say: 'The Minister for Housing made it clear today that he is determined to root out a row of workers' homes in Market Street.'

In other words, a newspaper can make the Minister seem progressive and thoughtful, or arrogant and ruthless.

Oral exercise

Study the letters, articles and/or news items in a newspaper. Find words which have an emotive effect. Bring the material to school and discuss in class the effect of the emotive words and the possible motives which the writers or newspapers had in using them.

10.6 Discussion

Discuss the statements below. They are taken from the work of examination candidates and are useful as warnings of attitudes to avoid.

1. *On the topic 'Truly great men are humble men':*
   'A great man is a tall man and tall men are usually humble because they are too big for people to attack.'

2. *On 'Ways of dealing with crime':*
   'As soon as a gangster is caught, he should be taken out and shot without wasting time and money on a fair trial.'

3. *On 'Parents and their children':*
   'A modern youth matures earlier than in former years. He can think with careful logic much earlier than did his imbecile counterpart of yesterday.'
   (Notice that 'his imbecile counterpart' will probably mark his examination paper.)

4. *On the equality of men and women:*
   'It is true that – on the whole – men are physically stronger than women, so it is reasonable to let them do the fighting when there is a war. However, there is no doubt that women are more caring, intelligent and compassionate than men. They are much better at seeing both sides of an argument. They can reason without becoming abusive or aggressive. For these (and many other) reasons, it makes sense to leave most planning and policy decisions to women. In this way, men and women can share the responsibilities of leading a country.'

5. *On character (two separate statements by one student):*
   a) 'It is absolutely futile to try to judge a man's character from his face. I think it was Shakespeare who said: "There's no art to find the mind's construction on the face".'
   b) 'Thus by looking at a person's face we see it is impossible to judge a person's character, except for people such as women, scientists, police officers and suspicious persons.'

10.7
Grammar: common errors

Exercise 1

Correct the errors in the use of verbs in these sentences.

1. My brother who working in a bank is studying to be an accountant.

2. It's late and Uncle hasn't come yet. Maybe he not coming this evening.

3. We are best friends for at least five years.

4. My nephew live in this country for a long time and is very happy here.

5. Michael has wrote to us to tell us about his life in London.

6. We are all very grateful to Mrs Wilson for everything she have done to help us recover from the fire.

7. Pollution from factories and vehicles increase the heat in the atmosphere and should be reduce as much as possible.

8. If I won a lottery, I will share my money with members of my family.

9. Some people do not look after their pets and allowed them to wander about the streets.

10. A novelist cannot write about anything unless he had experience of it.

11. If you tell me that you were coming, we would have meet you at the airport but we didn't know, so we didn't go there.

12. There are more than one way of repairing this pipe.

Exercise 2

Correct the errors in the use of verbs in these sentences

1. Thank you for your letter which is received on 4 August.
2. Members of the gang will be prosecuted if their crimes were discovered and somebody able to identify them.
3. When Miss Stewart had obtained what she wanted at the market, she goes home by bus.
4. It was about 5 p.m. when we reached Tanya's home. She was alone at home because her mother has gone out.
5. In parts of Canada it is so cold that only white people does live there.
6. Oxygen is a gas which make it possible for people to live on Earth. Without it, there have no people living here.
7. When we waiting for a bus, a lorry come by and splash us when it go through a puddle.
8. Francine was so tired that she fall asleep on the bus and did not woke up until the bus reached the terminus.
9. My mother told me that her parents had married for fifty years before they dead.
10. Why you didn't write me you was coming?
11. Do your brother want to come to the party on Saturday or is he having too much work to do?
12. You can eat this fruit now. It have all been wash very thoroughly.

10.8
Grammar: reflexive and emphatic pronouns (revision)

Make sure that you know how to use **reflexive pronouns** correctly.

- We can use them as the **object** of a verb or **after a preposition**. We do not use them as the subject of a verb. The pronouns are in bold type in the examples below.

Singular	Plural
I blamed **myself** for the mistake. Don't blame **yourself**, Mike. Earl cut **himself** by accident. Lana made **herself** a costume. The dog scratched **itself**. One must protect **oneself** at all times.	We were pleased with **ourselves** when we won. Don't blame **yourselves**, boys. It was my fault. The players congratulated **themselves**.

Notice that the plural forms end in '-ves' and never in '-fs'.

- We can also use these pronouns to emphasise a person or thing. Then we call them **emphatic** (or **emphasising**) **pronouns**. They often follow a noun or pronoun or refer to one, e.g.

  I know the rumour about Errol winning a lottery is true. He told me so **himself**.
  Coleen likes her new home but I'm not keen on it. The house **itself** is fine but the location is not so good. It's on a very busy road, so it's noisy.

  It was not a very good game to watch. It was very hot and the players **themselves** looked as if they were going to fall asleep at any minute.
  All right. Now I'll tell you what I **myself** think of the plan.

Over to you!

Exercise 3

Put in suitable reflexive or emphatic pronouns.

1. Mitzie made this doll all by ____. Nobody helped her.

2. If you're still hungry, girls, please help ____ to more food.

3. Don't lose ____ when you get into town, Peter.

4. Lorraine likes her new hair style but I ____ think it is too elaborate.

5. When we go out, we leave the dog at home by ____ to guard the house.

6. It's not easy to prepare a meal for eight people all by ____, especially if one has to do all the shopping as well as the cooking.

7. Don't get the vegetables mixed up with the meat. Cook them by ____.

8. Did your cousins enjoy ____ at the party last Saturday, Leela?

9. My mother and I went shopping and decided to treat ____ to a meal downtown.

140 *English Alive!*

10. Natoya ____ is a very friendly and unselfish girl but her cousin is not very nice.

11. Quacy went into the kitchen and got ____ a soft drink from the fridge.

12. Nobody was more surprised than Lall ____ when he won the cross-country race.

13. Be careful, Sharon! Don't cut ____ with that knife. It's very sharp.

14. Nadia bought two ice creams: one for her sister and one for ____

15. Can you repair this bike by ____, Dean, or do you need some help?

10.9
Writing a factual account (1)

These are common subjects of factual writing and we need special techniques to deal with them:

- **events/actions**: past, present and future, e.g. a science experiment, how to do something, a sports meeting, a visit to a place, a fire or an accident

- **places**, e.g. my country, region, town/village, home/school

- **objects**: how something works or its function/usefulness, e.g. a computer, a camera, television, a newspaper

- **people**, e.g. biography, autobiography, the achievements of a person

- **an organisation or society**, e.g. a school society or club, the UN, a Caribbean organisation

- **one's own activities**, e.g. hobbies, daily life, ambitions, strengths and weaknesses.

Factual writing is also involved in such school subjects as Science, Geography, History, Social Studies and Economics.

Unit 10 · *Bajan Entertainment*   141

Step 1: Who are you writing for?

Make sure that you know for whom you are writing. Is your factual account of a camera for a child aged 10 or a professional photographer? Is your account of an accident for the police, for a penfriend or for an insurance company – or for an examiner?

The language and techniques which you use will depend largely on your awareness of your reader.

Step 2: How much time have I got? How long should my account be?

In the CSEC examination, you may have one of these limits:

- 180–200 words in 25 minutes
- 300–350 words in 35 minutes
- 400–450 words in 45 minutes.

But study the instructions because these limits can always be changed.

Step 3: What is my theme?

Your theme is the central unifying idea on which the whole composition is based. In some ways, it is like a person's backbone – no backbone, no body; no theme, possible chaos.

In many cases, the theme will be given in an examination topic but you may need to work out a theme yourself, as the examples below show.

Examples of finding a theme

- *Exam question:* An overseas penfriend has sent you an email asking for information about your country. She says she knows nothing about it and would like to have a brief account of it. Write a suitable email to send to her.
  Theme: I will write an email (for an overseas penfriend) giving an account of my country. (On the question paper, I would underline 'overseas penfriend', 'about your country', 'account' and 'email'.)

- *Exam question:* You were a passenger in a car which was involved in an accident. Write a statement for the police, describing what happened before, during and after the accident.
  Theme: I will write a statement for the police, describing what happened before, during and after an accident involving a car in which I was a passenger.

- *Exam question:* Storms.
  Comment: For some students, this type of topic could be a disaster. They may fail to understand the topic and simply describe one storm.
  Theme: I will restrict the scope of the topic to 'Tropical Storms' and explain how they form and move, and the damage they can cause.

If you have to write about a topic such as 'Storms', you can find a theme by using PC FAT:

P = The **part** which something plays in our lives.
C = Give a **chronological** (time) account of the development of something.
F = Give a **factual** account.
A = Describe the different **attitudes** to a subject.
T = Describe different **types** of the topic.

In the third example on page 142, we have used T, C and F together.

Over to you!

Exercise 4

Write out a possible theme for each of the following topics. Express your theme in a single sentence each time.

1. A friend has written to you for advice on the best methods of choosing and keeping a pet. Choose any pet (e.g. a bird, a cat, fish, etc) and write a letter giving the necessary advice.

2. How does tourism affect your country?

3. The influence of climate on the occupations and habits of people in your country.

4. Describe some hobby or interest which you find both enjoyable and useful. Give your reasons for thinking that it is useful.

5. Give an account of a sports meeting in which you took part.

6. Farming.

10.10
Writing a factual account (2)

After you have found a **clear theme** for a factual topic, your next step is to **make a plan** based on your theme.

Step 4: Consider 4W + H

Sometimes 4W + H will give you an idea for arranging your points in a logical order:

- **What?** What was the event or what is the thing you are going to write about? Tell your reader as quickly as possible. You can give details of it later on.

- **When?** If you have to describe an event, say when it happened. Give the date and perhaps the time.

- **Where?** Where did the event take place? This may be unimportant or extremely important.

- **Who?** Who were the participants and what did each one do?

- **How?** How was the event caused?

Not all of these points will be useful, but some of them may help you to form a plan.

Step 5: Arrange your points in a logical order

Depending on the topic, we can arrange points in one of these ways:

- **in time order**, from the beginning to the end. This method is useful for a topic which involves past or future actions, e.g. when dealing with an accident, plans for a picnic, preparing a meal, doing an experiment, etc.

- **in place order**, showing what happened in different places, e.g. at a fun fair, at school

- **in order of importance**, e.g. when giving an account of the activities of a school club or any organisation

- **showing the good and bad aspects of a topic** or the advantages and disadvantages of it

- **divide and describe**, e.g. examine your topic to find the major factors, systems or parts of which it consists. List each one, explain its relationship to the whole, and describe it. We can apply this method to a topic such as 'The human body', 'Agriculture in your country' or 'Using a computer'.

There are other methods for arranging facts in a logical order, but you will probably find that one of the five given above will help you to make a plan.

Examples of themes and plans

Study these topics with their themes and plans:

- *Topic*: Discuss the problems facing teenagers or elderly people in the community.
  Theme: I will discuss (some of) the problems facing teenagers in the community.
  Note: Some careless candidates will write about *both* teenagers and elderly people. If you make a point of underlining key words on your question paper you are less likely to make this mistake.)
  Plan: opening: problems at home, at school, amongst friends
  home: mother, father, brother, grandparents
  school: Maths and Science
  friends: helping others
  end: problems less than the enjoyment or most problems will disappear in the future

- *Topic*: Consider the effects of tourism on your country.
  Theme: I will write about the (good and bad) effects of tourism on my country.
  Note: Be careful here. Some people (such as hoteliers and shopkeepers) are strongly in favour of tourism. Others are very critical. An extreme position – either way – is likely to upset the examiner.

> *Plan:* Advantages first; then disadvantages
>   advantages: improved airport, harbour, access roads
>   jobs in hotels, shops, taxis, guides, other services
>   many tourist facilities available to local people
>   helps economy, income for govt
>   medical/dental services improved
>   inward investment encouraged
>   disadvantages: (I can't think of any important ones, so I'll have to invent some.)
>   crowded areas sometimes – shops, rental cars/taxis
>   bad behaviour: some people drunk or on drugs
>   bad behaviour: sometimes rude in shops
>   end: advantages more important than disadvantages

Notice that the plans in the above examples are *not* completely realistic ones. In an examination, we would not write out complete words in a plan. A real plan would look more like this:

> adv 1st; disadv
> adv: better air, harb, rds
>   jobs – htls, sh, tax, gu, others
>   t fac for locals
>   hlp econ, income - govt

The notes have been written out in full here so that you can understand them more easily.

Over to you!

Exercise 5

Write out the theme and plan for *one* of these topics.
1. Explain clearly how a main food crop is grown and harvested.
2. Explain precisely how you made something at home or school.
3. Describe the effects of schools holidays on various people, e.g. on yourself, your teachers, your parents and others.
4. Give an account of methods of training for an important game or event.
5. The value of learning a foreign language (including English if it is not your mother-tongue).

Exercise 6

Write out the theme and plan for *one* of these topics.
1. Give an account of the ways in which you help the community – either in school or out of it.
2. Give an account of the system of discipline and punishments in a typical secondary school, pointing out what seem to you to be its good and weak or bad features.

3. The importance of water in the life of man
4. How has the development of air transport affected your country and others in the region?
5. How I should like to improve the district in which I live

10.11
Writing

Choose *one* of the topics below. Then do these things in not more than 35 minutes:

   a) Write your theme out separately.

   b) Write your plan (in note form) based on your theme.

   c) Write 300–350 words about the topic.

1. Explain how your country is governed.
2. How important is religion in the lives of people in your country?
3. Choose two school subjects: one at which you are good, and one in which you are weak. Attempt to explain why you are good at one subject but weak in the other.
4. What kind of life would you expect emigrants from your country to be able to lead in a foreign country after they have emigrated? What are the reasons for your opinion?
5. Consider the contribution of modern science to agriculture.

10.12
Enjoying poetry

Sometimes a poet can make a point just as powerfully in a short poem as in a long one. In fact, sometimes a short poem is the result of a strongly-felt view or emotion which the poet wants to share with people. This is the case in the first poem opposite. When you read it, think about these questions:

- What does the first line mean?
- What perhaps led the poet to write this poem?
- Do you agree with the point he is making?

Country

It is in the raw country that we come upon ourselves.
Here the hoe-man is no rejector of heaven,
And people wriggle their toes in the mud
And say:
5   Something for all of us here,
Come dig, time to plant up.

These people have never seen
Blood spilled over the charmed penny.

These people have never been
10 Where smoke is a law
And they persecute you with pen and ink
And most folks are sad
Because they have found out about things.

Raw, we say.

15 It is in the crude country that we come upon ourselves.

E. McG. Keane

Questions

When you try to answer the following questions, remember that sometimes we do not know exactly what a poet meant when he wrote a word or line. (In some cases, he was perhaps not sure himself.) Don't worry if your opinion is different from that of other people. As long as your opinion makes sense and is justified by the words in the poem, it is an acceptable one.

1. What does the poet want us to understand by the word 'raw'? Is the word used to refer to something good or not good?

2. Whom is the poet criticising in line 2?

3. In line 3, why do people 'wriggle their toes in the mud'? What is the poet trying to tell us by using this expression?

4. 'These people have never seen
   Blood spilled over the charmed penny.'
   Is the poet using 'charmed' sarcastically, bitterly or in praise of the penny?

5. What does the poet mean in line 11?

6. In the last line, does 'crude' mean 'rough and bad' or does it mean 'unspoilt by town life'?

7. In one sentence, say what the poet's theme is.

8. Do you agree with the poet? Does his theme still hold good in your country today?

The next poem is about Sir Lancelot. He was the son of the King of Brittany (in northern France) but he was stolen when he was a child and was taken to England. He was brought up at the court of King Arthur, where he was a model of bravery and chivalry. Unfortunately, he fell in love with Gwenivere, the beautiful wife of King Arthur. As a result of this love, there was a war and King Arthur died.

Lancelot bitterly regretted that he had been disloyal. He became a monk and died as a holy man. Queen Gwenivere entered a convent and became the abbess. When this poem starts, Gwenivere did not know that Lancelot was dead.

The Death of Lancelot, as Told by Gwenivere

Then, after many years, a rider came,
An old lame man upon a horse as lame,
Hailing me 'Queen' and calling me by name.

I knew him; he was <u>Bors</u> of Gannis, he,   **Lancelot's nephew**
5 He said that in his chapel by the sea
My lover on his death-bed longed for me.

No vows could check me at that dying cry,
I cast my abbess-ship and nunhood by …
I prayed, 'God, let me see him <u>ere</u> he die.'   **before**

10 We passed the walls of Camelot; we passed
Sand-raddled <u>Severn</u> shadowing many a mast,   **the River Severn**
And bright Caerleon where I saw him last.

Westward we went till, in an evening, lo,
A bay of bareness with the tide at flow,
15 And one green headland in the sunset's glow.

There was the chapel, at a brooklet's side.
I galloped downhill to it with my guide.
I was too late, for Lancelot had died.

I had last seen him as a flag in air,
20 A battle banner bidding men out-dare.
Now he lay dead: old, old, with silver hair.

I had not ever thought of him as old …
This hurt me most: his sword-hand could not hold
Even the cross upon the sacking-fold.

25 They had a garden-close outside the church
    With <u>Hector</u>'s grave, where robins came to perch.
    When I could see again, I went to search

    For flowers for him dead, my king of men.
    I wandered up the brooklet, up the <u>glen</u>;   *small valley*
30 A robin watched me and a water-hen.

    There I picked <u>honeysuckles</u>, many a bine   *a type of flower*
    Of golden trumpets, budding red as wine,
    With dark green leaves, each with a yellow spine.

    We buried him by Hector, covered close
35 With <u>these</u>, and elder-flower, and wild rose.   *the flowers in lines 31–3*
    His friends are gone thence now; no other goes.

    He once so ringing glad among the spears,
    Lies where the rabbit <u>browses</u> with dropped ears   *nibbles the grass*
    And shy-foot stags come when the moon appears.

40 Myself shall follow, when it be God's will;
    But whatso'er my death be, good or ill,
    Surely my love will burn within me still.

    Death cannot make so great a fire <u>drowse</u>;   *go out*
    What though I broke both nun's and marriage-vows,
45 <u>April</u> will out, however hard the boughs;   *Spring = love*

    And though my spirit be a lost thing blown,
    It, in its waste, and in the grave, my bone,
    Will glimmer still from Love, that will <u>atone</u>.   *make amends*

                    John Masefield

Questions

1. Why does the poet make the man and horse in line 2 lame?

2. What is the rhyme scheme in this poem?

3. What was the answer to the prayer in line 9? Suggest a reason for the answer.

4. Why is 'old' repeated in line 21?

5. What are we meant to understand in line 27 by 'When I could see again'?

6. What is the significance of 'dropped ears' in line 38?

7. Suggest a synonym for 'glimmer' in the last line.

8. What was the aim of the poet? Do you think he has achieved it?

11 O'Hare

11.1 Pre-reading

The passage in 11.2 contains two true stories. What are the links between them? One link is explained in the stories. Can you find the other link?

11.2 Reading

Story 1

During the Second World War, Lieutenant Commander Butch O'Hare, aged 28, was a fighter pilot on an aircraft carrier in the South Pacific. On one occasion, he set off with his squadron on a reconnaissance flight but soon discovered that he did not have enough fuel to complete his mission and return to his ship. His fuel gauge
5   showed that somebody had forgotten to top up his fuel tank after an earlier mission.

O'Hare's flight leader told him to return to the carrier. On his way back to the carrier, he saw Japanese bombers speeding towards the defenceless American fleet. O'Hare attacked the Japanese squadron and shot down five bombers before he ran
10 out of ammunition. Although his plane was damaged, he managed to land on his carrier safely. Film from the camera mounted on his plane confirmed what had happened to the bombers. Later that year, 1942, O'Hare became the first naval aviator to win the Congressional Medal of Honour. In the following year, he was killed in aerial combat. His home town would not allow the memory of their hero
15 to die. The airport at Chicago was named O'Hare Airport and today contains a memorial to Butch O'Hare and a statue of him.

Story 2

Some years earlier, there was a man in Chicago known as Easy Eddie. He was the lawyer for Al Capone, a gangster who virtually controlled Chicago. Easy Eddie was a very good lawyer. His skill at legal manoeuvring kept Big Al out of jail for a long
20 time. To show his appreciation, Capone paid him very well. He and his family lived in a fenced-in mansion that filled an entire Chicago City block. Eddie lived the high life of the Chicago mob and gave little consideration to the atrocities that went on around him.

However, Easy Eddie had one soft spot. He had a son whom he loved dearly. He ensured that his son had the best of everything: clothes, cars and a good education. Despite his involvement with organised crime, Eddie tried to teach his son to rise above his own sordid life. He wanted his son to be a better man than he was. Yet, with all his wealth and influence, there were two things that Eddie could not give his son: a good name and a good example.

One day, Easy Eddie made a difficult decision. Offering his son a good name was far more important than all the riches he could lavish on him. He had to rectify all the wrongs that he had done. He would go to the authorities and tell the truth about Scar-face Al Capone. He would try to clean up his tarnished name and offer his son some semblance of integrity. To do this he must testify against the Mob, and he knew that the cost would be very great. But more than anything, he wanted to be an example to his son. He wanted to do his best to make restoration and hopefully have a good name to leave his son. So he testified. Within the year, Easy Eddie's life ended in a blaze of gunfire on a lonely Chicago Street, as he had known it would. He had given his son the greatest gift he had to offer at the greatest price he would ever pay.

What do these two stories have to do with one another? Butch O'Hare was Easy Eddie's son.

11.3
Understanding

1. When O'Hare left an aircraft carrier in line 2, what did he intend to do?
2. How did negligence on the carrier nearly cost O'Hare his life?
3. Why was the American fleet defenceless (line 8)?
4. In what way was the camera on his plane helpful to O'Hare when he returned?
5. How old was Butch O'Hare when he was killed?
6. What was Easy Eddie's main work before the war?
7. What is meant by referring to Easy Eddie's life as 'high' in line 21?
8. In what way was Eddie's life 'sordid'? (line 27)
9. Explain why the decision in line 30 was 'difficult' for Eddie to take.
10. To what does 'the greatest gift' refer in line 39?

11.4 Vocabulary: meaning in context

Choose the word(s) which best show(s) the meaning of the underlined words as they are used in the passage in 11.2.

1. on a <u>reconnaissance</u> flight (line 3)
   - A. very long distance
   - B. extremely dangerous
   - C. to bomb enemy cities
   - D. to gather information

2. had forgotten to <u>top up</u> his fuel tank (line 5)
   - A. inspect carefully
   - B. empty and clean
   - C. refill by adding some more
   - D. check the contents of

3. before he <u>ran out of</u> ammunition (lines 9–10)
   - A. managed to avoid
   - B. escape from
   - C. had none left
   - D. started to use

4. the camera mounted on his plane <u>confirmed</u> what had happened (line 11)
   - A. verified
   - B. demonstrated
   - C. showed
   - D. contradicted

5. gave little <u>consideration</u> to the atrocities that went on around him (line 22)
   - A. care
   - B. pity
   - C. mercy
   - D. thought

6. Eddie tried to teach his son to rise above his own <u>sordid</u> life (line 27)
   - A. reckless and self-centred
   - B. mean and immoral
   - C. frantic and dangerous
   - D. hardly legal

7. all the riches he could <u>lavish on</u> his son (line 31)
   - A. give extravagantly to
   - B. invest on behalf of
   - C. save up for
   - D. waste by giving to

8. He had to <u>rectify</u> all the wrongs that he had done (line 31)
   - A. tell somebody about
   - B. keep quiet about
   - C. confess to
   - D. put right

9. He would try to clean up his <u>tarnished</u> name (line 33)
   - A. spoilt
   - B. unpopular
   - C. unjustified
   - D. slippery

10. offer his son some <u>semblance</u> of integrity (line 34)
    - A. confirmation
    - B. high reputation
    - C. slight appearance
    - D. belief

11. offer his son some semblance of <u>integrity</u> (line 34)
    - A. wisdom
    - B. honesty
    - C. skill
    - D. firmness

12. To do this he must <u>testify against</u> the Mob (line 34)
    - A. give evidence against
    - B. refuse to cooperate with
    - C. break away from
    - D. turn his back on

11.5 Vocabulary

Exercise 1

Choose the best answer for each of the following.

1. When workers are axed, they ____.
   A. have an accident
   B. lose their jobs
   C. receive an unexpected bonus
   D. are no longer unemployed

2. If you call somebody a dog in a manger, you mean that the person is ____.
   A. dishonest   B. selfish   C. hungry   D. weak

3. In a discussion, if we say that somebody is dead right, we mean that he is ____.
   A. no longer alive
   B. completely correct
   C. speaking without thinking
   D. jealous of other people

4. Miss Harrison was anything but happy when she was transferred to another branch. We can guess that she was ____.
   A. very pleased
   B. rather unhappy
   C. more confident than before
   D. surprised but pleased

5. 'I'm not going to put up with your attitude any longer,' the manager of a shop said to an assistant. Then he ____ her.
   A. dismissed   B. engaged   C. transfer   D. promoted

6. In question (5) above, 'put up with' means ____.
   A. question   B. discuss   C. criticise   D. tolerate

7. If somebody lives beyond his means, he ____.
   A. has a long way to travel to get to work
   B. finds that the demands of the job greatly exceed his ability
   C. will almost certainly get into debt
   D. enjoys an income which is greater than what he needs

8. The plot of the film was very complicated, so Luke had great difficulty in making ____ what it was all about.
   A. off   B. up   C. out   D. on

9. When recruits first join the Army, they are usually put ____ a rigorous course to get them fit and used to discipline.
   A. through   B. to   C. away   D. at

10. If you bury the hatchet, you ____.
    A. start a quarrel
    B. make peace
    C. cause harm to somebody
    D. become weaker

11. If a person is negligent at work, he may be dismissed because his ____ may cause a serious mistake or ____
    A. rudeness … error
    B. ignorance … correction
    C. carelessness … accident
    D. haste … trouble

12. In a competition, a ____ player is one who is expected to reach the final or semi-finals.
    A. branched
    B. rooted
    C. planted
    D. seeded

11.6
Grammar: relative pronouns (1)

We can use 'who', 'that', 'which', 'whom' and 'whose' as **relative pronouns**. Then they are the first word in an adjectival clause. They tell us something about a preceding noun or pronoun.

'who' or 'that' + a verb

Look at these examples:
  The man **who was Butch O'Hare's father** was Al Capone's lawyer.
  Do you know the girl **that is talking to Suresh?**

When we refer to people, we can use 'who' or 'that'. In speech, 'that' is more common than 'who' because it is easier to say. In a **non-defining clause**, we use 'who' and not 'that' when referring to a person. See 11.7.
The adjectival clause which starts with 'who' or 'that' comes after a noun and can be used early in a sentence or at the end.

Over to you!

Exercise 2

Complete the sentences below by putting in suitable clauses from the box.

who travel on cruise ships	who drive under the influence of alcohol
who try to smuggle drugs	who robbed a jewellery shop last week
who work in Caribbean hospitals	that is sitting just behind Donna
that works in a large hotel	who guides a liner into harbour safely
that dives at Spiny Bay	who raises a family by herself

1. Anybody ____ may be swept away by the strong current.

2. What's the name of the girl ____?

3. The man ____ is known as the pilot.

4. A woman ____ deserves a medal.

5. People ____ are a menace to other road users and to pedestrians.

6. Foreign countries are anxious to recruit nurses ____.

7. A chef ____ must be very experienced.

8. Tourists ____ often buy souvenirs to take home with them.

9. In Singapore and some other countries, people ____ may be hanged.

10. The police are still looking for the men ____.

Exercise 3

Combine each pair of sentences to make a single sentence containing 'who' or that'. Make any necessary changes, e.g.
>The fisherman stood at the rear. He owned the boat.
>*The fisherman who owned the boat stood at the rear.*

1. That is the lady. She is in charge of the exhibition.

2. What was the name of the actor? He played the part of the detective.

3. Can you recommend a lady? She can give my daughter piano lessons.

4. Those are the men. They built our house

5. The police are anxious to trace a youth. He started the fire.

6. The lady said we can get our money back. She sold me these tickets.

7. The manager is talking to the lady. She complained about a camera.

8. Shall we invite the boy? He has just come to live next to us.

9. Two of the players came from our school. They took part in the test match.

10. The watchman has been reprimanded. He fell asleep while on duty.

11.7
Grammar: defining and non-defining clauses
Defining clauses

Notice the different ways in which these sentences are (correctly) structured:
>The boy **who found the wallet** received a reward.
>Mr Harris gave some money to the boy **who found the wallet**.

We call the words in bold **defining clauses** because they define the boy, i.e. they show which boy we are referring to.

Non-defining clauses

However, sometimes we already know which person we are referring to. Then the adjective clauses are called **non-defining** because we do not need them to show which person we are referring to. We use 'who' (and not 'that') when referring to people in a non-defining clause, e.g.

My brother, **who found the wallet**, received a reward.

Mr Harris, **who was delighted to recover his wallet**, gave the boy who found it a big reward.

We use commas to mark off non-defining clauses. Here are more examples:

My eldest sister, **who is studying in Texas at the moment**, will be returning some time next month.

Lloyd's uncle, **who works for an overseas airline**, often sends him foreign stamps.

If you want to learn to swim, you could ask Delroy, **who is an excellent swimmer and a very patient instructor**.

Exercise 4

Study these sentences. Some contain defining clauses; some contain non-defining clauses. Put in commas where they are needed.

1. O'Hare Airport was named after Butch O'Hare who was a very brave military pilot.

2. O'Hare Airport in Chicago was named after a pilot who fought bravely in the Second World War.

3. The shop assistant who served us was very courteous and helpful.

4. Miss Wilson who served us herself was both courteous and helpful.

5. I'll introduce you to a lady who is a qualified accountant.

6. I'm sure that Nnke's brother who is a qualified accountant will be able to advise us.

7. Anybody who works in a bank has to speak reasonable English.

8. My sister who works in a bank has to speak good English.

9. Gerald Dixon who is acting as guide for the tourists has been employed by us for several years and is completely trustworthy.

10. Mr Ajmir Singh who gave evidence for the prosecution has decided to set up his own security company.

11.8

Grammar: relative pronouns (2)

'which' or 'that' + a verb

This sentence pattern is similar to those in 11.6 and 11.7 but we use it to refer to things and not people, e.g.

    The dog **which caused the accident** was unhurt but frightened.
    Our dog, **which is now nearly fifteen years old**, is not as energetic as it used to be.
    The manta ray **that swam just above us** seemed enormous.
    The road to Kingston, **that is usually packed with traffic during the rush hours**, was almost empty this morning.
    We were very surprised when Mother's car, **which is usually very reliable**, broke down yesterday evening.
    Any car **which is used a lot** is bound to break down eventually.

It does not matter whether we use 'that' or 'which'. However we do not use 'that' after a preposition. Then we use 'which', e.g.

    This is the bus stop **at which we wait nearly every morning**.
    We need a screwdriver or something strong **with which to get the lid off this tin of paint**.
    The store **from which we used to buy most of our groceries** has closed down.
    The *Jamaica Gleaner*, **in which our company often advertises**, is a very reliable newspaper and sets high standards.

Exercise 5

Complete the sentences below by putting in suitable clauses from the box.

which precedes 'q' in the alphabet	that was in its bowl
which measures small distances	that is landing now
that was supposed to leave at 2 p.m.	which make a poem more striking and effective
which almost always follows 'q'	which is known as The Rock and attracts tourists
which was said to be escape-proof	which contains both synonyms and antonyms

1. A micrometer is an instrument ____.

2. A thesaurus is a book ____.

3. The letter ____ is 'u'.

4. I'm sorry but the flight ____ has been cancelled because of the approaching storm.

5. Has the cat really eaten all the food ____? She must have been very hungry.

6. Al Capone was sent to Alcatraz, a prison ____.

7. The prison is on a small island ____.

8. One letter ____ is 'p'.

9. Similes and metaphors are two of the devices ____.

10. The plane ____ has just come from Miami.

11.9
Punctuation and setting out dialogue

Reminders:

- Put direct speech inside inverted commas.
- Each new speaker starts a new paragraph.
- Have a sense of humour. You will need it for the following exercise.

Exercise 6

Set the following passage out correctly, putting in all necessary punctuation marks and following the reminders above.

```
One night a woman woke up and discovered that her husband
was not in their bedroom she put on a dressing-gown and
went downstairs to look for him she found him sitting at
the kitchen table with a cup of coffee in front of him he
seemed to be deep in thought just staring at the wall she
watched him wipe a tear from his eye and take a sip of his
coffee whats the matter she asked why are you down here at
this time of night her husband looked up and said do you
remember many years ago when we were dating and you were
only 16 yes I do she replied he paused the words were not
coming easily do you remember when your father caught us
kissing and cuddling out on the verandah yes I remember
said his wife lowering herself into a chair beside him the
husband continued do you remember when he shoved his shotgun
in my face and said either you marry my daughter or I'll
send you to jail for 20 years yes I remember that too the
woman said quietly the man wiped another tear from his
cheek I would have got out today
```

11.10
Arranging a debate

In 11.14, you are going to hold a class debate. Sections 11.10–13 give guidelines on debating.

When a formal debate is held, there are usually two teams of speakers (one team speaking *for* the proposal (or 'motion') and one team *against* it). These teams agree on the rules or procedures to be followed, and there are several different systems which can be used.

Preliminary arrangements

1. A suitable topic is chosen. The teams draw lots to see whether they will propose or oppose the motion. In some cases, the organisers may tell them whether to propose or oppose it.

2. A neutral chairperson is chosen and invited.

3. Details of the place, time, date, etc. are settled.

4. The teams choose their speakers. We will use four speakers, two on each side, and we will call them P1 and P2 (proposers) and O1 and O2 (opposers). They can speak from brief notes or without notes but they should *not* read out their speeches.

5. The speakers prepare their material. If possible, research the motion in preparation for the debate. Useful sources include:

   - the internet, using your computer and a search engine – you will probably find more material than you can use!

   - the online archives of local and national newspapers

   - first-hand reports/comments from people who work in the field which will be discussed during the debate; information from this source may be invaluable and will enable you to speak with greater confidence and authority.

11.11
Debate procedure

The time limits shown here can be changed. They are only examples.

1. The chairperson welcomes the audience and introduces the speakers. He or she then calls on the first proposer, P1, to speak.

Unit 11 · *O'Hare*

2. P1, the first proposer, formally proposes the motion and speaks for 5 minutes in support of it. The chairperson *may* ring a bell at the end of 4 minutes to show P1 that he or she has only a minute left. At the end of 5 minutes, the chairperson will ring a bell, and the speaker *must* stop.

3. O1, the first opposer, will speak for 5 minutes, explaining to the audience why he or she opposes the motion. He or she may attack the arguments put forward by P1 but should also present positive ideas of his or her own.

4. P2, the second proposer, will speak for 5 minutes (or any shorter period which has been agreed by both teams).

5. O2, the second opposer, will speak for 5 minutes.

6. At this point, the debate may be 'thrown open to the floor', which means that members of the audience can speak on either side. A time limit of 2 minutes per speaker may be enforced by the chairperson. A period of 10 or 20 minutes may be allowed for all speakers from the floor.

7. O1, the first opposer, now replies to arguments put forward by P1, P2 and any speakers from the floor who supported the motion. He or she may be allowed to speak for 3 minutes only.

8. P1, the first proposer, answers arguments put forward by the opposition. He or she may be allowed to speak for 3 minutes only.

9. The chairperson may briefly sum up the arguments put forward by both sides, but sometimes this is not done.

10. The vote is taken, sometimes with the help of 'tellers' (people who count) from each side. The chairperson will then declare the motion carried or lost.

11. Somebody will briefly propose a vote of thanks to the chairperson, speakers and audience. Another speaker will briefly second this motion, and the debate will end.

11.12
The duties of speakers in a debate

Most speakers, and particularly the four major ones, will attempt to do some or all of these things:

- present constructive and interesting reasons in support of their argument
- attack and destroy the arguments put forward by opposing speakers
- anticipate the possible arguments of the opposition and try to destroy or minimise them
- speak clearly, vigorously and in an interesting manner

- use their hands (and sometimes visual aids) to help them to make their message more striking.

11.13
Judging a debate

There are many different ways of judging a debate. The main point is to make sure that the judges are given a simple system such as this one:

- Content (= ideas/opinions): 40%
- Organisation: 30%
- Delivery: 30%

These figures can be changed, depending on the factors which seem most important in any particular situation.

11.14
Topics for a debate

Choose a suitable topic and then hold a debate in class. Remember that everybody – all the speakers and members of the audience must stay cool, be courteous and be self-disciplined. One team can propose, and the other team can oppose the motion that …

1. Work at school should be compulsorily supplemented by some form of community service.

2. All forms of advertising should be subject to control by the Government.

3. Sport at school should not be compulsory.

4. Women are more honest and reliable than men.

5. Tradition is more of an obstacle than a guide.

6. Geography is a more useful and interesting subject than history.

7. At the present rate of global pollution, the destruction of the Earth as a habitat for humans is inevitable.

8. Upon conviction, the penalty for most crimes involving a weapon such as a gun or knife should be death.

9. Homework should be abolished.

10. Fathers should play a more responsible part in raising their children.

11. History proves that the sword is more powerful than the pen.

12. The subject matter of all school subjects should be adjusted to serve the needs of future citizens.

13. In the CSEC English Language examination, the study and examining of poetry should be optional and not compulsory.

14. People convicted of two criminal offences should lose the right to vote until such time as they are able to prove that they have reformed.

15. As a condition of becoming an MP, a man or woman should agree that his or her income is open to public scrutiny for as long as the person remains an MP.

16. To help local farmers, more should be done to encourage people to eat locally-produced food.

17. Scientific discoveries and inventions have done more harm than good to civilisation.

18. It is better to be comparatively poor and honest than wealthy and dishonest.

19. Caribbean countries should reject external influences and decide on their own system of government and style of living.

20. Television channels should aim to raise the quality of the programmes which they show and should accept more responsibility for influencing viewers in beneficial ways.

11.15
Enjoying poetry

Too Soon It Was My Allotted Task

Too soon it was my allotted task
to drag my father's past
from drawers and closets
to <u>see</u> him clothed again   **imagine**
5 in colours more splendid
than funeral blackness.

This was not the time
to bewilder myself with memories
but to pass on to others
10 the <u>providence of</u> a simple life   **things kept carefully during**

the bright suits and shirts;
shoes; dozens of neck-ties,
every colour from red to green
faded into an ashen grey;
15 stiff collars in a collar-box;
hats, a <u>cummerbund</u>, a cane: **wide waistband**

these and more would go
to the Veterans of Foreign Wars.
There were other things,
20 mementos that I have kept:
a pharmaceutical note-book
containing five formulae
and a slip of paper
with a detailed budget
25 marked simply, "July, 1938,"
the <u>economy</u> of yesterday in a proud hand,   **household economy or budget**
the present dead, riding forever
on a moment's wing;
two pairs of cuff-links,
30 and a small pocket-knife.

In the end, these will take on
their own magnificence,
perhaps when my son
will no longer wear his sleeves unbuttoned
35 now that there are silver links
to chain him to my past.

Edward Anthony Watson

Questions

1. Why does the poet say (in line 1) 'too soon'?
2. What is implied in line 2 by the use of 'drag' instead of 'take'?
3. What made the poet write 'This was not the time'? (line 7)
4. What do you understand by 'the providence of a simple life' in line 10?
5. Why did the poet plan to give some things to the Veterans of Foreign Wars?
6. What do lines 24–6 tell the reader about:
   a) the dead man?
   b) about the poet?
7. Express in your own words what you think the poet meant by lines 27 and 28.
8. What are the 'silver links' in line 35 and how can they 'chain' the poet's son to the poet's past?

11.16
Writing

Either: Write 400–450 words on topic (1) or (2) in about 45 minutes.
or: Write 250–300 words on topic (3) in about 30 minutes.

1. Choose *one* of the illustrations below. Then write a story closely linked to the scene shown in the illustration.

2. Make up or retell from memory a story involving bravery by a male or female.

3. Choose one of the debate motions in 11.14. Write a speech which a proposer might make in an inter-school debate. Start in this way:
   Madam Chair, honoured guests, fellow students: I am delighted to propose that …

164 *English Alive!*

12 The Penny Post

12.1
Pre-reading

In 12.1, we can read about how the first stamps were issued, in l840. The passage is interesting because it shows that even officials in high positions opposed any change in the existing system. All people need to adapt to make progress and meet new dangers or problems. Are you a person who is willing to try out something new: new clothes, new food, new machines? Or are you the type of person who hates any change and tries to obstruct progress?

How do modern forms of communication compare with the primitive ones in this passage?

12.2
Reading

The Penny Post

In the early part of the nineteenth century, there were no computers, email, telephones or radios. The only way of communicating with people in other villages, towns or countries was by sending a letter but at that time there was no efficient postal service. Letters were paid for by the recipient; delivery was slow and
5 uncertain; foreign delivery was often impossible; letters and packets were often lost or stolen.

From 1833 to 1836 an Englishman named Rowland Hill studied the incompetent post office in his country. In l836 he wrote a pamphlet urging that reforms should be carried out. Hill showed what the costs of a letter really were:
10 they were costs of handling, not of carrying for long distances. At that time, every letter had to be given to a postal clerk, who examined it studiously to see where it was going, and who then entered the postage due on it. Laboriously, he recorded in a ledger the fee to be collected on delivery. The letter was then passed to another clerk who, in all doubtful cases, checked to see whether it contained an enclosure
15 (which was strictly prohibited). Checking was done by 'candling', i.e. by holding the letter against the light of a candle in a dark room. In those days, there were no envelopes; letters merely consisted of folded and sealed sheets of paper.

In due course, the letters were despatched to the most convenient town (by slow-moving Royal Mail carriages). The local postman then had to find the address
20 of each addressee and hand the letter to him, first collecting the fee. This sometimes involved an argument and further loss of time. In an experiment to check on part of Hill's pamphlet, a postman delivered 67 letters in 1½ hours under traditional conditions, but 570 letters in half an hour when he just left them at the

addresses. Big post offices had to employ hordes of accountants and clerks for their book-keeping.

Hill then made various proposals which, at the time, many people regarded as sheer lunacy:

   (i) The postal rate should be so low that even poor people could send and receive letters. An increased use of the post would compensate for loss of revenue.

   (ii) The rate should be the same for all distances within the country.

   (iii) The rate should depend on the weight of the letter and not on the number of sheets.

   (iv) The rate for the minimum weight should be one penny.

   (v) All letters should be prepaid.

The proposals came as a shock. They abolished the whole machinery of collecting fees and accounting for them between post offices, replacing it with prepayment.

Hill suggested that the Post Office use 'a bit of paper just large enough to bear the (ink) stamp, and covered at the back with a glutinous wash, which the bringer might, by the application of a little moisture, attach to the back of the letter.'

The impact of Hill's pamphlet was sensational. People divided themselves into two groups: pro-Hill and anti-Hill. When a Government committee met to consider the proposals, the Chief Secretary to the Post Office said that Hill's scheme was 'fallacious, preposterous, utterly unsupported by facts, and resting entirely on assumption.' The Postmaster-General declared that the scheme was the most extraordinary of all the wild and visionary schemes he had ever heard of.

Despite this opposition, the penny post was started in 1840 and was soon followed by all other major countries.

12.3
Understanding

A Choose the best answer each time.
1. When a person wanted to send a letter in 1835, ____.
    A. there was a risk that the stamps would be stolen
    B. he had to deliver it himself
    C. he had to pay according to the distance involved
    D. it was not necessary for him to pay in advance

2. Hill proposed various reforms ____.
    A. but knew that they could never be carried out
    B. to increase the inefficiency of the postal service
    C. although he doubted whether they were practicable
    D. and hoped that they would be put into effect

3. We would expect a postal clerk of 1836 to oppose Hill's reforms because ____.
    A. they might deprive him of his job
    B. they were not based on an adequate study of the service
    C. he would be faced with much more work
    D. most people regarded them as sheer lunacy

4. The author implies that Hill's pamphlet was ____.
    A. not popular even with poor people
    B. justified by existing conditions
    C. unsuccessful despite its good points
    D. the product of an unsound mind

5. The most expensive aspect of the system used in 1836 appears to have been ____.
    A. the time wasted on 'candling'
    B. the need to collect money from the receiver
    C. connected with the absence of envelopes
    D. the need to use a large number of employees

6. Hill's proposals came as a shock because ____.
    A. they were quite different from the existing system
    B. he knew very little about the postal service
    C. the Chief Secretary to the Post Office was opposed to them
    D. the prepayment system caused considerable delay

7. The statement that Hill's proposals were 'resting entirely on assumptions' was ____.
    A. false, as the experiment with the delivery of letters shows
    B. untrue, because Hill proposed to use adhesive stamps
    C. correct, as was shown by later events
    D. accurate, because the proposals were wild and visionary

B Answer these questions about the passage.

1. What precautions were taken to ensure that nothing was put inside a letter?
2. Do you think that Hill's proposals were justified? Why (not)?
3. Which two of Hill's five proposals seem to you to be the best? Why have you chosen them?
4. Suggest a reason for the opposition of the Postmaster-General and the Chief Secretary to the Post Office.
5. a) By 1841, there was unanimous agreement that Hill's reforms were excellent. Why then was there opposition to them in 1836?
   b) What attitude to new ideas does this reveal?

12.4

Vocabulary: meaning in context

A Choose the word(s) which best show(s) the meaning of the underlined words as they are used in 12.1 and 12.2.

1. All people need to <u>adapt</u> to make progress (12.1, line 5)
   A. become educated
   B. speak out clearly
   C. follow traditional methods
   D. adjust to new conditions

2. there was no <u>efficient</u> postal service (12.2, line 3)
   A. profitable
   B. well run
   C. cheap
   D. available

3. Letters were paid for by the <u>recipient</u> (line 4)
   A. receiver
   B. sender
   C. postman
   D. postal clerk

4. Hill studied the <u>incompetent</u> post office in his country. (line 8)
   A. bureaucratic
   B. non-competitive
   C. inefficient
   D. competing

5. which was strictly <u>prohibited</u> (line 15)
   A. enforced
   B. safeguarded
   C. in favour
   D. not allowed

6. letters <u>merely</u> consisted of folded and sealed sheets of paper (line 17)
   A. only
   B. always
   C. often
   D. usually

7. many people regarded as <u>sheer</u> lunacy (line 27)
   A. dangerous
   B. complete
   C. costly
   D. astonishing

8. many people regarded as sheer <u>lunacy</u> (line 27)
   A. extreme foolishness
   B. waste of time and money
   C. arrogance
   D. unjustified boldness

9. They <u>abolished</u> the whole machinery of collecting fees (line 36)
   A. began to improve
   B. went to the heart of
   C. involved
   D. did away with

10. Hill's scheme was <u>fallacious</u> (line 44)
    A. far too expensive
    B. much too far-reaching
    C. based on misleading arguments
    D. infallible

B Match the underlined words from the passage with the meanings which they have in the passage.

Words from the passage	Meanings
1. the letters were <u>despatched</u> (line 18)	a) make up for
2. under <u>traditional</u> conditions (line 23)	b) sticky
3. employ <u>hordes</u> of accountants (line 24)	c) completely
4. would <u>compensate</u> for loss (line 29)	d) supposition
5. with a <u>glutinous</u> wash (line 39)	e) senseless
6. the <u>application</u> of a little moisture (line 40)	f) unreal
7. the scheme was <u>preposterous</u> (line 44)	g) sent
8. <u>utterly</u> unsupported by facts (line 44)	h) very large numbers
9. resting entirely on <u>assumption</u> (line 45)	i) use
10. <u>visionary</u> schemes (line 46)	j) customary

12.5
A cloze passage

Put a suitable word in each blank space.

(1) ____ to 1840, the postal service in Britain was clearly inefficient. The postal fee was (2) ____ by the receiver; delivery was slow and (3) ____. Sometimes (4) ____ was lost or stolen.

After (5) ____ the postal service for three years, a man named Rowland Hill proposed that a number of major (6) ____ should be (7) ____ out. He (8) ____ that the postal rate should be reduced, and that it should (9) ____ the same for all distances within the country, and depend on the (10) ____ of a letter (11) ____ than on the number of sheets. In addition, he suggested that the (12) ____ rate should be one penny because even a poor person could (13) ____ to pay that.

When an (14) ____ was performed to check on part of Hill's proposal, it was (15) ____ that a postman would (16) ____ far more letters if he (17) ____ the method proposed by Hill. The

Unit 12 · *The Penny Post* 169

public were divided in their (18) ___ to the proposals which
(19) ___ considerable opposition from officials whose influence
might be undermined. However, Hill's proposals were eventually
(20) ___ and the penny post was started.

12.6
Vocabulary: idioms

What do the following expressions mean? When would you use them?

1.
   a) to throw in the towel
   b) to take pot luck
   c) to take him down a peg
   d) to put off an event
   e) to put up with something
   f) to be at daggers drawn
   g) on the QT
   h) to be in clover
   i) to fall foul of somebody
   j) to get away with something

2.
   a) to turn over a new leaf
   b) to make a pig of yourself
   c) to grease somebody's palm(s)
   d) to sail near the wind
   e) to smell a rat (in a plan)
   f) to live in a fool's paradise
   g) to back out of something
   h) to be at the end of your tether
   i) to call a spade a spade
   j) to catch somebody red-handed

12.7
Grammar: inversion of subject and verb

When we start a sentence with 'never', 'never before', 'not only', 'no sooner', 'hardly' or 'scarcely', the following verb comes before its subject.

170 *English Alive!*

Check that you can use the words and expressions in bold type below:

Word/expression	Examples
never	**Never** had I heard such an incredible story.
	Never had Leela seen such a magnificent display.
never before	**Never before** has anybody run as fast as he did.
never again	**Never again** will I agree to lend him money.
not only	**Not only** did Paul score two goals but he helped the defence as well.
	Not only is she related to the managing director but she has a share in the firm as well.
	Not only does Miss Smith own this house but she owns two shops as well.
no sooner	**No sooner** had the game started than it poured with rain.
	No sooner had the two sides reached agreement than a fresh dispute arose.
hardly, scarcely	**Hardly** had we reached home when the telephone started to ring.
	Scarcely had we started the journey when the driver began to argue about the fare.
only	**Only in recent times** has it been accepted that women have the same rights as men.
	Only after several hours of questioning did the suspect admit that he had taken part in the raid on the bank.
	Only at the last minute did the man change his plea to 'Guilty'.

You need to recognise this type of pattern, but you may find that you do not have to use it in your own written work. We can always find an alternative method of expressing the same idea, e.g.

with inversion: Never had we met such a kind person.
without inversion: We had never met such a kind person.

with inversion: Only after queuing for an hour were we able to buy two tickets.
without inversion: We were able to buy two tickets but only after queuing for an hour.

Over to you!

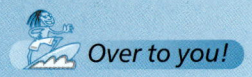

Exercise 1

Express the 14 examples on page 171 in a different way so that no inversion of subject and verb is necessary. In some cases, there are alternative ways of doing this.

12.8
Grammar: correcting errors

Exercise 2

Correct any mistakes in these sentences.

1. Most members of the committee thought only of their ownselves.
2. That is the woman with whom both of my cousins work with.
3. Most of our problems can be overcomed with a determined effort.
4. Ranjit felt all the more stronger after the rest.
5. The police could not get a single information from the suspect.
6. Unfortunately, the man drove round the bent far too quickly.
7. Some subjects are comparatively new. Examples, Economics, Botany, etc.
8. The effects of individualism on society is sometimes quite harmful.
9. Courtney ripped his shirt on a barbed wire fence, mainly because he was in such a hurry.

10. When he was young, Howard was both spoiled by his parents and his grandmother.
11. I spent three years in that school and other three years in another school.

12. Samantha spends a lot of time to help her younger sister with her homework.

13. Hardly need I remind you of the importance of adequate training.

14. The visitor's lengthy speech soon made us feel boring and anxious to go.

15. Michael is my brother. He is elder than I am.

16. According to the writer of a letter in today's newspaper, some young men lack in moral standards.

17. My aunt very much enjoyed on her holiday in Florida.

18. You should form it a habit to take plenty of exercise.

19. In the test, two marks were rewarded for each correct answer.

20. In a primary school, it is important to rouse up the curiosity of the pupils so that they will participate more fully in class activities.

12.9
Grammar: relative pronouns (3)

In Unit 11, we practised using 'who', 'that' and 'which' when they are the subject of an adjectival clause, e.g.

Do you know the girl **who/that is talking to Suresh?**
The lady **who/that is waiting to see the Principal** is one of Vimala's aunts.
Has anybody found the electrical fault **which/that started the fire**?

When a relative pronoun is the object of a verb, we use 'whom' or 'that' for persons, and 'that' or 'which' for things. In both speech and written work, the relative pronoun can be omitted, e.g.

Do you know the girl (whom/that) the car nearly hit?
What have you done with the video (which/that) Uncle gave you?

Over to you!

Exercise 3

Join each pair of sentences to make a single sentence containing an adjectival clause. Leave out any words which are not needed, e.g

This is the watch. Uncle gave me it.
*This is the watch **that** Uncle gave me.*
or *This is the watch Uncle gave me.*

1. Have you repaired the lock? You broke it.

2. We ate all the food. We had taken the food with us.

3. The mistake was not very serious. Aboise made the mistake.

4. The programme starts at seven o'clock. Mother likes that programme.

5. Nickesha has found the key. She lost the key last week.

6. Now we can visit interesting places. We never dreamt of visiting them before.

7. Have you still got the receipt? The sales assistant gave you a receipt.

8. What's the name of the player? The referee sent him off.

9. The girl comes from Antigua. Glenford married her.

10. That's the policewoman. We saw her in the supermarket yesterday.

11. What have you done with the book? I borrowed it from the library a couple of days ago.

12. Can you remember the name of the tourist? Uncle was talking to him for nearly an hour.

12.10
Grammar: relative pronouns (4) – using 'whose'

We can use the relative pronoun 'whose' to link two statements about a person, an animal or (more rarely) a thing. The most common pattern is **noun or pronoun + 'whose' + noun**, e.g.

Do you know the man **whose** car was damaged?
Michelle knows somebody **whose** sister works in that office.
What happened to the cat **whose** legs were hurt?

We can combine two sentences by using 'whose', e.g.

That's the girl. Her brother won the race.
That's the girl **whose** brother won the race.

Mrs Harris has promised to help us. Her husband is a doctor.
Mrs Harris, **whose** husband is a doctor, has promised to help us.

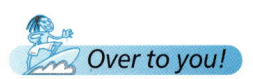

Over to you!

Exercise 4

Combine each pair of sentences to make a single sentence containing 'whose'.

1 That's the man. His boat sank in the harbour during the night.

2. The motorist was very angry. His car was damaged by a bus.

3. My brother grew these flowers. His hobby is gardening.

4. The fishermen have been rescued. Their boat was wrecked during the storm.

5. I feel sorry for the boy. His leg was injured during a game at school.

6. What's the name of the girl? Her bicycle was stolen during the night.

7. I think I know the name of the man. His dog chased us yesterday.

8. What was wrong with the player? You took his place in the second half of the game.

9. The girl won the first prize. Her costume was the most original and striking.

10. One group was barred from performing. Its players were half-drunk.

11. My friend is extremely good at science subjects. Her ambition is to be a doctor.

12. I got these stamps from a relative. Her job frequently involves travelling to foreign countries.

12.11
Grammar: synthesis

Exercise 5

Join each pair of sentences by using the words in brackets. Notice that you may have to change, add or omit words.

1. We won the game. Our centre-back was injured. (despite)

2. We arrived on time. There was a severe storm which partly flooded the road. (in spite of)

3. Donna helped us prepare for the party. She baked a lot of cakes and made many sandwiches. (by)

4. The Maroon hid in some bushes for twelve hours. He avoided capture. (by)

5. We could help them. They still won't reach the top of the mountain today. (even if)

6. Errol did not care about the dangers. He decided to swim to the land. (regardless)

7. The bicycle was not in perfect condition. He decided to buy it. (although)

8. Natoya was reluctant to get mud on her clothes. She agreed to help us. (despite)

9. The temperature could reach 35 degrees. The material still won't ignite. (even if)

10. The suspect continued to claim that he was innocent. He said, 'I didn't go near the shop.' (persisted)

11. Our country is not far from the equator. It is always very warm or hot. (therefore)

12. The small boat hit a sharp rock. It caused the boat to sink quite quickly. (which)

12.12
Writing: a simple report

Each year, many large firms make an assessment of their employees. This helps to show those who are most suitable for promotion. The assessment sometimes includes a form which lists those qualities of value in a particular job or company.

Copy the following form. Put your own name where it says 'Name of employee' and then assess your own character and abilities. Tick the appropriate columns.

As an optional activity, you can then ask a friend, classmate or relative to use your form and make his or her assessment of you, using a different colour/type of ink or pencil.

Name of employee:					
Qualities	**Very good**	**Good**	**Average**	**Weak**	**Bad**
Honesty					
Health					
Physical fitness					
Works hard					
Reliability					
Intelligence					
Mathematical skills					
Helpfulness					
Ability to work as a member or a team					
Ability to accept criticism					
Leadership					
Originality					
Personal appearance					
Courtesy to others					
Friendliness					

12.13
Writing: starting a composition

In section 4.8, we practised these ways of starting a story: SAD (**s**tatement, **a**ction, **d**ialogue). For other types of composition (e.g. argumentative, factual, imaginative, etc.), we can add three more ways of starting. Then we have six methods and can make the acronym DO PASS to remember them:

- **D** = **Dialogue.** In the opening sentence, use direct speech which is relevant to the theme and plan.
- **O** = **Opinion.** Give your opinion of your topic if it is an argumentative one or if it requires you to give an opinion.
- **P** = **Proverb** or quotation. Start with an apt proverb or quotation.
- **A** = **Action.** Start by describing relevant and interesting action.
- **S** = **State** your theme. This is an important method in some cases. Make your theme clear to your reader. Don't leave him or her to guess what you are writing about.
- **S** = **Story or anecdote.** Start by describing an incident or by telling a *short* story which illustrates your theme. This method is *not* recommended for the CSEC examination because your composition will not be long enough to introduce an anecdote unless you are very skilful.

In all cases, your main aim is to *make your theme clear to your reader as soon as possible*. Some students have a theme and base their plan on it but they do not make the theme clear to the reader.

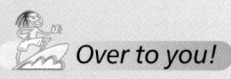

Over to you!

Exercise 6

Choose *one* of the topics below and then follow the instructions, but do not write the whole composition. Complete the exercise in under 20 minutes.

a) State your theme in a single sentence.

b) Give examples of *three* different ways of starting, and say which of the six methods you have used. For each of the three different methods write one or two sentences only.

1. Learning to swim.

2. How to keep fit.

3. Should gambling be prohibited?

4. Carnival time.

5. The contribution which a religion can make to the life of an ordinary person.

6. How to train for a sports event.

7. Myself in 20 years' time.

Exercise 7

Choose *one* of the topics below and then:

a) State your theme in a single sentence.

b) Give examples of *three* different ways of starting. One of the methods must be different from the three used in the previous exercise.

Complete this exercise in under 20 minutes.

1. An evening meal at home.
2. Describe a school fun fair (or similar event) in which you helped or which you visited.
3. Describe how you have been helped and hindered by relatives and friends in preparing for your public examination.
4. How has the history of your country influenced the way in which people live there now?
5. Describe and try to account for your attitude to members of the opposite sex at the present time.
6. What is your ambition and how are you going to try to achieve it?
7. In your own words tell the story of any myth or traditional tale which you read several years ago but which you liked and can still remember.
8. Discuss the advantages and disadvantages of being a member of a large family *or* a one-parent family.

12.14
Writing: ending a composition

Use as much skill at the end of a composition as you do at the start. First and last impressions are important. Your final paragraph should be well constructed and thoughtful – not just a hurried or tired farewell to the reader.

The acronym L CARS shows five possible ways of finishing a composition:

- **L** = **Look into the future** Consider the position of your topic in the future. This is a signal to the reader that the composition is coming to an end.
- **C** = **Climax** This method is used when writing short stories.
- **A** = **Air of finality** Make it clear that your final paragraph is the final one.
- **R** = **Repeat your theme** and show that you have proved your point.
- **S** = **Sum up** both sides of a problem or give a summary of your main points.

Practise these methods when you write the compositions required in the following units.

12.15
Writing

Either: Write 400–450 words on topic(1) or (2) in about 45 minutes.
or: Write 250–300 words on topic (3) in about 30 mintues.

1. Write a story based on the picture above.

2. Write a story which finishes with these words:
    … *That was a piece of advice which Nicolle never forgot.*

3. What do you consider to be the advantages and disadvantages of becoming a professional sportsperson in athletics, football, cricket, basketball or any other sport? Does this sort of career attract you or not?

Unit 12 · *The Penny Post*

13 Louis Pasteur

13.1
Pre-reading

The following passage is set out in a way which will give you practice in answering comprehension questions in an examination. For convenience, the passage is divided into sections, each of which is followed by questions.

This is how you should deal with the questions:

1. Imagine you are an examiner. Read the questions and the five possible answers given for each one. Decide which answers are correct, which are completely wrong, and how close the others are to being correct. Give each answer a mark following these guidelines:

   - For a correct answer, give 2 marks.
   - For a completely wrong answer, give 0 marks.
   - For the other answers, give 1½, 1 or ½ a mark, depending on how close they are to being correct.

   Note: There may be more than one completely right or completely wrong answer given for a question.

2. Read the comments which follow the questions to find out how well you did.

13.2
Reading

Louis Pasteur

In the 1860s, Pasteur set out to find the answers to three questions:
   a) Why do things putrefy?
   b) Is it possible to stop something from going bad?
   c) If something has gone bad, can we find a cure for the ailment?

5 Pasteur carried out a number of experiments and discovered that dust in the air contains germs which cause putrefaction. In one experiment he boiled soup for several minutes to destroy any germs it might contain. Then he opened flasks of the soup higher and higher up the side of a mountain. He found that when he went higher up the mountain, fewer of the flasks showed signs of putrefaction. He soon
10 concluded that dust in the air contained germs which could cause disease.

English Alive!

Remember to give up to 2 marks for each answer.

Questions

1. What does 'putrefy' mean in line 2?
   A. dead
   B. die
   C. It mean going bad.
   D. It means 'going bad'.
   E. going bad

2. What was in the flasks when Pasteur opened them?
   A. When Pasteur opened them, soup was in the flasks.
   B. The flasks contained boiled (sterile) soup.
   C. Some of the flasks contained soup showed signs of putrefaction.
   D. Soup which had been boiled to destroy any germs in it.
   E. Soup.

3. What did Pasteur's experiments on a mountain tell him about the quality of the air there?
   A. It showed him that the air was clean.
   B. They showed him that the higher he went, the fewer germs the air contained.
   C. Pasteur's experiments on a mountain told him about that the air at the top had more germs than the air at the bottom.
   D. It contained germs.
   E. Dust in the air contain germs which could course disease.

Comments

Question 1

A – 0 marks or ½ a mark. The instructions did not say that answers must be in complete sentences but 'putrefy' means 'going bad' and not dead already.

Unit 13 · *Louis Pasteur*

B – ½ a mark or perhaps 1 mark. The answer is not accurate, but 'die' is perhaps better than 'dead'.

C – 1 mark. Deduct half a mark for spelling 'means' wrongly. Deduct half a mark for omitting inverted commas.

D – 2 marks

E – 2 marks. A complete sentence is not needed here.

Question 2

A – 1 mark. The answer omits a key fact: the soup had been boiled to make it sterile.

B – 2 marks

C – 0 marks. When Pasteur opened the flasks, they had not yet been exposed to the air, so the soup had not putrefied. The answer shows that somebody did not read the question carefully. In the question, 'when Pasteur opened them' is a key expression.

D – 2 marks

E – 1 mark or ½ a mark.

Question 3

A – 0 marks or ½ a mark. The answer is too vague and suggests that somebody did not understand the question.

B – 2 marks. This is seen by the fact that fewer flasks became contaminated.

C – 0 marks. The answer has been copied from the passage, is ungrammatical and is factually wrong.

D – 1 mark. This is only half the answer. There is no mention of what happened when he went higher up the mountain.

E – 1 mark. Deduct half a mark for 'contain' (which should be 'contains') and for the mistake in spelling 'cause'.

How did your scores compare with those shown above? Were you too generous or not generous enough? Now read on.

> Pasteur had shown the role of germs in putrefaction and disease. His study of immunisation against diseases was accelerated by an accident. An injection of an old and weak stock of chicken cholera was given to two hens by mistake. They should have died but they lived. Assuming that they were immunised, he later injected
> 15 them with a killing dose of chicken cholera. They survived but two 'control' hens (which had not had a previous injection) died after receiving an equally strong dose.
> Pasteur had found a 'vaccine' for the most serious disease of the chicken farm.

His chicken cholera 'vaccine' was an 'attenuated virus', i.e. a living virus
20 weakened to the point of safety, but one which produced sufficient antibodies when injected to control disease-causing infection by the same kind of virus. Following up this discovery, he eventually found an attenuated virus for immunising sheep and cattle against anthrax – the scourge of the pastures since animal husbandry first began.

Questions

4. What was the 'role' mentioned in line 11?
   A. Germs in the air cause putrefaction.
   B. Putrefaction and disease are caused by germs.
   C. It was acclerated by an accident.
   D. The role was that germs carried dust which caused putefaction and disease.
   E. It was an important one.

5. Give a synonym for 'accelerated' in line 12.
   A. discover   B. discovered   C. hasten   D. hastened   E. caused

6. What does 'the most serious disease' refer to in line 17?
   A. In line 17, 'the most serious disease' refers to chicken cholera.
   B. It refer to 'chicken cholera'.
   C. chicken cholera
   D. It was anthrax.
   E. It killed chickens which caught it.

7. What was the function of the antibodies mentioned in line 20?
   A. It was injected into hens to fight chicken cholera.
   B. They killed chickens which contained them.
   C. There purpose was to protect chickens from chicken cholra.
   D. When injected to control disease-causing infection by the same kind of virus.
   E. They were able to protect a hen against the germs which caused chicken cholera.

Comments

Question 4

A – 2 or 1½ marks

B – 2 or 1½ marks.

C – 0 marks. The facts are wrong and there is a spelling mistake.

D – 0 marks or perhaps ½ a mark for trying! The facts are wrong and there is a spelling mistake.

E – ½ a mark. The student who made the mistake did not understand what is meant by 'role'.

Unit 13 · Louis Pasteur

Question 5

A and B – 0 marks. Wrong meaning.

C   – 1 or 1½ marks. The meaning is reasonable but the form of the verb is wrong.

D   – 2 marks

E   – 0 marks. Wrong meaning.

Question 6

A – 2 marks.

B – 1½ marks. Deduct half a mark for using 'refer' instead of 'refers'.

C – 2 marks.

D – 0 marks. Wrong disease.

E – 0 marks or ½ mark.

Question 7

A – 0 marks. The facts are wrong. Antibodies develop inside a hen. They are not injected into it.

B – 0 marks. The facts are clearly wrong. Antibodies protect; they do not kill the creature which produces them.

C – 1 mark. Deduct half a mark for 'There' (Their) and for spelling 'cholera' wrongly.

D – 0 marks or ½ a mark if you feel very generous.

E – 2 marks.

Now read on.

25 Pasteur next concentrated on the disease known as rabies, because dogs suffering from it become rabid. Human beings who were bitten by mad dogs raved, choked and died in the most horrible manner, their final agonies often being shortened by friends or relatives who suffocated them to death. The disease was invariably fatal.
    Pasteur succeeded in producing an attenuated virus but he realised that rabies
30 could not be controlled without immunising dogs on an impossible scale. There were too many of them and they could not all be caught. Immunisation was useful but a *cure* for rabies remained essential. At this point the obvious question was whether his emulsions, injected *after* infection, would prevent the development of the dreadful disease, since they prevented it if given before infection. His dilemma
35 was solved by a distraught mother who rushed her rabies-infected son from Alsace to Paris. Pasteur could not resist her pleas. The rabies injections were administered and the boy soon recovered.

Questions

8. What does 'rabid' mean in line 26?

9. Give *two* reasons why the use of 'dreadful' in line 34 is justified.

10. 'Immunisation was useful' (line 31). How is it useful in modern times?

11. Explain clearly what Pasteur's 'dilemma' (line 35) was and how it was solved.

12. What were the pleas (line 36) of the mother from Alsace?

13.3 Vocabulary: meaning in context

Choose the words which best show the meaning of the underlined words as they are used in the passage in 13.2.

1. He soon concluded that dust in the air contained germs (line 10)
   A. came to an end
   B. stopped (his experiments)
   C. decided, based on the evidence
   D. guessed

2. His study of immunisation against diseases (lines 11–12)
   A. a method of showing when somebody has caught (a disease)
   B. providing a defence to stop a person being affected by
   C. curing somebody who has been attacked by a disease
   D. giving people an early warning when a disease attacked them

3. Assuming that they were immunised (line 14)
   A. Knowing
   B. Believing without proof
   C. Hoping
   D. Wrongly guessing

4. the scourge of the pastures (line 23)
   A. relic
   B. common cause
   C. thing inherited
   D. cause of a calamity

5. since animal husbandry first began (line 23)
   A. experiments
   B. taming
   C. management
   D. slaughter

6. Human beings who were bitten by mad dogs raved (line 26)
   A. made wild noises
   B. played loud music
   C. applauded loudly
   D. liked a lot of noise

Unit 13 · Louis Pasteur

7. relatives who <u>suffocated them to death</u> (line 28)
    A. gave them medicines which did more harm than good
    B. killed them by preventing them from breathing.
    C. gave them so much food that they died
    D. hanged them by using a rope

8. His dilemma was solved by a <u>distraught</u> mother (line 35)
    A. worried
    B. very upset
    C. sad
    D. determined

9. Pasteur could not resist her <u>pleas</u>. (line 36)
    A. desperate requests
    B. pleasant nature
    C. offers of money
    D. advice

10. The rabies injections were <u>administered</u> and the boy soon recovered. (lines 36–7)
    A. set aside   B. given   C. reconsidered   D. effective

13.4 Vocabulary practice

Choose the word which best completes each sentence.

1. Pasteur boiled some soup to ____ any germs which might be in it.
    A. eliminate
    B. distinguish
    C. extinguish
    D. destruct

2. Pasteur discovered the ____ between germs and diseases.
    A. relative
    B. reference
    C. concern
    D. connection

3. When he was questioned, the suspect denied that he had ____ a crime.
    A. made
    B. done
    C. committed
    D. involved

4. After a robbery, the police will try to ____ the persons responsible for it.
    A. convince
    B. assess
    C. allege
    D. apprehend

5. When an Iranian town was hit by an earthquake, a man ____ under the rubble for 13 days before he was rescued.
    A. endured
    B. persisted
    C. revived
    D. survived

6. I'm sorry to tell you that the condition of the patient has not improved. In fact, his condition has ____ and he may not live much longer.
    A. collapsed
    B. deteriorated
    C. deterred
    D. afflicted

7. Donna wants to make a cake but she is not sure she has all the ____ to put in it.
   A. ingredients
   B. components
   C. utensils
   D. elements

8. In an industrial area, the ____ is usually not very pleasant for any residents.
   A. surrounding
   B. suburbs
   C. establishment
   D. environment

9. In the words 'homicide', 'suicide' and 'germicide', the root '–cide' means ____.
   A. illegal
   B. kill
   C. investigate
   D. protect

10. The woman told us that when she was young she ____ the dark but that now she does not worry about it at all.
    A. afraid
    B. terrified
    C. frightened
    D. feared

13.5
Writing summaries: good and bad

Study the following two summaries. Then say why one summary is good but the other one is bad.

Question

Using not more than 80 words, explain how Pasteur developed a successful vaccine for use on a patient who had been bitten by a rabid dog.

Summary 1

Pasteur boiled some soup and put it in seal flasks, then he took the flasks up a mountain and opened some of them. He tested the flasks and found that in some of them something had caused putrefaction, this show that there was harmful germs in the air. He injected two hens with a old and weak stock of chicken cholra. The hens did not die, so he had found a "vaccine" for the most serious disease of the chicken farm. Pasteur next concentrated on the disease know as rabies. He produced an attenuated virus and gave it to a boy from Alsace. The boy soon recovered, so Pasteur knew he had found a vaccine.

Summary 2

Notes:

soup – air– germs

accident – imm hens against ch-col – used weak form

used sim method – formed vaccine for rab

tested it v succ on boy with rab

The notes come to about 26 words; they could be up to about 40 words, half the length of the final summary.

Draft summary:

First Pasteur used boiled soup to prove that the dust in air contains harmful germs. Thanks to a lucky accident, he was then able to develop a way of immunising hens against chicken-cholera by using a weak form of the germ, which produced antibodies in the hens.

Stop and count the words: 47. We can use another 30 words. Continue:

He used a similar method to form a vaccine for rabies and tested it very successfully on a boy who had rabies.

Number of words: 69. We can leave the draft summary as the final answer or we can expand it slightly (if there is time to do this in an examination). If we expand it, the final summary will be as follows. The added words are in bold type here:

First Pasteur used boiled soup to prove that the dust in air contains germs **which can cause serious diseases**. Thanks to a lucky accident **involving hens**, he was able to develop a way of immunising hens against chicken-cholera by **developing and then** using a weak (**harmless**) form of the germ, which produced antibodies in the hens.

The rest of the draft summary will be unchanged.

Number of words: 78. But notice that it was *not* essential to expand 67 words to get nearer to the limit of 80.

Comments

The first summary is the bad one. It contains 35 words beyond the limit of 80. In addition, it contains material copied from the passage, as well as a number of mistakes. Did you detect these mistakes?

- line l: The comma after 'flasks' should be a full stop. 'seal' should be 'sealed'.
- lines 1–3 contain too much information after the discovery using soup.
- line 3: The comma after 'putrefaction' should be a full stop. 'show' should be 'showed'; 'was' should be 'were'.
- line 4: 'a old' should be 'an old'; 'cholera' is spelt wrongly.
- line 5: The expression 'the most serious disease of the chicken farm' is copied from the passage and is an unnecessary detail.
- line 6: 'know' should be 'known'.
- line 7 At the end, the summary does not make it clear that the boy was suffering from rabies.

Over to you!

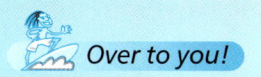

Exercise 1

In not more than 120 words, summarise the history of your country from the fifteenth or sixteenth century up to the time when it became independent. Do not copy from any books or a computer. You can use as many paragraphs as you think necessary. These notes *may* help you but they do not apply in exactly the same way to all Caribbean countries:

before 9th century: many Arawaks
1494 Columbus – Spaniards – Arawaks killed by weapons and disease
1517 – Spaniards imported slaves
17th century – British drove out Spaniards; British colony
immigrants from UK
more slaves – led to uprisings/wars
18th–19 centuries: sugar, bananas
1834: slavery banned; indentured labourers from India and China
1962: independence

13.6
Writing: rules and regulations

A man erected a swimming pool above ground in his garden. It was 1½ metres deep, 5 metres wide and 10 metres long. It stood above the ground and had a metal ladder which led into the pool.

To prevent damage to the pool and injury to children using the pool, the man prepared a set of rules and made the children read them. These are the rules:

Rules for using the swimming pool

1. Before you enter the pool, wash yourself with the hose. Make sure your feet are clean.

2. **Don't** go in the pool if you have a skin disease or an open wound.

3. **Don't** dive from the ladder or from the walls of the pool.

4. **Don't** stand on the walls. You can sit on them.

5. **Don't** go in the pool if there is a storm with lightning.

6. **Don't** play the fool in the water or endanger other swimmers.

7. Put away any rafts, balls, etc., which you have been using.

8. Each non-swimmer **must** be accompanied by a swimmer who will be personally responsible for his or her safety.

9. When you come out of the pool, make sure that you dry your ears and toes thoroughly.

10. After a meal, wait at least an hour before you swim.

Rules and regulations enable society to function efficiently and without avoidable risk. There are two main ways in which you can draw up a set of rules; sometimes we combine both methods:

- Write down, in time sequence or in any other logical order, all the things which people must do and all those which they are likely to do but must not do. Check that the list is complete and that the items are in a sensible order. If possible, go through the process (e.g. of swimming in the pool) yourself, and see if you have failed to deal with any vital point. Ask friends to study the proposed rules and to improve them if they can.

or

- Find somebody who has already prepared and used a set of rules for a similar situation. Borrow the rules, study them, improve them if possible, and then use them for your own situation.

Perhaps the best method is to use both ways. This is not possible in an examination but it is often possible in real life.

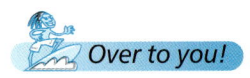

Over to you!

Exercise 2

There are ten rules above. Rearrange them in time order. Use these headings:

- Before you enter the pool
- In the pool
- After swimming.

Exercise 3

Draw up a list of advice to be given to *one* of the following people. Arrange your points under suitable headings and try to put them in a suitable order.

a) a baby-sitter
b) a form monitor
c) a library prefect
d) a temporary shop assistant
d) a security guard at a factory
e) the editor of a school magazine
f) a mechanic in a service station
g) a tourist visiting your country

13.7
Grammar: prepositions

Exercise 4

Put in any suitable word or take out the spaces to show that no word is needed.

1. Mrs Chan looked the boy ____ the eye ____ an attempt to see whether he was telling the truth or not.

2. Yesterday we spent most ____ our time packing things ____ boxes ____ preparation ____ our move ____ a new house tomorrow.

3. My friend was born ____ 1990, ____ the tenth ____ March to be exact.

4. Is your brother ____ the habit ____ going fishing ____ every evening?

5. Most ____ of the workers ____ that factory are ____ strike ____ support ____ a claim for higher pay. The dispute will probably be settled ____ arbitration ____ the near future.

6. You can't go home ____ this storm. You can stay ____ us tonight but phone your parents to let them ____ know where you are.

7. Mrs Williams left everything ____ her daughter ____ her will because she had not heard ____ her son ____ over twenty years and assumed that he had died.

8. According ____ local rumours, that man is heavily involved ____ selling drugs and is wanted ____ the police in three different countries.

9. If he is extradited ____ our country and has to face ____ trial overseas, he may soon find himself ____ jail ____ no chance of getting out ____ twenty years or more.

10. Some schools can help a student to change ____ a better person who will have a successful career and make a contribution ____ society.

11. If you like, I'll explain the proposal ____ detail, but I can give you a summary if you're ____ a hurry.

12. ____ my opinion, those two countries will be ____ war again ____ a few months' time. The proposals coming ____ both sides seem to have little or nothing ____ common.

13. There was an accident ____ the corner ____ the road ____ this morning. One of the passengers was trapped ____ a car and appeared to be ____ great pain. Eventually he was extricated ____ some firemen and taken away ____ ambulance.

14. Melinda likes to sit down and read ____ a quiet place because she is very interested ____ romantic novels and is thinking ____ becoming a writer when she is older.

15. We are bound to make a few mistakes ____ our way ____ life.

16. No action will be taken ____ Paul if he makes a full confession ____ his mistakes and apologises ____ the manager ____ them.

17. ____ view ____ objections ____ members ____ the public, we have agreed to defer consideration ____ it ____ the time being.

18. Learn to stand ____ your own feet and don't rely ____ others to get you out ____ trouble.

13.8
Grammar: using the Present Perfect tense (revision)

Forms

Form		Examples
Active	'has/have (not)' + a past participle	Have you finished your homework yet? Where has Leela gone? Have you seen her anywhere?
Passive	'has/have (not) been' + a past participle	Has your bike been repaired yet? Our school football team has not been defeated so far this year.
Continuous	'has/have (not) been' + a present participle	How long have you been waiting? We have been living here for nearly twenty years.

Uses

- For actions which have happened recently if we do not mention the time or date of the action. Compare these correct sentences:
    *time/date **not** stated:* Thank you for the parcel which **has arrived** safely.
    time/date mentioned: Thank you for the parcel which arrived yesterday.
    *time/date **not** stated:* Grandma **has been released** from hospital.
    time/date mentioned: Grandma was released from hospital an hour ago.
  As the examples show, we use the Simple Past tense (and not the Present Perfect tense) when we mention the time or date of a past action.

- With 'already', 'just', 'recently', 'now', 'never', 'yet' and (in questions) 'ever', e.g.
    The West Indies **has already produced** many famous sportsmen and women.
    What a nuisance! My printer **has just run out of** ink.
    Have you ever been up the Essequibo River?

- To express an action which began in the past and is still taking place, e.g.
    Father **has been working** for the Government for more than ten years.

Over to you!

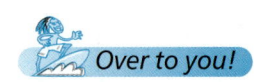

Exercise 5

Make short sentences with 'She ... it'. Put in the active form of the Present Perfect tense of the verbs below.

1. break	4. take	7. steal	10. hide	13. eat
2. find	5. light	8. leave	11. drink	14. repair
3. sharpen	6. choose	9. lose	12. clean	15. tear

Exercise 6

Put in the continuous form of the Present Perfect tense of the verbs in brackets.

1. Paul: Where have you been?
   Mike: I ____ just ____ (help) a friend to repair a punctured tyre. I hope you ____ not ____ (wait) very long.

2. Pa is very proud of his new car. He ____ (clean) it for the past twenty minutes.

3. Mother: What ____ you ____ (do), Vimala?
   Vimala: I ____ (just) ____ (tidy) up the kitchen. I ____ (put) everything back in its right place after the party last night.

4. Brian: What ____ members of the committee ____ (discussing) for so long? They ____ (talk) for nearly two hours so far.
   Olive: They ____ (study) a plan to try to prevent this district from being flooded. They ____ (argue) about the cost of the plan.

5. The cost of living ____ (rise) steadily for some time. Prices ____ (go) up and up.

6. Gopal ____ (attend) the Out-Patients Department of the new hospital for several weeks now. He ____ (receive) treatment for his back.

7. Those men ____ (sit) in that car for the last half an hour. I wonder what they're waiting for. They ____ not ____ (talk) much.

8. How long ____ your sister ____ (work) in that office?

9. Sometimes Grandma feels unwell after she ____ (travel) in a car for too long.

10. Sorry. I can't talk now. I ____ (work) in the yard. I've got to wash my hands.

Exercise 7

Express these sentences in a different way. Make the words in bold type the subject of the sentence. Use the passive form of the Present Perfect tense, e.g.

   Somebody has stolen **my bicycle**.
   My bicycle has been stolen by somebody.

194   *English Alive!*

1. Our company has opened **two new factories** recently.
2. An old tree has damaged **our fence**.
3. All the suppliers have increased **the price of petrol and kerosene**.
4. The police have arrested **one of the robbers**.
5. Miss Warren has offered **Tanya** a job in a lawyer's office.
6. Somebody has watered **those plants** already.
7. Experts have tested **this material** to make sure that it will not break.
8. Somebody has changed **the lock on this door** recently.
9. A skilled and very reliable mechanic has checked **this car** carefully.
10. The manager has reduced **the price of this necklace** by 20% already.

13.9
Enjoying poetry

This is a Hymn
– For Michael Granzen

For all who ride the trains
<u>all night</u>　　　　　　　　　　　　**because they have no homes**
sleep on sidewalks and park benches
beneath basements
5　and abandoned buildings
this is a hymn.

For those whose homes
are the great outdoors
the streets their one big room
10　for live men asleep in tombs
this is a hymn.

This is a hymn for bag women
pushing <u>rubbish babies</u>　　　　　　　**rubbish instead of real babies**
in ridiculous prams
15　dividing open lots
into elaborate architects' plans.

Mansions of the dispossessed
magnificence of desperate rooms
kings and queens of homelessness

20 die with empty bottles
    rising from their tombs.

    This is a hymn
    for all recommending
    a bootstrap as a way
25 to rise with effort
    on your part.
    This is a hymn
    may it renew
    what passes for your heart.

30 This hymn
    is for the must-be-blessed
    the victims of the world
    who know salt best
    the world tribe

35 of the dispossessed
    outside the halls of plenty
    looking in
    this is a benediction
    this is a hymn.
                    Lorna Goodison

Questions

1. Who do you think Michael Granzen was? Why?

2. What alliterating sound is used in the first stanza? In what way, if any, does the use of alliteration here contribute to the poet's hymn?

3. Explain the meaning of 'asleep in tombs' in line 10.

4. In line 20, how does the word 'empty' contribute to the poet's aim?

5. Is stanza five addressed to the same people as those in the previous stanzas?

6. Who are the people who have 'what passes for your heart'? (line 29)

7. In what way, if any, does the tone of the poet change in the fifth stanza compared with the tone in previous stanzas?

8. In line 33, 'who know salt best' may remind you of the expression 'the salt of the earth'. If that is so, what word can we use instead of 'salt' to make the poet's meaning quite clear (but less poetic)?

9. In a single sentence, say what we can infer about Lorna Goodison from this poem.

13.10 Writing

In not more than 35 minutes, write 300–350 words on *one* of the following topics:

1. What different careers are open to young people who would like to work in the field of (a) medicine and health *or* (b) science?

2. You are representing your country at a meeting of a worldwide sports body which is discussing where to hold its annual competition in two years' time. The competition will attract several thousand competitors and a big crowd of spectators.

    Write a speech in which you urge the delegates to choose your country as the best venue for the competition.

3. How do people become homeless? What can be done to help them?

14 AIDS

14.1
Pre-reading

Over millions of years, the human body has developed an immune system. When the body is attacked by a virus, the immune system creates antibodies to destroy the virus. If the immune system is impaired or destroyed, almost any harmful virus which enters a person's body can develop and cause death.

AIDS is an **acronym** for 'Acquired Immune Deficiency Syndrome', a potentially fatal disease which is believed to be caused by a virus called HIV (Human Immunodeficiency Virus). HIV is spread mainly by:

- unprotected sex with an HIV-infected person
- drug-users who share a needle
- transfusions of HIV-contaminated blood.

About half of the people who become infected by HIV develop AIDS within ten years. AIDS itself does not kill people. It weakens their immune system so that they die of an opportunistic infection, e.g. pneumonia, influenza, bronchitis, cancer.

14.2
Reading

AIDS

AIDS appeared, almost out of nowhere, in 1980 in the USA. In June 1981, the US Centers for Disease Control and Prevention published a report which stated: 'In the period October 1980 to May 1981, 5 young men, all active homosexuals, were treated for biopsy-confirmed *Pneumocystis carinii* pneumonia at three different
5 hospitals in Los Angeles, California. Two of the patients died.'

A month later, the *New York Times* reported that doctors in New York and California had diagnosed among homosexual men 41 cases of a rare and often rapidly fatal form of cancer. It added that eight of the victims had died less than 24 months after the diagnosis had been made. The report included this warning: 'The
10 cause of the outbreak is unknown, and there is as yet no evidence of contagion. But the doctors who have made the diagnoses, mostly in New York City and the San Francisco Bay area, are alerting other physicians who treat large numbers of homosexual men to the problem in an attempt to help identify more cases and to reduce the delay in offering chemotherapy treatment.'

15 The reaction to the new disease was slow and hesitant because the authorities did not realise the full potential of AIDS. But by the end of 1988 nearly 90,000 people in America had contracted AIDS and nearly 50,000 had died. By that time it had become clear that the USA was faced with an ever-spreading epidemic for which there was no effective treatment or cure.

20 By the mid-1990s, more than 500,000 Americans had been diagnosed with AIDS and more than half of them had died. By the end of the century, 40,000 new cases of HIV infection were being reported each year.

Outside the USA, the news is much worse. It is now known that at least 22 million people have died of AIDS throughout the world. According to the World 25 Health Organisation, more than 25 million people in sub-Saharan Africa are infected with HIV or AIDS. This is up to 30% of the adult population in some countries. More than 12 million African children have been orphaned by AIDS. Nearly 4 million Africans were newly infected with HIV in 2000. Worldwide, more than 40 million people are infected with the AIDS virus and an epidemiologist with 30 UNAIDS is convinced that the worst is yet to come.

In some African villages, a generation of adults has almost been eliminated, leaving behind large numbers of HIV-infected orphans to be cared for. Experts say that what has happened in Africa (which took just two decades) is only just beginning in Asia, where the disease is still very young. The epidemic in most 35 Asian countries began amongst drug-users. Infection rates soared from 1% to 40% among some drug-injecting communities in a single year. In China it is reported that there was a major scandal when contaminated blood was used in transfusions and infected hundreds of thousands of innocent victims.

Drug companies have devoted a lot of effort in attempts to find a cure or vaccine 40 for AIDS but have not been successful. At the moment, the best they can offer is an expensive cocktail of drugs which prolongs the life of an HIV sufferer. Experts fear that by 2010 there will be 25 million orphans in Africa, and that in the next 20 years, 70 million people throughout the world will be killed by AIDS.

14.3
Understanding

A Choose the best answer each time.

1. According to the information in 14.1, ____.
   A. AIDS precedes HIV
   B. HIV precedes AIDS
   C. HIV follows AIDS
   D. AIDS causes HIV

2. We learn from 14.1 that ____.
   A. the human immune system has developed an immunity to HIV but not yet to AIDS
   B. HIV is particularly dangerous to people whose immune system has been destroyed by AIDS
   C. the human immune system has not yet developed a foolproof defence against AIDS
   D. HIV is more dangerous than AIDS because people die sooner with HIV than with AIDS

3. Pneumonia is mentioned in 14.1 and again in 14.2 as an example of ____.
   A. a cause of HIV
   B. an opportunistic infection
   C. a consequence of AIDS
   D. a source of AIDS

4. Why did the *New York Times* report, in July 1981, what doctors had found?
   A. Most of the affected people lived in New York.
   B. There was an unusually high number of deaths from a rare disease.
   C. It is the newspaper that most doctors read.
   D. The Government had asked it to publicise the report.

5. One reason why the reaction to the new disease was not swift was that ____.
   A. nobody yet realised how dangerous AIDS was
   B. it was very expensive to prepare new drugs to fight AIDS
   C. it affected only two regions in the USA
   D. officials probably did not believe the newspaper reports

6. In less than ten years after 1988, the number of deaths from AIDS in the USA had increased by a multiple of about ____.
   A. ten   B. 250,000   C. 500,000   D. five

7. One example of a sub-Saharan African country is ____.
   A. Egypt   B. Kenya   C. Libya   D. Algeria

8. It seems highly likely that of the 12 million African children mentioned in line 27, ____.
   A. all of them have AIDS
   B. none of them has AIDS
   C. all of them have HIV
   D. some of them have HIV

9. An epidemiologist is a person who studies ____.
   A. the causes of unknown or rare diseases mainly
   B. outbreaks of diseases affecting many people
   C. possible links between HIV and AIDS
   D. ways of protecting children from the diseases of adults

10. If we judge by the next to last paragraph, as far as AIDS is concerned, the outlook for parts of Asia is probably ____.
    A. far from good
    B. rapidly improving
    C. better than expected
    D. impossible to predict

B Answer these questions about 14.1 and 14.2:

1. In 14.1, line 3, what is the difference between 'impaired' and 'destroyed'?

2. Explain how pneumonia can be 'opportunistic' (last line of 14.1).

3. In line 9 of 14.2, what is a diagnosis?

4. Why do you think the epidemiologist thinks that 'the worst is yet to come'?

5. Suggest *two* reasons why in future the number of deaths from AIDS in Africa may be far higher than deaths from the same cause in Europe or North America.

14.4
Vocabulary: meaning in context

Choose the word(s) which best show(s) the meaning of the underlined words as they are used in 14.1 and 14.2.

1. the human body has developed an <u>immune</u> system (14.1, line 1)
   A. aggressive
   B. protective
   C. unaffected
   D. very great

2. AIDS is an <u>acronym</u> (line 5)
   A. used only in medical and official writing as a convenient abbreviation
   B. made by using the initial letters of two or more words
   C. which is opposite in meaning to the words it is made from
   D. made up by doctors to help their patients

3. a <u>potentially</u> fatal disease (line 5)
   A. almost always
   B. invariably
   C. which can be
   D. occasionally

4. <u>transfusions</u> of HIV-contaminated blood (line 10)
   A. the transferring
   B. the transfixing
   C. investigation
   D. enquiry into

5. HIV-<u>contaminated</u> blood (line 10)
   A. obtained
   B. extracted
   C. derived
   D. made impure

6. and there is <u>as yet</u> no evidence (14.2, line 10)
   A. so far
   B. apparently
   C. it is said
   D. however

7. no evidence of <u>contagion</u> (line 10)
   A. catching a disease by touch or other physical contact
   B. a disease being caught by the movement of a virus in the air
   C. any known cure being found
   D. any explanation for what has happened

8. (the doctors are) <u>alerting</u> other physicians (line 12)
   A. informing
   B. seeking help from
   C. making aware
   D. corresponding with

9. an epidemiologist with UNAIDS is <u>convinced</u> that the worst is yet to come (line 30)
   A. afraid
   B. certain
   C. worried
   D. unsure

10. a generation of adults has almost been <u>eliminated</u> (line 31)
    A. badly affected
    B. affected
    C. handicapped
    D. wiped out

14.5 Vocabulary practice

Exercise 1

In each case, choose the most suitable word or expression.

1. In the past, villages developed because of the need for ____ protection.
   A. one another
   B. each other
   C. integral
   D. mutual

2. If a shopkeeper is ____, he or she is quite prepared to deceive customers.
   A. unscrupulous
   B. inhibited
   C. unmitigated
   D. indispensable

3. A hunter used a dead goat to try to ____ a man-eating tiger into a trap.
   A. encourage
   B. deceive
   C. persuade
   D. lure

4. A clean and well-run town or city is usually a sign of the ____ pride of its inhabitants.
   A. urban
   B. urbane
   C. civic
   D. civil

5. A study of urban or rural life usually ____ the sociable nature of people clearly.
   A. illustrates
   B. designs
   C. demonstrate
   D. depict

6. We have studied all the evidence in this case, but we do not agree with the ____ which you have drawn from it.
   A. ending
   B. final
   C. conclusion
   D. gist

7. Sometimes people buy a new car mainly because a neighbour has one and they want to ____ with him.
   A. make up
   B. keep up
   C. take up
   D. do up

8. The plants ____ and soon died because of lack of water.
   A. dwindled
   B. shrunk
   C. diminished
   D. withered

9. What a ____ he did not pass his driving test! I know he was very anxious to pass.
   A. sadness
   B. sorrow
   C. grief
   D. pity

10. A doctor is a member of the medical ____.
    A. craft
    B. occupation
    C. vocation
    D. profession

14.6 Vocabulary: problem words

Appendix 6 contains examples of the correct usage of several hundred problem words.

Exercise 2

In each case, choose the right word from the brackets.

1. Anybody who emigrates to a foreign country must learn to (adapt, adopt) himself or herself to conditions in that country.

2. A new environment will probably (affect, effect) an emigrant at first but it will not take long before he becomes accustomed to it.

3. If we include substitutes or reserves, our team for tomorrow's game consists of 16 players (all together, altogether).

4. In tennis and table-tennis, the players hit the ball (alternately, alternatively).

5. This letter is urgent. Please (assure, ensure) that you post it in the morning.

6. The Prime Minister presented (awards, rewards) for bravery at a ceremony yesterday. Each person received a special certificate of appreciation.

7. You can't go out now. It's raining heavily. (Beside, Besides) you haven't finished your homework.

8. For many elderly people, ill-health is a burden which has to be (born, borne) patiently.

9. If a shopkeeper needs to (borrow, lend) money, he will usually find a bank willing to (borrow, lend) him some at a suitable rate of interest.

10. Take a deep (breath, breathe). That's right. Now (breath, breathe) out slowly.

Exercise 3

In each case, choose the right word from the brackets.

1. We keep our (cloth, clothes) in this wardrobe to prevent insects from damaging (it, them)

2. Each team entering the tournament must have its proper (complement, compliment) of players (age, aged) under 16.

3. If you are buying a new car on hire purchase, the finance company will insist that you have a (comprehension, comprehensive) insurance policy to cover it against all risks.

4. The evidence in this case shows quite (in conclusion, conclusively) that the accused man is innocent.

5. Our coach has been trying to build up the (confidence, confident) of the players so that they have a more (negative, positive) approach to the game.

6. A (conscious, conscientious) person has a responsible attitude to his or her work.

7. A man who is frequently drunk and disorderly will probably be regarded as (contemptuous, contemptible) by his neighbours.

8. If an action happens all the time without stopping (like the orbit of the moon around Earth), we say that it is a (continual, continuous) action.

9. Hurricane Andrew caused a great deal of (damage, damages) when it moved across our country, leaving a (trial, trail) of devastation behind it.

10. According to the doctor, the old man has been (dead, died) at least 72 hours. The doctor thinks he probably (dead, died) last Thursday night.

14.7
Writing a speech of thanks

A nurse, Miss Angela Smith, came to your school and spoke to your class about AIDS and other health problems facing teenagers. The talk was very interesting and helpful.

Miss Smith mentioned that she hoped that all schools would try to raise funds to help children who had been made orphans by the AIDS epidemic in South Africa. She left behind the name and address of a society in Johannesburg, AIDS Relief, which runs schools and clinics for orphans in South Africa. Miss Smith is a voluntary worker for AIDS Relief. She came to the school on her day off from work.

Your teacher has asked you to thank Miss Smith, on behalf of your class. Write a speech of 5–10 lines, thanking Miss Smith for her talk and saying that you will try to raise funds to help AIDS Relief.

This photo shows a little girl in the Catholic Nazareth House orphanage, Cape Town, South Africa.

14.8
Writing a letter

After the talk by Miss Smith, a group of students at your school volunteered to organise an event to raise funds for AIDS Relief. You have been elected secretary of the group.

Write a formal letter to the Principal of your school, seeking permission to use school premises for a charity event to raise money for AIDS Relief.

- Explain where the money will go and what it will be used for.
- Suggest two or more events which would attract parents and the public.
- Say what rooms and/or open space you would like to use.
- Give some idea of a possible date and time.
- Say whether an admission fee will be charged.
- Add any other information which will enable your Principal to discuss your request with the Board of Governors and/or the Parent–Teacher Association.

14.9
Equivalent (similar) sentences

Exercise 4

Choose the sentence which is nearest in meaning to the given sentence.

1. The cause of the outbreak is unknown, and there is as yet no evidence of contagion.
   A. Nobody has been able to find out why this outbreak is not contagious.
   B. The cause of this disease has not yet been discovered but at the moment we have not found any proof that it is infectious.
   C. Although this disease cannot be spread by touch, it is unknown for the cause to break out.
   D. Nobody has been able to find out what caused the start of this disease, and so far we have not seen anything to suggest that it is caught by physical contact.

2. The reaction to the new disease was hesitant because the authorities did not realise the full potential of AIDS.
   A. The people responsible for public health did not fully comprehend what AIDS could do, so they were somewhat uncertain about how to react to it.
   B. When the authorities realised how dangerous AIDS could be, they took more urgent action to face the threat.
   C. The initial reaction to the new disease lacked conviction because even experts did not have the time and money to deal with a new problem.
   D. The authorities reacted to the new disease in a way which showed that they did not realise the danger involved.

3. Outside the USA, the news concerning AIDS is much worse.
   A. The news concerning AIDS is bad outside the USA but quite good inside it.
   B. The news of AIDS outside the USA is much worse than it used to be inside the USA.
   C. Compared with the AIDS situation in the USA, things are much worse beyond the USA.
   D. The USA has had more deaths and HIV infections than other countries have had.

4. Nearly 4 million Africans were newly infected with HIV in 2000.
   A. In 2000 there were just under 4 million new cases of HIV in Africa.
   B. Nearly 4 million people in Africa caught AIDS for the first time in 2000.
   C. By the end of the last century, there were approximately 4 million AIDS victims in Africa.
   D. In 2000 just under 4 million Africans developed AIDS after having been infected with a new kind of HIV.

5. In some African villages, a generation of adults has almost been eliminated by AIDS.
   A. In African villages, all the people in one age group have been nearly killed by AIDS.
   B. AIDS has been responsible for the death of most people in one generation in certain villages in Africa.
   C. Almost all the elderly people have died of AIDS in a number of African villages.
   D. As a result of AIDS, the age gap between generations has been almost eliminated in some African villages.

6. The AIDS epidemic in most Asian countries began amongst drug-users.
   A. The cause of the global epidemic of AIDS was Asian drug-users.
   B. Asians who used drugs were responsible for the start of the global AIDS epidemic.
   C. In the majority of countries in Asia, people who took drugs were the ones who first showed signs of AIDS.
   D. AIDS has affected only drug-users in most Asian countries.

7. In China there was a major scandal when blood contaminated with HIV was used in transfusions and infected hundreds of thousands of people.
   A. In China there was a big scandal when blood containing HIV was collected from hundreds of thousands of people and used in transfusions.
   B. Very large numbers of people were infected with HIV when they were given contaminated blood during transfusions in China; this led to a big scandal.
   C. Hundreds of thousands of people died of AIDS in China when they received blood containing HIV during a transfusion, and this became a major scandal.
   D. HIV contaminated by blood was used in transfusions in China, and this caused the death of hundreds of thousands of people, which was a major scandal.

8. Drug companies have devoted a lot of effort to attempts to find a cure or vaccine for AIDS but have not been successful.
   A. Neither a cure nor a vaccine for AIDS has been found despite considerable effort on the part of firms which manufacture drugs.
   B. Drug companies have tried hard to find a vaccine or cure for AIDS but have met with only partial success as yet.
   C. AIDS victims have devoted a lot of time to persuading drug companies to seek a cure or vaccine for AIDS but have not been successful.
   D. Drug companies have been reluctant to spend time or money searching for a cure or vaccine for AIDS, so they have failed so far.

14.10
Grammar: the Past Perfect tense

Forms

Form	Examples	
Active	he had (not) caught	they had (not) invited
Continuous	he had (not) been catching	they had (not) been inviting
Passive	he had (not) been caught	they had (not) been invited

Uses

- **To show which of two past actions happened first.** This tense is not often used by itself. It is used with a verb in the Simple Past tense to show us that one action happened before the other, e.g.
  Leela realised that she **had lost** her keys.
  We were glad to see that the bridge **had been repaired**.
  I wondered where my brother **had gone**.
  We went for a drive when Pa **had repaired** his car.
  Kevin asked me how long I **had been waiting**.

Sometimes the two actions are mentioned in separate sentences:
  At last I discovered the truth. He **had bought** a new car.
  We could not open the door. Somebody **had locked** it.

- **In indirect speech to replace a verb which, in the original speech, was in the Present Perfect or Simple Past tense**, e.g.
  The woman told us that she **had lost** her passport.
  Colin told us that his brother **had flown** to London two days earlier.

- **In conditional sentences which refer to a past time** (sometimes called 'impossible conditions' because the events cannot be changed), e.g.
    If you **had come**, we could have all gone for a picnic (but you didn't come).
    I could have scored if you **had passed** the ball to me (but you didn't pass it).

- **After 'I wish', 'I would rather' and 'I would sooner' when speaking about a past event**, e.g.
    I wish I **hadn't spent** all my money. Now I've got nothing left.
    I would rather you **hadn't told** Paul about the party.

Exercise 5

Complete these sentences in any sensible way. Use a verb in the Past Perfect tense. Make one sentence only but the example shows some different ways of completing a given sentence, e.g

    Dave knew that …   the rain had stopped/started.   Paul had gone.
                        the last bus had gone already.   Lall had arrived.
                        he had made a mistake.   the plane had landed.

1. I realised that …
2. Francine found out that …
3. I knew that …
4. She was quite sure that …
5. Did anybody notice that …?
6. Mr Chan noticed that …
7. Leela asked me where …
8. He remembered that …
9. Marcia wondered whether …
10. My mother wanted to know where …

Exercise 6

Join each pair of sentences to make one sentence. Find the action which happened first, and put the verb into the Past Perfect tense. When necessary, add 'when' or 'after', e.g.
    Miss McKay locked the door. She went to bed.
    *When Miss McKay **had locked** the door, she went to bed.*
    or *Miss McKay went to bed after she **had locked** the door.*
    Shellyann finished her homework. She watched a film on television.
    *After/When Shellyann **had finished** her homework, she watched a film on television.*
    or *Shellyann watched a film on television after/when she **had finished** her homework.*

1. Marlon repaired a puncture in his bicycle. He rode to his friend's home.
2. A man came to repair our TV set. My father telephoned the shop.
3. The storm went. We went outside to clear up the yard.
4. David posted the parcel. He weighed it at the Post Office.
5. I went to see my friend. I washed and dressed properly.
6. The patient was discharged from hospital. He recovered completely.

7. We ate the food. We washed the dishes and put them away.

8. The men repaired our telephone. I rang my cousin to tell him that the phone was working again.

9. Wayne told us about the accident. We realised that it was not his fault.

10. The plane left. We felt sad.

11. We drove for about half an hour. We reached the beach.

12. She finished the painting. She left it to dry.

13. We followed a path through the forest for nearly an hour. We sat down to have a rest.

14. Uncle and Auntie left on the long flight home. Our home seemed much quieter but less cheerful.

15. Mother washed the fish thoroughly. She showed us the best way to cook it.

14.11

Punctuation: using an apostrophe (revision)

Contractions

We can use an apostrophe to show that one or more letters have been omitted, e.g.

it's = it is or it has   o'clock = of the clock   won't = will not
I'd = I had/should/would   didn't = did not   shan't = shall not
can't = cannot   he's = he is/has   I'm = I am

We often use contractions when we speak and when we write dialogue. In other cases, we use the full form.

Possession

- Don't put an apostrophe on a verb ending in 's' or any other letter.

- Don't put an apostrophe on a plural noun unless the apostrophe means 'of' or 'of the'.

- When you want to show possession, add 's' to a singular noun or to a plural noun which does not end in 's', e.g.
    This is Leela's bicycle. = the bicycle of/for Leela
    What's that boy's name? = the name of that boy
    There is a children's concert at school next week.
    Those are fishermen's nets.

- If a plural noun ends in 's', put an apostrophe after the last letter, e.g.
  Those are the boys' bicycles. = the bicycles of the boys
  There must be somebody at home. I can hear ladies' voices inside the house.

- If somebody's name ends in 's' or 'z', you can use either of these forms:
  Charles' speech   or   Charles's speech
  Aziz' parents   or   Aziz's parents

Over to you!

Exercise 7

Put in an apostrophe *when necessary*. Sometimes no apostrophe is needed.

1. Dont go in that car. Theres something wrong with its steering-wheel.

2. The papaws on those trees are not ripe yet.

3. I like the brides dress. Its one of Miss Rodrigues creations.

4. In the struggle, the policemans hat was knocked off and rolled under the wheels of one of the cars.

5. My friends name is Sharnette. Her parents are teachers. She is very kind and friendly, so she is popular with other students in our class.

6. Mother said she has gone to talk to a neighbour and will be back in ten minutes time but I doubt whether she will return in less than an hours time.

7. Sherlock Holmes friend was Dr Watson. The two men solved many crimes.

8. A farmers life is never easy, especially when bad weather affects his crops and forces him to find other ways of earning a living.

14.12
Enjoying poetry

Dives

Before they built the <u>deep water harbour</u>   in Barbados
sinking an island to do it
we used to row out in our boats

to the white liners, great ocean-going floats,
5 to dive for coins. Women with bracelets,
men with expensive <u>tickers</u> on their wrists,   watches

watched us through bland sun glasses
so that their blue stares never blinked.
They tossed us pennies. The spinning flat
10 metallic bird would hit the water with a little

    flap and wing zig-zagging down the water's track.
    Our underwater eyes would watch it like a cat
    as it dark bottomed soundwards like a pendulum
    winging from side to side, now black
15 now bright, now black, now bright,
    catching the dying daylight down
    the coal dark sides of the ship
    every shadow we saw was a possible shark

    but we followed that flat dark light
20 even if the propellers would suddenly turn
    burning the water to murderous cold
    we would never come nearer to gold.

Edward Braithwaite

Questions

1. Does it make any difference if we set the first few lines of the poem out in continuous prose? Does writing prose in short lines turn it into poetry?

2. How does the poet emphasise the difference between the tourists and the boys?

3. What dangers do the boys face?

4. Suggest a reason why the poet uses 'cat' in line 12. (See line 10.)

5. At what point would you say a more 'poetical' tone appears in the poem?

6. Did the poet originally write 'soundwards' or 'downwards' in line 13? Or did he perhaps write 'sideways'?

7. What is the alliterating sound in lines 16 and 17?

8. Study the (lack of) punctuation in lines 17–22. Is the absence of punctuation deliberate? Does it help or hinder the reader here?

9. What is the main feature of the poem? (On which point does the poet apparently lavish more care and attention?)

14.13
Writing

Either: Write 400–450 words on topic (1) or (2) in about 45 minutes.
or: Write 250–300 words on topic (3) or (4) in about 30 minutes

1. Write a story which includes the scene shown in the illustration above.

2. Write a story which starts with these words:
   The news came as a shock to the rest of our family. ...

3. Give an account of a time when you (or a relative or friend) recovered from an illness or injury.

4. Write an account of a person (living or dead) whom you admire. Explain why you admire the person.

15 Moving On

15.1
Pre-reading

The passage in 15.2 is an extract from one of the finest novels of the twentieth century, *The Grapes of Wrath* by John Steinbeck, who also wrote *The Pearl*. To understand, the extract you need to know the following:

- The book deals with the plight of poor farmers in Oklahoma, a state in the USA. After years of growing the same crop, the fertility of the fields was weakened so much that strong winds easily picked up the top soil and formed huge clouds of dust. The region became known as the dust bowl of America. The crops deteriorated and farmers found it almost impossible to make a living.

- In order to survive, the farmers borrowed from local banks. When they were unable to repay the loans, the banks decided to take the farms, amalgamate them and use huge tractors to farm them.

In the extract, employees of a bank have arrived at a poor farm to tell the family to pack up and leave. The farmers sit around on the dusty ground and listen to the bank's employees telling them to go. Notice how the bank employees (the 'owner men') refer to their bank as an impersonal monster for which they are not responsible.

15.2
Reading

Moving On

Some of the owner men were kind because they hated what they had to do, and some of them were angry because they hated to be cruel, and some of them were cold because they had long ago found that one could not be an owner unless one were cold. And all of them were caught in something larger than themselves. If a
5   bank or a finance company owned the land, the owner man said, The Bank – or the Company – needs – wants – insists – must have – as though the Bank or the Company were a monster, with thought and feeling, which had ensnared them. The owner men sat in the cars and explained. You know the land is poor. You've scrabbled at it long enough. God knows.
10   The squatting tenant men nodded and wondered and drew figures in the dust, and yes, they knew, God knows. If the dust only wouldn't fly. If the top would only stay on the soil, it might not be so bad.
    The owner men went on leading to their point: You know the land's getting poorer.

15 You know what cotton does to the land: robs it, sucks all the blood out of it.
   The squatters nodded – they knew, God knew. If they could only rotate the crops they might pump blood back into the land. Well, it's too late. And the owner men explained the workings and the thinkings of the monster that was stronger than they were. A man can hold land if he can just eat and pay taxes; he can do that.
20 Yes, he can do that until his crops fail one day and he has to borrow money from the bank.
   But – you see, a bank or a company can't do that, because those creatures don't breathe air, don't eat side-meat. They breathe profits; they eat the interest on money. If they don't get it, they die the way you die without air, without side-meat.
25 It is a sad thing, but it is so. It is just so.
   The squatting men raised their eyes to understand. Can't we just hang on? Maybe the next year will be a good year. God knows what price cotton will bring. Don't they make explosives out of cotton? And uniforms? Get enough wars and cotton'll hit the ceiling. Next year, maybe. They looked up questioningly.
30 We can't depend on it. The bank – the monster has to have profits all the time. It can't wait. It'll die. No, taxes go on. When the monster stops growing, it dies. It can't stay one size.
   The squatting men looked down again. What do you want us to do? We can't take less share of the crop – we're half starved now. The kids are hungry all the
35 time. We got no clothes, torn an' ragged. If all the neighbors weren't the same, we'd be ashamed to go to meeting.
   And at last the owner men came to the point. The tenant system won't work any more. One man on a tractor can take the place of twelve or fourteen families. Pay him a wage and take all the crop. We have to do it. We don't like to do it. But the
40 monster's sick. Something's happened to the monster.
   But you'll kill the land with cotton.
   We know. We've got to take cotton quick before the land dies. Then we'll sell the land. Lots of families in the East would like to own a piece of land.
   The tenant men looked up alarmed. But what'll happen to us? How'll we eat?
45 You'll have to get off the land. The plows'll go through the dooryard.

If you ever hope to become a writer, make sure that you read the whole of *The Grapes of Wrath*. You can learn a lot from Steinbeck's skill as a story-teller.

15.3
Understanding

A Choose the best answer each time.

1. We learn from lines 4–8 in 15.1 that ____.
    A. Oklahoma became too heavily populated
    B. Poor people from the east coast of the USA were sent to Oklahoma as indentured labourers but become farmers

C. The farmers did not rotate their crops
   D. Oklahoma became known as the windy capital of the USA

2. The dust storms in Oklahoma had ____ effect on the livelihood of farmers there.
   A. very little
   B. a beneficial
   C. an adverse
   D. only a temporary

3. When the banks enforced the decision mentioned in line 10 of 15.1, huge tractors became necessary because of ____.
   A. a lack of labour
   B. the size of the new farms
   C. the poor quality of the soil
   D. a change to a different crop

4. Referring to the bank as a monster is an example of ____.
   A. assonance
   B. euphemism
   C. litotes
   D. personification

5. The coldness mentioned in lines 3 and 4 of 15.2 implies a lack of ____ on the part of the banks.
   A. a hard and objective attitude
   B. business
   C. compassion
   D. strictness

6. Steinbeck stations the owner men in their cars and the poor farmers on the ground in order to stress ____.
   A. the resentment which the hungry farmers felt
   B. the inferiority of the farmers in their time of difficulty
   C. the fact that the owner men knew how worthless the farmers might become
   D. the love which the farmers had for the land

7. The expression 'and drew figures in the dust' is intended by the author to ____.
   A. indicate that the farmers did not know that the bank owned the land
   B. add realism to the scene
   C. stress the futility of the owner men
   D. remind us of the harm done to the land by dust storms

B Answer these questions about the passage.

1. Why have the owner men come to the farms?

2. What does 'scrabbled' imply in line 9?

3. In line 25, what does the first 'so' mean?

4. In line 37, the owner men said 'the tenant system won't work any more'. For whom won't it work? What are the consequences?

5. What evidence is there in this extract that the tenant men had a deeper concern for the land than the owner men had?

Unit 15 · Moving On   215

15.4 Vocabulary: meaning in context

Choose the word(s) which best shows the meaning of the underlined words as they are used in 15.1 and 15.2.

1. *The Grapes of* Wrath by John Steinbeck (15.1, line 2)
   A. sorrow   B. distress   C. hunger   D. anger

2. the plight of poor farmers (line 4)
   A. difficulties
   B. needs
   C. distressing condition
   D. lack of luck

3. the fertility of the fields was weakened (line 5)
   A. good drainage
   B. ability to produce crops
   C. protection from the wind
   D. depth of the soil

4. The crops deteriorated (line 7)
   A. refused to grow
   B. worsened
   C. grew too rapidly
   D. had to be rotated

5. take over the farms, amalgamate them and use huge tractors (line 10)
   A. improve
   B. investigate
   C. diversify
   D. bring together

6. which had ensnared them (15.2, line 7)
   A. attracted
   B. trapped
   C. lured
   D. deceived

7. If they could only rotate the crops (line 16)
   A. give fertiliser to
   B. choose the best
   C. improve the quality of
   D. grow different ones in turn

8. Get enough wars and cotton'll hit the ceiling (line 29)
   A. go to its highest
   B. cause trouble and pain
   C. become far too expensive
   D. no longer become available

9. We can't depend on it. (line 30)
   A. completely agree with
   B. be responsible for
   C. rely on
   D. accept without doubt

10. we'd be ashamed to go to meeting (line 36)
    A. too frightened
    B. very reluctant
    C. nervous about doing something
    D. feeling embarrassed by inadequacy

216 *English Alive!*

15.5
Writing: style

If you look at the words in 15.4, you will see that half the words come from the Pre-reading section. That is because John Steinbeck writes so simply and clearly that there are not many difficult words to ask questions about. Consider this and say whether you agree with it:

- It is necessary to *understand* some comparatively difficult words because they may occur in questions in the CSEC examination, and because you may eventually meet them in newspapers and books, *but*

- If you want people to understand what you say and write, a simple style is the best way to go. You can find a simple style in the Bible, and in the works of such writers as John Bunyan, Ernest Hemingway, John Steinbeck, Somerset Maugham, V.S. Naipaul and Peter Abrahams.

Read this essay by a child aged 10. Although some of the statements are rather odd, the language is admirably simple:

A Bird and a Beast

```
The bird that I am going to write about is the Owl. The Owl
cannot see at all by day and at night is as blind as a bat.
  I do not know much about the Owl so I will go on to the
beast which I going to choose. It is the Cow. The Cow is a
mammal. It has six sides — right, left, an upper and below. At
the back it has a tail on which hangs a brush. With this it
sends the flies away so that they do not fall into the milk.
The head is for the purpose of growing horns and so that the
mouth can be somewhere. The horns are to butt with, and mouth
```

is to moo with. Under the cow hangs the milk. It is arranged for milking. When people milk, the milk comes and there is never an end to the supply. How the cow does it I have not yet realised, but it makes more and more. The cow has a fine sense of smell; one can smell it far away. This is the reason for the fresh air in the country.

The man cow is called an ox. It is not a mammal. The cow does not eat much, but what it eats it eats twice, so that it gets enough. When it is hungry, it moos, and when it says nothing it is because its inside is all full up with grass.

You do not have to write like the child above but when you are tempted to use long or difficult words in your own compositions, think of the English in the Bible, and in any of the books by the authors mentioned above. … And remember the cow!

15.6 Vocabulary practice

In each case, choose the word which best completes the sentence.

1. When the two teams started fighting, the referee decided to ____ the game.
   A. desertB. adjournC. abandonD. postpone

2. The firm decided to ____ the contract when they found this it was unprofitable.
   A. terminateB. dismissC. nullD. deny

3. My uncle has recently been ____ to the post of manager.
   A. risenB. increasedC. promotedD. lifted

4. Grandma is very ____ and is very reluctant to change her mind.
   A. rigidB. convictedC. firmlyD. stubborn

5. The police had to use tear gas to ____ the mob who were attacking the dance-hall.
   A. disperseB. dischargeC. disposeD. dislocate

6. Donna has too much work to do. I doubt whether she will be able to ____ the strain much longer.
   A. doB. payC. sitD. stand

7. The deputy manager was ____ of his post because of suspected dishonesty.
   A. takenB. movedC. derivedD. relieved

8. Vehicles have been ____ to a side street because the main road is blocked by an accident.
   A. deportedB. convertedC. divertedD. rooted

9. There are too many hotels here already, so there is not much ____ for another one.
   A. range   B. scope   C. place   D. dimension

10. The dog ____ its tail to show its happiness at seeing us again.
    A. swishes   B. flipped   C. waved   D. wagged

11. The new system is extremely ____ and saves us a lot of time.
    A. sufficient   B. laborious   C. time-consuming D. efficient

12. Maria is normally a very nice person, so we ought to ____ her very unusual outburst of temper.
    A. overlook   B. outlook   C. look over   D. look out

15.7
Vocabulary: problem words

Exercise 1

In each case, choose the right word from the brackets.

1. We decided to continue the game (despite, in spite) of the heavy rain.

2. Pasteur (discovered, invented) many harmful bacteria on dust in the air.

3. People who are asked to investigate allegations of corruption in a company should be (uninterested, disinterested) as far as the transactions of the company are concerned.

4. In the Second World War there was sometimes a (dual, duel) between the pilots of warring planes.

5. The Minister said that the (economic, economical) news showed signs of a recovery in the country's finances.

6. If a film is (interested, interesting), the viewers will not be (bored, boring).

7. Kwesi's (older, elder) brother is four years (elder, older) than he is.

8. Mr Wilson's complaint to the supermarket should (elicit, illicit) a speedy reply because of the publicity involved.

9. Anybody aged 14–18 is (eligible, illegible) to take part in the competition provided that he or she is a citizen of the country.

10. According to the news on television, there is an (eminent, imminent) danger of structural damage as the hurricane draws nearer.

11. The Ministry has made an (exhausted, exhaustive) inquiry into the cause of the collapse of the bridge and will publish its report shortly.

12. (Famous, Infamous) is more similar in meaning to 'notorious' than (famous, infamous) is.

Exercise 2

In each case, choose the right word from the brackets.

1. Christina Harrison was (formerly, formally) crowned Miss Universe at the pageant last night.

2. She will (rain, reign) for the forthcoming year ending 31 December.

3. In this district, pollution is caused by both a factory and by vehicles. The former (is, are) not as great an offender as the latter (is, are).

4. All of the furniture in this apartment (is, are) brand new.

5. Anybody convicted of robbery is almost certain to be sent to (goal, gaol).

6. My aunt says she is extremely (grateful, thankful) to the doctor and nurses at the hospital for enabling her to recover from the accident.

7. A farmer has to work (hard, hardly) if he wants to support a family on five acres of land.

8. Take no notice of his boasting; it is mainly hot (air, water) intended to impress people.

9. Between you and (I, me) I think she has made a mistake in marrying Mike.

10. I suspect that she was (indoctrinated, infatuated) with Mike and will soon discover what he is really like.

11. An (industrial, industrious) person is somebody who works (hard, hardly).

12. (Invaluable, worthless) is similar in meaning to 'priceless'.

15.8
Grammar: reporting orders and requests (revision)

We saw in earlier books that we can report orders in these ways:

Direct speech	Indirect (reported) speech
She said to me, 'Put **your** books away.'	She told me to put **my** books away.
'Lend **me** $50,' Dave said to Anna.	Dave asked Anna to lend **him** $50.
'Tell **me** what **you saw**,' the man said.	The man told me to tell **him** what **I had seen**.
'Don't open **my** letters,' Anna said to her brother.	Anna told her brother not to open **her** letters.
I reminded Dave, 'Don't be late or we**'ll** miss the show.'	I reminded David not to be late or we **would** miss the show.
'Don't forget to thank Uncle for the present he sent **you**,' my mother reminded me.	My mother reminded me not to forget to thank my uncle for a/the present he had sent **me**.

Notice the changes in verb forms and in words such as 'you', 'your, 'me' and 'my'.
When we use indirect speech, we have to make the identity of the various persons clear.

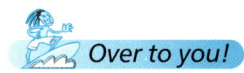

Over to you!

Exercise 3

Change these sentences into indirect (reported) speech.

1. The man told me, 'Take the second turning on your left.'
2. The nurse at the clinic said to Ram, 'Come back and see me if you get a pain in your throat again.'
3. 'Please get some salted fish when you go out,' Mr Menon said to his wife.
4. 'Tell me when you're ready to use the computer,' Peter reminded his sister.
5. 'Explain why you were absent on Friday,' Miss Johnson said to Suresh.
6. 'Don't forget to post my letter when you go out,' Mrs Taylor said to Francine.
7. 'Don't start smoking. It can kill you,' Grandma said to Howard.

8. 'Don't leave your clothes on your bed,' Mrs Blake told her son.

9. The guide told Ian, 'Don't dive down to the wreck without taking a companion with you. The currents are dangerous down there.'

10. The security guard warned us, 'Don't leave luggage unattended in the airport.'

11. 'Don't forget to tell Mother that I've gone fishing,' Noel said to his sister.

12. 'Read the form carefully before you sign it,' the woman told Tanya. 'Check the small print and make sure that you understand it.'

15.9

Grammar: reporting statements (indirect speech) (revision)

In earlier books, we saw that when we report a statement we may have to make these changes:

- As in 15.8, change pronouns ('I', 'me', 'he', 'you', etc.) and possessive adjectives ('my', 'your') to make the identities of the people clear.

- Probably change words showing time. (This depends on how soon after a speech you report it.) These are likely changes:

In direct speech	In reported speech
now	then, that day, at that time
today	that day, yesterday
tomorrow	the next/following day
yesterday	the previous day
last year	the previous year

- Probably change words showing place to make the situation clear, e.g.

In direct speech	In reported speech
here	there (or name the place)
there	(perhaps name the place)
in my home	in his/her home
at your school	at my/our school

Most of the changes are a matter of common sense.

- If the action in the direct speech has not yet happened or is still happening, it will probably not be necessary to change the tense of any verbs. However, if the action has happened, you may need to make changes like these:

In direct speech	In reported speech
She said,	She said that
it's raining	it was raining
I know the place	she knew the place
I'll help you	she would help me/us
he's gone	he had gone
I lost it	she had lost it
I can do it	she could do it
we must go now	they had to go then
I was waiting	she had been waiting

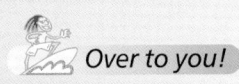

Over to you!

Exercise 4

Change these sentences into reported (indirect) speech.

1. 'I'll bring your bicycle back tomorrow,' Nadia told her friend. 'I'm grateful to you for letting me use it.'

2. 'Open your mouth wide,' the dentist told Stacy. 'Don't worry. This won't hurt you.'

3. Uncle said, 'I'll repaint the kitchen when I've finished dealing with a leak in the roof. I'll finish both jobs by the end of the week, I hope.'

4. One of the tenant farmers said, 'I can't pay my rent now but I'll pay in three months' time if the bank agrees.'

5. 'Sorry,' the man from the bank said. 'It's too late. The monster can't wait. Tractors will be here in five days' time. You've got to get off before then.'

6. The owner man told the farmers, 'You can go west to California. You can find work picking fruit. There's no future for you here.'

7. He told the farmers, 'The bank'll bring in tractors. We'll make very big farms and grow cotton until the soil is useless. Then we'll sell the land to people from the East Coast.'

8. When he was 22, Delroy told his mother, 'I've made up my mind. I'm off to London next week. A friend has offered me a good job over there.'

9. Delroy's mother said to him, 'I lived in London when I was a little girl. It's crowded and noisy over there but it will be easier for you to get a decent job.'

10. The TV announcer said, 'Hurricane Andrew has changed course and is unlikely to come our way. It's taken a more westerly route and will have little effect on us.'

15.10
Grammar: indirect questions (1)

Many questions start with 'How' or a word starting with 'W', e.g. 'What', 'When', 'Why', etc. We follow these guidelines when we report them:

- Use a full stop and not a question mark after an indirect question:
  direct: The lady asked me, 'How old are you?'
  indirect: The lady asked me **how** old I am.
  direct: 'When does the game start?' my friend asked me.
  indirect: My friend asked me **when** the game starts.

- Do not use inverted commas in an indirect question. Do not put a comma after 'asked'.

- Put the subject *before* the verb and not after it, e.g.
  direct: 'What's your name?' the woman asked me.
  indirect: The woman asked me **what my name is**.
  direct: 'Where's your brother?' Mike asked Nadia.
  indirect: Mike asked Nadia **where her brother was**.

- Make any necessary changes in pronouns, possessive adjectives and words showing time or place, as in 15.9.

- Move the tense back in time *if this is necessary*, as in 15.9.

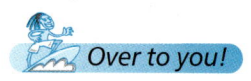

Over to you!

Exercise 5

Change the following into indirect questions.

1. 'How much is a flight to Miami?' Mike asked the woman.

2. 'When does the procession start?' Stacy asked us.

3. 'What's the record for the 100 metres?' Daljit asked me.

4. 'Where's the rest of the money?' Inspector Daley asked the suspect.

5. Miss Dosman asked Victor, 'Why haven't you done your homework?'

6. 'How many tickets do you want?' the man asked us.

7. 'Which ring do you prefer?' Pathma's aunt asked her.

8. 'How much will it cost to extend our house?' Miss Reid asked a builder.

9. We said to the stranger, 'What do you want?'

10. Colin asked me, 'What's the score?'

15.11
Grammar: indirect questions (2)

We use 'if' or 'whether' when we report a question starting with a verb, e.g.
    direct: 'Can you swim?' the woman asked Wayne.
    indirect: The woman asked Wayne **if he could swim**.
    direct: 'Did you answer all the questions in the test?' Fiona asked Mike.
    indirect: Fiona asked Mike **whether he had answered all the questions in the test**.

In most cases, it does not matter whether we use 'if' or 'whether' in this type of indirect question.

Over to you!

Exercise 6

Change these direct questions into indirect ones.

1. 'Have you seen Nnke recently?' Natoya asked me.

2. 'Are there alligators in the river?' one of the tourists asked the guide.

3. 'Do you like coffee?' Alicia asked her new friend, Francine.

4. The sales assistant said to me, 'Can I help you?'

5. Deena said to her mother, 'Is Pa going to Florida again next month?'

6. The police sergeant asked Maria, 'Did you see the accident happen?'

7. The tourist enquired, 'Is the Carnival held at the same time every year in Trinidad?'

8. 'Has your young brother started school yet?' a neighbour asked Samantha.

9. 'Will it take long to repair my car?' Miss Simms asked the mechanic.

10. Paul said to his brother, 'Can I use the computer when you've finished, please?'

11. 'Am I as tall as your sister?' Nadia asked Peter.

12. 'Does your sister still work in a bank?' Miss Wilson asked Mike.

15.12

Writing: summary

Question

Read sections 15.1 and 15.2 again and summarise the problems of the tenant farmers and how they were forced to leave. Do not use more than 130 words.

Action by you:

Read the two summaries below. This time, neither of them contains errors of language. Which summary is good and which is bad?

Hint:

These are the main factors to be included in a summary:

poor – had to borrow from banks
grew cash crop, cotton, repeatedly – to get money for bank
fertility of soil deteriorated – less crop
wind blew top soil off – dust everywhere
bank decided to foreclose – make profit from big farms
bank required tenants to leave

Summary 1

The farmers in Oklahoma were poor, so they had to borrow money from a bank. In order to repay the bank, they grew cotton, a cash crop, and did not rotate their crops. Inevitably, the fertility of the soil deteriorated and the financial return was less. At the same time, the poor quality of the soil made it possible for strong winds to blow across the fields and carry the top soil away. Eventually the bank decided to foreclose to try to recover the money lent to farmers. It sent men to tell the farmers to leave the land and move elsewhere because the bank intended to form very big farms and get a profit from them as long as it could.

Summary 2

The main problem of the farmers in Oklahoma was the dust storm which frequently swept across their fields, carrying away the valuable top soil and leaving them only with semi-useless sub-soil. In this way the fertility of the fields was weakened so much that strong winds easily picked up the top soil and formed huge clouds of dust. The region became known as the dust bowl of America. The crops grew worse and the farmers found that the dust made it impossible for them to make a living. At this time, there was a demand for cotton because it was needed to make explosives and uniforms. There wasn't a war all the time, so the farmers could not always sell their crop.

In which summary can you find the following:

a) a major factor entirely omitted? What is the factor?

b) a great deal of material copied from the original? Where is it done?

c) information inserted which was not in the original material. What has been inserted?

d) repetition. Where?

15.13
Enjoying poetry

The following poem deals with three stages of a son's life:

- the time before he was born
- his 'employment' as a gangster
- preparations for his inevitable death through violence.

The poem is a very powerful indictment of the way in which some people live.

The Woman Speaks to the Man Who Has Employed Her Son

Her son was first made known to her
as a sense of unease, a need to cry
for little reasons and a <u>metallic tide
rising in her mouth each morning</u>.   known as 'morning sickness'
5 Such signs made her know
that she was not alone in her body.
She carried him <u>full term</u>   i.e for 9 months
right up under her heart.

She carried him like the poor
10 carry hope, hope you get a break
or a visa, hope one child go through
and remember you. He had no father.
The man she made him with had more
like him, he was fair-minded
15 he treated all his children
with equal and unbiased indifference.

She raised him twice, once as mother
then as father, set no ceiling
on what he could be doctor,
20 earth healer, pilot take wings.
But now he tells her he is working
for you, that you value him so much
you give him one whole submachine gun
for him alone.

25 He says you are like a father to him
she is wondering what kind of father
would give a son hot and exploding
death, when he asks him for bread.
She went downtown and bought three
30 and one-third yards of black cloth
and a deep crowned and veiled hat
for the day he draws his bloody salary.

She has no power over you and this
<u>at the level of earth</u>, what she has   on Earth, at a physical level
35 are prayers and a mother's tears
and at knee city she uses them.
She says psalms for him

228 *English Alive!*

> she reads psalms for you
> she weeps for his soul
> 40   her eyewater covers you.
>
> She is throwing a partner
> with Judas Iscariot's mother
> the thief on the left-hand side
> of the cross, his mother
> 45   is the banker, her draw though
> is first and last for she still
> throwing two hands as mother and father.
> She is prepared, she is done. Absalom.
> Lorna Goodison

Questions

1. How does the tone of the poet change in the third stanza? Why does it change?

2. Comment on the poet's choice of words in line 16.

3. What is the attitude of the poet to her son's 'employer'?

4. What does the poet mean in lines 44–6?

5. For what is the mother prepared in line 48?

6. As far as you can judge, how relevant is the poem to modern life?

15.14 Writing

Either: Write 400–450 words on topic (1), (2) or (3) in about 45 minutes.
or: Write 250–300 words on topic (3) or (4) in about 30 minutes.

1. Write a story about a teenager who gets involved with bad company but manages to free himself or herself and lead a better life.

2. Write a story which starts in the following way:
    Nobody expected that Donna would achieve much in life but …

3. Attempt to explain what has caused the situation about which Lorna Goodison writes in her poem in 15.13.

4. How far is the saying 'When in Rome do as the Romans do' relevant and wise for people who emigrate to North America or Europe from the Caribbean?

16 People

16.1 Pre-reading

In Unit 16, we will study ways of describing people. We can begin by looking at the following extract from *The Dragon Can't Dance* by Earl Lovelace. At the start of his novel, the author makes it clear that Miss Cleothilda, the Queen of the Band, is going to be a major player in the story. Notice how he skilfully brings her to life for the reader. (Notice also – *but don't try to imitate until you become a skilful writer* – the length of the opening sentence. The author is certainly not using the style of 'A Bird and a Beast' in 15.5!)

16.2 Reading

Miss Cleothilda

For the whole year here in the yard on Alice Street, Miss Cleothilda, the mulatto woman occupying the two front rooms upstairs in the main house, has lived, tending her flowers and fern hanging in wire baskets from the ceiling of the narrow verandah, scolding her brown and white pup over its toilet training, fussing, and
5   criticising everything – the ugliness of the area, the noise of the children climbing the governor plum tree – making a nuisance of herself to everybody, strutting about the yard with her rouged cheeks and padded hips, husbanding her fading beauty, flaunting her gold bangles and twin gold rings that proclaim that she was once married, wearing dresses, showing her knees, that if you give her a chance will
10 show her thighs, walking this street on her way from market with her overflowing basket, displaying her more expensive purchases – the crab and the callaloo bush and the bound legs of the white chicken and the fat fingers of yellow plantains – her nose lifted above the city, her long hair plaited in two plaits, like a schoolgirl, choking with that importance and beauty which she maintained as a queenship
15 which not only she, but the people who shared the yard with her, had the duty to recognise and responsibility to uphold. She owned a little parlour stocked with goods ranging from haberdashery to groceries, and she ran it as if she were doing a favour to the Hill rather than carrying on a business from which she intended to profit: closing and opening whenever she pleased, holding up the steady stream of
20 customers to lecture anyone who dared come in without first saying good morning, leaving her enduring customers unattended to go and feed her dog or chat with one of her old friends who periodically dropped in, reserving the full cutting mischief of her tongue for anyone who dared suggest that she should hurry.

All year long she carried on hostile, superior and unaccommodating, refusing

25 still from the height of her presumed gentility to give even recognition far less encouragement to Philo, the calypsonian across the street, who, by whatever miracle of endurance and shamelessness and hope, after seventeen years still nursed this passion for her, dismissing him with that brisk turn of her head, the raising of her eyelashes and the sucking of her teeth, in one fluid gesture of disgust
30 that she could perform better than anybody else. But, now that it was Carnival season, Miss Cleothilda was getting friendly with everybody. In the same swirling spasm of energy that fuelled her earlier pose, she had become a saint almost, giving away sweets to the children, questioning them about their lessons, advising them against the perils of the Hill in a voice loud enough so that adults nearby could
35 hear, holding the little boys and girls speechless and tame, their round eyes printed on her face, which she knew how to so wonderfully change to dramatise whatever point she chose to make.

She had already made her journey to the steelband tent, a few streets farther up the Hill, to view the sketches of the masquerade costume the band would appear in
40 for Carnival, and had given her decision: she would portray the queen – queen of the band – though the Hill was by now certain that she would never appear in any other costume; for the Hill knew that it was not only a habit – she had been playing queen for the last eleven years – but that she could afford it; the Hill knew what she knew: that to her being queen was not really a masquerade at all, but the
45 annual affirming of a genuine queenship that she accepted as hers by virtue of her poise and beauty, something acknowledged even by her enemies.

The description of Miss Cleothilda continues for several pages. We learn what other people think of her and how she interacts with them.

16.3
Writing: starting a story

We saw earlier in this book that three useful ways of starting a story are by using SAD (**s**tatement, **a**ction, **d**ialogue). Which method does the author use in 16.2? He could have started in one of these ways:

- with action, e.g.
  With her nose lifted above the city, Miss Cleothilda marched across the yard on her return from the market …

- with dialogue, e.g.
  'Good morning, Miss Cleothilda,' Philo said hopefully, half-wondering whether the queen of his dreams would condescend to recognise him.

Using one of the three methods shown by SAD, suggest another way of starting the story.

16.4 Understanding

A Choose the best answer each time.

1. We can infer from the passage that Miss Cleothilda criticised everything because ____.
   A. she had no children to worry about
   B. she had never married and that had made her critical of people
   C. she felt superior and had a right to make her views known
   D. the yard was a noisy and ugly place

2. The expression 'strutting about the yard' is meant to convey an impression of ____.
   A. pride   B. poverty   C. inferiority   D. loneliness

3. Why do you suppose Miss Cleothilda flaunted her gold bangles?
   A. She did not want other people to see them.
   B. They were a sign to people that she was a married woman.
   C. She wanted to impress and attract Philo.
   D. She liked to impress other people.

4. In line 14, 'choking with' is better than 'showing' or 'displaying' because ____.
   A. it gives us a better idea of the size of the woman
   B. it implies that Miss Cleothilda found it difficult to impress other people
   C. it intensifies Miss Cleothilda's feelings and attitude
   D. it shows us how a schoolgirl would act in that district

5. The author probably brought in Miss Cleothilda's 'little parlour' ____.
   A. as a device for revealing her character more fully
   B. to make the story longer
   C. to make readers feel greater affection and understanding for Miss Cleothilda
   D. because he realised that most readers are interested in shopping

6. In line 22 'cutting mischief' shows that Miss Cleothilda had a ____ tongue.
   A. friendly   B. sociable   C. sharp   D. still

7. Philo probably felt ____ Miss Cleothilda.
   A. disgusted by
   B. antagonistic towards
   C. rebuffed by
   D. uninterested in

8. Children apparently viewed Miss Cleothilda with something approaching ____.
   A. awe   B. anxiety   C. disrespect   D. great fear

B Answer these questions about the passage.

1. Why does the author mention the things Miss Cleothilda bought at the market?
2. Explain why the customers in line 21 are described as 'enduring'.
3. Why was Miss Cleothilda 'unaccommodating'? (line 24)
4. What evidence is there to explain why Miss Cleothilda had enemies? (line 46)

English Alive!

16.5
Vocabulary: meaning in context

Choose the word(s) which best show(s) the meaning of the underlined words as they are used in 16.2.

1. <u>husbanding</u> her fading beauty (line 7)
   - A. conserving and looking after
   - B. looking back at
   - C. letting people know about
   - D. concealing her worry about

2. had the duty to recognise and responsibility to <u>uphold</u> (line 16)
   - A. agree with
   - B. support
   - C. tolerate
   - D. object to

3. leaving her <u>enduring</u> customers unattended (line 21)
   - A. regular
   - B. remaining
   - C. suffering
   - D. patient and understanding

4. she carried on hostile, superior and <u>unaccommodating</u> (line 24)
   - A. not willing to do what people want
   - B. unwilling to provide a home for people
   - C. eager to find fault with what people are doing
   - D. not interested in what might happen to her

5. from the height of her <u>presumed</u> gentility (line 25)
   - A. what she has claimed to have
   - B. not acceptable to others
   - C. causing trouble for her
   - D. leading to resentment

6. from the height of her presumed <u>gentility</u> (line 25)
   - A. kindness to others
   - B. higher social status
   - C. noble birth
   - D. previous experiences

7. In the same swirling <u>spasm</u> of energy (line 32)
   - A. time
   - B. lack
   - C. source
   - D. burst

8. that <u>fuelled</u> her earlier pose (line 32)
   - A. caused
   - B. led to
   - C. provided power for
   - D. spoilt

9. her earlier <u>pose</u> (line 32)
   - A. difficulty
   - B. assumed attitude
   - C. problem with neighbours
   - D. way of sitting for a photograph

10. she would <u>portray</u> the queen (line 40)
    - A. give advice to
    - B. inform
    - C. offer criticism to
    - D. assume the role of

11. the annual <u>affirming</u> of a genuine queenship (line 45)
    - A. confirmation
    - B. imitation
    - C. cooperation
    - D. search for

Unit 16 · People

12. by virtue of her <u>poise</u> and beauty (line 46)
    A. self-control even when provoked by enemies
    B. admirable way of holding herself
    C. mental skill in dealing with critics
    D. physical fitness despite increasing age

16.6 Vocabulary practice

In each case, choose the word which best completes the sentence.

1. A scientist has discovered a clear ____ between poor hygiene and premature death.
   A. reference   B. relative   C. join   D. relationship

2. The tourists put all their ____ in a taxi.
   A. baggages   B. luggages   C. crate   D. luggage

3. When their ship sank during a storm, three members of the crew managed to ____ in a small boat until they were rescued.
   A. endure   B. prolong   C. survive   D. revive

4. Did you happen to hear the weather ____ on the radio last night?
   A. prospectus   B. forecast   C. foretell   D. prophecy

5. The firemen were praised for their ____ to duty despite the dangerous situation.
   A. devotion   B. enthusiasm   C. passion   D. inspiration

6. The price of raw materials has risen since we gave you an estimate for the work, so we are forced to ____ our estimate now.
   A. devise   B. undertake   C. rise   D. revise

7. Any increase in the price of petrol from the refineries is bound to be ____ in a similar increase at the petrol pump.
   A. deflected   B. proceeded   C. reflected   D. affected

8. If he lets the ____ out of the bag, everybody will know about our secret.
   A. mouse   B. dog   C. cat   D. hen

9. Try not to be prejudiced against the plan. Keep an ____ mind until you know all the details.
   A. open   B. empty   C. honest   D. even

10. The magistrate said that he was prepared to give the defendant the benefit of the ____ in view of the conflict of evidence.
    A. luck   B. question   C. sentence   D. doubt

16.7 Vocabulary: problem words

Exercise 1

In each case, choose the right word from the brackets.

1. Look at that ship. It has a lot of damage on (its, it's) starboard side.
2. In most countries, the government (is lacking, lacks) the money to provide free medical and dental treatment for everybody.
3. When we entered the room, we saw an old man (laying, lying) on the floor.
4. A doctor said that the body must have (laid, lain) on the floor for at least 48 hours.
5. Anybody who drives a car while under the influence of alcohol is (reliable, liable) to be sent to prison.
6. The woman (went, looked) in her purse and took out two coins.
7. If you try to take a short cut, make sure that you don't (lose, loose) your way.
8. There (is, are) not (many, much) traffic on the road right now, and there (is, are) not (many, much) ships in the harbour.
9. The majority of the months in a year (has, have) 31 days. April is not the only one which (has, have) 30 days.
10. Uncle says that (maybe, may be) he will come on Saturday but he (maybe, may be) late if there (is, are) a lot of cars on the road.
11. During a war, the (moral, morale) of a victorious side is usually higher than that of the defeated side.
12. Francine is late. She must (have, of) missed the bus.
13. According to Selva, there (is, are) more than one way of getting to his village.
14. When you see (mother, Mother), please tell her that Mrs Wilson phoned while she was out.
15. The storm hovered over our district for several days. Out of (necessary, necessity) we had to rely on tinned food on the fourth day.
16. At Sting last year, the crowd became (noisy, noisily) and (violent, violence) broke out.
17. Only by banning guns, (can Jamaica, Jamaican can) hope to (kerb, curb) violence throughout the country.
18. Father has just lost his job, so a holiday in Florida is (beyond, off, out) of the question for the time (being, been).

19. Don't try to (take over, overtake) a car on a sharp bend or on the (cress, crest) of a hill.

20. While Nadia was waiting outside the shop, some boys ran (pass, past, passed) her.

16.8
Writing: composition length – a reminder

In the CSEC English A examination, you may have to write these compositions:

		No. of lines at 10 words per line
Basic Proficiency:	180–200 words in 25 minutes	18–20
	300–350 words in 35 minutes	30–35
General Proficiency:	250–300 words in 30 minutes	25–30
	400–450 words in 45 minutes	40–45

As suggested earlier, it is a waste of time to count the *words* in an examination. Before you take the examination, work out the average number of words which you write per line. Then count the number of lines in an examination. If you write an average of 10 words per line, you will need to write the number of lines shown above.

If you have not done it already, find out the average number of words you write per line.

16.9
Writing: descriptions of people in a short story

In his book *The Dragon Can't Dance,* Earl Lovelace uses about six pages (2500 words) to describe Miss Cleothilda. That is roughly 2½ per cent of the whole book. 2½ per cent of 400 words is 10 words, so:

- for literary purposes, we can study ways of describing people *in a novel*

but

- we have to use a much more concise method when writing a short story of 400–450 words.

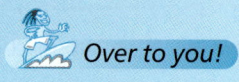

Over to you!

Exercise 2

Imagine that (in an examination) you are writing a short story in which Miss Cleothilda plays a major part.

1. How many lines can you use to describe Miss Cleothilda if your total must be 40–45 lines?

2. Write a description of Miss Cleothilda in not more than two lines. Here is an example:
   Miss Cleothilda was a proud but ageing beauty who could never forget that she was queen of the band.

3. Try again. Write a different description of Miss Cleothilda, based on information in 16.2. Do not use more than two lines.

4. Look back at Unit 6. In two lines, write a description of Colonel O'Reilly.

16.10
Writing: different attitudes

Learn to describe a person from different angles of approach. For example, we can describe a beggar in any of these ways:

- **as seen by an anonymous writer**, e.g.
  The beggar shuffled into the shop almost apologetically, holding out half a coconut shell with sad persistence …

- **as a first person description**, e.g.
  I watched the beggar thoughtfully and wondered whether he earned more than I did from his earnest entreaties to elderly tourists …

- **as seen by his own daughter**, e.g.
  The scene always puzzled Mitzie, young as she was. She watched her father take off the clean clothes he wore at home, and put on some old and dirty rags.
  'It's his work,' her mother explained nervously. 'He works in a very dirty place, and he doesn't want to spoil his good clothes.'
  For a moment, Mitzie wondered where her father worked, but she did not dare ask. Little did she know that in about an hour's time she was going to come face to face with him in the street.

- **as an autobiography**, e.g.
  If it makes you feel happy, you can call me a 'beggar'. I am too old and tired to worry about names. I am what I am …

- **as seen by a hard-hearted police officer**, e.g.
  'Scum!' the policeman said to his colleague. 'That's what they are – scum. Too lazy to work! Too idle to wash …'

We might get different attitudes and descriptions from a social worker or a tourist or a jealous, competing beggar, etc.

If you want to write about a person (or a place or thing), think carefully about the angle of approach you will use.

Over to you!

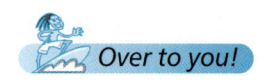

Exercise 3

Write the opening one or two sentences of a description of your school. Illustrate three different approaches to your school, choosing from the following people who are describing it.

a) you
b) a teacher
c) a nurse
d) a school inspector
e) a local shopkeeper
f) a local police officer
g) your Principal
h) your parent(s)
i) the local MP

Exercise 4

Choose one of the following people in List A below. Then assume that the people in List B are going to describe the person you have chosen. Choose two people from List B (or any others) and give three different descriptions of the person from List A. In each description write no more than five lines.

List A	List B
a neighbour	a school student
a friend	a historian
a singer	a friend or admirer of the person
a musician	somebody who is jealous or hostile
an actor/actress	a writer of short stories
Tessanne Chin	a biographer of the person
a politician	the person himself or herself
a shopkeeper	a news reporter
Nelson Mandela	a gossip columnist
President Bush	
Brian Lara	
Marcus Garvey	
Queen Nanny	
Bob Marley	

English Alive!

16.11
Writing: what does 'describe' mean?

Notice that in an examination the words 'Describe' and 'Give a description of' do not always refer to descriptive topics. They may introduce descriptive, narrative or factual topics. Each type needs different treatment.

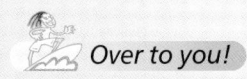

Over to you!

Say whether the following topics require descriptive, narrative or factual writing.

1. Describe how a mobile telephone works.//
2. Describe your first day in a new class or school.
3. Describe the home of one of your friends.
4. Give a description of an imaginary politician, as seen by two different people.
5. Give a description of the main sources of revenue for your country.
6. Describe any amusing incident which you witnessed or in which you played a part.
7. Describe any carnival which you have watched or in which you have played a part.
8. Describe the struggle for the independence of your country.
9. Describe a quarrel between two people which ended peacefully.
10. Describe the view from a window of your home.

16.12

Writing: describing people – a checklist

A writer can use a number of techniques when describing somebody in a novel. We can describe a person by referring to:

- his/her clothes
- his/her general appearance (age, height, build)
- details of his/her face, neck, hands or body
- the way in which the person walks or sits
- the person's character, thoughts and motives
- any mannerisms or significant details
- his/her actions
- what the person says
- what other people say to and about the person
- what we are told by the author.

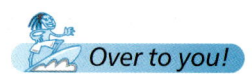

Over to you!

Exercise 5

Read the passage about Miss Cleothilda again. Then say which of the above techniques Earl Lovelace used to describe Miss Cleothilda.

Exercise 6

Read the following extract from *Great Expectations* by Charles Dickens. Say which of the above techniques Dickens used to describe

a) Mrs Joe

b) Joe Gargery.

An orphan, named Pip, is describing his sister (Mrs Joe Gargery) and her husband, who brought him up. He has just been to a cemetery, in a churchyard, to visit the grave of his parents. He has returned home late.

> My sister, Mrs Joe Gargery, was more than twenty years older than I and had established a great reputation with herself and the neighbours because she had brought me up 'by hand'. Knowing that she had a hard and heavy hand, and was much in the habit of laying it upon her husband as well as upon me, I supposed
> 5 that Joe Gargery and I were both brought up by hand.

240 *English Alive!*

She was not a good-looking woman, my sister, and I had a general impression that she must have made Joe Gargery marry her by hand. Joe was a fair man, with curls of flaxen hair on each side of his smooth face and with blue eyes. He was a mild, good-natured, sweet-tempered, easy-going, foolish, dear fellow – a sort of Hercules in strength, and also in weakness.

My sister, Mrs Joe, with black hair and eyes, had such a red skin that I sometimes wondered whether it was possible that she washed herself with a nutmeg-grater instead of with soap. She was tall and bony, and almost always wore a coarse apron which was stuck full of pins and needles in front.

Joe's forge adjoined our wooden house. When I ran home from the churchyard, the forge was shut, and Joe was sitting alone in the kitchen. Joe and I being fellow-sufferers, Joe hurried to give me the news as soon as I raised the latch of the door and peeped in.

'Mrs Joe has been out a dozen times, looking for you, Pip. She's out now.'

'Is she?'

'Yes, Pip,' said Joe, 'and what's worse, she's got Tickler with her.'

At this dismal news, I twisted the only button on my coat round and round, and looked miserably at the fire. Tickler was a wax-ended piece of cane, worn smooth by collision with my sensitive frame.

'Has she been gone long, Joe?' I asked.

'Well,' said Joe, glancing at the clock, 'she's been out about five minutes, Pip. She's coming now! Get behind the door and hide behind the towel.'

I took the advice. My sister threw the door wide open, and finding an obstruction behind it immediately used Tickler. Then she picked me up and threw me at Joe who, glad to get hold of me, stood me in the fire-place, and quietly fenced me up there with his great leg.

'Where have you been, you young monkey?' said Mrs Joe, stamping her foot. 'Tell me directly what you've been doing to wear me away with fret and fright and worry, or I'll have you out of that corner if you were fifty Pips, and he was five hundred Gargerys.'

'I've only been to the churchyard,' I said, crying and rubbing myself.

'Churchyard!' repeated my sister. 'If it weren't for me you'd have been to the churchyard long ago, and stayed there. Who brought you up by hand?'

'You did,' I said.

16.13
Writing: significant detail

The most significant thing about Mrs Joe was that 'she had a hard and heavy hand'. Can you remember anything else striking about her?

When you describe a person, you can sometimes obtain realism and vividness by describing a detail such as a person's mouth or eyes, or the way in which the person walks (e.g. Miss Cleothilda). Here are some examples of descriptions of significant features of people and places:

- His **mouth** told me everything I needed to know. Its message was clear, long before he spoke: a closed mind, no discussion, no tolerance, no mercy. It was a thin, tight line set in a tense and angry face.

- I was fascinated by the way in which she used her **hands**. She spoke with them – and seemed to have an endless vocabulary. They rose to emphasise a point, fluttered to show uncertainty, clawed the air when she lost a missing word, and drooped limply when she lost a point or could not get her way. I heard her speak but hardly listened. My eyes followed her hands and received a message twice as eloquent as any of her words.

- The shop was dirty and neglected. The owner sat (or dozed) on a rough wooden box behind the counter. His **vest** had not been washed for weeks and the same convenient policy seemed to apply to the whole shop.
  When I entered, the owner hardly bothered to glance at me. I wandered along the counter and stopped to watch **a column of ants dragging a dead cockroach** away from some dried fish.

- The bicycles told me what to expect inside the school. They were scattered around the compound in **no definite order**: a few near the gate, a group in the shade of a convenient tree, some leaning against a fence, and one or two sprawling across the path so that a stranger had to step over them to find his way to the school office. There were **no signs** to show where the office might be. Visitors were evidently not welcome.

Look for significant details (of people and places) in daily life. You may be able to use them in descriptive writing.

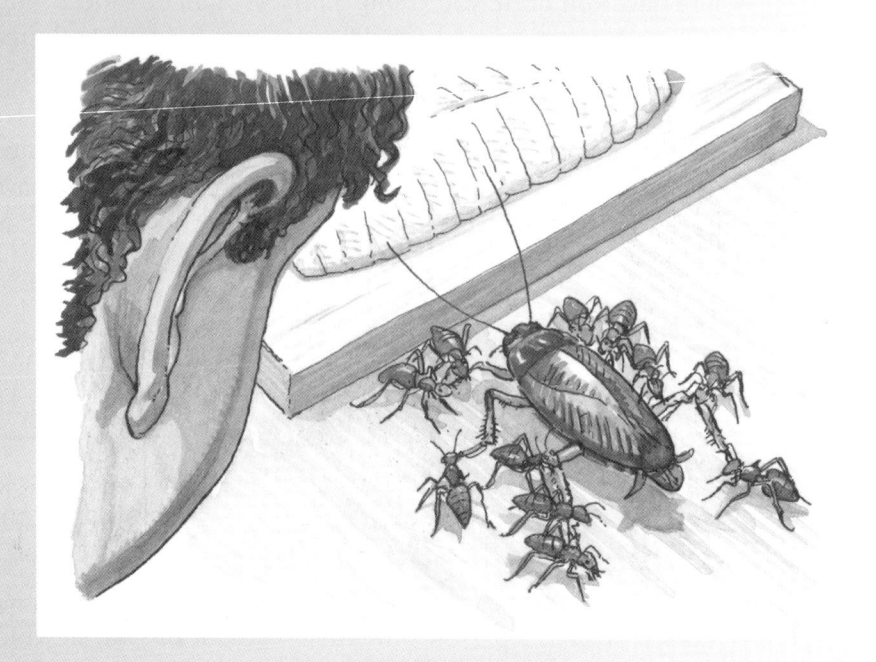

Over to you!

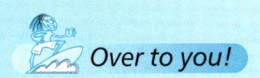

Exercise 7

1. Think of *two* or more people. In each case, write down what seems to you to be a significant detail of the person because it gives you a clue to the person's character.
2. Think of
   a) a room at school
   b) a room at home or in somebody else's home.

In each case, write down what seems to you to be a significant detail of the room.

Exercise 8

Rewrite this description to create an *unfavourable* picture of the girl concerned.

```
She was rather tall and had long black hair which shone like
silk. She carried herself well, but with the fitness of an athlete
rather than the assumed arrogance of a professional model. Her
mouth was well formed and seemed always on the point of bursting
into a smile. She had a small, almost dainty, nose, and a perfect
complexion. But what struck us most forcefully were her eyes:
large, brown and dancing with life. They twinkled with
friendliness when she spoke, and gazed at you with interest when
she listened. In conversation, it was clear that she was
interested in whatever you said and did not interrupt to relate
her own problems and experiences.
```

16.14
Enjoying poetry

The poem below comes from *Still Standing*, a book of poems by Michael C. Pintard. The Dedication (at the front of the book) helps to explain why the poem was written. The poet wrote:

```
'To my mother, Laura P. Hepburn.
My life has been phenomenally eventful, and as I have moved
from the extreme of lawlessness to discipline, I've done so
with similar passion.
Mom, you and the source of your faith have been the
stabilizing constants I've needed. I love you Mom.'
```

The poems in *Still Standing* show Pintard's awareness of the many troubles affecting Africans in Africa and the problems facing people of African descent worldwide. Amidst the turmoil of his thoughts and experiences, he values a moment of peacefulness.

Scarce Resource

I kneel next to my bed
hands propping up my head
elbows dug comfortably into the mattress.
The thermostat creates a warm   **controlling the central heating**
5   soothing environment,
a marked contrast to the freezing
air gusts beyond my window.

Flowery curtains chilled by air
seeping between the window seams,
10   then warmed, ever so slightly, by gentle
light rays, as they filter through
forecasting dawn's arrival.

In the darkness I can only faintly
make out the furniture's silhouette.
15   Memory though, positively identifies
them all.
All is quiet still,
except for the light rustling of old pipes
running in the vistas of this
20   late-Victorian house.

Fluorescent light in the hallway
meets the darkness
just under my door.
A sigh escapes.
25   Air exits my nostrils,
piercing the silence
as it sways my mustache
en route to anonymity.

I wish
30   this early morning serenity
was a global phenomenon.

Michael C. Pintard

Questions

1. Which expression of five words in the Dedication probably explains why the poet was kneeling in line 1 of the poem?

2. Where do you think the poet was when he wrote this poem? What evidence is there in the poem to support your answer?

3. At what time of the day was the poet kneeling by his bed? What is the evidence for your reply?

4. In line 10, what is warmed and by what?

5. What might be a better word than 'rustling' in line 18?

6. What is your reaction to lines 24–8?

7. What perhaps led the poet to write lines 29–31 and, perhaps, the whole poem?

You can read two more poems by Michael C. Pintard in 22.11.

16.15
Writing

Write 300–350 words in not more than 35 minutes on *one* of these topics:

1. Myself in ten years' time.

2. Describe any living person whom you particularly admire.

3. How far is it true to say that the lyrics of modern songs are the modern form of poetry?

4. Write a story which starts with these words:
    They say that a leopard can't change its spots. Well, I know one that did, fortunately. …

5. In what ways has the movement for the equality of sexes affected communities in your country?

17 Rebecca

17.1 Pre-reading

In almost all Caribbean countries there are a number of large old plantation houses: some in ruins but others renovated and in good condition. In 17.2 a woman dreams of a time when she lived in a large house called Manderley. A long drive led to the house and at the entrance to the drive there was a lodge, a small house for the man whose job was to open and close the gate.

The extract in 17.2 comes from the well-known romantic novel *Rebecca* by Daphne Du Maurier. Study the detailed description of the drive and notice how the writer creates the impression of years of neglect.

17.2 Reading

Rebecca

Last night I dreamt I went to Manderley again. It seemed to me I stood by the iron gate leading to the drive, and for a while I could not enter for the way was barred to me. There was a padlock and a chain upon the gate. I called in my dream to the lodge-keeper, and had no answer, and peering closer through the rusted spokes of
5 the gate I saw that the lodge was uninhabited.

No smoke came from the chimney, and the little lattice windows gaped forlorn. Then, like all dreamers, I was possessed of a sudden with supernatural powers and passed like a spirit through the barrier before me.

The drive wound away in front of me, twisting and turning as it had always done,
10 but as I advanced I was aware that a change had come upon it; it was narrow and unkempt, not the drive that we had known. At first I was puzzled and did not understand, and it was only when I bent my head to avoid the low swinging branch of a tree that I realised what had happened.

Nature had come into her own again and, little by little, in her stealthy, insidious
15 way had encroached upon the drive with long, tenacious fingers. The woods, always a menace even in the past, had triumphed in the end. They crowded, dark and uncontrolled, to the borders of the drive. The beeches with pale, naked limbs leant close to one another, their branches intermingled in a strange embrace, making a vault above my head like the archway of a church. And there were other trees as
20 well, trees that I did not recognise, squat oaks and tortured elms that straggled cheek by jowl with the beeches, and had thrust themselves out of the quiet earth, along with monster shrubs and plants, none of which I remembered.

    The drive was a ribbon now, a thread of its former self, with gravel surface gone, and choked with grass and moss. The trees had thrown out low branches, making an impediment to progress; the gnarled roots looked like skeleton claws. Scattered here and again amongst this jungle growth I would recognise shrubs that had been land-marks in our time, things of culture and of grace, hydrangeas whose blue heads had been famous. No hand had checked their progress, and they had gone native now, rearing to monster height without a bloom, dark and ugly as the nameless parasites that grew beside them.

    On and on, now east now west, wound the poor thread that had once been our drive. Sometimes I thought it lost, but it appeared again, beneath a fallen tree perhaps, or struggling on the other side of a muddled ditch created by the winter rains. I had not thought the way so long. Surely the miles had multiplied, even as the trees had done, and this path led but to a labyrinth, some choked wilderness, and not to the house at all.

    I came upon it suddenly, the approach masked by the unnatural growth of a vast shrub that spread in all directions, and I stood, my heart thumping in my breast, the strange prick of tears behind my eyes.

    There was Manderley, our Manderley, secretive and silent as it had always been, the grey stone shining in the moonlight of my dream, the mullioned windows reflecting the green lawns and the terrace. Time could not wreck the perfect symmetry of those walls, nor the site itself, a jewel in a hollow of the land.

    The terrace sloped to the lawns, and the lawns stretched to the sea, and turning I could see the sheet of silver, placid under the moon, like a lake undisturbed by wind or storm. No waves would come to ruffle this dream water, and no bulk of cloud, wind-driven from the west, obscure the clarity of this pale sky. I turned again to the house, and though it stood inviolate, untouched, as though we ourselves had left but yesterday, I saw that the garden had obeyed the jungle law, even as the woods had done …

    Nettles were everywhere, the vanguard of an army. They choked the terrace, they sprawled about the paths, they leant, vulgar and lanky, against the very windows of the house. They made indifferent sentinels, for in many places their ranks had been broken by the rhubarb plant, and they lay with crumpled heads and listless stems,

55 making a pathway for the rabbits. I left the drive and went on to the terrace, for the nettles were no barrier to me, a dreamer. I walked enchanted, and nothing held me back.

Moonlight can play odd tricks upon the fancy, even upon a dreamer's fancy. As I stood there, hushed and still, I could swear that the house was not an empty shell
60 but lived and breathed as it had lived before.

17.3
Understanding

A Choose the best answer each time.

1. It seemed to the dreamer that the lodge had been ____.
   A. demolished   B. abandoned   C. replaced   D. displaced

2. The dreamer called to the lodge-keeper ____.
   A. to have a chat with him
   B. to see if the lodge was inhabited
   C. to open the gate
   D. because she had no answer

3. In line 6, we are told that the lattice windows 'gaped forlorn'. This strongly suggests that ____.
   A. somebody had broken the windows
   B. the windows were open
   C. the windows were all closed
   D. it was summer time

4. Why did the dreamer want to go through the gate?
   A. The writer does not explain this mystery.
   B. A spirit appeared and guided her.
   C. She wanted to visit the lodge.
   D. She dreamt she had gone through it.

5. It quickly became clear to the dreamer that the drive had been ____.
   A. diverted   B. lengthened   C. shortened   D. neglected

6. The idea that Nature had 'come into her own again' (line 14) is echoed later in the same paragraph by the expression ____.
   A. had triumphed in the end
   B. making a vault
   C. had thrust themselves
   D. none of which I remembered

7. In line 25, 'impediment' is used with the meaning ____.
   A. 'welcome'
   B. 'closed door'
   C. 'strange guide'
   D. 'obstacle'

8. In line 37, 'it' refers to ____.
   A. the drive   B. the lodge   C. a labyrinth   D. Manderley

9. In line 39, the 'tears behind my eyes' were a sign of ____.
   A. strong emotion
   B. awakening from the dream
   C. pain caused by thorns
   D. an unpleasant shock

248 *English Alive!*

10. In line 43, 'symmetry' is similar in meaning to ____.
    A. impressive height
    B. construction
    C. beautiful shape
    D. age

B Answer these questions about the extract.

1. What seems to have been the dreamer's attitude to Manderley?

2. Why did the writer say, 'At first I was puzzled and did not understand'? (line 11)

3. Explain the meaning (in line 48) of 'it stood inviolate'.

4. Write down three words which the writer uses to sustain a metaphor about the nettles in lines 51–57.

5. What do the words 'the house was not an empty shell' imply about Manderley?

17.4
A writer's skill (1)

When the author set out to write about the drive and Manderley, what was her main aim? How does she seek to achieve it? How far would you say she succeeded?

17.5
Vocabulary: meaning in context

A Choose the word(s) which best show(s) the meaning of the underlined words as they are used in 17.2.

1. the little lattice windows gaped <u>forlorn</u> (line 6)
    A. sad
    B. sadly
    C. sadden
    D. sadness

2. it was narrow and <u>unkempt</u> (line 11)
    A. uncombed
    B. unused
    C. unpolished
    D. neglected

3. in her <u>stealthy</u>, insidious way (line 14)
    A. skilful
    B. furtive
    C. evil
    D. criminal

4. in her stealthy, <u>insidious</u> way (line 14)
    A. relentless and cannot be stopped
    B. not showing mercy or pity
    C. deceitful and wanting to be undetected
    D. aggressive and demanding

5. had <u>encroached upon</u> the drive (line 15)
    A. a clear effect upon
    B. managed to reach
    C. done some damage to
    D. wrongly moved onto

6. with long <u>tenacious</u> fingers (line 15)
   A. unwilling to release
   B. thin but powerful
   C. greedy
   D. liable to cause damage

7. The woods, always a <u>menace</u> even in the past (line 16)
   A. nuisance   B. threat   C. enemy   D. trouble

8. I did not recognise, squat oaks and <u>tortured</u> elms (line 20)
   A. painful   B. pained   C. twisted   D. dying

9. that straggled cheek by <u>jowl</u> with the beeches (line 21)
   A. force   B. cheek or jaw   C. luck   D. cunning

10. the <u>gnarled</u> roots looked like skeleton claws (line 25)
    A. very old or ancient
    B. thin but strong
    C. distorted or twisted
    D. long-lasting and strong

B Match the underlined words with the meanings which they have in the passage.

Words from the passage	Meanings
1. this path led but to a <u>labyrinth</u> (line 35)	a) imagination
2. <u>placid</u> under the moon (line 45)	b) partly cover
3. to <u>ruffle</u> this dream water (line 46)	c) almost lifeless
4. <u>obscure</u> the clarity of this pale sky (line 47)	d) somewhat inefficient
5. the <u>vanguard</u> of an army (line 51)	e) as if with magical powers
6. They made <u>indifferent</u> sentinels (line 53)	f) guards
7. They made indifferent <u>sentinels</u> (line 53)	g) maze
8. and <u>listless</u> stems (line 54)	h) leading soldiers
9. I walked <u>enchanted</u> (line 56)	i) disturb
10. odd tricks upon the <u>fancy</u> (line 58)	j) calm

17.6
A writer's skill (2)

Look at the last two paragraphs of the extract from *Rebecca* in 17.2 and study line 59. What will perhaps happen next in the book?
To be able to write like Daphne Du Maurier, you need certain skills, e.g.

- excellent powers of observation

- experience of the world (in this case of trees and plants)

- a good imagination

- a wide vocabulary
- determination to become a writer.

Since this book is a romance, you also need a good understanding of a range of different types of people of both sexes.

If you look at the patterns which the writer makes with her sentences, you will see that she does not normally use long sentences. Many of the expressions and sentences follow this pattern:

.... and ....

For example:

No smoke came from the chimney *and* the little lattice windows gaped forlorn.
It seemed to me I stood by the iron gate leading to the drive *and* for a while I could not enter …
The terrace sloped to the lawns, *and* the lawns stretched to the sea
I walked enchanted *and* nothing held me back.

Often the two parts of a sentence achieve a balance, which makes it easy to say and read the sentences. At times, John Steinbeck uses a similar style in *The Pearl* and in *The Grapes of Wrath*. Find more examples of this type of balancing sentence in 17.2.

17.7
Writing: describing places

Why are you describing the place?

The method you use to describe a place will depend on your reason for describing it. You might want to do any of these things:

- give a brief account of a place in an examination composition
- describe an accident scene in a statement to the police
- describe a house which is going to be sold, bought or repaired
- describe a single room which is going to be changed.

There are many more reasons for describing a place. Your method will depend upon the situation.

Arranging your points in a logical order

These are possible ways of arranging your points (but the method you choose will depend on the type of place you are describing and your reasons for describing it):

- from the foreground to the background (when describing a picture)
- from the left to the right (of a picture or view)

Unit 17 · *Rebecca*

- from the bottom to the top (of a picture or photo)
- from a significant feature outwards.

You can easily think of other methods. The main point is that you should use a method which is obvious to your reader and helps him or her to understand. In 17.2, the writer worked forwards from the gate to the house.

Using your senses

As in all descriptive writing, try to use as many of your five senses as you can to make your description realistic and stimulating. We can use these five senses:

- **sight**: what we can see at a place
- **sound**: what we can hear at a place
- **smell**: what we can smell, especially at a market or in a kitchen
- **touch**: the texture of something
- **taste**: what something tastes like.

Which sense did Daphne Du Maurier use mainly in her description of the drive?

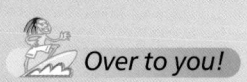

Over to you!

Exercise 1

Imagine that you have to describe some of the following places. Choose *three* of the places. In each case, say which sense you could use and give an example for each sense, i.e. if you mention the sense of smell, say what smells you might describe.

a) a market

b) a store

c) a ship at sea

d) a carnival procession

e) a place of worship such as a church, temple or mosque

f) a factory or an industrial building

g) a sports stadium

h) a restaurant

17.8 Writing: arranging ideas

Consider these two examples:

- Imagine that you are helping the owners of a hotel to prepare a brochure which can be sent to travel agents overseas. The aim of the brochure is to give information which will attract guests to the hotel. In what order can you arrange the various points? Perhaps:
    1. Interesting places in the locality
    2. Interesting places in the region
    3. Facilities in the hotel and outside it?

    Or you could change the order to 3, 1, 2. Can you think of a different way of arranging the main points?

- A relative overseas has just inherited a house in your country. He has asked you to inspect it and let him know what condition it is in and what repairs or improvements are needed before he advertises for a new tenant. In what order can you arrange the various points? Perhaps outside → inside:
    1. the yard/land/garden/field and any fencing
    2. inside: downstairs, upstairs and/or front to back
    3. the building: roof, walls, windows, etc?

    Or you could change the order to 1, 3, 2 *or* to 2, 1, 3.

Sometimes there is no ideal way of arranging your points. The important thing is that you use a logical method and make it clear to the reader.

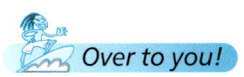

Over to you!

Exercise 2

Write down how you would arrange your points for *three* of the following topics.

1. An overseas relative or friend has written to you and asked you to describe the vicinity in which you live (but not the house).

2. An older relative is thinking of applying for a job at your school. She has written to you for information about your school.

3. The editor of your school magazine wants to have a feature entitled 'My favourite place for a picnic'. She has asked you to send in your contribution.

4. Describe your local market or a general store. You need the information to give a short talk to the class.

5. In an examination, you have to write a composition with the title 'My room'.

6. In an examination, you have to write a composition describing any place of worship, e.g. a church, temple or mosque.

17.9 Spelling

The words below are often spelt wrongly. Check that you can spell them correctly. Then your teacher can test you on them or divide the class into two parts and have a competition.

accommodation	conscientious	exhibition	occurred	similarly
appropriate	continuously	foreigner	pedestrian	simultaneously
beginning	convenient	immediately	privilege	superfluous
behaviour	definition	interested	pronunciation	superstitiously
beneficial	develop	necessarily	received	surprising
committed	embarrassment	neighbours	relatives	temporary
competition	exclamation	occasionally	reservoir	until

17.10 Punctuation: using a question mark (revision)

Put a question mark after a **direct question** but *not* after an indirect question.

Direct question (with a question mark)	Indirect question (without a question mark)
What's her name?	I wonder what her name is.
What's the matter now?	He wants to know what the matter is now.
How did he do it?	I'm not sure how he did it.
When does the game start?	Nobody knows when the game starts.
Where are my keys?	She asked me where her keys are.
Is Uncle coming tomorrow?	He asked me if Uncle is coming tomorrow.

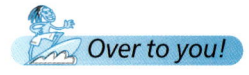

Over to you!

Exercise 3

Put a question mark or a full stop at the end of these sentences.

1. He wants to know if the food is ready yet

2. Try to find out what his phone number is

3. Had Kedeshia entered the competition, she would probably have won

4. Had you finished all the test when the bell rang

5. What we should do next has not yet been decided by the committee

6. Tell us where you would like to study microbiology

7. Please find out what the woman wants

8. Are you sure that this watch is Deena's

9. What he told you is not necessarily the whole truth

10. When will members of the committee let us have their decision

11. Please let us know if there is anything we can do to help

12. Is this the way to the General Hospital

13. Please let us know when Uncle goes into hospital for his operation

14. Is there any doubt about the man's guilt

15. Does anybody know where Kimani is now

16. Miss Davis wants to know where Kimani was yesterday

17. The woman told us what her name is and where she comes from

18. Mr Clarke could not understand how he had lost so much money

19. What we really need to know is where Sharnette lives now

20. Why he has gone to Florida suddenly is something of a mystery

17.11
Grammar: giving advice

One way of giving advice is by using 'You had better (not) …'. In speech, the 'had' is shortened to 'd'. Sometimes when people say 'You'd better' or 'I'd better', they speak quickly. Then the sound of /d/ almost disappears. This wrongly leads some people to omit the 'd' in speech and writing. Compare these sentences:

wrong: If you're tired, you better go to bed.
right: If you're tired, you'd better go to bed.
wrong: The game starts at 4.30, so we better hurry up.
right: The game starts at 4.30, so we'd better hurry up. We'd better not be late.

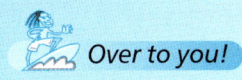

Over to you!
Exercise 4

Use 'he'd better', 'she'd better', 'you'd better' or 'I'd better' to give advice.

1. John said to you, 'I've got toothache. It's really painful.' Reply to him.

2. Your sister is speaking to you. She said, 'Poor Grandpa. You know he's a bit absent-minded. He went out shopping with Ma. Now he's discovered that he accidentally put a book in his bag and walked out without paying for it.' What do you suggest?

3. We haven't got much food in the house. There's a hurricane due here tomorrow. What do you suggest?

4. A friend said, 'I was in our car yesterday when my dad had to stop suddenly. I wasn't wearing a seat belt, so I really hit my head on the dashboard.' Tell him/her what to do in future.

5. You notice that a brother or sister has a nasty cut on one leg. There is no covering on the cut and you are worried that germs might get into it. What can you suggest?

6. You have a new student in your class. He says that he is somewhat deaf. Where should he sit? Tell him.

7. You notice that some windows are open at home. It has just started to rain heavily. What will you think to yourself?

8. A neighbour has just parked her car outside her house. You notice that one of her rear tyres is nearly flat. You suspect that she has not noticed it. What can you suggest to her?

9. You have two young brothers/sisters. The floor is nearly covered with toys they have been playing with. Your mother will return home and she is very strict about not having toys on the floor. What can you tell your brothers/sisters?

10. You: What's the matter, Ana? Why are you shaking that radio?

    Ana: I bought it in a cheap sale at the store yesterday. Now I can't get a single station on it. I've changed the batteries and checked everything but it doesn't work.

    What do you suggest?

17.12
Asking questions

Check that you know which verb to use when you ask a question.

Questions about present time

am	**Am** I in your way?	When **am** I going to get a turn?
is	**Is** this pen yours?	Where **is** your brother going?
are	**Are** you ready to go?	Why **are** you looking sad?
does	**Does** this shirt fit you?	How much **does** salted fish cost now?
do	**Do** those men work here?	What **do** those tourists want?

English Alive!

Exercise 5

Complete these questions by inserting 'am', 'is', 'are', 'do' or 'does'. Use a capital letter when necessary.

1. ____ any of your friends taking part in the competition?

2. ____ Lucy work in the same office as your sister?

3. ____ this the right path to Francine's village?

4. ____ your uncle still grow sugar cane?

5. ____ many people in Belize speak Spanish?

6. How often ____ your sister in Canada write to you?

7. Which of these cameras ____ your brother use at work?

8. Where ____ you usually play badminton with your friend?

9. How much ____ the ferry trip across the river cost?

10. When ____ I going to get a reply to my letter?

11. ____ there any poisonous or harmful snakes in Antigua?

12. ____ everybody ready to leave now?

Questions about past actions

was were	**Was** the answer correct? **Were** the men caught yesterday?	What **was** the right answer? Where **were** you at 9 p.m. last night?
has have	**Has** Mother gone shopping? **Have** your friends gone yet?	What **has** happened? What **have** you lost?
did	**Did** Leela pass the test?	How **did** you break it?

Unit 17 · Rebecca   257

Exercise 6

Complete these questions by inserting 'was', 'were', 'has', 'have' or 'did'.

1. ____ you post my letter when you went out?
2. ____ anybody phone while we were out?
3. ____ there many people at the game yesterday?
4. ____ the driver injured in the crash yesterday?
5. ____ the manager of the shop replied to your letter yet?
6. How ____ the prisoners manage to escape from jail last night?
7. What ____ you done with my keys? I can't find them.
8. Where ____ you leave the keys? I haven't seen them.
9. Why ____ two of the players sent off the field. ____ they fighting?
10. When ____ you last hear from Uncle? We haven't heard from him for months.

17.13
Is it similar?

In the CSEC examination, you may have to decide which of four sentences is most similar in meaning to a given sentence. In this (and the following units) we will consider the skills involved in this type of work.

Imagine that we have a line of five girls. We pick out one (Girl A) and then ask, 'Which of the other four girls is most similar to this one?'

- Girl B may look the same but be slightly taller.
- Girl C may be slightly heavier.
- Girl D may have a different hair style.
- Girl E may have a different mouth or nose.

In a similar way, you may be given four sentences which *seem* to be similar to a given sentence but which are different in *one* (or more than one) way. Follow these guidelines to find the matching sentence.

> **Guidelines for deciding similar sentences**
> 1. Read the first sentence very carefully and make sure that you understand the whole of it.
> 2. Read the four following sentences carefully. Look for one or more ways in which each sentence is different from the original one.
> 3. Delete the wrong answers. The remaining sentence should be the correct one.

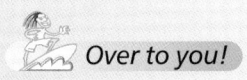

Over to you!

Exercise 7

Which sentences are similar in meaning to the sentence in bold type? Be careful. Some, none or all may be similar in meaning.

1. **Many spectators left the stadium before the end of the game.**
   A. Before the match finished, a lot of the people watching the game had gone.
   B. When the game finished, many of the spectators left.
   C. Not many of the spectators left before the end of the match.

2. **The judge decided that the taxi-driver was not responsible for the death of two passengers.**
   A. In the opinion of the judge, the two passengers did not have any responsibility for the death of the taxi-driver.
   B. The responsibility for the death of two passengers did not rest with the driver of the taxi, according to the judge.
   C. The judge was of the opinion that it was not the taxi-driver who could be said to bear the responsibility for the death of the three passengers.

3. **Francine is not only intelligent but she is very kind too.**
   A. Francine is neither intelligent nor very kind.
   B. Francine is very kind but not intelligent.
   C. Francine is intelligent but not very kind.

4. **When the price of fuel went down, the profits of the transport company increased.**
   A. A reduction in the cost of fuel proved to be good for the transport company's profits.
   B. The profits of the transport company led to a decrease in the price of fuel.
   C. A decrease in the price of fuel was accompanied by a fall in the profits of the transport company.

17.14 Enjoying poetry

Sometimes when we read a poem we may think, 'Hm! I wonder what that means. It might mean this or it might mean that.' This is one of those poems.

The Castle

His mother told him of the king's
enormous thick-walled castle where
with lots of yellow courtiers
he kept his yellow court of fear.

5   The bold knight hopped a milk-white horse.
spurred fiercely, keen as anything;
resolved, this honourable knight,
to slay that fearful king.

The <u>giddy</u> knight rode hard and fast.   **foolish**
10 At dusk he heaved a dreadful sigh:
at last, that frightful yellow flag
against the darkening sky!

LIVING IS FEARING. Tired, he read
the writing on the castle wall,
15 and braced himself to slay that king
who terrifies us all.

The drawbridge down, the knight spurred hard,
galloping into battle;
but as he neared, the bridge pulled up
20 with a disdainful rattle.

Too late to stop, he took the plunge;
<u>accoutred</u> well, he couldn't float;   **dressed and equipped in armour**
and, loud exclaiming 'Death to Fear!',
he drowned himself in the moat.

Mervyn Morris

Questions

1. Is the poet serious (and, if so, what about) or is he just amusing himself in a clever way?

2. Do the words 'hopped' (line 5) and 'disdainful' (line 20) give you any clue to the poet's attitude?

3. Who *might* be the king? Consider lines 3 and 4 (the colour yellow), 13, 16 and 23 before you give your answer.

4. Is there a moral in this poem? If so, what might it be?

17.15
Writing

In not more than 45 minutes, write 400–450 words on *one* of these topics:

1. Describe *one* of the two pictures below.

2. For an overseas relative or friend, describe what you saw when you ventured outside your home when the eye of a hurricane was passing over the region where you live.

3. Write a story which ends with these words:

    … And so, as they say, all is well that ends well.

4. Write a story in which somebody is charged with a crime which he/she did not commit but the person is quite happy to plead 'Guilty' to the charge.

5. On the whole, are you sorry or not that your ancestors came to the Caribbean?

18 Letters to the Editor

18.1
Pre-reading

If you use your computer and go to www.jamaica.gleaner.com you can read the news, sports reports, overseas news and many other items. One of the most interesting sections is the one headed 'Letters to the Editor'. Readers write to praise, criticise, complain and offer comments on the news. Some of the letters are amusing; some are very emotional. The letter in 18.2 is an excellent example of how to present a complaint in a clear and sensible manner.

If you write a letter to the editor of a newspaper, start with 'Dear Sir' or 'Dear Sir or Madam' or (if you know that the editor is a woman) 'Dear Madam'. Some newspapers expect readers to start a letter with 'THE EDITOR, Sir:' as shown below. You can finish your letter in any way you like. In modern times, most people end with 'Yours sincerely' but you can use 'Yours faithfully' if you prefer it. A traditional ending many years ago was 'I am, Sir, Your obedient servant' or 'I am, Sir, Yours faithfully' but very few people use those endings today.

18.2
Reading

THE EDITOR, Sir:
A year and a half has passed since my last trip home to Jamaica for vacation. I was so happy to be home that I decided not to join in the usual all-night partying; instead I planned to enjoy the more natural aspects of Jamaica. First stop, rafting on the Rio Grande in Portland.

5   It was all going wonderfully, snapping pictures of unbelievable natural images, basking in the serenity, trying not to talk too loudly out of reverence for the peacefulness. About 30 minutes into our trip I noticed the calm turquoise water steadily changing from slightly cloudy to a muddy brown. The water change was accompanied by the jarring noise of a bulldozer and dump truck, which quite
10 effectively suppressed the sounds of the water, splashing fish and chirping birds. I was not expecting the scene that appeared around the next bend in the river.

Of all the places in this land of wood and water, someone has decided to mine sand in the Rio Grande's river bed. Our relaxing ride on a bamboo raft along the river took us right past a bulldozer, digging in the river and dropping sand into the
15 back of a truck that then took its load to a large mechanical sieve located on the banks of the river which made even more noise than the truck and bulldozer combined.

Our raft captain informed us that the organised body of captains had complained to those who supposedly authorised the mining. The response to the captains was 'the two things must exist together'. In a bizarre and deeply disturbing way, the two do exist together. Among my collection of picturesque images of my ride on the river are pictures of this unnatural and horrendous travesty against our natural resources. Part of my memories of this trip along the river is having to shout above the machinery to carry on a conversation.

The damage to the river and its banks is also obvious. Every time it rains heavily, as it does frequently in Portland, the river eats away more of the land on the river banks. Ironically, the mechanical sieve sits precariously near to the edge of the river. According to our captain, 'One day after one big rain dem nah come back de come see it.'

How many Jamaicans vacation at home, and take the time to enjoy the absolutely remarkable natural resources and beauty we have available here at home? I am deeply disappointed at the decision-making process that allows sand mining and a tourist attraction to co-exist in such a destructive way.
Yours sincerely,
Sheri-Marie Harrison
Graduate student, University of Miami

18.3
Understanding

A Choose the best answer each time.

1. Ms Harrison came to Jamaica ____.
   A. to study at a university
   B. to make a complaint
   C. to recover from an illness
   D. on holiday

2. In line 3, the writer uses 'more natural' to make a comparison with ____.
   A. rafting
   B. partying
   C. city life
   D. Jamaica

3. In lines 6 and 7, the idea of 'serenity' is best echoed by the word ____.
   A. unbelievable
   B. basking
   C. natural
   D. peacefulness

4. It seems likely that the first mechanical noise which the writer heard on the river was made by ____.
   A. a sieve
   B. a dump truck
   C. a bulldozer
   D. the birds

5. It seems likely that at the site where sand was being mined, ____.
   A. the mine had gone partly under the river-bed
   B. rafts could not move up or down the river
   C. the water was comparatively shallow
   D. a sieve was used to separate sand and water

6. The 'two things' mentioned in line 20 are ____.
   A. sand mining and the peacefulness of natural beauty
   B. the bulldozer and the sieve
   C. the sieve and the dump truck
   D. wood and water

7. In line 25, the writer uses 'also' because of the prior reference to ____.
   A. sand   B. a sieve   C. noise   D. a raft

B Answer these questions about Ms Harrison's letter.

1. What was probably Ms Harrison's main aim in writing to the newspaper?

2. In which direction was the raft probably going? What is the reason for your answer?

3. What is the danger to the sieve?

4. Why is the writer opposed to sand mining?

18.4
Vocabulary: meaning in context

Choose the word(s) which best show(s) the meaning of the underlined words as they are used in the letter.

1. to enjoy the more natural <u>aspects</u> of Jamaica (line 3)
   A. rivers   B. wild life   C. features   D. enjoyments

2. <u>basking</u> in the serenity, trying not to talk too loudly (line 6)
   A. taking great pleasure   C. becoming involved
   B. swimming and bathing   D. contemplating

3. basking in the <u>serenity</u>, trying not to talk too loudly (line 6)
   A. tranquillity   B. happiness   C. warmth   D. freedom

4. out of <u>reverence</u> for the peacefulness (line 6)
   A. joy   B. respect   C. fear   D. surprise

5. The water change was accompanied by the <u>jarring</u> noise of a bulldozer (line 9)
   A. irregular   C. unnaturally loud
   B. throbbing   D. harsh and unpleasant

6. which quite effectively <u>suppressed</u> the sounds of the water (line 10)
   A. surpassed   C. obliterated
   B. rivalled   D. accompanied

7. captains had complained to those who <u>supposedly</u> authorised the mining (line 19)
   - A. presumably
   - B. in error
   - C. wrongfully
   - D. wilfully

8. those who supposedly <u>authorised</u> the mining (line 19)
   - A. controlled
   - B. approved
   - C. made the arrangements for
   - D. gave financial backing to

9. In a <u>bizarre</u> and deeply disturbing way (line 20)
   - A. very strange
   - B. very surprising
   - C. almost illegal
   - D. almost unique

10. The damage to the river and its banks is also <u>obvious</u>. (line 25)
    - A. serious
    - B. harmful
    - C. avoidable
    - D. clear

11. the mechanical sieve sits <u>precariously</u> near to the edge of the river (line 27)
    - A. unwisely
    - B. dangerously
    - C. foolishly
    - D. extremely

12. that allows sand mining and a tourist attraction to <u>co-exist</u> in such a destructive way (line 33)
    - A. exist again
    - B. exist together
    - C. continue to exist
    - D. exist but conflict

18.5 Vocabulary practice

In each case, choose the most suitable word or expression to complete the sentence.

1. If somebody is not really suitable for a job, we can call him a ____ peg in a round hole.
   - A. thick
   - B. thin
   - C. circular
   - D. square

2. It's a waste of time asking him for money. He hasn't got any, so don't try to get blood out of a ____.
   - A. tree
   - B. sponge
   - C. stone
   - D. hen

3. Mitzie has lost her boyfriend but we told her not to worry because he's not the only fish in the ____.
   - A. river
   - B. pool
   - C. sea
   - D. pond

4. There's something wrong with this message. I can't make head or ____ of it.
   - A. sense
   - B. meaning
   - C. foot
   - D. tail

5. Be careful! Don't put all your ____ in one basket and rely on him alone. You may be disappointed.
   - A. papaws
   - B. mangoes
   - C. bananas
   - D. eggs

6. Don't be afraid of Mr Harris. He's not as fierce as he seems. His ____ is worse than his bite.
   A. bark   B. threat   C. tooth   D. sting

7. That's a good idea. We can post your parcel and then buy the vegetables on our way home. We can kill two ____ with one stone.
   A. people   B. birds   C. jobs   D. chickens

8. Every evening she is in the ____ of going for a walk at about 6 p.m., when the temperature is not so high.
   A. routine   B. tradition   C. practise   D. habit

9. Before an operation, a doctor always ensures that the instruments have been properly ____.
   A. immunised   B. sterilised   C. pasteurised   D. purefied

10. The landslide threatened to bury several homes, so the occupants were ____ as a safety precaution.
    A. evacuated   B. retreated   C. withdrawn   D. retired

11. The lecturer showed complete ____ of his subject and answered all questions successfully.
    A. conquest   B. mastery   C. victory   D. triumph

12. We were surprised to see a long ____ of ants leading from the food cupboard to the window.
    A. pillar   B. file   C. column   D. nest

13. History shows that when a ruler becomes ____ he is likely to be removed from his throne.
    A. cosmopolitan B. decent   C. decadent   D. competent

14. The ____ of this block of apartments have formed an association to look after their interests.
    A. inhabitants   B. dwellers   C. inmates   D. residents

15. The medical authorities will take drastic action if SARS or another serious disease suddenly breaks ____ in our country.
    A. down   B. up   C. about   D. out

16. In written work, a ____ expression will probably be put in brackets or marked off by commas.
    A. quoted   B. foreign   C. doubtful   D. parenthetical

17. ____ lucky you were to win the first prize!
    A. What   B. Very   C. How   D. Why

18. When a ship approaches a foreign port, a ____ usually comes on board to bring the ship safely into port.
    A. captain   B. pilot   C. inspector   D. mate

19. It is impossible to steer a ship properly if its ____ has been badly damaged.
    A. anchor   B. funnel   C. galley   D. rudder

20. Farming land sometimes ____ to forest or jungle if it is completely neglected.
    A. reverts   B. converts   C. restores   D. relapses

18.6 Vocabulary: problem words

In each case, choose the right word from the brackets.

1. When my mother was young, she did not (owe, own) any property but now she (owes, owns) two houses and a shop.

2. Most of the (personnel, personal) in our company are highly (train, trained).

3. An auditor has to follow several basic (principals, principles) if he or she is going to do an honest and (through, thorough) job.

4. The price of many items has (raised, risen) steadily in recent years. The price of petrol is expected to continue to (raise, rise) because of a tight control over supplies.

5. If you live a (respectable, respectful) life, people will probably be (respectable, respectful) in their dealings with you.

6. It has rained heavily for at least four days (walking, running, going).

7. A doctor may give you an antibiotic to take if you have a cut which becomes (sceptic, septic).

8. When Donna first arrived in London during the winter, the freezing winds made her (quiver, tremble, shiver) until she put on warmer clothes.

9. We haven't heard from Uncle (for, since) several weeks.

10. The (sauce, source) of this river is somewhere up in the mountains.

11. Our country (composes, comprises, consists) of two islands, one larger than the other.

12. What time does the (sport, sports) meeting start?

13. This part of the harbour usually (teams, teems) with small fish.

14. Between you and (I, me), I doubt whether their plan will succeed.

15. It's time the game (start, started, starts). It's ten minutes late (all ready, already).

16. Go and (awake, wake) Mike up. It's time he (getting, got) up.

17. When (you, your, you're) ready, I'll help you to repair the puncture in (you, your, you're) bike.

18. There's an (abundance, abundant) of wild life in the forest of St Lucia and (until, so) this was pointed out in a recent article, (it, they) was not fully appreciated.

18.7

Answering comprehension questions

Read this letter to a newspaper and then study the questions (and answers) about it.

The Editor, Sir:
It has been quite evident that crime in this country is increasing at a high rate each day, and unemployment plays a major role in this aspect for the saying goes 'Idle dog eats sheep'.
   How do we tackle the problem? I personally believe that with the expertise we
5 have in this country no outside help should be sought.
   Based on the observation that males are the predominant offenders, my suggestions are:
1. Draft into the Army boys between the age of 15–25 years (those not pursuing higher studies or not employed) where the respective skills could be taught, e.g.
10 auto mechanics, craft, construction, welding, agriculture, etc.
2. After one year's training they should be dispatched to areas where those skills would be required whether in the government service or privately.
3. The trainees to receive a stipend monthly.
4. An assessment to be done at the end of the year as to the feasibility of such
15 training.

There has got to be a start somewhere, for, if the situation of crime continues, we will all be heading for destruction.
Yours sincerely,
Dean Archer
St Elizabeth

Questions

Study each question and the possible answers below. Award 2 marks for each correct answer. Deduct marks for errors of fact and/or expression.

1. What does the writer assume when he uses 'quite evident' in his opening sentence?
   A. Crime in the country is increasing at a high rate each day.
   B. The writer assume that his guess is right.
   C. When he uses quiet evident in his opening sentence, the writer assumes that crime increasing.
   D. He assumes that his readers are aware of the amount of crime being committed.
   E. He assumes that people who read the newspapers and watch television are familiar with the rise in the amount of crime.

2. What does 'aspect' refer to in line 2?
   A. It refers to a major roll.
   B. It refers to the increase in the amount of crime.
   C. In Line 2, 'aspect' refer to unemployment.
   D. increasing at a high rate each day
   E. Refers to the saying 'Idle dog eat sheep'.

3. To what or whom is the writer referring when he mentioned 'idle dog' in line 3?
   A. He is referring to a dog which have no work to do.
   B. unemployed males
   C. He is referring to young unemployed males.
   D. He is refering to dogs and young men that have no work to do and cause trouble.
   E. He is thinking of young men who have no jobs and are likely to get into trouble.

4. What is the 'problem' mentioned in line 4?
   A. It is how to find employment for young males.
   B. The problem mention by the writer is how to prevent the rate of crime from increasing.
   C. The problem is how to reduce the amount of crime.
   D. Draft boys aged 15–25 into the army for a year to learn skills.
   E. It is what to do with males because they are the worst offenders.

5. What does 'predominant' mean in line 6?
   A. worst
   B. It means 'main'
   C. It means main.
   D. It means 'strongest'.
   E. The majority of offenders are males.

Unit 18 · Letters to the Editor   269

6. In line 8, what does the writer imply by using 'draft' instead of 'enrol' or 'admit'?
   A. He implies that the scheme must be compulsory because some boys would not want to join the Army.
   B. He implies: make the boys join even they don't like it.
   C. He implies that the Army won't be happy to have all the young men in it.
   D. He uses 'draft' to show the it will be compulsory for males aged 15–25 to serve in the Army (with some exceptions).
   E. He knows that the army is part of the military.

18.8
Writing: making a summary

You are an intern (a learner) working in the office of a newspaper and hoping to become a journalist. This week you are working in a department which deals with letters from readers. Your supervisor has asked you to read each email or letter which comes in and let her have a summary of it in about 50 words.

You received this letter:

Dear Sir

I wish to complain about EPS Electrical Stores in Market Street. A week ago I bought a radio at the store. It seemed to work quite well in the store but soon after I took it home, it stopped working. I could not get any radio station on it and even the clock on it did not work. I was busy for a few days, so I could not go back to the store immediately.

Eventually, I took the radio back to the store and asked to see the manager. After waiting nearly an hour, I was able to speak to the manager. He demanded that I show him the receipt. When I could not produce this (having lost it), he refused to exchange the radio and said, "You can sue us if you like. You can't prove that you bought it here. Sorry. I can't help." I'll never go back to that store and I'm telling all my friends about it.

Yours sincerely

Ivbin Dunn

You wrote this summary for your supervisor:

Somebody is complaining about an electrical store which, so he claims, refused to exchange a faulty radio which he had bought at the store. He had lost the receipt, so he could not prove that he had bought the radio at the store. The manager refused to help him.

English Alive!

Over to you!

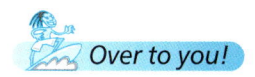

Exercise 1

Remember that you are an intern working in the offices of a newspaper, as explained opposite. Make summaries (of about 50 words each) for your supervisor of each of the letters in 18.2 and 18.7.

18.9
Slander and libel

- **Slander** is *saying* something which is harmful and untrue about a person. It is also called 'defamation of character'. If you slander somebody, the person may sue you in a law court and be awarded damages against you.

- **Libel** is *writing or printing* something which is harmful and untrue about a person. Defaming a person on the radio or on television is also called libel because many people may hear what you say. If you libel somebody in a letter or a report, the person may sue you and obtain damages against you, *so be careful what you say and write!* The penalty for libel is more serious than the one for slander.

18.10
Writing: making a complaint

Follow these guidelines when making a complaint:

Guidelines for making a complaint

1. If possible, make your complaint in person or on the telephone before you put anything in writing. It is usually much quicker and more efficient to get in touch with somebody on the phone or through email. A formal written letter may involve other people and cause a lot of trouble. Keep the world peaceful and happy if possible!

2. Check your facts very carefully before you make a written complaint. You may discover that you are partly at fault.

3. Don't accuse somebody of dishonesty or negligence unless you have evidence which will be acceptable in a court of law.

4. Say (a) what you think is wrong and (b) what you want somebody to do about it. Give the relevant time, date and facts. Be as simple and clear as possible.

5. Keep a copy of your complaint.

Look at the following examples.

Example 1

```
I enclose your invoice number 547/16D for $585 dated 14 August.
Please note that I paid this invoice on 12 July and have your
receipt, number 64431, dated 17 July.

Will you please explain why you have sent me another invoice
although the original invoice was paid a month ago?
```

The last paragraph is not necessary but it may force the receiver to investigate the matter.

Example 2

```
In August last year, I bought a set of reference books published
by your company. Since then I have received many unwanted
catalogues and brochures about other books. In April, I wrote to
your company, asking you NOT to send any more material. However,
last week I received a copy of WORLD ART from your company, along
with a request for $249.50 in payment.

Please note that I did not order this book and do not want it. I
estimate that the cost of the return postage will be about
$35.00, and I shall be happy to return the book if you send $35.00
for the postage. If I do not hear from you within 10 days, I shall
charge 50c a day storage fee in addition to the return postage.

Yours faithfully
```

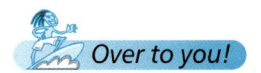

Over to you!

Exercise 2

Write *one* of these letters of complaint:

1. You sent some films to be developed by post. You have not received the prints and have received no reply to an earlier letter of enquiry. Make up the dates and other details.

2. To the editor of a newspaper about unnecessary details of violence which appeared in a report in the newspaper. Make up the date, page number, headline and other details.

3. You bought a camera which was guaranteed for a year. Three months after you bought the camera, it developed a fault. You took it back to the shop but the shopkeeper said he could not repair it because he had no spare parts. He refused to exchange the camera for a new one. You have found the address of the overseas maker of the camera. Write a letter to the maker.

English Alive!

4. Write a letter of complaint based on your own experiences or on those of a relative or friend.

18.11
Is it similar?

Exercise 3

Look at each sentence in bold type below. Then say whether the sentences below it are similar in meaning to the given sentence or not.

1. **A year and a half has passed since my last trip home to Jamaica for vacation.**
   A. I have not been to Jamaica on holiday for the past 18 months.
   B. The last time I went home to Jamaica on holiday was 18 months ago.
   C. During the past year and a half, I have not been home for a holiday.

2. **I was so happy to be home that I decided not to join in the usual all-night partying.**
   A. It was not because I was happy to be home that I decided not to take part in an all-night party.
   B. I did not take part in the customary all-night partying because I was unhappy about being home.
   C. I skipped the usual business of going partying all night because I was really delighted to be home.

Unit 18 · Letters to the Editor

3. **I was not expecting the scene that appeared around the next bend in the river.**
   A. We did not expect to go round the next bend in the river and be able to view the scenery.
   B. I had not in any way anticipated what we saw when we rounded the next bend in the river.
   C. When we went round the next bend in the river, we saw something which I had not anticipated seeing .

4. **At this site, the very strong current makes diving fun for experienced divers but difficult or even dangerous for novices.**
   A. Inexperienced divers will find that the strength of the current here is more suitable for divers with considerable experience.
   B. Experienced divers will find that the considerable strength of the current at this place provides them with fun but beginners will find diving here presents them with some difficulty and even with danger.
   C. At this site, the current is very strong; this may make experienced divers laugh but it could kill beginners.

5. **One consequence of the defeat of the Taleban in Afghanistan is that the supply of opium has risen dramatically.**
   A. The Taleban succeeded in eradicating the production of opium in Afghanistan by punishing offending farmers.
   B. Farmers in Afghanistan rebelled against the Taleban because they wanted to be free to grow poppies and produce opium from them.
   C. In Afghanistan, much more opium is now being produced because the Taleban have been overthrown.

6. **The rapid spread of AIDS in large areas of Africa is having an extremely adverse effect on the economy of some countries.**
   A. Economic conditions in some African countries are worsening very considerably as a result of the swift spread of AIDS there.
   B. AIDS has swept across some countries in a large part of Africa, causing the death of many people and creating thousands of orphans.
   C. The economy of some African countries in a large area of the continent has been affected by the gradual spread of AIDS throughout the region.

18.12 Enjoying poetry

The Fringe of the Sea

We do not like to awaken
far from the fringe of the sea,
we who live upon small islands.

We like to rise up early,
5 quick in the agile mornings
and walk out only little distances
to look down at the water,
to know it is swaying near to us
with songs, and tides, and endless boatways
10 and <u>undulate</u> patterns, and moods.   *rising and falling*

We want to be able to saunter beside it
slowpaced in burning sunlight,
barearmed, barefoot, bareheaded,

and to stoop down by the shallows
15 sifting the random water
between the <u>assaying</u> fingers   *testing*
like farmers do with soil,

and to think of turquoise mackerel
turning with <u>consummate</u> grace,   *perfect, very great*
20 sleek and <u>decorous</u>   *dignified*
and elegant in high blue chambers.

We want to be able to walk out into it,
to work in it,
dive and swim and play in it,

25 to row and sail
and pilot over its sandless highways,
and to hear
its calls and murmurs wherever we may be.

All who have lived upon small islands
30 want to sleep and awaken
close to the fringe of the sea.

A.L. Hendriks

Questions

1. What literary device does the poet use in line 2?
2. Does 'agile' apply to the poet or the morning?
3. Suggest a reason why the poet uses 'undulate' (a comparatively rare word) in line 10.
4. What does line 15 mean?
5. Where are the 'high blue chambers' of line 21? What figure of speech is used here?
6. Where, how and why does the poet vary the rhythm of the poem?

18.13
Writing

Either: Write 400–450 words on topic (1) or (2) in about 45 minutes.
or: Write 250–300 words on topic (3) or (4) in about 30 minutes.

1. Write a story in which a river plays an important part.
2. Why do people write letters to a newspaper? Give a brief account of some of the more common topics mentioned in letters to a newspaper.
3. What is your favourite book? Give a brief account of it and say why you like it.
4. Give an account of at least one place in your country where the environment has been adversely affected (or may be affected in future) by the activities of mankind.
5. Discuss the importance (or lack of it) of rivers in your country.

19 In Court

19.1
Pre-reading

Before the Second World War, E.R. Braithwaite went to England from the Caribbean to do postgraduate studies. When war broke out in 1939, he joined the Royal Air Force and served as an aircrew member. After the war, he became a teacher in one of the toughest parts of London, the East End.

One of Braithwaite's students, a boy called Patrick Fernman, got into trouble with the law. His grandmother sent him to a barber to sharpen a knife. On his way, he was stopped by a bully, who tried to steal the knife. In the ensuing struggle, Fernman cut his hand on the knife but stabbed the bully. The police arrested Fernman and charged him with malicious wounding.

In the following extract from Braithwaite's book *To Sir, With Love*, the Chairman of the Magistrates deals with the case – and is very critical of the school where Braithwaite is teaching.

19.2
Reading

The Law at Work

Now all informality vanished from the little courtroom as the clear, vibrant voice of the Chairman of Magistrates rose and fell in measured delivery. Here was the law at work, as dignified, severe and remote as its representative who seemed to grow larger and graver as he spoke.

5 'The court has read and heard the statements of the boy and his parents, and we are in no doubt that this youth did not arm himself with the weapon, but was sent out to have it sharpened; a simple enough errand one might think, but one which had serious consequences …

'I want to warn you, Patrick Fernman, and to advise you against the use of
10 weapons, any type of weapons. This frightening experience should be a severe lesson to you and to your unhappy parents.'

Then the Chairman turned his attention to Fernman's school. He did not mention it by name, but to anyone familiar with the area there could be no doubt that he meant Greenslade. His voice was harsh and cuttingly sarcastic as he
15 referred to the evils of 'free discipline' in general and the particular practice of it at 'a certain school in this vicinity'. In his opinion such schools were the brood-pens of delinquency, attested by the frequency with which children, boys and girls, from that school appeared before the Juvenile courts on one charge or another.

He felt that certain cranks and dreamers were doing more harm than good to the

20 youth of the area by pursuing an educational course which over the years of trial had achieved nothing to recommend it; rather it had encouraged among the youth a vicious licence to do evil, and a continued disregard for established social institutions.

'Those people,' continued the Chairman, 'to whom the education and
25 development of these youths is entrusted, cannot hope to escape the final responsibility for the natural result of their ill-conceived schemes. I sometimes am persuaded that justice would be better served if they were made to answer the charges for the offences which, one might say, they have by proxy committed.'

He turned his attention once more to the boy, who had sat bemused and silent at
30 this angry tirade; this time, however, the voice was kindly and rather paternal. He told Fernman that he was sure that his own evident grief and the sorrow which he had brought to his parents was punishment enough; however, for his own good, a supervision order would be made which would require that he report to a probation officer once weekly for a period of one year. He then discharged the boy
35 into his parents' keeping, and the little group left the court, reunited and trying to smile through their tears of relief.

19.3
Understanding

A Choose the best answer each time.

1. It seems very likely that before Braithwaite went to England ____.
   A. he had been a magistrate
   B. his father had taught him to fly
   C. he had already attended a university
   D. his mother was a teacher in London

2. In the word 'postgraduate', the prefix 'post' means ____.
   A. for   B. before   C. not yet   D. after

3. As far as we can judge, the injury to the bully was ____.
   A. self-inflicted   C. his own fault
   B. a minor one   D. a fatal one

4. Evidently the Chairman of the Magistrates was ____ man.
   A. an impressive   C. an irritating
   B. a merciless   D. an insignificant

5. In the expression 'but one which' (line 7), the word 'one' refers to ____.
   A. a reader   C. a listener
   B. the knife   D. the errand

6. In line 11, the parents were unhappy because ____.
   A. their son was sent to prison
   B. the judge blamed them
   C. their son killed somebody
   D. their son had broken the law

7. In line 14, Greenslade was apparently ____.
   A. the name of the bully
   B. Braithwaite's school
   C. one of the injured boys
   D. a district in London

8. Why was the Chairman of Magistrates so critical of Fernman's school?
   A. The boy had injured a bully.
   B. Too many of its pupils had been in trouble with the law.
   C. Both Fernman and the bully came from that school.
   D. It was the place where delinquent offenders in the district were sent.

9. In line 16, 'brood-pens' is similar in meaning to ____.
   A. results of
   B. opposites
   C. places which produce
   D. main causes

10. In the expression 'it had encouraged' (in line 21), 'it' refers to ____.
    A. Greenslade
    B. more harm than good
    C. years of trial
    D. a particular type of education

B Answer these questions about 19.2.

1. In your own words, explain the meaning of 'we are in no doubt that the youth did not arm himself with the weapon' (lines 5–6).

2. In the opinion of the Chairman of Magistrates, what should Patrick Fernman learn from his court case?

3. What made the Chairman think that the schemes at Greenslade were 'ill-conceived'?

4. Explain the meaning of 'offences… they have by proxy committed' (line 28).

5. What caused the 'tears of relief' in the last line of the extract?

19.4

Vocabulary: meaning in context

A Choose the word(s) which best show(s) the meaning of the underlined words as they are used in 19.1 and 19.2

1. In the <u>ensuing</u> struggle (19.1 line 7)
   A. bitter   B. following   C. unexpected   D. desperate

2. charged him with <u>malicious</u> wounding (line 9)
   A. intending to cause harm
   B. extremely serious
   C. not allowed by law
   D. quite superficial

Unit 19 · In Court 279

3. the clear, vibrant voice of the Chairman of Magistrates (19.2, line 1)
   A. loud   B. lively   C. musical   D. memorable

4. one which had serious consequences (line 8)
   A. dangers   B. threats   C. warnings   D. results

5. His voice was harsh and cuttingly sarcastic (line 14)
   A. very sharply   C. deliberately
   B. somewhat   D. reluctantly

6. His voice was cuttingly sarcastic (line 14)
   A. contrasting good and bad   C. not saying what he really thought
   B. meaning less than he said   D. mockingly scornful

7. a certain school in this vicinity (line 16)
   A. bad area   C. neighbourhood
   B. with bad habits   D. respect

8. such schools were brood-pens of delinquency (line 17)
   A. being absent from school   C. not knowing what your duty is
   B. anti-social or illegal conduct   D. lack of trust and confidence

9. attested by the frequency with which children … appeared (in courts) (line 19)
   A. demonstrated   C. examined
   B. put under a strain   D. found to be false

10. He felt that certain cranks and dreamers (line 19)
    A. amateurs who are not familiar with the subject they write or speak about
    B. people who hold an opinion with which you do not agree
    C. people who hold and advocate views considered unacceptable by the community
    D. beginners who do not know very much about a subject and do not want to know

B Match the words from the passage with the meanings as used in the passage.

Words from the passage	Meanings
1. a vicious licence to do evil (line 22)	a) permission
2. a vicious licence to do evil (line 22)	b) obvious
3. their ill-conceived schemes (line 26)	c) fatherly
4. by proxy committed (line 28)	d) confused
5. had sat bemused and silent (line 29)	e) released
6. this angry tirade (line 30)	f) concerned with a trial period
7. rather paternal (line 30)	g) badly thought out
8. his own evident grief (line 31)	h) savage/malicious
9. a probation officer (line 34)	i) bitter outburst/speech
10. He then discharged the boy (line 34)	j) through another person

19.5
Vocabulary: proverbs and sayings (revision)

In Unit 9 we saw that:

- you may have to write about a proverb or saying in an examination

- most proverbs have two meanings: a literal, surface meaning, and a broader metaphorical meaning.

In an examination, write about the broader (metaphorical) meaning and do not take the proverb literally, e.g.
question: Write a story based on the saying: 'The grass is always greener on the other side of the hill'.
the wrong approach: I will write a story about a farmer, his cows and grass on a hill. *(This is based on the literal, surface meaning of the saying.)*
a suitable approach: The saying means: 'Conditions are always better in another place', so I will write a story about somebody who emigrated and found that the saying is (not) true.

Over to you!

Exercise 1

Imagine that you have to write a story based on each of the sayings in bold type below. Say whether each possible theme is suitable or not.

1. **Every cloud has a silver lining.**
   A. I will write about the effect of sunlight on clouds.
   B. I will write about how the shape of a cloud affected somebody's life badly.
   C. I will describe a time when a misfortune brought good to somebody.

2. **It never rains but it pours.**
   A. I will write a humorous story about a day when somebody was very unlucky and encountered several minor misfortunes.
   B. I will write about the heavy rain which comes with a hurricane.
   C. I will point out that tropical rain is often very heavy.

3. **The early bird catches the worm.**
   A. I will write about somebody who did well by being quick to seize an opportunity.
   B. I will describe a group of bird-watchers observing birds feeding.
   C. I will describe how several young men loved a very beautiful girl but were too scared to approach her. One young man was not scared and made his feelings known to the girl. She married him.

4. **Don't put the cart before the horse.**
   A. I will describe what happened when a silly young man put a horse behind a cart and expected it to push the cart.
   B. I will write a story which stresses the importance of doing things in the right sequence.
   C. I will describe a plan which nearly failed because the planner did not get things in the right order.

5. Now think of some Caribbean proverbs and explain their meaning.

Exercise 2

Match the following expressions with their meanings. Use each phrase in a complete sentence to show that you understand its meaning

Expressions	Meanings
1. a close shave	a) It is up to you to take action now.
2. a red herring	b) something which is unwanted and expensive to maintain
3. to play second fiddle	c) to be greedy and eat or take too much
4. a chip off the old block	d) something (bad) that is being concealed deliberately
5. a white elephant	
6. a square peg in a round hole	e) to be in an inferior position compared with another person
7. The ball is in your court now.	
8. to make a pig of yourself	f) to break a promise or an agreement
9. to go back on your word	g) a narrow escape
10. a skeleton in somebody's cupboard (or closet)	h) somebody in an unsuitable job or position
	i) a child that is like a parent in some way
	j) something intended to distract or to deceive

19.6

Grammar: conditional sentences (1)

In 19.6 and 19.9, check that you can use:

- the sentence patterns involved
- the correct tense of the verbs concerned.

We can use conditional expressions for various purposes, e.g.
  to give advice: If I were you, I would accept the offer.
  to give information: If a hurricane approaches, stay at home.
  to state a condition: Leela won't go to the party unless you go too.
  to promise: If you lend me $100, I'll repay you next week.
  to threaten: If you don't keep quiet, you'll be in big trouble.
  to warn: Be careful! If you touch that cable, you may get a shock.

There are four kinds of conditional sentences. We will study two of them in this section, and two more in 19.9.

Habitual or routine actions

In this sentence pattern, we use **'if' + Simple Present + Simple Present**. 'If' here is similar in meaning to 'when', e.g.

> If you leave fish out of a fridge, it soon goes bad.
> In North America, if it snows, workmen put salt and/or grit on the roads.
> If people get drunk, they sometimes start to fight.
> If you don't water plants, they soon die.
> Plants soon die unless you water them regularly.
> It takes me half an hour to get to school unless our bus breaks down.

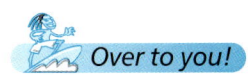

Over to you!

Exercise 3

Complete these sentences to show what usually or sometimes happens. You can use words from the list in the box below *or* you can choose your own way of completing the sentences.

1. During a football match, if the referee sees a foul, he ____.

2. If a dog sees a cat, it ____.

3. If you heat an iron bar, ____.

4. If somebody breaks the law, ____.

5. If you expose phosphorus to the air, ____.

6. If you forget to put butter back in a refrigerator, it ____.

7. If somebody has painful toothache, ____.

8. If you have a deep cut on your hand or leg, it may become infected unless ____.

9. The river is rising and may soon flood the land unless ____.

10. I usually go to bed by 11 p.m. unless ____.

Possible ways of finishing the sentences in Exercise 3
These expressions are *not* in the right order.
a) he or she usually goes to see a dentist.
b) the police usually arrest him.
c) blows his whistle.
d) I have a lot of work to do.
e) you put some antiseptic ointment on it.
f) it expands.
g) the rain stops soon.
h) it bursts into flame.
i) begins to melt or go soft.
j) usually chases it.

Specific situations

This is a common pattern when we refer to a specific situation and say what may or will happen:

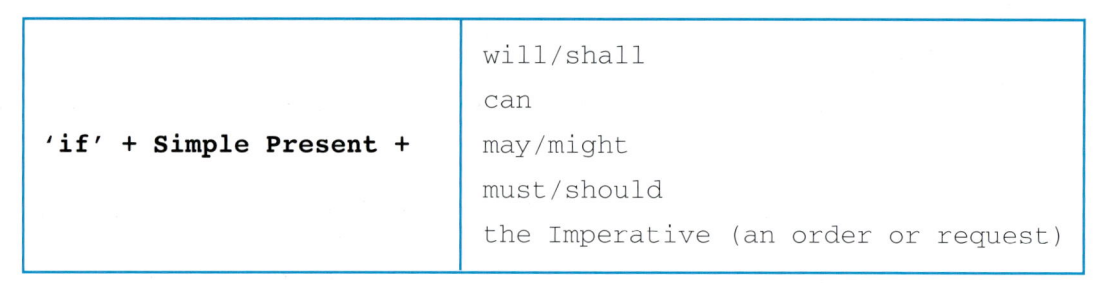

'if' + Simple Present +	`will/shall`
	`can`
	`may/might`
	`must/should`
	`the Imperative (an order or request)`

Examples:
    If it rains next Saturday, the Sports Meeting will be cancelled.
    If your parents agree, you can stay with us during the holidays.
    If the pain doesn't disappear, you must/should see a doctor.
    If you see Durai, please ask him to phone me.
    If those shoes are too tight, change to a more comfortable pair.

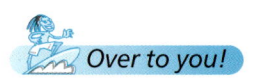

Over to you!

Exercise 4

1. Complete these sentences in any sensible way *or* choose a suitable expression from the list in the box below.
   a) If tourists stop coming here, ____.
   b) If you hold the mouth of a test-tube towards you while you are heating it, ____.
   c) Be careful! That dog is vicious because it has been treated badly. If you go too near it, ____.
   d) If creatures from another planet land on Earth, ____.
   e) If the Government needs to increase its revenue, ____.
   f) If the price of petrol is doubled because of a global shortage, ____.
   g) If I ever win the first prize in a lottery, ____.
   h) If I see burglars breaking into a neighbour's home, ____.
   i) If you can run 100 metres in under 9.8 seconds, ____.
   j). If those shoes hurt your feet, ____.

2. Make five sentences of your own, using the structure in the box above.

Possible expressions for Exercise 4
Use your own expressions if you can.
  i) I will share the money with my family.
  ii) many people may lose their jobs.
  iii) they will have a big surprise.
  iv) bus fares will go up.
  v) you will win a gold medal.
  vi) I will inform the police immediately.
  vii) you should get a larger pair.
  viii) it may bite you.
  ix) something may spit out at you.
  x) it can double the tax on new cars.

19.7

Grammar: what's wrong?

Exercise 5

Say or write the letter which shows where there is something wrong or unacceptable in the following sentences. In some cases, there may be no error.

1. I'm <u>sorry about</u> the mistake in the advertisement but there <u>really isn't nothing</u> we
          A   B
   can do <u>to correct it</u> at this late stage because it has already been printed. <u>No error</u>
               C   D

2. The manager of the shop told <u>both of us</u> that he is out of stock <u>temporary</u> but he has
                                         A   B
   promised to order <u>more supplies from</u> the manufacturer if that is possible. <u>No error</u>
                             C   D

3. <u>With the help of volunteers</u>, the police combed the area of the forest <u>adjacent to the</u>
           A   B
   scene of the crime, <u>left no stone unturned</u> in the quest to find evidence. <u>No error</u>
                              C   D

4. <u>Between you and me</u>, the couple are unlikely to <u>get married</u> in the near future
           A   B
   because they are <u>quite satisfied</u> with their present relationship. <u>No error</u>
                         C   D

5. After the accident, witnesses discovered the <u>driver of the vehicle</u> not far away,
                                                                A
   <u>laying on his right side</u> and <u>suffering from</u> injuries to his head and legs. <u>No error</u>
           B   C   D

6. If you <u>had told</u> us last month that you were <u>short of cash</u>, we <u>would have helped</u>
            A   B   C
   you by lending you whatever you needed. <u>No error</u>
                                               D

7. Donna heard <u>womens' voices</u> outside, so she walked to the window and <u>peered out</u>
                      A   B
   cautiously, anxious to see without <u>being seen</u>. <u>No error</u>
                                       C   D

8. We can't use the library this <u>week, it is</u> closed to allow senior students to make
                                                   A
   <u>an inventory</u> and find out how many books <u>are missing</u>. <u>No error</u>
        B   C   D

Unit 19 · In Court   **285**

9. Our Maths teacher explained that there <u>were</u> more than one method <u>of solving</u> the
                                                                       A   B

   equation but that one method was much <u>less simple than</u> the other. <u>No error</u>
                                                            C   D

10. In order to stay healthy, the human body needs <u>various kinds</u> of <u>food vegetables</u>,
                                                                 A   B

    meat, fish, salt, sugar, etc., so a <u>varied diet</u> is highly desirable. <u>No error</u>
                                         C   D

19.8
A cloze passage

Complete this passage by choosing the best words from the items given below the passage. In 19.2, a magistrate criticised a school. This is part of the headmaster's defence.

In the (1) ____ of the law, a teacher stands 'in loco parentis' to his (2) ____ her students. That is to say, the teacher is regarded as (3) ____ in the place of a parent. It (4) ____ that the attitude of a teacher to his students should be (5) ____ of a reasonable parent to his sons and daughters.

In some schools, this is a (6) ____ difficult task. Many students (7) ____ from homes where (8) ____ is only one parent. Some students do not (9) ____ know who their father is. In addition, a mother who is (10) ____ with the task of earning money to buy food and clothes does not always (11) ____ enough time (12) ____ which to look after her children adequately. Thus many students (13) ____ affection and concern for (14) ____ welfare at home, so the teacher has to try to (15) ____ for this deficiency and help children to develop to the (16) ____ of their ability.

1. A. view
   B. teeth
   C. eyes
   D. rules

2. A. or
   B. and
   C. besides
   D. also

3. A. stood
   B. work
   C. standing
   D. worked

4. A. means
   B. tells
   C. imply
   D. show

5. A. like
   B. that
   C. similar
   D. fond

6. A. special
   B. particularly
   C. extremely
   D. exceptional

7. A. coming
   B. are come
   C. come
   D. has come

8. A. it
   B. she
   C. father
   D. there

9. A. to
   B. even
   C. never
   D. ever

10. A. face
    B. facing
    C. faced
    D. faces

11. A. want
    B. had
    C. need
    D. have

12. A. at
    B. in
    C. through
    D. for

13. A. lacking
    B. needed
    C. lack
    D. show

14. A. his
    B. her
    C. a
    D. their

15. A. compensate
    B. overcome
    C. enhance
    D. ignore

16. A. good
    B. better
    C. best
    D. rest

English Alive!

19.9
Grammar: conditional sentences (2)

In 19.6, we studied two of the four main ways of using conditional expressions. In this section, we can study the other two methods.

General statements and unlikely events

We can use this pattern when we:
- make a general statement without referring to a particular person or thing
- refer to something which is unlikely to happen:

`'if' + Simple Past +`	`might`
	`could`
	`should`
	`would`
		`+ an infinite without 'to'`

Examples of general statements:
   If motorists drove more carefully, there would be fewer accidents.
   If men showed more respect for women, there would be fewer quarrels at home.

Examples of unlikely events:
   If I were you, I wouldn't go to the party.
   If we had enough money, we could go to Florida for a holiday.

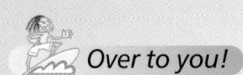

Over to you!

Exercise 6

1. Put in a suitable form of the verbs in brackets. Study each situation to see what form of the verb is needed.
   a) There would be various problems if many people living in apartments ____ (keep) large dogs. It ____ (be) difficult to give the dogs enough exercise. The dogs ____ (make) a lot of noise. Then people ____ (complain) about them.
   b) This camera is no good. There's something wrong with it. If I ____ (be) you, I ____ (take) it back to the shop. I ____ (ask) for a replacement.
   c) We wouldn't have to leave home so early if we ____ (live) near our school or if we ____ (have) a car to take us to school.
   d) What would you do if you ____ (win) millions of dollars in a lottery? ____ you ____ (spend) the money or ____ you ____ (save) it? I think I ____ (share) the money with members of my family but I ____ also ____ (give) some to my church.
   e) If I ____ (be) you, I ____ not ____ (mention) racial prejudice in your letter to the editor. It is a very complex topic. If I ____ (be) you, I ____ (omit) that sentence.
   f) There would probably be fewer crimes if there ____ (be) more police officers.

Unit 19 · *In Court*

2. Make eight sentences of your own to practise this structure. Use each of 'might', 'could', 'should' or 'would' in two sentences.

Commenting on past events which cannot now be changed

This type of sentence is used when we want to say what might/would/could/should have happened if somebody had acted differently at some past time. We cannot change what has already happened, so these expressions are often called **impossible conditions**.

The normal sentence pattern is:

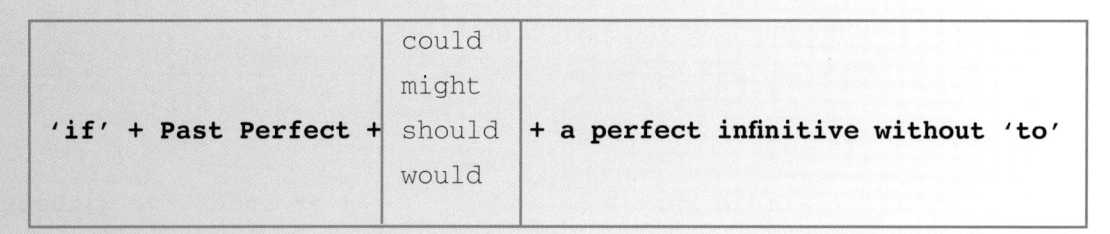

'if' + Past Perfect +	could might should would	+ a perfect infinitive without 'to'

Examples:

I'm glad you didn't throw that old chair away. If you had done so, Grandpa would have been upset because it's his favourite chair.

If you had told me that you were going to the cinema yesterday, we could have gone together. Instead of that, we went separately.

If Wayne had played in our team, we might have won. Unfortunately, he was ill, so he could not play and we lost the game.

Uncle was very lucky. If he had gone on that plane, he might have been killed when it crashed. I'm glad he decided not to go.

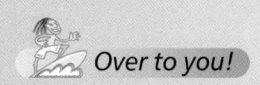

Over to you!

Exercise 7

Answer the questions about the sentences in bold type.

1. **Carlotta would have been disappointed if she had failed to get the job.**
    a) Did Carlotta get the job?
    b) Was she disappointed?

2. **If Marlon had scored his third goal, we would have won by 5-4. Then we would have finished top of the league instead of being runners-up.**
    a) How many goals did Marlon score?
    b) What was the final score?
    c) Did Marlon's team win, lose or draw?
    d) Which team was next to the top of the league?

3. **If somebody had told me a month ago that John would be working in England now, I would never have believed him.**
   a) Was John working in England a month ago?
   b) Is he working there now?
   c) Did somebody tell the speaker about John's work a month ago?

19.10
Enjoying poetry

A Fairy Tale

Openly he says: Sir, when I grow up
I want to be a fine man; someone like you.
Secretly he says: You old fool, I'll join
a gang like Applejackers or Navarones
5   and if we catch you in the street
we will break all your bones.
You say you teach me about life
but you don't know that life is strife
between mother and father.

10 Life is nothing to eat when morning comes;
life is no money to buy books and uniforms.
No this, no that, no taking part
in so many things you say make life.
Life is a drunk father on payday,
15 and mother with her feller on Saturday.
Life is sickness and no cash for doctor.
What you teach as life is just a fairy tale.

Anson Gonzalez

Questions

1. How typical or accurate is this poem when applied to the teenagers you know?

2. The speaker/narrator assumes that the 'old fool' in line 3 does not know about domestic strife or hardship or gangs. For example, in line 8, he says, 'but you don't know that life is strife'. What does this imply about the speaker?

3. What is the mood of the speaker throughout the poem? How can we account for this mood? Will it last?

4. The speaker has a problem. What is his problem and how does he intend to deal with it? What can we guess about the future prospects of the speaker?

5. Explain clearly why the poet has chosen the title 'A Fairy Tale'.

6. What is *your* attitude to the speaker or your opinion of him? Why?

19.11
Writing

Either: Write 400–450 words on topic (1) or (2) in about 45 minutes.
or: Write 250–300 words on topic (3), (4) or (5) in about 30 minutees.

1. Write a story in which the person(s) shown in *one* of the photos on these pages plays an important part.

2. Write a story which ends with the words:
   *… And so, you see, sometimes it **is** true that the grass is greener on the other side of the hill.*

3. If you were the Prime Minister of your country (and leader of the strongest political party) what changes and/or improvements would you seek to make? Where would you get the money to finance them? (Be realistic. Don't put forward changes which the country cannot afford.)

4. Describe some of the problems which you have faced, or are now facing, in preparing for the CSEC examinations, and explain how you have tried to deal with them.

5. Try to account for the different attitudes which people have towards the development of tourism in your country.

20 English in Business (1)

20.1 Pre-reading

After working in London for more than 30 years, Grandpa Blake has returned to Barbados to retire. In 20.2 he is talking to a grandson, Errol, about his early days in London.

20.2 Reading

That Opened My Eyes

Errol: What was your first job, Grandpa?
Grandpa: I worked for a shipping firm. Nowadays, you could call me a shipping executive but in those days I was just a junior clerk or an office boy. I used to do filing, outgoing mail and all sorts of odds and ends.
5 **Errol:** Did you enjoy it? Was it interesting? What did the shipping company do?
Grandpa: Hey, slow down a bit. Yes, the work was OK, fun at times – especially at Christmas. Our company supplied fuel to ships. We had maybe twenty depots overseas. We bought coal in the UK and from India. Then we chartered ships and sent the coal out to our overseas depots, along with supplies of oil. In those days,
10 many ships used coal as their fuel but some used oil. If a ship was sailing from the UK to, say, New York, Trinidad, Singapore or Australia, there was no way it could possibly carry enough fuel for the whole voyage, so it had to stop somewhere to take on more fuel. That's when a ship would call at one of our depots to get fuel.
Errol: Like a petrol station for cars on land?
15 **Grandpa:** Yes, that's right but one thing puzzled me for a long time …
Errol: What was it?
Grandpa: I was just trying to tell you! Every week I had to go to our bank, cash a cheque for £300 (which was a year's pay for an adult in those days) and bring back nice new banknotes. Then the chief clerk packed them in a registered and insured
20 envelope and I had to take them to the Post Office.
Errol: Weren't you worried about being robbed on the way?
Grandpa: No. There was very little crime where I worked. Anyway, I could take care of myself with any two robbers, so I wasn't bothered. Then one day I asked the chief clerk why we were always sending cash overseas.

English Alive!

25 **Errol:** Yeah. I was just going to ask you about that. What did he say?
Grandpa: Not much. He told me to take out one of the files and read the letters in it. When I had a chance, I took out this file and, I tell you, that really opened my eyes. When a ship called at some of our depots, the depot manager had to give the Chief Engineer or the Captain or both of them a £10 note.

30 **Errol:** What for? Was it a bribe? Coo!
Grandpa: Yes, you're right. If we didn't bribe the right man on a ship, the vessel would slow down deliberately and arrive a day or two late at its destination. The Chief Engineer would send in a long report, claiming that the coal was poor quality and it created a lot of ashes. He would say that it contained a lot of stone and other
35 material that would not burn. Then he would claim that the ashes and stones clogged the furnaces and reduced the heat for the boilers. As a result, so he claimed, the ship slowed down and arrived late. Then the shipowner sent us a nasty claim for demurrage and additional expenses.

Errol: 'Demurrage'? What's that? I've never heard of that word before.
40 **Grandpa:** It's like a fine. If a ship arrives late at a port, it may miss cargo and have all sorts of problems. Then the shipowner is going to sue whoever caused the ship to be late. The charge for a single day's delay was hundreds of pounds, so we simply had to bribe the ship's officers at some depots. It was dirty work but we had no choice.

45 **Errol:** Did that happen at all your depots?
Grandpa: No, only at a few, mainly in the Far East. We supplied the same quality coal to perhaps a dozen depots but only three or four of them required weekly parcels of cash. Mind you, I suspect that we got our money back by increasing the price of fuel supplied at places where we had to pay bribes. Anyway, that was my
50 introduction to how the wheels of industry are sometimes greased. We've got to stop now. It's time for lunch. One day, I'll tell you a few more 'business' secrets.

Unit 20 · English in Business (1)

20.3 Understanding

Choose the best answer for each of the following.

1. It seems ____ that Errol's grandfather was born in the Caribbean region.
   A. likely
   B. very likely
   C. unlikely
   D. very unlikely

2. In line 4, 'odds and ends' is similar in meaning to ____.
   A. strange tasks
   B. unwanted tasks
   C. peculiar activities
   D. minor jobs

3. In line 7, 'depots' is particularly suitable because ____.
   A. things were stored at the places
   B. they were overseas
   C. they were in foreign countries
   D. only ships used them

4. Fuelling depots were essential to ____.
   A. ships relying on their sails
   B. provide work for coal-miners
   C. vessels making a long voyage
   D. enable passengers to board ships

5. In line 19, presumably the envelope was insured ____.
   A. against loss and theft
   B. because it was registered
   C. in case Grandpa died or had an accident
   D. to protect the cheques inside it

6. The expression 'really opened my eyes' (lines 27–28) implies that Grandpa ____.
   A. nearly fell asleep at the time
   B. strongly disapproved of something
   C. had poor eyesight when he was young
   D. had quite a surprise

7. By slowing down his ship a Chief Engineer intended to punish ____.
   A. the captain and crew
   B. the owners of the ship
   C. the supplier of fuel
   D. agents at the next port of call

8. It appears from Grandpa's account that the 'quality' of coal supplied to some ships depended on ____.
   A. where it had come from
   B. the amount required
   C. whether or not a bribe had been paid
   D. how long it had been stored at a depot

9. In line 50, 'greased' is used with a ____ meaning.
   A. derogatory
   B. technical
   C. clinical
   D. complimentary

10. What was Grandpa's role in the bribery of ship's officers overseas?
    A. He originated the scheme.
    B. He was simply a messenger.
    C. He played no part in it at all.
    D. He attempted to stop it or wipe it out.

20.4 Vocabulary: meaning in context

Choose the word(s) which best show(s) the meaning of the underlined words as they are used in 20.1 and 20.2.

1. Grandpa Blake has returned to Barbados to <u>retire</u>. (20.1, line 2)
   A. live
   B. stop working
   C. live and die
   D. find a different job

2. I was just a <u>junior</u> clerk or an office boy (20.2, line 3)
   A. of lower rank
   B. poorly paid
   C. temporary
   D. ignorant

3. I used to do <u>filing</u> (lines 3–4)
   A. sharpening tools
   B. making things smooth
   C. putting papers away in the right place
   D. sending attachments to an email

4. I used to do filing, <u>outgoing</u> mail and all sorts of odds and ends (lines 3–4)
   A. positive and cheerful
   B. departing
   C. advertising and persuasive
   D. arriving

5. We had <u>maybe</u> twenty depots overseas. (line 7)
   A. roughly
   B. perhaps
   C. approximately
   D. at least

6. Then we <u>chartered</u> ships and sent coal out (line 8)
   A. hired
   B. bought
   C. built
   D. obtained

7. so I wasn't <u>bothered</u> (line 23)
   A. accosted
   B. scared
   C. concerned
   D. mugged

8. ashes and stones <u>clogged</u> the furnaces (line 36)
   A. extinguished
   B. opened widely
   C. smothered
   D. choked

9. the shipowner is going to <u>sue</u> whoever caused the ship to be late (line 41)
   A. find out
   B. blame
   C. take legal action against
   D. complain strongly to

10. how the wheels of industry are sometimes <u>greased</u> (line 50)
    A. prevented from functioning well
    B. made to work smoothly
    C. slowed down by something
    D. impeded by corruption

20.5
Vocabulary: business expressions (1)

1. Explain what each of these is or does.
   a) a pay-roll, piece work, a bonus, commission, wages, salary
   b) overhead charges (overheads), depreciation, 'fair wear and tear'
   c) capital, income, net profit, gross profit, dividends
   d) a consumer, a shareholder, an investor, an investment
   e) a Service Department, a Human Resources Department, a Customer Relations Department

2. Find out and discuss in class what happens in each of these cases when:
   a) a company goes into voluntary liquidation
   b) a person is declared bankrupt
   c) a person or an animal is put in quarantine
   d) an embargo is put on the goods of a foreign country
   e) import tariffs are raised or lowered
   f) a unilateral decision is made
   g) a bilateral agreement is signed
   h) a machine is serviced
   i) a guarantee is declared null and void
   j) a cheque is returned with a note on it saying, 'Refer to Drawer'
   k) a person goes to a bank to ask for an overdraft
   l) a firm accepts a contract on a 'cost plus' basis
   m) somebody goes to a bank to get a first or second mortgage on a house
   n) an insurance company notifies a person that the premium on his/her car insurance has been increased
   o) an insurance company asks a person whether he/she is entitled to a 'no claims bonus'

20.6
Vocabulary: business expressions (2)

1. Explain briefly the difference between these words:
   a) a deputy, an assistant
   b) leasehold property, freehold property
   c) a consignor, a consignee
   d) a deposit account, a current account

2. a) What is a trademark?
   b) What is meant by saying that Firm X 'infringed the trademark' of Firm Z?

3. Explain what each of these is or means:
   a) an agenda
   b) the minutes of a meeting
   c) an amendment
   d) a resolution

English Alive!

e) a motion
f) a proposer
g) a seconder
h) unanimously
i) nem con (*nemine contradicente*)
j) to abstain from voting

20.7
Using the internet: email

When you use a computer, remember the saying: 'There are two problems in life. One is how to get money (= food, clothes, a home, etc.). The other is how to keep it.' You will come across many advertisements when you use the internet. Remember that the aim of most advertisers is to get your money. Be on your guard!

Sending an email

If you want to send or receive an email, you need an ISP (internet service provider) such as AOL, Hotmail, etc. Once you have got one, you can follow the procedure set out below. Check to see if this is the procedure that *you* follow:

1. Click on the email icon (little picture or symbol) to open your email software program.

2. Click on 'Work online'.

3. Click on 'Create mail'.

4. In the box marked 'To', insert the email address of your intended receiver.

5. In the box marked 'Cc', insert the email address of anybody to whom you want to send a copy of your email *or* leave this box empty.

6. In the box marked 'Subject', put a simple subject or – to a friend – just put 'Hi!'

7. Type your message – see 20.9 .

8. If you want to attach a file already prepared in MS Word, click on 'Insert' and then on 'File attachment'. Then select and click on the right file. K on 'Attach'.

9. Click on 'Send' or 'Send/Receive'.

10. Click on 'Yes' when you see 'Would you like to go online now?'

11. Enter your user name and password if it doesn't appear automatically. Click on 'Connect' and wait.

12. Once you are online and connected to your ISP, your email will be sent. If you are worried that perhaps the email did not go through, click on 'Sent items' to check or confirm that it has disappeared from your 'Outbox'.

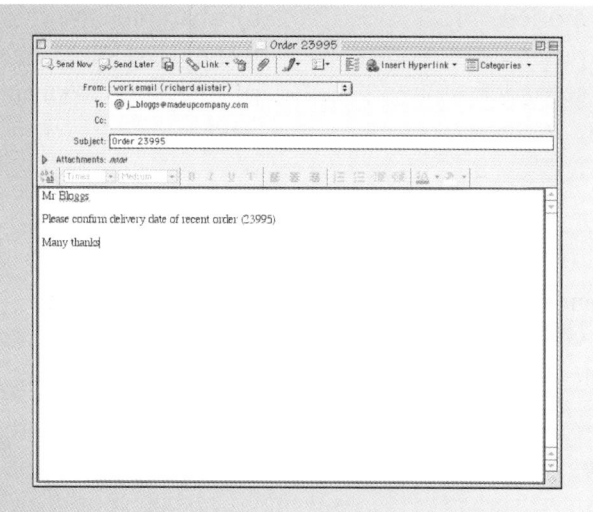

Receiving an email

1. Open your email software program using the email icon and connect to your ISP.

2. The computer may automatically download incoming email or you may need to click on 'Send/Receive'.

3. Use your mouse to highlight any email you want to read.

4. Use the 'return' key to make an email fully visible.

5. Click on the 'Print' icon if you want to print an incoming email.

6. Disconnect unless you want to reply to the email immediately.

20.8
Writing: making a summary

Read the conversation in 20.2 again. Then in not more than 100 words make a summary of how Grandpa Blake found out about bribery in the company for which he was working. Summarise how and why the bribery was carried out.

20.9
Using the internet: writing an email to a friend

Starting

You can start in any way you like. These are common methods:
Dear (name), e.g. Dear Francine,
Hi!
Hello!

Body of your email

This depends on you. In many cases, the email will contain information about yourself and family, and information about anybody or anything in which your receiver is interested.

Ending

You can end in any way you like. These are possible endings:
> I've got to go now but I'll write again later.
> Please do write when you get a chance.

20.10
Using the internet to obtain information

'One of the aims of the CSEC English syllabus is to develop knowledge of various sources of information. In modern times, your computer is by far the best source of information. If you connect to the internet and go to **Google**, you can find out almost everything you need to know. For example, there are over 30,000 entries for *Lorna Goodison*; over 89,000 for the *Barbados Crop Over Festival*; over 12 million for *Creole*; over 89 million for *Guyana*; over 108 million for *Trinidad*, and over 497 million for *English Language*.'

20.11
Writing business letters: basic points

Check that you are familiar with these basic points about business letters:

- Keep a copy of any letter or report you write.

- If necessary, put 'Miss', 'Mrs', 'Ms' or 'Mr' in brackets after your name, especially if people cannot easily tell whether you are a male or female by looking at your name. Write your full name at the end of a letter – not just your initials.

- Make your letter as short and clear as possible. Do not give unnecessary details.

- Remember that your letter can become a legal document. Don't make accusations, offers, orders or remarks unless you are prepared to see them used in a law court.

- If you write to a company about different topics, consider writing two separate letters. Then each letter will go to the right department. For example, you may need to write to a company which sells computers. You want to (a) get somebody to repair your computer, and (b) obtain details of the latest model. The first letter will be dealt with by the Service Department; the second letter will be answered by the Sales or Marketing Department.

- If you put two topics in one letter, one of your points may be overlooked.

- Companies rely very much on reference numbers. If you have an account, membership or reference number, put it in the heading of your letter or somewhere where it is very clear.

- Give a heading to your business letter. You can use numbered paragraphs and subheadings if they are helpful.

20.12
Writing business letters: layout

A letter to a business company may look like this:

```
                                          26 Fifth Avenue
                                          Aranguez
                                          Trinidad
Tel: 234-5678

                                          1 April 2008
The Manager
Better Builders Ltd
240 Brick Road
Port of Spain
Trinidad

Dear Sir

Alterations to 26 Fifth Avenue

I confirm our telephone conversation with you this morning and
would be grateful if you would give me a quotation for the
following alterations to this house:

1. Build an extension consisting of two rooms and a bathroom.
2. Supply and install two 1-HP air-conditioners.
3. Supply and install bath, shower, etc. for the new bathroom.
I suggest that you phone me to arrange for a suitable time when
you can send somebody to meet me here and make a note of the
precise details involved in the work.
Yours sincerely

Kevin Lall

Kevin Lall
```

English Alive!

Notes:

1. Since the letter is within Trinidad, we can omit 'Trinidad' in both addresses.

2. The modern trend is to omit commas in an address. You can put them in if you like.

3. At one time, a letter started some way in from the left margin. Because of the influence of computers, most business letters now start at the left margin. Then the closure and signature are also at the left margin.

4. Americans put the month before the day, e.g. 4.1.2008 or April 1, 2008.

5. Americans put a colon (instead of a comma) after the greeting.

6. Americans put 'Yours' as the second word at the end of a letter, e.g. 'Sincerely yours'.

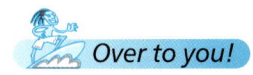

Over to you!

Exercise 1

Imagine that you work for Better Builders. Write a reply to Mr Lall. Do these things:

a) Thank him for his letter.

b) Say that, as arranged with him, Mr Jagjit Singh will be visiting him on 10 April to collect all the necessary information.

c) You will send Mr Lall a quotation shortly after Mr Singh has obtained all the necessary information.

d) Thank him for the opportunity to quote for the work.

20.13
Writing business letters: ordering goods

Some or all of this information may be necessary:

- a description of the goods
- a catalogue number, if known
- the number (quantity) ordered
- the delivery date and method (for business companies)
- the cost and method of payment.

A description may be difficult. For example, if you order a book, you will have to give the title, the author's name, the name of the publisher and (if you know it) the ISBN number. You will also have to say whether you want a hard-cover edition (more expensive) or a paperback. If you are writing to an overseas supplier, you will have to make arrangements for paying, perhaps by credit card. An overseas supplier will not normally send goods unless he receives the money first.

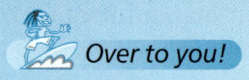

Over to you!

Exercise 2

Answer *one* of these questions.

1. Write a letter to an overseas company. Order spare parts for something made by the company but not available locally. Give details of the parts you need. Explain how you will pay for the goods before they are sent to you.

or

2. A relative is opening a new (but small) restaurant. You are helping him/her. On behalf of your relative, write to a local furniture company and order 12 tables and 60 chairs. If you like, the letter can be written confirmation of a verbal order you gave at the furniture factory when you visited it.

20.14

Writing business letters: asking for further information

You saw this advertisement in a newspaper:

WANTED

Intelligent students (male and female) to act as guides/tutors for parties of visiting overseas students during the holidays.

Duties include travelling within the country, explaining local places and events, helping with shopping, etc. Some knowledge of the local music scene would be an advantage but is not essential. Full time or part-time work available.

Send SAE for details to Box 844, The Daily Chronicle.

English Alive!

You could write:

```
                                                    [your address]
[your telephone number]

                                                    [the date]

Box 844
The Daily Chronicle
Dear Sir or Madam

Part-time Guides

I refer to your advertisement in "The Daily Chronicle" of 17
June and would be grateful if you would please send me details
of the above vacancy.

I enclose a stamped, addressed envelope.

Yours sincerely
(your signature)
(your printed name) (Miss)
```

What did SAE mean in the advertisement? What type of envelope would you send? What would you write on the envelope?

Useful expressions:

> Please send me …
> I should be grateful if you would send me details of …
> Would you please send me information about … ?

Imagine that the advertiser sent you details of the above part-time job and invited you to register your name as somebody available 'on call' for work of the type mentioned in the advertisement. The registration fee is the local equivalent of US $20. Would you register with the advertiser? If you cannot make up your mind, see the first paragraph of section 20.7.

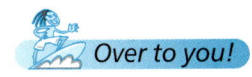

Over to you!

Exercise 3

Answer *one* of these questions.

1. At school you are doing a project on something which is controlled by a government department or government body. Write and try to obtain information about it. Explain what you want and why you want it.

or

2. You saw the following advertisement in a magazine.

THE CHEAPEST AIR FARES AVAILABLE

Join our travel club and you automatically become eligible for the lowest discount fares available in the Caribbean. Convenient travel times on scheduled or charter flights. Lowest prices on rental cars at your destination.

Exclusive discount rates at hotels within the Caribbean, in North America and in Europe.

You can't afford to miss this GREAT DEAL.

For full details and an application form, write **Box 784, Air Travel**.

You know that a relative often has to travel to foreign countries, so you decide to send for details of this travel club in case they are of interest to him or her. Write the necessary letter. Make up the address of the magazine.

20.15
Writing business letters: making an enquiry

When you make an enquiry, explain exactly what you want to find out. These examples show possible enquiries:

```
Can you please tell me whether you are still the agents for
FLYCRAFT model aeroplanes? If you are, do you stock spare parts
XC3 and KJ14 for the SPECTRA HELICOPTER? I would be very
grateful if you could send me a list of spare parts available
for FLYCRAFT models or let me know where I can obtain them.
```

```
In a week's time, members of my family are going on a tour of
Europe, which will include a visit to the island of Cos, in
Greece. Can you please tell me whether it is (a) essential or
(b) desirable for them to be inoculated against typhoid before
they leave? I enquire on their behalf because of the recent
reports of typhoid on the island.
```

What headings would you use for the above letters?

If you want to ask several questions in a business letter, it is better to number them and set them out separately, as in this example:

```
TOURS OF NORTH AMERICA

I refer to your advertisement in "The Daily Chronicle" of 26
July and would be grateful if you could answer the following
questions:

1.   Do the prices include all return air fares?
2.   What meals are included in the prices?
3.   We are thinking of forming a family group of 8 adults and 4
     children aged 12-16. Is there any discount for this group?
4.   Do the prices include airport taxes throughout the tour?
5.   Can you please send me details of the dates when the
     tours leave here?


Thank you for your help.


Yours sincerely


(signed)


(printed name)
```

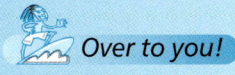

Over to you!

Exercise 4

Write only the body of a letter to obtain the information required below.

You are helping to arrange a visit to Miami by members of a school organisation. Write to the Rooms Division Manager, Lido Hotel, Miami. Ask him/her if he/she can reserve standard accommodation for the group.

Give full details of the number of people, the date of arrival and departure, and ask whether or not transport can be provided at the airport and (at the end of the visit) from the hotel to the airport. Enquire about the cost, based on two people sharing a room. Ask for the cost of a single supplement for anybody who does not share a room.

21 English in Business (2)

21.1
Memos

'Memo' is short for 'memorandum'. The plural forms are 'memos', 'memoranda' and 'memorandums'. A memo is a short note or message used inside a company or another organisation. Here is an example:

```
MEMO


From: Leela, Features Editor          Date: 17 May 200—
To: Earl Dawkins, Intern


Please find out as much as you can about CANASOL. I believe it is
a drug made from ganja (cannabis) and used to treat glaucoma.
Look in the archives and see what you can find out. Then let me
have a report by Friday morning.

Find out who discovered it, when, why and how. What is the
present position?

Keep your report down to about 2 pages maximum. No details,
please.

Leela
```

Memos can be written by hand on printed pads or you can use a computer. Each memo will contain the name of the receiver (and perhaps his/her department), the name of the writer (and perhaps his/her department), the date and an informal message of some kind. Some printed memos have boxes which the sender can tick, e.g.

☐ File.   ☐ For action by you.   ☐ I have replied.
☐ See me.   ☐ For information only.   ☐ Check and pay.
☐ Please check.   ☐ Please note and return.   ☐ Is this yours?
☐ URGENT   ☐ Please deal with this.   ☐ Please explain.

306 *English Alive!*

Over to you!

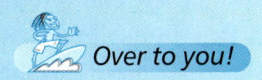

Exercise 1

Write a short memo for each of the following:

1. You work in the vehicle department of a large insurance company. A clerk brought you several files. Between the files you found a letter enquiring about the insurance of a shop against fire. The letter is a recent one and has not apparently been answered. You want to send it to a colleague in the Fire Department of your company. Explain where you found the letter.

2. The Managing Director of your company is returning by air from a business trip to North America. A secretary has just told you that the MD will arrive at the airport at 1430 local time tomorrow. The secretary wants you (or somebody else) to meet the MD with a car at the airport. You know that a colleague usually does this type of job, but you are not sure whether he/she will go or you should go. The computers in the office are down, and your colleague is not answering his/her phone. Send your colleague a suitable memo.

3. You work in the Accounts Department of a large company. You are checking recent accounts and have come across a request from a colleague for payment of US $128 for 'travelling expenses'. You are not sure what the money was spent on. Write a suitable memo to get the necessary information from your colleague in another department.

21.2

Pre-reading

Look again at the memo in 21.1. Earl used his computer to search the archives of his newspaper. In addition, he made various enquiries about Canasol. Then he wrote the report you can see in 21.3. He sent it with a memo which said:

```
MEMO

To: Leela, Features                          Date: 19 May 200—
From: Earl, Intern

CANASOL

As requested by you in your memo of 17 May, I am now sending a
report on CANASOL. I have a lot of additional details. Please
let me know if I can be of further help.


Earl
```

Earl suspected that Leela wanted the report on Canasol so that she could write an article about it. However, he did not try to write a news article himself because he thought Leela might resent this. He was asked to write a factual report, so that is what he set out to do. You can read the result in 21.3.

21.3 Reading

Canasol

What?

Canasol is a drug made from ganja (cannabis) in Jamaica and is used very successfully to treat glaucoma, a disease which adversely affects the eyes. Without proper treatment, glaucoma
5 causes blurred vision, destroys the retina and eventually causes blindness. Canasol has many qualities to recommend it. It acts much more swiftly than other forms of treatment; it is easy to use and it has no unpleasant side-effects. Consequently, it is markedly superior to other forms of
10 medication for glaucoma.

Why?

Glaucoma can affect black people comparatively early in life, and it causes major deterioration of the eyesight faster among black people than amongst other people. Out of the 3 million
15 people in Jamaica, about 100,000 are affected by glaucoma, and there are hundreds of thousands of cases in the USA, Europe, Africa and Asia.
   Cannabis is readily available in Jamaica and medical researchers are keen to produce safe, ganja-based medications
20 to fight glaucoma, asthma, arthritis and other serious ailments. With the cooperation of the government, high quality ganja is used in experiments intended to produce health-sustaining drugs.

Who?

25 The creators and leading researchers who produced Canasol were Professor Manley West and Dr Albert Lockhart. Professor West is an emeritus professor of pharmacology at the University of the West Indies. Dr Lockhart is an eminent consultant ophthalmologist. Both men are highly experienced researchers.

30 **When?**

In the early 1970s, Professor West became aware that Jamaican fishermen regularly used ganja to improve their eyesight before

going out to sea. Dr Lockhart was able to demonstrate that the use of cannabis led to lower pressure in the eyes. The two men
35 devoted much of their time to experiments designed to show the beneficial effects of some of the constituents in cannabis while excluding and rejecting substances which were psychoactive.

In 1983, the Jamaican government approved the new drug and
40 gave it official certification. Since then, thousands of vials of Canasol have been produced and exported. Unfortunately, the drug has not yet been officially approved for use in the USA. The main obstacle is that the USA Food and Drug Administration (FDA) does not recognise tests performed outside the USA. The
45 cost of replicating the tests in the USA runs to millions of US dollars and is beyond the resources of the Jamaican company set up by the two researchers.

Future Prospects
At the moment, about 30,000 vials of Canasol are produced each
50 year but increasing demand will be met by plans for improved production. Meanwhile, the two researchers are working on a number of other ganja-based medications which will help Caribbean people as well as sufferers in other countries. When Canasol was first produced, it was met by scepticism because it
55 had been created by scientists outside the USA and Europe. Not surprisingly, critics feared that it would contain the psychoactive agents which make cannabis a drug banned in many countries. However, now that Professor West and Dr Lockhart have found a way of excluding the psychoactive elements in
60 cannabis, experts believe that a whole range of valuable drugs will be produced from ganja and a growing manufacturing plant will be set up in Jamaica.

21.4
Understanding

A Study each question and give it up to a maximum of 2 marks. Discuss your marks in class and justify or amend them.

1. In her memo to Earl Dawkins, Leela called him an 'intern'. What is an intern?
   A. reporter
   B. He is a reporter.
   C. He is like an apprentice or somebody learning a job.
   D. He is a type of clerk.

2. Leela told Earl to 'look in the archives'. What are archives?
   A. They are a place where copies of past papers (and other documents) are stored.
   B. Big medical book.

Unit 21 · *English in Business (2)* 309

       C. They are magazines from other countries.
       D. A place on a computer where you can find out about things.

3. Why didn't Earl write an article on Canasol?
   A. Leela had ask him to write a report, not an article.
   B. He think Leela migh resent him.
   C. He didn't know how to write a article.
   D. He knew that it was his job to write a report.

4. What did Earl want to do in his first paragraph?
   A. He wanted to explain what Canasol was and how it was useful.
   B. He wanted to explain what glaucoma and Canasol are.
   C. He want to show that glaucoma is a bad disease and that Canasol is the best treatment for it.
   D. Canasol has many qualities to recommend it.

5. What percentage of the people in Jamaica are said to have glaucoma?
   A. Just over 3%.
   B. About 30%.
   C. The percentage of the people in Jamaica have glaucoma is 33%.
   D. In Jamaica, just over 3% of the people are said to have glaucoma.

6. In creating a drug based on cannabis, what elements of cannabis did the researchers want to remove?
   A. psychoactive
   B. They wanted to remove anything which affected the mind.
   C. They wanted to remove constituents.
   D. We cannot tell from Earl's report.

7. What was the attitude of the US FDA to Canasol?
   A. It approved the new drug in 1983.
   B. It promised to approve the drug after tests in the USA.
   C. The attitude of the US DFA to Canasol was unhelpfull.
   D. It declined to approve the drug.

8. Suggest a reason why the FDA does not recognise tests performed outside the USA.
   A. Maybe it does not like foreigners.
   B. A reason why the FDA does not recognise test proformed outside the USA is that the tests are different than the US tests.
   C. Perhaps the US government thinks that foreign tests are not always reliable or adequate.
   D. Maybe the tests in the USA are stricter than tests in other country.

B   Answer these questions:

1. Using only information in Earl's report, suggest *three* reasons why the Jamaican government supported the work of Professor West and Dr Lockhart. Express each reason in a separate sentence.

2. Suggest (a) one reason why somebody suffering from glaucoma in New York might *not* want to use Canasol, and (b) one reason why somebody living in New York might be *glad* to use Canasol.

21.5
Vocabulary: meaning in context

A Choose the word(s) which best show(s) the meaning of the underlined words as they are used in 21.2 and 21.3.

1. he thought Leela might resent this (line 3 above 21.3)
   A. reject
   B. do better than
   C. not want or expect
   D. be annoyed by

2. a disease which adversely affects the eyes (21.3, line 4)
   A. in a harmful way
   B. to some extent
   C. sooner or later
   D. in a painful manner

3. Without proper treatment (line 4)
   A. urgent
   B. correct
   C. careful
   D. immediate

4. glaucoma causes blurred vision (line 5)
   A. indistinct
   B. failing
   C. double
   D. improved

5. Consequently, it is markedly superior to other forms of medication (line 9)
   A. to a significant extent
   B. in some respects only
   C. somewhat
   D. alleged to be

6. Consequently, it is markedly superior to other forms of medication (line 9)
   A. higher than
   B. better than
   C. more expensive
   D. better known

7. it causes major deterioration of the eyesight (line 13)
   A. improvement
   B. alteration
   C. worsening
   D. change

8. Cannabis is readily available in Jamaica (line 18)
   A. rarely
   B. easily
   C. sometimes
   D. from time to time

9. ganja-based medications to fight glaucoma (line 19)
   A. reports by experts
   B. careful experiments
   C. types of drugs or medicines
   D. the effects of ailments

10. to produce health-sustaining drugs (lines 22–23)
    A. influencing
    B. maintaining
    C. improving
    D. affecting

Unit 21 · *English in Business* (2)

B Match the underlined words with the meanings which they have in 21.3.

Words from the passage	Meanings
1. professor of <u>pharmacology</u> (line 27)	a) intended, fashioned
2. an <u>eminent</u> consultant (line 28)	b) substances contained
3. to <u>demonstrate</u> the use of (line 33)	c) too great for
4. <u>designed</u> to show the (line 35)	d) prohibited
5. the <u>beneficial</u> effects (line 36)	e) showing doubt
6. the <u>constituents</u> in cannabis (line 36)	f) affecting the mind
7. <u>excluding</u> and rejecting (line 37)	g) well known as an expert
8. <u>replicating</u> the tests (line 45)	h) good
9. <u>beyond</u> the resources (line 46)	i) the study of drugs
10. met by <u>scepticism</u> (line 54)	j) keeping out
11. the <u>psychoactive</u> agents (line 57)	k) show, prove
12. <u>banned</u> in many countries (line 57)	l) doing again in the same way

21.6
Vocabulary: problem words

Exercise 2

Choose the correct words from the brackets.

1. Milk and cheese are known (as, like) (daily, dairy, diary) products.

2. Francine makes a (diary, daily) entry in her (daily, diary, dairy).

3. Most young people in Barbados are (literate, literal) in at least one language.

4. We must (adapt, adopt) the plan to meet changed circumstances.

5. The proposal finally (adapted, adopted) by the committee is a very sensible one.

6. We can buy envelopes and notepaper at a (stationary, stationery) shop.

7. My cousin used to be a security (guide, guard) but now he is a tourist (guard, guide) and takes groups of visitors to (the, a) number of beauty spots.

312 *English Alive!*

8. In most language examinations, there (is, are) a test of the (comprehensive, comprehension) ability of students.

9. If a car is covered by a (comprehensive, comprehension) (assurance, insurance) policy, the owner will be paid when the car is destroyed by fire.

10. Mr Harris works (hard, hardly) (expect, except) on Sundays.

11. The fire caused (extensive, intensive) (damage, damages) to machinery in the factory.

12. When the fire started, Uncle (preceded, proceeded) to telephone the police as (quick, quickly) as possible.

13. There is an (industrious, industrial) dispute at that factory.

14. Complete this form clearly. If your writing is (illegible, eligible) you will be (ineligible, illegible) to enter the competition.

15. Accountancy is regarded by most people as a (respectable, respectful) occupation (however, whereas) modelling is not always seen as (respectable, respectful) by some people.

21.7
Writing reports

In some jobs, people write more reports than letters. For example, these people have to write reports about the following things:

- **police officers:** traffic accidents, burglaries, domestic troubles, assaults and thefts, hooliganism, robberies and murders
- **store managers:** daily/weekly sales, shoplifting and losses, customers' requests
- **teachers:** students' progress, accidents at school, school clubs.

Depending on the situation, a written report can be in one of these forms:

- a letter, e.g. a testimonial for an employee or a student
- on a special form, e.g. a report on the mechanical condition of a car

- on a separate sheet of paper, e.g. a report on the year's activities of a Drama Club
- on 50–1000 sheets of paper, e.g. a report about setting up a new business in a country; an investigation into the collapse of a bank.

Follow these guidelines:

Guidelines on writing reports

1. All reports should include:
   - a heading or title
   - the date
   - the names of the writer and recipient.

2. The facts or points *must* be arranged systematically, e.g. in one of these ways:
   - in time order (an accident)
   - in place order (a report on AIDS throughout the world)
   - points for and against (a report on a new machine)
   - in order of importance (comparing sites for a proposed factory)
   - showing the cause, events and results (some industrial accidents)
   - or in any other logical order which fits the situation.

3. Points or paragraphs can be numbered for easy reference.

4. Diagrams, graphs or other things can be included in the body of a report or attached as appendices.

5. In some cases (e.g. criminal cases and traffic accidents), it is important to include dialogue and write down exactly what somebody said (instead of using reported speech or a summary).

6. A long report will probably need a list of contents and perhaps an index.

7. The writer *must* understand the difference between facts, opinions and guesses.

8. A long report may need one or both of these:
   - a summary at the start so that a reader can quickly see what the report is about
   - a final section giving conclusions or recommendations to improve something in future.

Here is an example of a report:

To: Mrs Dionne Edwards, Chief Examiner (English Language)
From: Mr Jagjit Singh, Assistant Examiner
Date: 8 June 200—

Composition Scripts

As requested by you, I have carefully examined the composition scripts of candidates 67005, 67486, 68531 and 68993. I give my views below.

1. All four candidates chose to write about topic 2(b), i.e. an original story involving a stray dog.
   a) All four compositions have exactly the same opening paragraph.
   b) With a few minor differences, 90% of the four compositions are identical. Sentences which are omitted in one script usually occur in two or three of the others.
   c) All four compositions are 420—430 words long and finish in exactly the same way.

2. It is clear that the four candidates have used a <u>memorised</u> model answer of some kind. This infringes the examination regulations since:

   a) candidates know that they are examined on what they themselves can do, and

   b) the question clearly asked for 'an original short story' but the answers of these candidates are NOT original.

3. I therefore have no alternative other than to recommend that all four candidates be disqualified for a breach of the regulations.

(signed)

Jagjit Singh

Here is an example of a report on a form. It is a report on the facilities of a hotel. It was made by a company which publishes travel books for tourists overseas.

Name of hotel: HAPPY TOURISTS HOTEL		**Date:** 1 April 200–
Address: Sea View Road, Trinibago		

Use the following grades:
A — outstanding   C — reasonable   E — below average; unacceptable
B — very good   D — fair to mediocre   F — unsatisfactory

AREA	GRADES	COMMENTS
Rooms for guests	B	Luxurious and clean; TV, phone, fridge, air-con
Food	A	A wide variety of local and US food; excellent quality and quantity
Public rooms	C	Rather cramped but adequate and clean
Reception	D/E	Insufficient staff; long wait at times; this will annoy some guests; inadequate reservations system
Prices	E	Too high compared with other hotels at a time when there is a surplus of good hotel accommodation
Facilities	C	Nothing special: tours, hire cars; left luggage; computer room, fax machine.
Staff:		
Friendliness	B	No complaints
Appearance	B	Always a high standard
Promptness	C	Room service fair only; slow at times
Experience	B	–

GENERAL COMMENTS
On the whole, the facilities are between reasonable and first class but the prices are 20% to 30% higher than those in similar hotels in the vicinity. Recommended for travellers if cost is not a problem. Budget-conscious travellers should look elsewhere.

Reporters: Abiose Johnson and Don Clarke

Over to you!

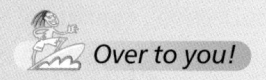

Exercise 3

Design a form which can be used to give a report on *one* of these occasions. Notice that you are *not* asked to complete the report. This is a test to see if you can work out what headings are needed.

1. You work for a company which buys and sells used vehicles. Design a form which can be used by employees to record the condition of a car which somebody wants to sell to the company. Include a simple grading system and list the main parts or areas to be inspected and reported on.

or

2. You work in the Personnel (Human Resources) Department of a very large company which owns many shops. Design a form which the manager or manageress of each shop can use to make a simple annual report about each member of staff.

Exercise 4

You are a monitor or prefect at your school. You witnessed an accident. These are the notes you made:

```
students going downstairs after school
student at top slipped and fell forward
other students knocked down
Paul Morris fell and fractured left leg
other students — cuts and bruises
nobody's fault — an accident
```

You have been asked to write a report for the Principal of your school, explaining what happened. Write your report on a separate sheet of paper which you can hand in at the school office with a simple covering letter. It is *not* necessary to write the covering letter now.

Exercise 5

Write a report to the Principal of your school on practical improvements which could be made to *one* of the following:

a) safety in science laboratories

b) the school canteen

c) the school library

d) sports training and activities

e) activities to help people in the nearby community.

21.8

Punctuation practice

Exercise 6

Put in apostrophes when necessary. In some cases, no apostrophe is needed.

1. Miss Smiths dog likes to chase cats but it is scared of Mr Kissoons children.

2. One should always try to keep ones word and remember that it is bad to break promises.

3. I'll be back in a few minutes time. I'm just going to my friends house to return some books which she lent me a couple of days ago.

4. Sometimes a writer deliberately leaves a lot to the readers imagination and expects him or her to work out what happens next.

5. These new schemes should increase the prosperity of both farmers and workers in our cities.

6. That is not Uncles car. It must be somebody elses.

7. After half an hours delay, all the passengers boarded the plane and it left for Trinidad.

8. The price of vegetables usually rises after a storm because there is a temporary shortage. A similar situation applies to fish and marine products.

9. When Mrs Menon took her baby to the clinic, two nurses recorded the babys weight and checked its health.

English Alive!

10. The suns rays are stronger in the tropics than they are in temperate regions.

11. The profits of the company have increased in the past year, so each worker will receive a bonus of a months salary. It will be paid in three months time.

12. Is that Miss Chans car or her neighbours?

Exercise 7

Punctuate the following sentences correctly. Notice that some of them may be correct already, so no changes will be required.

1. We stopped to watch some men. Repairing a burst water pipe not far from our school.

2. Those men make many souvenirs for tourists. For example dolls, statues, small boats etc.

3. The price was too high, therefore Miss Walker decided not to buy the car, it was several years old already.

4. We must buy enough food this afternoon, then we won't have to try to get some tomorrow. When the hurricane is getting nearer.

5. The bus service is being improved. Thus enabling people to travel more easily.

6. I haven't seen your sister for months, how is she now.

7. Oh, she's fine, she's got a job in an insurance company in town.

8. It's no good trying to follow fashion blindly, fashions are always changing, then the designers and businessmen make money.

9. The woman asked me how far it is from Trinidad to Tobago? I told her it is about 21 miles.

10. She wanted to know how long it would take to sail to Tobago? We told her that depended on the type of boat she used. And of course on the weather at the time.

21.9

Enjoying poetry

The Despairing Lover

    Distracted with care
    For <u>Phyllis the fair</u>,   a girl
    Since nothing could <u>move</u> her   make her change her mind
    <u>Poor Damon</u>, her lover,   a male
5 Resolves in despair
    No longer to languish
    Nor bear so much anguish;
    But, mad with his love,
    To a precipice goes,
10 Where a leap from above
    Would soon finish his woes.
    When in rage he came there,
    Beholding how steep
    The sides did appear,
15 And the bottom how deep;
    His torments projecting,
    And sadly reflecting,
    That a lover <u>forsaken</u>   abandoned, rejected
    A new love may get,
20 But a neck when once broken
    Can never be set;
    And, that he could die
    Whenever he would,
    But that he could live
25 For as long as he could:
    How grievous whatever
    The torment might grow,
    He scorned to endeavour
    To finish it so.
30 But bold, unconcerned
    At thoughts of the pain,
    He calmly returned
    To his cottage again.
              William Walsh

Questions

1. What is the tone of this poem?

2. Give a synonym for 'distracted' in line 1.

3. What caused the anguish in line 7?

4. Give a synonym for 'precipice' in line 9.

5. Why did Damon go to a precipice?

6. What made him change his mind?

7. To what does 'it' refer in line 29? ('To finish it so')

8. What can we conclude about Damon's love for Phyllis?

9. What moral does this poem contain for males and females aged 12–32?

10. What did Phyllis say when she heard about Damon? We could perhaps add a few lines to the poem:
    Well, one thing I can say
    (And tell him you may)
    When faced with the choice   *or*   If losing a wife
    Of an end to his voice   Is the end of his life,
    His love lasts
    Hardly a day.

Can you think of what Phyllis perhaps said when she heard about Damon's visit to the precipice?

21.10
Writing

Either: Write 400–450 words on topic (1), (2) or (3) in about 45 minutes.
or: Write 250–300 words on topic (4) in about 30 minutes.

1. Write a short story in which a computer plays a significant role.

2. Describe your ideal home. Deal with its location, its garden or yard, and the house itself.

3. Write a story about what happened when a small group of students found a sealed packet and realised that it contained copies of the CSEC Maths paper which they were expecting to take the next day.

4. What is your ambition and how do you hope to achieve it?

22 History?

22.1
Pre-reading

To the leaders of al-Qaeda, the men who flew planes into the World Trade Center in New York in 2001 were brave martyrs who sacrificed themselves for a holy cause. To the USA and many other countries, they were terrorists who showed no mercy to innocent women and children.

There are always two sides to any historical event. The British had one opinion of Paul Bogle – they hanged him. Modern Jamaicans have a very different opinion of him – they regard him as a national hero.

Read and compare the two different accounts of the same event in 22.2.

22.2
Reading
Mutiny or patriotic uprising?

Passage A

The Indian Mutiny started in 1857 and lasted only eighteen months. Indian soldiers shot their European officers, refused to obey lawful orders and restored the old and discredited Moghul Emperor Bahadur Shah II. The mutiny started as a result of a simple mistake. In order to fire a new type of rifle, soldiers first had to bite through
5   the paper cartridge. Through a misunderstanding on the part of the suppliers, the cartridges had been smeared with a grease containing a slight amount of animal fat. This deeply offended a number of Indian soldiers. The cow is sacred to Hindus, while the pig is unclean and offensive to Muslims.

European officers, unaware of the source of the fat, at first denied that it was
10 derived from animals. Later, vegetable fats were used but the change was too late to stop the mutiny. The rebels soon captured Delhi, slaughtering British women and children. These and other cruel atrocities angered the British troops, who fought back bravely. Delhi was recaptured after bitter fighting. Bahadur Shah was captured but his life was spared to show the mercy of the British. Reinforcements were sent
15 from Britain and, with the aid of loyal forces, the rebellion was quickly put down.

As a result of this incident, the system of administration in India was improved and greater promotion opportunities were created for Indian soldiers.

Passage B

The first great Indian Patriotic Uprising occurred in 1857. The British imperialists had for years attempted to destroy the traditions, culture and religions of India, and
20 to replace them with a language and society alien to patriots. The underlying cause of the uprising was the opposition of an enslaved people to their colonial exploiters. This hatred reached bursting point when British officers deliberately ordered Indian troops to lick animal fats. Nothing could restrain the justified anger of the troops.
25   For many months, loyal troops defeated the British on all fronts, despite a frantic call by the British for reinforcements. The imperialist troops fought with desperate savagery, adding further to their crimes against our great country. When at last they managed to recapture Delhi, three unarmed descendants of Bahadur Shah were shot in cold blood. Regardless of sex or age, no Indian was spared as the British
30 marched arrogantly across the country, seeking revenge for their humiliation. Eventually the loyal forces were betrayed by ambitious traitors, and the uprising was put down in 1858.
    Although the gallant patriotic movement did not succeed, it forced the British to pay far more attention to the rightful claims of our people.

22.3 Understanding

A Choose the best answer each time.

1. Compared with the second passage, Passage A is ____.
   A. more pro-Indian
   B. more personal
   C. less emotional
   D. less restrained

2. The major way in which the second passage differs from the first is ____.
   A. by describing the British forces as imperialists
   B. in its use of a greater number of emotional adjectives and adverbs
   C. by its failure to show the real causes of the event
   D. by viewing the event from an Indian point of view

3. What effect is achieved in the first passage by saying that the event 'lasted only eighteen months' and by referring to it as an 'incident'?
   A. These seek to show that it was the Indians who were in the wrong.
   B. They make the British position seem stronger than it really was.
   C. They seek to reduce the importance of the event.
   D. They remind us that other things were happening in India at this time.

4. Which of these expressions in Passage A shows some concern for the Indian point of view?
   A. lawful orders (line 2)
   B. deeply offended (line 7)
   C. bitter fighting (line 13)
   D. his life was spared (line 14)

5. Why do both accounts mention animal fats?
   A. They were probably written by the same person.
   B. These were the immediate cause of the trouble.
   C. Both sides wanted to blame the makers of the rifles.
   D. Both parties were looking for an excuse to start a war.

6. In the sentence (lines 12–13) 'These and other cruel atrocities angered the British troops, who fought back bravely' which word can be omitted without altering the meaning of the sentence?
   A. cruel
   B. other
   C. fought
   D. bravely

7. In their references to Bahadur Shah, both passages ____.
   A. show their appreciation of the old emperor
   B. contain untrue information intended to deceive readers
   C. reveal an understanding of European history and its effect on Indians
   D. use the event for propaganda purposes

8. In line 15, loyal forces are mentioned. These men are referred to as ____ in the second passage.
   A. imperialists
   B. aliens
   C. patriots
   D. traitors

9. In the expression (lines 2-3), 'they restored the old and discredited Moghul Emperor Bahadur Shah II', 'restored' means ____.
   A. put back
   B. improved
   C. renovated
   D. got rid of

10. Two animals are mentioned in these passages. From the references, we can conclude that ____.
    A. neither Hindus nor Muslims like to drink milk
    B. both Hindus and Muslims are vegetarians
    C. Hindus will not kill cattle and Muslims will not eat pork
    D. neither Hindus nor Muslims will eat beef

11. '(The fat) was derived from animals' (line 10). Here, 'derived' means ____.
    A. stolen
    B. borrowed
    C. obtained
    D. kept away

12. The likely purpose of using the expression 'Through a misunderstanding on the part of the suppliers' (line 5) was to ____.
    A. show the type of confusion which can arise during a war
    B. reduce the responsibility of the British government for the cause of the conflict
    C. emphasise that it was the Indians who were responsible for starting the conflict
    D. stress the incompetence of arms manufacturers

B Answer these questions about the two passages.

1. In Passage A, what does the writer seek to achieve by using the following words and expressions?

a) discredited (line 3)
   b) 'a simple mistake' (line 4)

2. In Passage B, what does the writer seek to achieve by using the following words and expressions?
   a) deliberately ordered (lines 22–3)
   b) frantic (line 25)

3. Suggest a reason why 'greater promotion opportunities were created for Indian soldiers' (line 17).

22.4
Vocabulary: meaning in context

A Choose the word(s) which best show(s) the meaning of the underlined words as they are used in 22.1 and 22.2.

1. were brave <u>martyrs</u> who sacrificed themselves (22.1, line 2)
   A. people who take unnecessary risks
   B. people who lose their lives unnecessarily by mistake
   C. victims of religious persecution
   D. people who voluntarily die for religious or other beliefs

2. they <u>regard</u> him as a national hero (22.1, line 7)
   A. esteem
   B. view
   C. venerate
   D. remember

3. The Indian <u>Mutiny</u> started in 1857 (22.2, line 1)
   A. refusal to obey the orders of those in authority
   B. defence of cherished religious or cultural ideals
   C. patriotic uprising against illegal occupying forces
   D. struggle for freedom from imperialists

4. bite through the paper <u>cartridge</u> (line 5)
   A. bullet made of lead or iron
   B. shell used in large guns in battle
   C. case holding an explosive charge
   D. wrapping round a new rifle

5. the cartridges had been <u>smeared with</u> a grease (line 6)
   A. lightly covered with a thin film of
   B. covered with a thick layer of
   C. manufactured by using
   D. protected against heavy rain by

6. The cow is <u>sacred</u> to Hindus (line 7)
   A. considered to be of value
   B. important to agriculture
   C. special
   D. holy

7. The cow is sacred to Hindu, <u>while</u> the pig is unclean and offensive to Muslims (line 8)
   A. during
   B. for a period of time
   C. and in addition
   D. although

Unit 22 · History? 325

8. The rebels soon captured Delhi, <u>slaughtering</u> British women and children (line 11)
   A. capturing and killing
   B. killing in a brutal and merciless way
   C. imprisoning under harsh conditions
   D. but not deliberately harming

9. These and other cruel <u>atrocities</u> angered the British troops (line 12)
   A. wounds caused during fighting
   B. insults and offences
   C. racially-motivated injuries
   D. cruel or wicked deeds

10. Delhi was recaptured after <u>bitter</u> fighting (line 13)
    A. lasting a long time
    B. involving the use of bad language
    C. determined and hotly contested
    D. in which no prisoners were taken

B Match the words from the passages with the meanings which they have in them.

Words from the passages	Meanings
1. <u>Reinforcements</u> were sent (line 14)	a) way of life
2. the aid of <u>loyal</u> forces (line 15)	b) with excessive pride and boasting
3. greater <u>promotion</u> opportunities (line 17)	c) foreign, distasteful, strange
4. <u>occurred</u> in 1857 (line 18)	d) warranted, deserved
5. <u>culture</u> … of India (line 19)	e) fundamental, basic
6. society <u>alien</u> to patriots (line 20)	f) advancement to a higher post
7. The <u>underlying</u> cause (line 20)	g) without pity or mercy
8. Nothing could <u>restrain</u> (line 23)	h) loss of pride and self-respect
9. the <u>justified</u> anger of the troops (line 23)	i) additional soldiers
10. were shot <u>in cold blood</u> (line 29)	j) took place
11. marched <u>arrogantly</u> (line 30)	k) hold back
12. revenge for their <u>humiliation</u> (line 30)	l) faithful (to their employers)

22.5
Vocabulary: what's the difference?

'Broad' and 'deep' are similar in that they are both measurements. They are different because 'broad' refers to distance measured horizontally, whereas 'deep' refers to vertical (downwards) measurement. So what is the difference between 'deep' and 'tall'?

Over to you!

Explain how these words are (a) similar and (b) different in meaning.
1. a house and a hotel
2. annoyed and furious
3. an acquaintance and a friend
4. shivering and trembling
5. greedy and hungry
6. a stream and a river
7. a stranger and a foreigner
8. uncommon and abnormal
9. a magistrate and a judge
10. murder and manslaughter

English Alive!

22.6 Vocabulary: definitions

Do not take these definitions too seriously:
>   *history:* a record of events which should never have happened
>   *crook:* a business rival who has just left the room
>   *oratory:* the art of making a loud noise seem like a deep thought
>   *forger:* a man who makes a name for himself
>   *consult:* to seek another person's advice on a course of action already decided upon

Exercise 1

1. Give serious definitions of any *three* of the following. You can consult a dictionary but do not copy from one.
    a) surgery
    b) a dentist
    c) modern
    d) democracy
    e) fashion
    f) a hypocrite
    g) a tourist
    h) beautiful

2. Give humorous definitions of any *three* of these:
    a) a tailor
    b) a newspaper
    c) a telephone
    d) dance-hall
    e) carnival
    f) a computer
    g) cricket
    h) rugby

Unit 22 · History?

22.7 Grammar: future actions (revision)

Check that you know these ways of expressing future actions. In each case, make up *two* more examples:

- The **Simple Future** tense is used for both planned and unplanned future actions, e.g.
  What time **will** Karen **arrive** from Miami?
  Which team **will win** on Saturday?

- The **Simple Present** tense is often used for regular schedules, e.g.
  The plane to London **leaves** in two hours' time.
  We'd better hurry. Uncle's plane **arrives** in less than an hour and it may be early.

- The **Present Continuous** tense is sometimes used for planned future movements and actions which show an intention, e.g.
  We**'re having** a party next Saturday. Would you like to come?
  I**'m meeting** Leela for lunch later on. I'll ask her about the wedding when I see her.

- We can use 'going to' to show an intention or that something is likely to happen, e.g.
  Father says he is **going to** buy a new car next month.
  Look at all those dark clouds. I'm sure it's **going to** rain any minute.

- We can also use 'about to' to show that something will happen very soon, e.g.
  Hurry up! The news is **about to** start on TV.
  Don't go near that wall. It looks as if it's **about to** fall down.

- We can use a **passive infinitive** ('to be' + a past participle) to give an order about the future or to refer to a planned future event, e.g.
  Now make sure that there are no mistakes. The tourists are **to be met** at the airport. They are **to be taken** to their hotel by coach. Each person is **to be given** a copy of the programme for the coming week.
  This letter is **to be delivered** to Miss Collymore by ten o'clock tomorrow morning without fail.

- The **Present Perfect** tense can be used to refer to the future after such words as 'when', 'before' and 'until', e.g.
  Don't forget to put all your books away when you **have finished** your homework. Don't leave them spread out all over the table.
  You can't go out until you **have done** your homework.

- The **Future Perfect** tense is used to express a completed action at the time of speaking or at some future time:

Active:	will/shall have finished
Passive:	will/shall have been repaired
Continuous:	will/shall have been waiting

Examples:
> We're late. By the time we get to the party, all the food **will have gone**.
> Yes, you're right. If my brothers are there, all the food **will have been eaten**. That's for sure.
> At the end of next month, my father **will have been working** for the same company for 25 years.

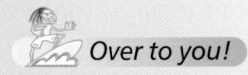

Over to you!

Exercise 2

Answer these questions in complete sentences.

1. What time will you wake up tomorrow morning?
2. What time will you have breakfast tomorrow?
3. When will you leave home tomorrow? Where will you go?
4. If it takes four men a week to put up a fence, how long will it probably take eight men to put up a similar fence?
5. What are you going to do after the CSEC examinations are finished?
6. Do you think the Olympic Games will ever be held in a Caribbean country? What is the reason for your answer?
7. When will you be 21?
8. Where do you think you will be in ten years' time?

Exercise 3

Complete these sentences by putting in a suitable form of the verb in brackets.

1. Uncle's plane left here several hours ago, so he … (reach) Miami by now.
2. Two men escaped from prison during the night but the police say they … (soon catch).
3. We … (go) rafting on the Rio Grande on Saturday. Would you like to come with us?
4. … you … (take) part in the Carnival next week?
5. These spare parts are needed urgently in Guyana. They are … (send) on the first plane tomorrow. Make sure you don't forget to take them to the airport in time.
6. Don't worry about what happens when you arrive at London Airport. Don and Francine … (wait) for you and they … (look) after you.

7. Donna: What's the matter, Leela?
   Leela: I … (lose) my money, so I … (have) to walk home.
   Donna: Don't worry. I … (lend) you whatever you need.

8. Don't be late for the picnic. If you're late, you … (find) that all the food … (eat) before you get there.

9. According to the news, the price of petrol … (increase) next Monday.

10. Hurry up! The 400m relay is about … (start). I hope our team … (do) well because then our school … (win) the shield.

22.8
Public relations work

Many large companies employ a public relations officer (PRO) or a public relations (PR) firm. The task of a PRO is to present the organisation to the public in the best possible light. A PRO is usually an expert in using language to avoid or ignore unpleasant facts and to expand or exaggerate favourable ones. On a busy day, a PRO may have to write or say a number of 'compositions' on behalf of his or her firm.

The aim of this section is not to teach you to become a PRO, but to make you alert and thoughtful so that you do not accept publicity statements unthinkingly. Many famous actors, actresses and pop stars employ a PR firm to handle their relations with the public.

Consider these fictitious examples:

- The famous singer Doodle Burde is found drunk on the floor at a bar. The police are called. Doodle is taken off to hospital. Her secretary or personal assistant (PA) phones her PRO. The PRO thinks quickly and issues a statement to the press:
  'Last night Doodle was quietly celebrating the completion of her new album "All For You" when she slipped in a restaurant and hit her head a glancing blow on a table. Although knocked unconscious by the blow, Doodle is now recovering at Plushmore Hospital and is expected to return home this evening. She will wear a bandana for the next few days until the slight wound has healed. The new album, to be released by Maxima Musica on 1 April, is already heading up the charts and is likely to be Number 1 by the end of the week. …'
  The PRO thinks to himself, 'We must make the most of every publicity opportunity we can get.' There will be no mention of drink or drunkenness.
  Imagine that you were Doodle's PRO. What statement would you make to the press? How would you reply if a reporter said, 'Was Doodle drunk?'

- A building contractor was building a large block of flats when the unfinished building collapsed, injuring several workmen. A PRO is immediately called in to deal with embarrassing questions from the press or public. In reply to a question about the cause of the collapse or a direct question about unsuitable materials or careless work, this type of statement may be issued:
  'The engineer in charge of the project is Mr Kwite Blanke, who holds four degrees in civil engineering, and studied for eight years in the USA, the UK and Australia.

Before commencing work on this site, he had been responsible for building 720 housing units to a value of US $600 million. He was also responsible for the new industrial complex at Newtown, sewage disposal schemes in Belize and Tasmania, and other large projects of international standard.'

You will notice that the PRO has seized on one point on which he knows he cannot be attacked – the qualifications of the engineer. He has said nothing about the causes of the collapse. If he knew that copper pipes had been used for the internal plumbing, he could have added a paragraph about the high quality of the pipes – and have ignored the key issues.

If you had been the PRO employed by the building company, what points would you have made or stressed in your press release?

- There has been a massive leak of oil into the harbour, with oil slicks polluting the beaches, killing fish and birds, stopping fishing, and causing a great deal of damage. The leak has been traced to a particular ship. On behalf of the owners of the ship, a PRO may issue a statement of which this is part:

    'Considerable efforts are now being made to deal with the situation. The new fireboat, *Harbour Cleanser*, is releasing anti-pollutants specially flown from Miami and New York during the past 24 hours. The *Harbour Cleanser* was built in Korea two years ago. It is eighty feet long, thirty feet wide and has a maximum speed of 20 knots. Its machinery was installed in Trinidad after extensive tests in Hamburg and London.'

    The PRO can describe in unnecessary detail the type of vessel being used to deal with the oil, the detergent or other material being sprayed on the oil, the men in charge – anything except the oil and the damage it is causing. His aim is to minimise the unpleasant aspects of the leak, and to distract public attention from the problem.

Not all PROs would issue this type of statement, but those who present the whole truth openly will probably not rise far in their profession.

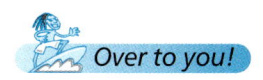

Over to you!

Exercise 4

Study the following situations and then explain, orally, what type of statement you would make if you were a PRO employed by the company concerned. Assume that you have to issue a statement to the press. Do *not* write out your statement.

1. A factory belonging to your firm has been burnt down. Several witnesses have claimed there were insufficient exits. Five workers were killed in the fire, so this is a very serious matter.

2. Your company owns many hotels. At one of them, 15 guests have just been taken to hospital with suspected food poisoning. Fifty other guests have left the hotel hurriedly.

3. Your factory has been caught discharging polluted material into the sea or a river, and has been fined US $10,000 for the offence.

4. Your firm manufactures a so-called tonic which is said to give people extra strength and vitality. A report by a consumer group in an overseas newspaper quotes an analysis by scientists who claim that the tonic is worthless.

22.9

A cloze passage

Complete the following passage by choosing the correct word for each blank space.

Not long ago, some unarmed engineers and (1) ____ set off to make (2) ____ way through the jungle in Trinidad. They were heading for a valley (3) ____ the Government hoped (4) ____ would (5) ____ possible to build a dam. They intended to (6) ____ and photograph the land in (7) ____ to establish whether or not it was (8) ____ for this purpose. There (9) ____ four young men altogether, and they were not (10) ____ with the territory, so they (11) ____ a guide closely. They knew that their guide was completely (12) ____ and would not (13) ____ them astray.

After (14) ____ about two miles, they came across a very (15) ____ snake lying motionless in a clearing. (16) ____ that the snake was (17) ____, one of the men kicked it. Much to his surprise, the snake resented this (18) ____ attack and reared up to (19) ____ him. The men waved their sticks at the snake (20) ____ hesitated and then slithered away. 'You were lucky,' their guide told them. 'That was a python. It was big enough to kill any of us if it had wanted to.'

1. A. tailors
   B. surveyors
   C. fishermen
   D. salesmen

2. A. they
   B. they're
   C. there
   D. their

3. A. what
   B. where
   C. which
   D. that

4. A. it
   B. he
   C. them
   D. him

5. A. do
   B. make
   C. be
   D. easy

6. A. grow
   B. survey
   C. plant
   D. look

7. A. valley
   B. means
   C. jungle
   D. order

8. A. present
   B. suitable
   C. well
   D. build

9. A. are
   B. is
   C. was
   D. were

10. A. familiar
    B. aware
    C. knowing
    D. informed

11. A. took
    B. followed
    C. employed
    D. paid

12. A. hopeless
    B. liable
    C. hopeful
    D. reliable

13. A. lead
    B. make
    C. cause
    D. do

14. A. walked
    B. gone
    C. walking
    D. travelled

15. A. dead
    B. big
    C. tame
    D. small

16. A. Assuming
    B. Thought
    C. Knowing
    D. Believed

17. A. died
    B. sleep
    C. dead
    D. decease

18. A. unprovoked
    B. unexpecting
    C. surprised
    D. mild

19. A. attract
    B. poison
    C. sting
    D. attack

20. A. as
    B. it
    C. which
    D. what

22.10
Say it another way

Exercise 5

Express these sentences in a different way. Start with the given words.

1. It is pointless to argue with her.
   There is …

2. Donna could not unscrew the top of the bottle and Leela could not unscrew it either.
   Neither …

3. There is a rumour that he is a very wealthy man.
   It …

4. I am not sure that we will win on Saturday.
   I doubt …

5. Nadia can send an email very quickly.
   It does not …

6. Although some members of the committee objected, the plan was approved.
   Despite …

7. Sharon suggested going for a stroll to the river.
   Sharon suggested that …

8. My parents let me do anything at the weekend.
   I am …

9. An electrical fault probably caused the fire.
   The fire …

10. Grandma does not like to watch shows on television.
    Grandma dislikes …

Exercise 6

Express these sentences in a different way, using the words in brackets.

1. Let me know what you think of this agreement. (opinion)
2. When were you born? (birth)
3. Do those shoes fit you? (right size)
4. Do you mind going without us? (objection)
5. I know the family living in that house. (who)
6. We couldn't swim across the river because the current was too strong. (so)
7. When it is humid, people feel tired. (humidity)

Unit 22 · History? 333

8. We have much pleasure in welcoming you. (welcome)

9. Donna found difficulty in saving money. (difficult)

10. Victor asked me, 'Have you seen my brother anywhere?' (whether)

22.11

Enjoying poetry

In 16.14, we read a poem by Michael C. Pintard. Go back to that section and read the introduction again. In his book *Still Standing,* he wrote: '*Still Standing* was written in the most turbulent and painful period in my life ... The page kept my fingers on the pencil, leaving no space for the trigger.'

Here are two more poems by Michael Pintard:

How Could We?

When satan
knock
on my door
I don't run an hide
5   I does cause him trouble
for tryin' to get inside.

Ya see,
I wan
poke him
10 choke him
broke him
stronghold
regain control
cause him pain
15 call him by his name
mr. profanity
creator of calamity
liar, thief
causer of grief
20 author of false belief
accuser
woman-abuser
how could I choose a
nasty critter
25 like him
the author of sin?

How could we ...?
Michael C. Pintard

Extracts from *I Ain't Turnin' Back*

I ain't turnin' back
Back where?
To fornication, degradation
worrying bout pregnancies
5 and disease
my reputation,
please!

I ain' turnin' back!
To no splif in my mouth
10 reddin' up my eye
scared to die,
sad
but, too macho to cry,
stupid enough to believe
15 I could fly.
Man!

Don't turn back!
to gern with friend
ta thief,
20 causing mummy grief,
too petrified to go to sleep.
Don't turn back
to being self-reliant,
Openly defiant
25 to God our creator
serving the great imitator
whose only ploy
is to
kill, steal and destroy
30 Hey!
Don't turn back!
    Michael C. Pintard

Questions

1. Complete the question 'How could we …?' at the end of the first poem.

2. Look back to 16.14 and the dedication Michael Pintard wrote to his mother. To what does 'the source of your faith' refer? How can we tell this from *both* of the poems in this section?

3. What is the attitude of the poet in both poems? What *two* influences have taken him away from 'the extreme of lawlessness' to discipline?

4. In line 13 of the first poem, what does the poet mean by 'regain control'?

5. In what ways are the two poems similar?

6. In the first poem, what name does the poet give to 'the great imitator' (mentioned in line 26 of the second poem)?

7. What do these words mean in the poems?
   a) In 'How Could We?': (i) profanity (line 16), (ii) calamity (line 17)
   b) In 'I Ain't Turnin' Back': (i) fornication (line 3), (ii) degradation (line 3), (iii) petrified (line 21), (iv) ploy (line 27)

22.12
Writing

Either: Write 400–450 words on topic (1), (2) or (3) in about 45 minutes.
or: Write 250–300 words on topic (4) or (5) in about 30 minutes.

1. Write a short story which illustrates the truth of the saying 'You will reap what you sow'.

2. For your school magazine, write an account of any game in which you took part as a member of a school team. Your account can be true or imaginary.

3. Write a short story in which an intelligent pet plays a part.

4. In what ways, if any, have computers affected people's daily lives?

5. Discuss the view that television does more harm than good to viewers.

23 Reporting the News

23.1
Reading

A Newspaper Reporter at Work

The life of a newspaper reporter is a demanding one. Amongst his (or her) problems in tracking down the news, he must take precautions against three common dangers.

The first of these is the law of libel. A reporter has to ensure that he writes nothing defamatory about an innocent person. This is a greater danger than it may appear, and legal records are littered with cases in which an error of judgement has proved very expensive.

A reporter may know or strongly suspect that somebody is corrupt but if he cannot prove this, he dare not print it. An accusation may be made at a public meeting, and a reporter may record it faithfully. His editor will then decline to print it because the accusation is not supported by facts. If he printed the claim, he might turn slander into libel. For a similar reason, a man is described as having been arrested for 'alleged burglary' and not for burglary itself. To say that he has been 'arrested for burglary' is to assume that the man is guilty. The newspaper may expect to hear from the man's lawyers if, in fact, he is acquitted by a court.

In a similar way, when the police are hunting for a murderer, they do not always say this. Instead, they announce that they are looking for a man 'who may help us with our enquiries'.

The need for caution is important when a reporter sets down an account of an event which he has not seen himself. He must be absolutely certain that he records facts and not theories or opinions. He cannot safely accept the views of eye-witnesses since they are notoriously prone to exaggerate.

Agency reports and Press releases from government and business sources sometimes turn out to be less than reliable. In 2003, there was a report of the dramatic rescue of a female American soldier in Iraq. Private Jessica Lynch had apparently been injured and captured during a gun-battle with Iraqi forces. A US helicopter led a filmed mission which showed American commandos breaking into an Iraqi hospital to rescue Pte Lynch. It later turned out that Pte Lynch had been injured in an accident and not in a gunfight. Medical treatment given at the Iraqi hospital had saved her life, and the doctors at the hospital had offered to hand her over peacefully but the US rescuers had insisted on breaking down the hospital doors to reach her.

On another occasion, a VIP was expected to arrive at an airport late at night. Instead of going to witness the scene, a reporter cheerfully invented the usual

35 details of the arrival and these were printed. The next morning he was embarrassed when he learnt, from a rival newspaper, that the plane had been delayed and that the celebrated visitor had not yet arrived.

Finally, a reporter has to cast a watchful eye on the advertisers in his newspaper. It is from advertisements that most newspapers obtain the greater part of their
40 income, and it is not unknown for businessmen to threaten to withdraw their costly advertisements unless they, their families, their business and their products are given a friendly reception by the newspaper. The son of a major advertiser may be involved in a very unpleasant court case of public interest, but no details of it may appear in some papers. A medical committee may declare that the medicines
45 sold by some companies are valueless, but this statement – if printed at all – may be summarised in such a way as to be harmless to the advertiser.

Not all newspapers, of course, are prepared to select, dilute or suppress the news in this way, nor do all advertisers attempt to exert pressure in this fashion, but the average reporter can never ignore a possibility which he probably meets
50 more than once in a long and varied career.

23.2
Understanding

A Choose the best answer each time.

1. A 'demanding' life (line 1) ____.
   A. asks a lot of the person involved
   B. is always full of variety
   C. brings a high salary for hard work
   D. involves constantly asking for sums of money

2. 'Amongst his (or her) problems in tracking down the news, he must take precautions against three common dangers.' (lines 1–3) From this we know that ____.
   A. three reporters are commonly dangerous
   B. three common precautions are taken against reporters
   C. reporters may meet three dangers which often occur
   D. some dangerous reporters are not particular common

3. From the second paragraph, we may infer that a person who has been libelled ____.
   A. has committed a criminal offence
   B. can seek financial compensation
   C. has written something unpleasant or harmful
   D. may be fined for littering

338 English Alive!

4. The 'slander' mentioned in line 12 has presumably been made by ____.
   A. the person who made a charge at a meeting
   B. the reporter himself
   C. the editor of a newspaper
   D. the person who printed the original accusation

5. An 'alleged burglar' is a person who ____.
   A. has committed burglary
   B. has been convicted of burglary
   C. has been a burglar for a long time
   D. is accused of burglary or said to have committed it

6. Paragraphs three and four stress the need not to ____.
   A. prejudge an event
   B. be influenced by advertisers or important people
   C. check facts and eye-witness reports very carefully
   D. make a report of an incident which the reporter has not personally seen

7. The case of Private Jessica Lynch is mentioned to illustrate ____.
   A. the problems which arise when incidents are reported during a war
   B. the occasional unreliability of the source of a news item
   C. the bravery of a female soldier and her rescuers
   D. the importance of helicopters during a war

8. From the last two paragraphs we may safely assume that a successful reporter ____.
   A. would attempt to exert pressure on advertisers
   B. would probably know the major advertisers in his paper
   C. does not allow himself to be influenced by advertisements
   D. ignores unpleasant possibilities when doing his or her work

9. In line 46, what might be the main reason for making a summary of a statement issued by a medical committee?
   A. There might not be enough space in the paper to print even a summary.
   B. The statement might be several years old.
   C. An editor might believe that the statement was important.
   D. The warning contained in the statement could be suppressed or weakened.

10. The 'possibility' mentioned in line 49 is concerned with ____.
    A. editors trying to influence advertisers
    B. reporters trying to influence editors
    C. newspapers being influenced by advertisers
    D. advertisers being influenced by reporters

B Answer these questions about the passage.

1. Both slander and libel are mentioned in line 12. What are they and what is the difference between them?

2. A man has been killed in Spanish Town. The police strongly suspect that Mr XYZ was the murderer. Give *two* possible reasons why the police inform reporters that they wish to 'interview Mr XYZ in connection with the case' rather than say that they are hunting the murderer, Mr XYZ.

3. May we safely conclude from the passage that eye-witnesses are always reliable? What is the reason for your answer?

4. Assume that you are the editor of a newspaper. The reporter mentioned in line 34 works for you. What would you say to him if he submitted a report of an incident which never occurred?

5. How important are advertisers to a daily newspaper?

6. In line 42, what do you understand by the expression 'a friendly reception'?

7. According to the passage, what might cause an editor or a reporter to 'dilute' news (line 47)? In this case, what does 'dilute' mean? What figure of speech is used here?

23.3
Vocabulary: meaning in context

In each case, choose the word(s) which best show(s) the meaning of the underlined words as they are used in the passage in 23.1.

1. ensure that he writes nothing defamatory about an innocent person (line 5)
   A. exaggerated
   B. harming the reputation
   C. rude
   D. which might be correct

2. legal records are littered with cases (line 6)
   A. are made wasteful
   B. contain many
   C. are made to appear untidy with
   D. are polluted or spoilt by

3. strongly suspect that somebody is corrupt (line 8)
   A. involved in dishonest acts
   B. immoral
   C. acting in an arrogant manner
   D. acting like a bully

4. His editor will then decline to print it (line 10)
   A. hasten
   B. hesitate
   C. offer
   D. refuse

5. having been arrested for 'alleged burglary' and not for burglary itself (line 13)
   A. claimed or said to be
   B. minor, not serious
   C. attempted but not completed
   D. contrary to the law

English Alive!

6. to <u>assume</u> that the man is guilty (line 14)
   - A. be able to prove
   - B. state publicly
   - C. believe but not be able to prove
   - D. be quite convinced

7. they are notoriously <u>prone</u> to exaggerate (line 22)
   - A. anxious
   - B. opposed
   - C. unlikely
   - D. liable

8. Agency reports and press <u>releases</u> from government and business sources (line 23)
   - A. leaks
   - B. confidential information
   - C. statements or reports
   - D. inside stories

9. from a <u>rival</u> newspaper (line 36)
   - A. competing
   - B. envious, jealous
   - C. inferior, of lower quality
   - D. more modern

10. that the <u>celebrated</u> visitor had not yet arrived (line 37)
    - A. long awaited
    - B. delayed for some time
    - C. successful at singing or in music
    - D. well-known

11. prepared to select, dilute or <u>suppress</u> the news (line 47)
    - A. distort in some way
    - B. prevent the publication of
    - C. make more striking
    - D. manipulate

12. nor do all advertisers attempt to <u>exert</u> pressure in this fashion (line 48)
    - A. prevent
    - B. minimise
    - C. apply
    - D. maximise

23.4
Vocabulary: expressions using 'take'

Check that you know how to use the expressions in italics below.

a) Suggest other ways of expressing a similar meaning without using the expressions in italics.

b) Make up your own sentences using the given expressions.

1. Reporters must *take precautions against* common dangers.

2. We've promised to *take care* of these things for Mr Lall while he is away on holiday.

3. Please don't *take offence at* what Santokh said.

4. Mr Williams is a good carpenter and *takes a pride* in his work.

5. Francine *took pity on* the stray kitten and gave it some food.

6. *Take no notice of* what he says; he is exaggerating.

7. Sometimes customers don't even *take the trouble* to count their change.

8. You should *take heed of* what Uncle says about the need for training.

9. We *took great pains to* decorate the hall in an attractive way for the concert.

10. Please *take charge of* the class until I return.

11. You should have *taken your opportunity* when you had the chance to get the job.

12. Donna has suddenly started to *take an interest* in growing flowers.

13. Many people *take* their health *for granted* and do not realise how lucky they are.

14. It will *take some time* to persuade him that he is wrong.

15. There's no hurry. *Take your time.*

16. Leela *took up* tennis about a year ago. She's quite good already.

Exercise 1

Use the correct form of one of the above expressions in these sentences.

1. Ignore what he says. He's only jealous, so ____ of him.

2. Natoya has suddenly ____ in dressmaking and started to design her own clothes.

3. Mr Daljit Singh is going to ____ of our hockey team, so we expect the standard to rise.

4. If malaria is finally eradicated, we shan't have to ____ against it any more.

5. Tanya's work is always neat and accurate. She ____ in everything she does.

6. It's a pity Paul didn't ____ to check his facts. Half of them are wrong.

7. The speaker was very critical of the arrangements made for the football tournament, and several of the officials ____ at his remarks and accused him of being unfair.

8. My mother is very kind and always ____ on any stray animals she sees.

9. Do you think you could ____ of our cat for three days while we're away?

10. I think you can ____ that you will get the job. Miss Robertson told me that she has decided to appoint you.

11. Could you please check these invoices for me? There's no hurry, so ____.

12. This composition is full of mistakes because you didn't ____ to check it for errors.

23.5
Vocabulary: from the newspapers

Exercise 2

Explain the meaning of the words and expressions in italics, which have been taken from daily newspapers.

1. Both sides in the dispute are trying to reach *a compromise solution* in an effort to solve the *deadlock*.

2. Mr Y, a shipping *magnate*, criticised the decision to raise *freight rates* and complained that it would make exports less competitive while increasing the cost of imported goods.

3. X, a police *supervisee*, was jailed for three months today.

4. The dispute involving bus-drivers has been *referred to arbitration*.

5. 'Coconut *pilot scheme* soon' (a headline)

6. The *Coroner*, in recording a *misadventure verdict*, said that the authorities concerned should make 'aquatic training' a *prerequisite* for all future marine policemen.

7. The first of the coaching sessions will last for four *consecutive* weekends. The *venue* will depend on the requirements submitted to the honorary secretary by *affiliated* clubs.

8. Two men escaped the *gallows* yesterday when their death sentences for *arson* were *commuted* to 30-year jail sentences.

9. As ambitious as they are *footloose*, over 9000 Jamaicans emigrated to the USA and UK last year.

10. Not so long ago some of our recently installed street lamps started to *act up*.

23.6
Writing: making a summary

Read the following passage about the work of consumer associations. Then, in not more than 120 words, summarise the main features of a typical consumer magazine.

In the past thirty years, consumer associations have become increasingly popular. The larger ones publish their own magazine, which relies on the subscriptions of members plus, in some countries, a government grant. No advertisements are accepted, so the magazine is entirely objective and cannot be influenced by advertisers.

A major aim in a typical consumer magazine is to reveal the 'best buys' in each category, e.g. TV sets, digital radios, mobile phones, dish-washers, vacuum cleaners, cars, etc. Within a specific category, each item is tested and then ranked as to its reliability, quality, price, etc. If an item is faulty – perhaps because it breaks down, is too noisy or doesn't do what its makers claim it does – the fault is exposed and backed by careful testing and research. Most consumer associations keep up-to-date information on their web site, so it is easy for a buyer in the market for, say, a car or a TV set, to check the consumer reports and get full information before making a decision about which item to buy.

In addition to the extensive testing of new items, the consumer association will give details of items and companies to avoid. It will warn readers of dishonest plumbers and electricians, cowboy builders who overcharge, financial advisers who are more interested in their own profit than that of their clients, insurance policies that look good but aren't, guarantees that are not worth the paper they are printed on, and a host of other tricks in what is loosely called the 'business world'.

In a consumer magazine we can also expect to see interesting letters from readers, warning the public of some new scam or seeking help with their own problems. For example, a reader may buy an air-conditioner or a suite of furniture and then find that the goods are not as advertised. She can write to the consumer magazine and receive guidance as to her legal rights. In addition, the magazine will print regular articles on common legal issues such as getting deposits refunded, dealing with threatening letters from suppliers, and other problems about which many consumers are ignorant.

When a consumer association carries out its tests and/or research, it sends employees out to buy or test equipment. They may use secret cameras or recorders to make a reliable record of each transaction, so that there can be no legal action by manufacturers when their goods are listed as unsatisfactory or far from being a 'best buy'.

Undoubtedly, consumer associations are a powerful influence for good. Not only do they help consumers in the ways described above, but they keep manufacturers on their toes. No manufacturer likes to see his goods described as 'dangerous for children' or 'having no value as medicine' or 'twice as expensive and half as good as the best buy'. Manufacturers know that consumer associations are watching them and that these associations are backed by both the public and the government.

23.7
Writing

Exercise 3

You are put in charge of the correspondence column in a newspaper. Write brief replies (which will be printed) to these letters. Your replies can be serious or humorous but not offensive. If you antagonise your readers, you may be dismissed or demoted to sweeping the floor. Each reply should not be more than five lines long.

1. Dear Editor,
   I want to be an air stewardess. What qualities do you think I need?
   Mitzie

2. Dear Sir,
   Why do schools waste so much time on sports? Think of all the extra knowledge the pupils could acquire if they didn't play any games. Isn't this a waste of public money?
   Anxious Parent

3. Dear Sir or Madam,
   What do you think about all this nonsense of ghosts haunting schools? My friend takes it all seriously but I think it is a load of rubbish. What do you think?
   Colin

23.8
Say it another way

Exercise 4

Rewrite each sentence so that you keep as closely as possible to the meaning of the original sentence but use the word in brackets or a suitable form of it.

1. I have lent my pump to my friend. (borrow)
2. The editor declined to print my report of the fire. (said)
3. The magistrate said the defendant was not guilty. (acquit)
4. The need for caution in reporting news is important. (cautious)
5. One cannot safely accept the views of witnesses. (safety)
6. I don't like that kind of joke. (appeal)
7. The government took away some of his land. (deprive)
8. He did not go to the fire, but made up a false report about it. (Instead)
9. I suddenly thought of a solution. (occur)
10. The magazine does not accept any advertisements. (No)

23.9

Grammar: 'a', 'an' and 'the' (revision)

When do we use 'an' instead of 'a' before a word?

These examples will help you to answer the question:

| an X-ray | an S-bend | an 'm' | an hour | an honest woman | an umbrella |
| a uniform | a xylophone | a large island | a 'u' | a European country | a hill |

When do we use 'the' before the name of a country?

We often use the names of these countries as nouns. Which of these normally have 'the' before them?

| USA | France | Philippines | Guyana | Netherlands |
| UK | Italy | New Zealand | Spain | Mexico |

Exercise 5

In each blank space, put in 'a', 'an' or 'the' *or* leave the space empty to show that no word is needed.

1. There are ____ number of reasons why people write ____ letter to ____ editor of ____ newspaper. Sometimes they want to make ____ complaint or draw ____ attention of ____ government to ____ need for ____ action.

2. People are beginning to think about landing on ____ Mars in much ____ same way as ____ landings already made on ____ Moon.

3. When astronauts first landed on ____ Moon, ____ few decades ago, some cynics suggested that ____ landing was ____ fake. They claimed that ____ 'landing' had been made in ____ deserted part of ____ USA. However, ____ scientists do not accept this claim and say it was ____ malicious attempt to belittle ____ achievement of ____ space agency NASA.

4. Tomorrow there is going to be ____ important conference on ____ international cooperation in ____ field of ____ tourism, with special emphasis on ____ Caribbean. Delegates are expected from ____ USA, ____ Canada, ____ Europe and ____ Asia. I shall be very interested to see what ____ outcome of ____ conference is.

5. In a football match last week, ____ captain of ____ visiting team set ____ bad example on ____ field. He was warned by ____ referee, who threatened to send ____ adverse report to ____ Disciplinary Committee of ____ League.

6. There is no doubt that many people now lead ____ much better life than their ancestors did ____ century ago but in some countries ____ very poorest people have not felt ____ benefit which people in ____ town enjoy.

7. Where can we find out ____ effect which ____ nitrates have on ____ development of ____ healthy crops? If you keep on growing ____ same crop on ____ same piece of land, ____ yield will decline steadily, and ____ crops will be more likely to be affected by ____ debilitating disease.

8. ____ electricity brings ____ light and ____ power to us. Oil lamps are really ____ nuisance and ____ source of ____ danger, especially during ____ storm such as ____ one we had ____ few weeks ago.

23.10
Grammar: using participles

An expression with a **present** or **past participle** can come at the start of a sentence, in the middle or at the end. If you use a participle expression at the beginning of a sentence, make sure that your meaning is not ambiguous, e.g.

ambiguous: Getting out of the car, Michael saw an old man.
Who was getting out of the car: Michael or the old man?
clear: Michael saw an old man getting out of the car.
clear: When he was getting out of the car, Michael saw an old man.

- **At the start of a sentence**, e.g.
  Not **knowing** where the other boys had gone, Courtney decided to go home.
  Nearly **overcome** by the heat, two of the firemen sat down to rest for a moment.

- **In the middle of a sentence**, e.g.
  The lady **sitting** in the back of the car is Toyin's mother.
  A lot of fruit **grown** in Barbados is now available in our stores.

- **At the end of a sentence**, e.g.
  We heard two men **arguing** about a football match.
  Nakiesha has decided to buy the computer **recommended** by your cousin.

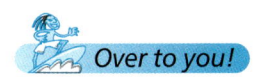

Over to you!

Exercise 6

Use a participle to change each pair of sentences into one longer sentence. Make any other necessary changes.

1. Abiose hurried to meet the postman. She hoped that he had a parcel from Canada for her.

2. The lorry-driver was dazzled by the lights on an oncoming vehicle. He swerved and nearly hit a tree.

3. Wayne thought that his mother had left her keys behind. He grabbed them up and rushed after her.

4. Pillai climbed slowly out of the water. He was nearly exhausted by his efforts to save the drowning child.

5. In 2003, Americans invaded Iraq. They thought that the Iraqi leader was preparing to use weapons of mass destruction.

6. The stranger hurried down the alley. He was looking anxiously behind him.

7. Three shops were damaged by the fire. They will be closed for two weeks at least.

8. We went to bed early. We did not expect Peter to arrive that night.

9. There was a tree blocking the road. It was soon removed by a gang of workmen.

10. Some food was contaminated by cockroaches. It was thrown away.

23.11
Grammar: making comparisons

Exercise 7

Correct the errors in these sentences. They illustrate common mistakes in expressing a comparison.

1. The medicine had the opposite effect of what he had expected; it merely made him feel worst than he had felt the day before.

2. Which is the most longest river in Guyana?

3. Travelling by air is much more swifter than going by sea.

4. Watch me and I'll show you a best way to get a tyre off a wheel.

5. I'm fairly sure that Amanda is a year older then your sister is.

6. That type of mobile phone is superior than the other kinds.

7. We all admired Fiona's wedding-dress. It was the most perfect we had ever seen.

8. Travelling by rail is much comfortable than going by car.

9. According to Francine, tourism is the second large industry in her country and may soon be the largest.

10. This method of cooking fish is much easier and natural than the old-fashioned one.

23.12
Enjoying poetry

The Washerwomen

Down where the river beats itself against the stones
And washes them in clouds of frothy spray,
Or foaming fumbles through them with the thousand tones
Of an orchestra,
5   The women wash, and humming keep a sort of time;
And families of bubbles frisk and float away
To be destroyed,
Like all the baffled hopes that had their little suns,
Tossed on the furious drifts of disappointments.
10 But all the tide
Cradles these clinging bubbles ever still, alike
The friendly little hopes that never leave the heart.

In this big hall of rushing waters women wash
And with the sound of washing,
15 With the steady heaving of their slender shoulders
As they rub their stubborn rags upon the boulders,
They keep a sort of time

With their thoughts. These were unchanging
Like the persistent music here,
20 Of swirling waters,
The crash of wet clothes beaten on the stones,
The sound of wind in leaves,
Or frog croaks after dusk, and the low moan
Of the big sea fighting the river's mouth.

25 The ever-changing patterns in the clouds
Before their dissolution into rain;
Or the gay butterflies manoeuvering
Among the leafy camouflage that clothes the banks
And hides their spent remains when they collapse and die,
30 Are symbols of their hopes and gaudy plans
Which once they dreamt. But finally they learn to hope
And make plans less elaborate.
It was the same
With those that washed before them here
35 And passed leaving the soap-stained stones
Where others now half stoop like devotees
To pagan gods.

They have resigned themselves to daylong swishing
Of wet cloth chafing the very stone;
40 And the big symphony of waters rushing
Past clumps of tall stems standing alone,
Apart, like band-leaders, or sentinels,
They must hear the heavy hum
Of wings of insects overgrown,
45 Cleaving the air like bombers on a plotted course.
They must hear the long 'hush' of the wind in leaves
As dead ones flutter down like living things
Until the shadows come.

Owen Campbell

Questions

1. What alliterating sound is used in lines 3 and 6? What effect does the poet seek to achieve by using it?

2. With what does the poet compare the 'families of bubbles' in lines 8–9?

3. In what way were the thoughts of the washerwomen said to be 'unchanging' (line 18)?

4. In line 35, which is better: 'passed leaving' or 'passing left'?

5. In line 29, the poet writes about butterflies which 'collapse and die'. Where is a similar idea expressed near the end of the poem? What point is the poet making by referring to the death of the insects?

6. How effective is the simile in lines 36–7? How does the simile fit into the picture which the poet has painted in the whole poem?

7. What is the attitude of the poet to the washerwomen? Is he hostile to them, sympathetic, pitying, scornful, understanding or totally objective? How does he show that attitude?

23.13
Writing

Either: Write 400–450 words on topic (1) or (2) in about 45 minutes.
or: Write 250–300 words on topic (3) in about 30 minutes:

1. a) Write a story in which the scene shown opposite plays a part. **OR**

   b) Pretend that you are a newspaper reporter. Write a news report based on the scene shown in the picture.

2. Write a story in which the help of a friend proves to be very important.

3. How reliable or accurate is the news which we see on television, listen to on the radio or read about in newspapers? Give reasons for your opinions.

24 The Persuaders

24.1 Reading

The Persuaders

They're out there – the hidden persuaders – and they're going to get you! You may see the results of their work when you watch advertisements on television or read them in a paper or magazine. You can hear them at work on the radio or when a politician or salesperson speaks. They know you and they start with a list
5   something like this one. It shows what most people desire.

Most people desire to:
1. have or obtain a comfortable home
2. be accepted and liked by other people, especially their peers
3. be respected or admired for their physical, intellectual or musical ability
10 4. be regarded as successful – at work, at home, in the community
5. get on well with, or even impress, members of the other sex
6. be in a secure job and see a secure future ahead
7. be healthy and find speedy remedies for temporary illnesses
8. protect their family
15 9. be happy, enjoy life and avoid avoidable tasks
10. be able to deal confidently with (common) problems
11. be up-to-date, in fashion or even ahead of others.

In addition, many (but not all) people desire to:
12. follow the guidelines of their religion and thus
20 13. be moral, honest, courageous and caring persons whose careers are worthwhile because they lead to helping others in the community.

Write down the numbers of the items in the list which do not apply to you. Discuss the results in class. Does the list omit anything important?

The aim of the persuaders is to make you part with your vote or your money by convincing you that they are fulfilling your desires. The persuaders work for supermarkets, politicians, advertisers, salespeople and companies. They employ
25 a variety of techniques, including some which are so subtle that the victims – you and I – are unaware of what is happening. These are some of the methods used to persuade you to do something:

Supermarkets

1. (1950) Provide baskets so that shoppers can pick up goods (which they did not intend to buy) as they stroll past the shelves. (1950s onward) Provide trolleys as well as baskets.
2. Put 'own brand' goods at waist or chest height, where they can be seen easily. Put popular brands lower or higher so that a shopper has to search for them.
3. Make shoppers join a queue and wait a few minutes before they can check-out the goods in their trolleys. Then shoppers may buy small items such as batteries or chocolate from the shelves by the check-out counter.
4. Use '2-for-1' and similar bargains to persuade people that they will get a bargain if they buy things that they did not particularly want.

Politicians

5. Exaggerate to make their opponents seem worse than they are. Exaggerate to make promises which they know they cannot keep.
6. Use any of the tricks in 5.1 and 10.5 to persuade people to vote for them. (Look back at these sections if necessary.)

Advertisers, salespeople and companies

7. Also use the tricks in 5.1 and 10.5 to persuade people to buy things.
8. Adjust their language and methods to suit the age range, sex and social class of the market. Thus they may use simple words and ideas when appealing to children or comparatively uneducated people, but more sophisticated language and ideas when trying to persuade better educated or older people.

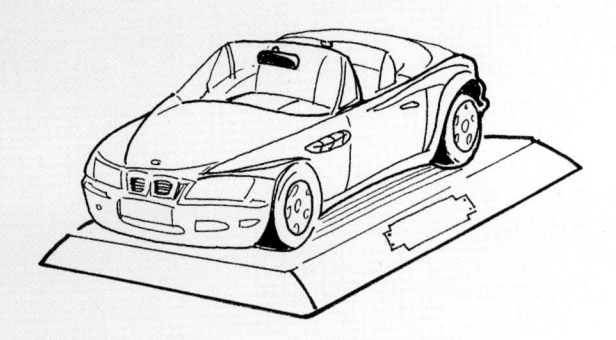

(for children)
Fun for you! Beautifully-made models of real cars, buses and vans.
Build your own collection at home! Control the traffic!
Just the thing to decorate a shelf! Show your friends and swop models with them.

(for educated adults)
A shrewd investment with guaranteed future appreciation. Buy now while stocks last. Display them or store them and wait for them to increase in value. Auction prices show up to 30% appreciation p.a. in recent years. Limited production ensures future gains.

9. Use veiled threats to imply that if you don't buy something now, you will regret it later on.

60 *Protect yourself against gobblonia with KONKIT.*
    Stay slim with FATOFF. (If you don't,
    you'll become obese.)
    Keep the flu at bay with UGHSTUFF!

10. Use irrelevant but attractive pictures of strong men and pretty girls to make you identify the image with the product even if this is illogical.

65 11. Misuse figures and statistics for their own purposes. 8% can become 'up to 25%'. 52% can become 'the great majority' if it suits an advertiser.

12. Produce 'recommendations' (which cannot be checked) from 'satisfied' customers.

13. Repeat the same point, using different words or expressions.

70 14. Attempt to impress the public by the use of technical or pseudo-technical terms, e.g. 'equipped with the ultra-modern RFID for greater security'.

15. Use emotive words designed to influence readers or listeners.

24.2
Understanding

A Choose the best answer in each case.

1. Judging from the passage as a whole, the 'results' mentioned in line 2 are likely to be ____.
   A. stupid   C. malicious
   B. clever   D. thoughtless

2. In line 4, 'know' is used with the meaning ____.
   A. are members of your family   C. are probably close friends
   B. have met you before   D. think they understand

3. As a result of item (1) in line 7, we might expect ____.
   A. advertisers to try to sell furniture   C. the price of new houses to fall
   B. people to have smaller families   D. there to be less demand for electricity

4. As a result of item (2) in line 8, we might expect advertisers to make use of ____ in some advertisements.
   A. peer pressure
   B. more mixed metaphors
   C. advice on how to look like other people
   D. warnings about advice from strangers

5. Some people will buy a security system as a result of item ____ in the list of things which people desire.
   A. 3   B. 7   C. 8   D. 12

6. The people least likely to desire item 12 are probably ____.
   A. male teenagers
   B. musicians
   C. elderly people
   D. atheists

7. The use of 'so subtle that' in line 25 implies that ____.
   A. the hidden persuaders have criminal tendencies at times
   B. some of the persuaders may be cleverer than the writer and reader
   C. honesty does not always pay
   D. sometimes the persuaders are too clever for their own good

8. The introduction of shopping baskets and trolleys in supermarkets probably ____.
   A. had to be stopped because these items were frequently stolen
   B. interfered with the normal shopping habits of people and annoyed them
   C. improved business and profits in supermarkets
   D. meant that paper or plastic bags were no longer necessary

9. 'Own brand' goods were put level with the waist or chest of an average shopper in order to ____.
   A. make it easier for shoppers to buy them
   B. stop shoppers from becoming tired when picking them off the shelves
   C. discourage shoppers from preferring them to more popular brands
   D. make it more convenient for shelf-stackers to replace them

10. In line 37, '2-for-1' is similar in meaning to ____.
    A. each couple of people can buy one only
    B. buy one, get one free
    C. every second shopper can have one of these free
    D. the price of some items has been doubled

B Answer these questions about the passage.

1. What do you think readers of a magazine published by a consumers association might think of the passage? Why?

2. How are the tricks in 5.1 and 10.5 related to the theme of this passage?

3. What do the illustrations and text in item 8 after line 49 demonstrate?

4. What threat is implied in line 62 ('Keep the flu at bay ...')?

5. How can emotive words influence people who read or watch an advertisement?

24.3 Vocabulary: meaning in context

Choose the word(s) which best show(s) the meaning of the underlined words as they are used in 24.1.

1. liked by other people, especially their <u>peers</u> (line 8)
   - A. relatives
   - B. employers
   - C. members of an extended family
   - D. people of similar age or standing

2. <u>intellectual</u> or musical ability (line 9)
   - A. ability to think and understand
   - B. skill with figures and numbers
   - C. appreciating literature
   - D. ability to write and appreciate poetry

3. even <u>impress</u>, members of the other sex (line 11)
   - A. do better than
   - B. keep away from
   - C. be equal in status and ability
   - D. have a quite favourable effect on

4. <u>remedies</u> for temporary illnesses (line 13)
   - A. signs or symptoms
   - B. ways of coping with
   - C. cures
   - D. excuses

5. be <u>moral</u>, honest, courageous and caring persons (line 20)
   - A. kind
   - B. virtuous
   - C. thoughtful
   - D. self-sufficient

6. by <u>convincing</u> you that you are fulfilling your desires (line 23)
   - A. trying to persuade you
   - B. explaining the need to you
   - C. making you feel certain
   - D. trying to prevent you from

7. as they <u>stroll</u> past the shelves (line 30)
   - A. walk
   - B. go
   - C. walk in a leisurely way
   - D. move impatiently

8. more <u>sophisticated</u> language and ideas (line 48)
   - A. worldly-wise
   - B. cunning
   - C. relevant
   - D. deceitful

9. a <u>shrewd</u> investment (line 51)
   - A. long-term
   - B. beneficial
   - C. cautious
   - D. well-made

10. with guaranteed future <u>appreciation</u> (line 52)
    - A. understanding
    - B. interest
    - C. increase in value
    - D. prestige

11. Use <u>veiled</u> threats to imply (line 58)
    - A. intimidating
    - B. frightening
    - C. dangerous
    - D. partly concealed

12. even if this is <u>illogical</u> (line 64)
    - A. upsetting
    - B. contrary to reason
    - C. disturbing
    - D. not in good taste

24.4

Vocabulary: prefixes

Pseudo

This prefix means 'false(ly)' or 'pretended', so 'pseudo-technical terms' are terms which appear to be technical but are made-up words (sometimes used to confuse people). e.g.

Our sugar has been processed through **anti-bacterial imaging** to ensure purity.

Ultra

This prefix means 'beyond' or 'to the greatest possible extent' and is an **intensifier**. Thus 'ultra-modern' means 'extremely modern' or 'as modern as anything can possibly be'. In advertising, people usually think that the more modern something is, the better it is. Sometimes, 'ultra-modern' is used with a pseudo-technical expression to impress people, e.g.

This ultra-modern camera makes use of **telesonic resonance** and **astral macrovision** to bring you pictures of superlative quality.

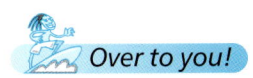

Over to you!

Exercise 1

How many words can you find which use the prefixes given below? Try to find at least two more examples in each case.

Prefix	Meaning	Example
1. anti	against	antibiotic (able to halt the growth of bacteria or to destroy them)
2. auto	self	automobile (a vehicle which can move by itself, without being pulled by horses)
3. bene	good, well	benevolent (doing or wishing well to others)
4. dia	across	diaspora (the scattering of people; scattered people)
5. equi	equal	equation (an expression with one side equal to the other side)
6. ex	former(ly)	an ex-international player
7. hyper	excessive, more than normal	a hyperactive person
8. mal	bad(ly)	malevolent (intending/thinking/doing bad things)
9. pan	all, united	a pan-African conference (attended by representatives from all or many African countries)
10. trans	across	a transatlantic flight

Exercise 2

Choose the word(s) which best show(s) the meaning of the prefixes in bold type below.

1. A **quadri**lateral has the same number of sides as a rectangle.
   A. two
   B. four
   C. six

2. If you **bi**sect something, you cut or divide it into two equal parts.
   A. cut
   B. part
   C. two

3. A ship may hit a **sub**merged wreck because it is below the surface and cannot be seen.
   A. under
   B. large
   C. dangerous

4. An **octo**genarian is most unlikely to win an event at the Olympic Games.
   A. old
   B. tired
   C. eight

5. **Ex**ports help to earn the foreign currency needed to buy goods overseas.
   A. made in a factory
   B. grown in a field
   C. going out

6. An **omni**vorous creature will eat meat, fish and vegetables
   A. all
   B. hungry
   C. growing

7. In the words **arch**bishop and **arch**-enemy, 'arch' is used with the meaning ____.
   A. ancient
   B. chief
   C. dedicated

8. When people visit a country, Customs officers will confiscate any **contra**band goods that they may have.
   A. against
   B. smuggling
   C. harmful

9. Is there any difference between the **circum**ference of an area and its perimeter?
   A. half
   B. height
   C. around

10. A **poly**gon has more than two sides.
    A. five
    B. seven
    C. many

24.5
Discussion: advertising

1. You work for an advertising agency which has a contract to prepare newspaper display advertisements for a new Honda Accord saloon car. Write down some words which you think would be useful in a display advertisement. Your aim is to attract the attention of readers and make them want to inspect a new Honda Accord. If possible, make a draft of a possible advertisement

2. You are helping an elderly relative who wants to sell her car. Prepare the draft of a classified (small) advertisement. Mention facts which you hope will make the advertisement appealing to anybody looking for a used (pre-owned) car.

3. This is not easy but try your best. You are working for an advertising agency which is going to advertise a type of food on a television channel which children like to watch. Choose the type of food you are going to advertise. Then suggest a way of advertising it on television. You can use live actors or animated ones. You can use a single display advertisement or a short story or anything which will interest children but not take up too much time. What do you suggest?

4. You work for a large insurance company which wants to get more customers to insure their homes, their cars and themselves. Write down some words which you could include in your advertisement to attract potential customers. If you have time, prepare a draft of the whole advertisement and let others criticise it.

24.6

Understanding: graphs

Study these two graphs and then answer the questions about them.

Monthly sales, 200– (US $)   **Cost of advertising, 200– (US $)**

Questions

1. How many advertising campaigns did the company have during the year?

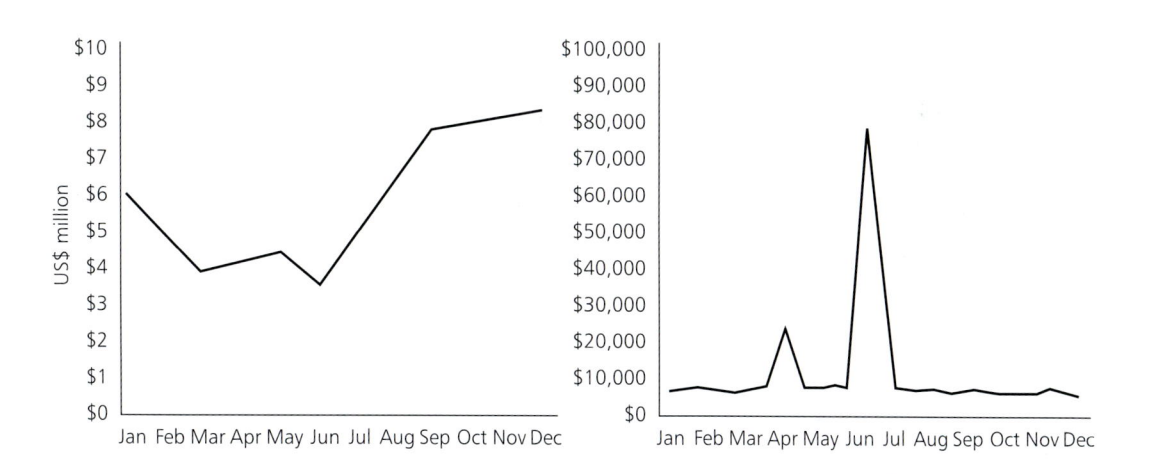

2. Which of the two campaigns was the more successful? How do you know that?

3. The company makes a net profit of about 10 per cent of the product of sales, i.e. for every $100 in sales, it makes a profit of $10. Did the second advertising campaign pay for itself?

4. In its budget for the following year, how much money is likely to be spent on advertising in the whole year? What are your reasons for your answer?

5. In what way are graphs like these of value to the company?

24.7

Meetings: convening a meeting

'To convene' means 'to summon, to call together'. Here is an example of a letter convening a meeting of the committee of the Music and Drama Club of a school.

[address]
[phone number]
[email address]
[date]

Members
Music and Drama Club Committee

Dear Colleague

Please note that there will be a meeting of the Committee of the Music and Drama Club at 5 p.m. on Friday, 14 October, in Room 14 of the school.

The agenda is enclosed.

I hope you will be able to attend.

Yours sincerely
Suresh Kissoon
Hon. Secretary

Music and Drama Club Committee

Agenda for meeting on 14 October

1. Apologies for absence
2. Minutes of the last meeting
3. Chairperson's announcements
4. Election of a representative to the school Student Council
5. Report by the Hon. Treasurer
6. Celebration of the school's 50th anniversary
7. Concert to raise funds to replace old and broken instruments
8. Any other business

Notes

- When all members of a committee belong to the same school, company, etc., it may not be necessary for the secretary to give his/her address.

- A telephone number and email address are useful in case members wish to report that they cannot attend or have a query.

- The greeting ('Dear …') and ending ('Yours sincerely') can be omitted.

- The agenda can be set out on a separate piece of paper enclosed with the letter or it can be sent later.

- 'Any other business' is sometimes shortened to 'AOB'.

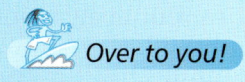

Over to you!

Exercise 3

You are the secretary of the school Student Council. Say or write a letter convening a meeting of the Council. Make up any necessary details but do not include an agenda.

24.8

Meetings: the agenda

'Agenda' is a Latin word meaning 'ought to be done or dealt with'. An agenda is a list of things which a committee (or any other body) will consider at a meeting (see the example in 24.7).

- The first item on an agenda is usually called 'Apologies for absence'. The secretary and/or members will give the names of members who have apologised for being unable to attend. This is an unimportant formality.

- Near the start of the meeting it is necessary to look at the secretary's Minutes (= written record) of the last meeting and, if approved, to vote to confirm them as correct. Sometimes the Chairperson, the Secretary or a member may wish to report on an item in the Minutes, e.g. to say that something proposed at the last meeting has been carried out. Sometimes a member may object to something in the Minutes. Then the Committee will have to decide whether or not to amend them.

- The Chairperson's announcements may come as the second or third item on the agenda.

- The last item on an agenda is usually called 'any other business' (AOB).
    - A date for the next meeting will be agreed.
    - The rules of many organisations will not allow a member to raise a proposal unless 7 (or more) days' notice has been given. This will prevent members from bringing

up and voting on a proposal about which absent members have not been warned. For example, a majority of the members may try to vote themselves a payment to cover alleged 'expenses'. If other members had been warned of this, they might have attended the meeting to block the proposal.

If you become a member of a committee, make certain that you know the constitution and rules. Then you can help to stop anything bad from being done. In a sense, the constitution is the law. Make sure the law is on your side.

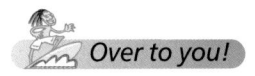

Over to you!

Exercise 4

Make up an agenda for a meeting of the Student Council of your school *or* for any other club or organisation of which you are an active member. Use your imagination and experience to decide what topics may be discussed at the meeting.

24.9
Meetings: the Minutes

The Minutes of a meeting are a record of the meeting. There are several different ways of writing minutes. If you become the secretary of an organisation and have to write the minutes, consult the chairperson. Find out which way he or she wants you to write the minutes. For example, consider this situation

> You are the secretary of the Student Council. During a meeting, you reported that the Principal had referred to the Council the case of a student call John Blank. He was accused of bullying at school, copying the homework of another student, telling lies to his teacher and of behaving badly in class. The Principal wanted the Student Council to consider the case of John Blank and make a recommendation concerning what to do with him.
>
> There was a long discussion and various points of view were put forward. Eventually the Council agreed to recommend that John Blank should be suspended for a week and put on probation for a month.

Possible minute (1):

```
The secretary reported that the Principal had referred to the
Council the case of John Blank. After considerable discussion,
the Council agreed to recommend that Blank should be suspended
for a week and put on probation for a month.
```

Possible minute (2):

In some cases, each person's views may be included in the minutes. Sometimes a member may ask to have his/her views recorded in the minutes:

The secretary reported that the Principal had referred to the Council the case of John Blank whose conduct had been unsatisfactory.

Derrick Allen felt that Blank's conduct was intolerable and that he should be expelled. Tyrone Robertson agreed, feeling that this was in the best interests of the students as a whole.

Inez Smith felt that expulsion was too severe and felt that a period of suspension, followed by probation, was more suitable. Three members agreed with her.

After further discussion, the matter was put to the vote, and the Council voted by 7–3 to recommend that Blank should be suspended for a week and then put on probation for a month.

Most organisations prefer the shorter type of minute, as in (1) above.

Below you can see possible minutes for the meeting of the committee of the Music and Drama Club for 14 October. The agenda is given in 24.7.

Minutes of the 12th meeting of the Committee of the Music and Drama Club held on 14 October at the school

12.1 Apologies for absence were received from Francine Walters and Durai Nathan.

12.2 The minutes of the meeting held on 2 October were considered and it was agreed to change 'all' to 'most' in line 2 of minute 11.6. The minutes were then confirmed and signed by the Chairperson.

12.3 The Chairperson announced that:
  a) Arising from minute 10.4, the Principal has agreed to allow the Committee to use Room 14 for future meetings and Room 12 for rehearsals and practice.
  b) Discussions are continuing with Docent Productions for a well-known actress to come and stage a show at the school some time in December.
  c) Shellyann Simms has resigned from the committee prior to her departure for the USA. The Chairperson has invited Jennifer Forbes to join the committee as a replacement, subject to approval by the committee. The invitation was approved.

12.4 The Chairperson explained that the committee had been invited to nominate a representative to sit on the Student Council. After a brief discussion, the Chairperson was approved as the committee's representative on the Student Council.

12.5 The Hon. Treasurer submitted her report, showing that the committee has a credit balance of $2,885.60 at present and has contingent liabilities of under $200. The Treasurer was thanked and her report was approved.

12.6 Items 6 and 7 on the agenda were considered together and a number of suggestions were made by members of the committee. It was resolved to appoint an Executive Committee to consider both events and to report back to the committee at its next meeting. Members of the Executive Committee will be the Chairperson, the Secretary and the Treasurer, with Natoya Williams and Julius Richardson.

It was agreed that the next meeting of the committee will be at 5 p.m. on Friday, 28 October in Room 14 of the school.

There being no further business, the committee adjourned at 7 p.m.

Respectfully submitted
Suresh Kissoon
Hon. Secretary

Notes:

- So that it will not be confused with the minutes of a clock, some people prefer to write 'Minute' instead of 'minute'. You can please yourself which method you use.

- Since this was the 12th meeting of the committee, the Minutes are numbered 12.1, 12.2, etc. As you can see from line 2 of 12.2 and line 2 of 12.3(a), this is useful because the Secretary does not have to put in the date of previous meetings each time they are mentioned. However, you can omit '12' if you like.

- Some people prefer not to give 'Apologies' a number. Then they start their numbering at what is now 12.2. It will become '1' or '12.1'.

- Each of items 12.2 to 12.6 could be made much longer by giving details of what was said by members. The Minutes might then consist of several pages but most organisations prefer the shorter form given on page 363.

- Americans normally insert 'Respectfully submitted' above the signature of the Secretary at the end of the Minutes, but these two words can be omitted if you like.

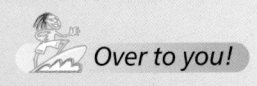

Over to you!

Exercise 5

This was the agenda for a meeting of the Committee of the PTA (Parent-Teacher Association) of your school. Read the agenda, use your imagination, and write the Minutes of the meeting to show what might have happened.

```
[name of school] Parent—Teacher Association

Agenda for meeting on 1 April

1. Apologies for absence

2. Minutes of the last meeting

3. Chairperson's announcements

4. Road safety near the school

5. Arrangements for meeting with teachers

6. Open Day

7. Treasurer's report

8. Any other business
```

24.10
Discussion

- If you have to write about an argumentative topic in an examination, study the wording of the question carefully. You may have to do one of these things:
  – oppose a proposal
  – support a proposal
  – discuss a proposal (= consider both sides)
  – give your own views (= discuss = consider both sides).
  Underline the key word ('discuss', 'support', 'oppose', 'against', 'own views') on the question paper, and then base your plan on it.

- Look to see what format you have to use, e.g. a letter, a speech, an article, a composition. If necessary, *underline* the word that indicates the format.

- Remember that a proposal may be good in some cases, so it may not be wise to be totally in favour of or opposed to a proposal. For example, you may be asked to say whether you agree or disagree with the view that parents should decide which television programmes children can watch and which they cannot watch. Obviously they should control what very young children watch, but the children may need greater freedom of choice when they grow older. A similar argument may apply when considering other topics, so be ready to use 'in some cases' when deciding on your plan.

Over to you!

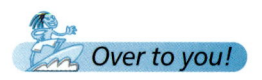

Exercise 6

Discuss each of these topics and make notes of the main arguments you could use when writing or speaking about the topic.

1. Is it fair to permit professionally-trained people such as nurses, teachers and police officers to emigrate to a foreign country? Is it fair or practical to stop them from emigrating? What is your view?

2. Should parents play a greater part in deciding the type of education which their children receive, e.g. by exercising more control over schools? What is your opinion?

3. 'Corporal punishment should be prohibited in schools and in the home.' Write a letter to the editor of a newspaper opposing or supporting this point of view.

4. 'Tourism should be given greater government support because of the many benefits which it brings to the host country.' Are you in favour of or against this statement?

5. 'Helping the community' should be a recognised subject at school and the achievements of each student in this respect should be formally stated on each secondary school leaving certificate. To what extent do you agree with this?

6. People who commit murder in circumstances which leave no doubt in the mind of a jury or judge should be put to death by an injection of lethal drugs. Prepare a speech in which you support or oppose this proposal.

24.11
Writing

Choose *one* of the topics in 24.10 and then write 250–300 words about it in not more than 30 minutes.

24.12
Grammar: using gerunds

A **gerund** is a noun formed from a verb. It can consist of one, two or three words, as the examples below show.
In the following sentence, 'bananas' is a noun:
    I like bananas.
We can use a gerund instead of the noun 'bananas':
    I like **inviting** people to a party.
    I like **being invited** to a party.

English Alive!

In the following sentence, 'accusation' is a noun:
   The man denied the accusation.
We can use a gerund instead of 'accusation':
   The man denied **having stolen** a watch.
   The man denied **having been involved** in a robbery.

Types of gerunds	Examples	
Present (active)	stealing	biting
Present (passive)	being stolen	being bitten
Perfect (active)	having stolen	having bitten
Perfect (passive)	having been stolen	having been bitten

Gerunds and participles sometimes have the same form but we use them in different ways. We can put a noun in place of a gerund but *not* in place of a participle, e.g.
   gerunds: **Smoking** is bad for your health.
      She is opposed to **smoking**.
   participles: I saw a man **smoking** outside a shop.
      Thinking that Peter had come home already, I locked the door.

Some uses of gerunds

- **As the subject**, e.g.
  Swimming is a good form of exercise.
  Sending an email does not take very long.

- **As the object**, e.g.
  Siva enjoys **hiking** with his friends.
  The man admitted **having tried** to steal a car.

- **After a preposition**, e.g.
  We look forward to **meeting** your new friend.
  My father is good at **repairing** television sets.

- **As the complement**, e.g.
  Her hobby is **making** clothes.
  His job is **repairing** cars and trucks.

Over to you!

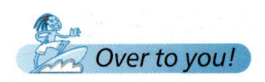

Exercise 7

Put in suitable gerunds ending in '-ing' made from the verbs in brackets.

1. The driver said he couldn't avoid (hit) the dog.
2. I was busy (write) a letter when you phoned.
3. We congratulated her on (win) the competition.
4. We didn't have much difficulty in (find) the beach.
5. Many people do not enjoy (cook) but most enjoy (eat).
6. Donna is very honest. She is incapable of (tell) lies.
7. The police officer insisted on (see) the man's driving licence.
8. We look forward to (visit) Canada during the holidays.
9. He showed us two ways of (repair) the lock.
10. My friend suggested (go) for a walk along the stream.

Exercise 8

Express these sentences in a different way, using the words in brackets and making any necessary changes.

1. For some reason, Tanya would not speak to us. (avoided)
2. My aunt hates to be late for work. (can't bear)
3. The man confessed that he had deceived his employer. (having)
4. The suspect said that he had not stolen the money. (denied having)
5. We did not expect to meet him again so soon. (foresee)
6. Will the new job force you to move to Port of Spain? (involve)
7. It is useless to try to make him change his mind. (no use)
8. We are sorry that we did not send you a receipt. (regret not)
9. The owner of the car said that he had not been involved in an accident. (denied having)
10. It's a good idea to wait until the new model comes out. (worth)

25 Offences

25.1
Pre-reading

The passage in 25.2 is an extract from *The Chrysalids* by John Wyndham. The events take place at some future time, long after a major disaster – such as a war involving atomic bombs – has devastated much of the world. The narrator is a boy who lives on a farm with his very strict parents.

Apparently radiation from nuclear weapons caused mutations amongst surviving plants, animals and humans. The people in the boy's district believe that any abnormality, such as a child with six fingers or toes, is an Offence or a Blasphemy and must be destroyed to preserve the purity of living things.

In this extract, the boy explains 'Offences' and then describes outlying areas of the region in which he lives.

25.2
Reading

Offences

It was because my father was a careful and pious man with a keen eye for an Offence that we used to have more slaughterings and burnings than anyone else, but any suggestion that we were more afflicted with Offences than other people hurt and angered him. He had no wish at all to throw good money away, he pointed out. If our neighbours were as conscientious as ourselves, he had no doubt that their liquidations would far outnumber ours; unfortunately there were certain persons with elastic principles.

So I learnt quite early to know what Offences were. They were things which did not look *right* – that is to say, did not look like their parents, or parent-plants. Usually there was only some small thing wrong, but however much or little was wrong it was an Offence, and if it happened among people it was a Blasphemy – at least that was the technical term, though commonly both kinds were called Deviations.

Nevertheless, the question of Offences was not always as simple as one might think, and when there was disagreement the district's inspector could be sent for. My father, however, seldom called in the inspector; he preferred to be on the safe side and liquidate anything doubtful. There were people who disapproved of his meticulousness, saying that the local Deviation-rate, which had shown a steady overall improvement and now stood at half what it had been in my grandfather's time, would have been better still but for my father. All the same, our Waknuk district had a great name for Purity.

Ours was no longer a frontier region. Hard work and sacrifice had produced a stability of stock and crops which could be envied by some communities to the east of us. You could now go some thirty miles to the south or south-west before you came to Wild Country – that is to say parts where the chance of breeding true was less than 50%. After that, everything grew more erratic across a belt which was ten miles wide in some places and up to twenty in others, until you came to the mysterious Fringes where nothing was dependable, and where, to quote my father, 'the Devil struts his wide estates, and the laws of God are mocked.' Fringes country, too, was said to be variable in depth, and beyond it lay the Badlands about which nobody knew anything. Usually anybody who went into the Badlands died there, and one or two men who had come back from them did not last long.

It was not the Badlands, but the Fringes that gave us trouble from time to time. The people of the Fringes – at least, one calls them people, because although they were really Deviations they often looked quite like ordinary human people if nothing had gone too much wrong with them – these people, then, had very little where they lived in their border country, so they came out into civilized parts to steal grain and livestock and clothes and tools and weapons, too, if they could; and sometimes they carried off children…

In my father's childhood, mothers used to quieten and awe troublesome infants by threatening: 'Be good now, or I'll fetch Old Maggie from the Fringes to you. She's got four eyes to watch you with, and four ears to hear you with, and four arms to smack you with. So you be careful.' Or Hairy Jack was another ominous figure who might be called in '… and he'll take you off to his cave in the Fringes where all his family lives. They're all hairy, too, with long tails; and they eat a little boy each for breakfast every morning, and a little girl each for supper every evening.' Nowadays, however, it was not only small children who lived in nervous awareness of the Fringes people not so far away. Their existence had become a dangerous nuisance and their depredations the cause of many representations to the Government in Rigo.

25.3

Understanding

A Choose the best answer in each case.

1. In 25.1, the effects of radiation are given as ____.
   - A. a supposition
   - B. an undeniable consequence
   - C. a fact
   - D. a regrettable result

2. In line 8 of 25.1 the thing that must be destroyed is ____.
   - A. six fingers
   - B. an abnormal child
   - C. six toes
   - D. the boy's district

3. The narrator's father was apparently ____ in his dealings with Deviations.
   A. lenient
   B. zealous
   C. tolerant
   D. inconsistent

4. In line 1, the use of 'pious' is supported by a reference later in the extract to ____.
   A. the laws of God
   B. preferring to be on the safe side
   C. being hurt and angered
   D. hard work and sacrifice

5. The 'slaughterings' mentioned in line 2 are echoed in the later use of the word ____.
   A. suggestion
   B. angered
   C. liquidations
   D. certain persons

6. The mention of throwing 'good money away' in line 4 is a reference to ____.
   A. using the wrong farming methods
   B. a refusal to use bribery
   C. the constant need for economy
   D. the cost of liquidations

7. Some people were said to have 'elastic principles' (line 7) because they did not always ____.
   A. attend church regularly
   B. cooperate with others
   C. pay taxes due to the government
   D. identify and remove Offences

8. The use of 'Blasphemy' (in line 11) implies ____.
   A. the presence of religion in the community
   B. that the law was more lenient in dealing with people than in dealing with animals
   C. a lack of moral principles on the part of the law-makers
   D. that Offences were more serious than Deviations

9. We learn from the first three paragraphs that some people think that the narrator's father ____.
   A. is not firm enough in dealing with Deviations
   B. should make greater use of the opinions of the district inspector
   C. is not as zealous as his own father had been earlier
   D. was too strict in his interpretation of what constituted an Offence

10. In lines 18–19, we are told that 'the local Deviation-rate … now stood at half what it had been'. This means that ____.
    A. more Offences were detected
    B. fewer Offences occurred
    C. only half the Offences were detected
    D. Purity was half as good as it had been

B Answer these questions about 25.1 and 25.2.

1. As far as we can tell, why did these Deviations occur in and near Waknuk?
2. What was the attitude of the people in Waknuk to Deviations?
3. What information in 25.1 probably explains the Badlands (line 30)?
4. Suggest a reason why the Fringes caused more trouble to Waknuk than the Badlands did.

25.4 Vocabulary: meaning in context

A Choose the word(s) which best show(s) the meaning of the underlined words as they are used in 25.1 and 25.2.

1. has <u>devastated</u> much of the world (25.1, line 3)
   - A. made great changes to
   - B. laid waste
   - C. completely destroyed
   - D. shocked

2. who lives on a farm with his very <u>strict</u> parents (line 4)
   - A. insisting on following certain principles very closely
   - B. prone to bullying and beating children at the slightest opportunity
   - C. determined not to listen to other people's point of view
   - D. showing no interest in their own children and acting selfishly

3. <u>Apparently</u> radiation from nuclear weapons (line 5)
   - A. step by step
   - B. beyond any doubt
   - C. as far as one can tell
   - D. inevitably

4. nuclear weapons caused <u>mutations</u> amongst surviving plants (line 5)
   - A. alterations
   - B. deaths
   - C. injuries
   - D. wounds

5. believe that any <u>abnormality</u> (line 7)
   - A. improvement
   - B. favourable factor
   - C. injury
   - D. change from a customary state

6. my father was a careful and <u>pious</u> man (25.2, line 1)
   - A. studious and hardworking
   - B. humble and unambitious
   - C. solemn
   - D. respecting God

7. we were more <u>afflicted with</u> Offences (line 3)
   - A. sympathetic towards
   - B. inactive concerning
   - C. suffering from
   - D. lenient towards

8. if our neighbours were as <u>conscientious</u> as ourselves (line 5)
   - A. dutiful
   - B. concerned
   - C. hard-working
   - D. fearful

9. he had no doubt that their <u>liquidations</u> would far outnumber ours (line 6)
   - A. detections
   - B. killings
   - C. afflictions
   - D. supplies of water

10. there were certain persons <u>with elastic principles</u> (line 7)
    - A. who interpreted laws freely to suit themselves
    - B. who followed the law too tightly
    - C. who were inflexible in their application of the law
    - D. who were not willing to move away from the letter of the law

English Alive!

B Match the underlined words with the meanings which they have in 25.2.

Words in the passage	Meanings
1. it was a <u>Blasphemy</u> (line 11)	a) absence of change
2. both kinds were called <u>Deviations</u> (line 13)	b) fill with fearful wonder
3. his <u>meticulousness</u> (line 18)	c) walks and acts arrogantly
4. produced a <u>stability</u> of stock (line 23)	d) changeable
5. could be <u>envied</u> by some (line 23)	e) raids and damage caused by them
6. grew more <u>erratic</u> (line 26)	f) thoroughness
7. the Devil <u>struts</u> his wide estates (line 29)	g) frightening
8. to quieten and <u>awe</u> (line 40)	h) speaking or acting against God
9. another <u>ominous</u> figure (line 43)	i) made the object of jealousy
10. their <u>depredations</u> (line 49)	j) (unacceptable) changes from the normal

25.5 Vocabulary practice

Exercise 1

Choose the most suitable word(s) in each case.

1. I ____ my mistake. I'll be much more careful next time.
   A. regret for   B. apologise   C. sorry   D. regret

2. Please ____ me that bottle. I can't reach it.
   A. each   B. past   C. deliver   D. pass

3. After being ____ of a serious driving offence, Mr Smith was ____ from driving for a year.
   A. convicted … disqualified   C. accused … unqualified
   B. committed … unqualified   D. charged … disqualified

4. What was the ____ when your uncle's company was ____ by a foreign company last month?
   A. come out … taken over   C. come out … overtaken
   B. outcome … overtaken   D. outcome … taken over

Unit 25 · Offences   **373**

5. When Hira Singh helped the police to arrest a robber, he was given ____ for his service to the ____
   A. a reward … society
   B. an award … community
   C. an award … environment
   D. a reward … bravery

6. It was raining heavily, so my friend suggested ____ at home and wait ____ the rain had stopped.
   A. we stay …until
   B. us to stay … till
   C. we staying … till
   D. to stay … until

7. The ____ of our school said that we could ____ with our plan to form a Drama Club.
   A. principal … precede
   B. principle … proceed
   C. principle … precede
   D. principal … proceed

8. As a young man, Father was a good athlete but now he is so out of ____ that he can scarcely run fifty metres.
   A. fitness   B. condition   C. health   D. habit

9. Very few people believe in the ____ of supernatural creatures.
   A. occurrence   B. incident   C. accuracy   D. existence

10. The heavy rain during the night ____ the road conditions even worse.
    A. made   B. did   C. caused   D. created

11. When you start work in this company, take ____ not to offend the manager.
    A. caution   B. precaution   C. effort   D. care

12. The bridge was unsafe, so the soldiers decided to ____ back to their camp.
    A. retreat   B. retire   C. go   D. return

13. Tomorrow the magistrate will have to consider the conflicting ____ given by the various witnesses.
    A. proof   B. evidence   C. events   D. remarks

14. Her success in her examinations last year has ____ her to study even harder.
    A. inspired   B. resulted   C. effected   D. pulled

15. I wish you wouldn't ____ your papers all over the table.
    A. stray   B. spray   C. straggle   D. spread

16. A diluted solution of a substance is a comparatively ____ one.
    A. concentrated   B. fragile   C. rare   D. weak

17. If you want a baby to grow properly, you should make sure that he gets ____ food.
    A. supporting
    B. nourishing
    C. advancing
    D. maintaining

18. After Abiose had been working for the firm for a year, she ___ up the courage to ask for an increase in salary.
    A. plucked B. raised C. pulled D. made

19. Villages often ___ up at the meeting-place of two rivers.
    A. develop B. spring C. establish D. evolve

20. In many countries, the coming of the railways changed the whole ___ of village life.
    A. stamp B. frame C. pattern D. design

Exercise 2

Choose the most suitable word(s) in each case.

1. When we were walking through the mountains, we ___ upon a remote village quite ___ chance.
   A. bumped … on
   B. tumbled … with
   C. tripped … at
   D. stumbled … by

2. When an animal dies in the forest, its body begins to ___ quite quickly because of the heat.
   A. decay B. decompose C. ripen D. depreciate

3. When we heated the compound in a test-tube, it gave ___ a foul-smelling gas.
   A. up B. away C. across D. off

4. These new machines should ___ us to increase ___ at the factory considerably.
   A. able … production
   B. enable … output
   C. help … come
   D. allow … outflow

5. Errol decided to ___ from voting at the meeting because he could not make up his mind whether to vote for or against the proposal.
   A. restrain B. avoid C. decline D. abstain

6. Did the Minister ___ anything about taxes in his speech?
   A. speak B. tell C. mention D. inform

7. High humidity often makes the heat really ___.
   A. oppressive B. odious C. repulsive D. repugnant

8. The injured man did not complain ___ his injuries although they ___ him great pain.
   A. of … made
   B. concerning … took
   C. for … created
   D. about … caused

9. After all the changes that have occurred in recent years, it is good to have ___ economic conditions at last.
   A. stable B. deteriorating C. rigid D. stationary

10. Last week the newspaper published a special ____ dealing with the problems of agriculture in South America and the Caribbean region. It was distributed free with the paper.
    A. complement   B. compliment   C. supplement   D. increment

11. It is wise to keep some tinned food at home to provide an emergency supply ____ some unexpected disaster turns ____.
    A. maybe … out
    B. in case … up
    C. against … down
    D. if … on

12. Mr Blank was dismissed because his bad work showed that he was ____.
    A. incompetent
    B. incomplete
    C. insufficient
    D. inadvisable

13. This low-lying area could probably be ____ into rice country with proper drainage.
    A. transformed
    B. replaced
    C. cultivate
    D. develop

14. This is the ____ season for tourists, so you won't find many of them here.
    A. away   B. down   C. out   D. off

15. In some countries, people who live in remote areas tend to be out of ____ with development in other parts of their country.
    A. feel   B. touch   C. sight   D. hearing

16. If a country is self-____ as far as rice or fruit is concerned, it does not need to ____ any.
    A. sustaining … grow
    B. adequate … buy
    C. supporting … import
    D. reliable … purchase

17. Last month, Mrs Wilson helped us. Then yesterday we were delighted to help her. As Mother said, 'One good turn deserves ____.'
    A. everybody
    B. everything
    C. other
    D. another

18. Better irrigation schemes can increase the ____ of rice in some areas.
    A. yield   B. produce   C. gain   D. product

19. If water in a small pool does not move, it may become ____.
    A. scattered   B. stagnant   C. malignant   D. restive

20. Farmers hope that they can increase rice production by using new ____ of rice.
    A. assortments
    B. branches
    C. strains
    D. breeds

25.6
Grammar: infinitives (revision)

We can use an **infinitive** with 'to' or without 'to', depending upon the type of sentence, e.g.

with 'to': Melissa likes to cook the food for the whole family.
without 'to': We must cook the food now.

In the following examples, 'to' is in brackets to show that we must leave it out in some sentences.

Present	push	make
Active	(to) push	(to) make
Passive	(to) be pushed	(to) be made
Continuous	(to) be pushing	(to) be making
Perfect		
Active	(to) have pushed	(to) have made
Passive	(to) have been pushed	(to) have been made
Continuous	(to) have been pushing	(to) have been making

Examples using the verb 'make':

Don't **make** too much noise. Grandma is asleep.

This type of camera used **to be made** in Italy. Now it is made in China.
Mom is in the kitchen. She might **be making** a cake for Mitzie's birthday.
Paul ought **to have made** his new kite by now. He started several hours ago.
Anna: I wonder if our curtains are ready yet.
Tanya: I expect so. They ought **to have been made** by now.
When we arrived, Vimala was watching television but she ought **to have been making** a handbag for her sister.

Unit 25 · *Offences*

Over to you!

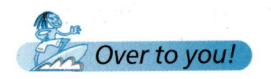

Exercise 3

Put in a suitable infinitive of the verb in brackets.

1. What's the time, Deena? I must ____ (leave) my watch at home by accident.

2. That wooden step is dangerous. It could break at any time. It needs ____ (repair).

3. It's nearly 2 a.m. What are you doing in the kitchen at this time of night? You ought ____ (sleep) now, not wandering around the house.

4. Anybody who drives while uninsured should ____ (fine) and his car should ____ (confiscate).

5. The magistrate scolded the accused men and told him, 'You were not paying attention to oncoming traffic. You ought ____ (see) a bus approaching when you tried ____ (overtake) a lorry.'

6. Before you went to bed last night, you ought ____ (check) both doors ____ (make) sure that they were locked.

7. The guest in Room 433 asked ____ (call) at 5.30. She has to catch an early plane.

8. After the earthquake, more people might ____ (rescue) if the rescuers had arrived earlier. They must ____ (delay) by all the traffic on the road after the quake. The police should ____ (clear) a way for them.

9. In 2004, Lennox Lewis said he was going ____ (retire) as undefeated heavyweight boxing champion of the world. He likes ____ (visit) Jamaica because that is where his family came from.

10. It's 3 p.m. UK time, so Uncle's plane should ____ (approach) Heathrow Airport now. It was due ____ (arrive) at 3.10 p.m. His wife is going ____ (meet) him at the airport, so she should ____ (wait) for him now.

Exercise 4

Put in a suitable infinitive of the verb in brackets.

1. The starter will fire a gun ____ (tell) you when ____ (start).

2. When do you intend ____ (buy) a decent bike?

3. What do you want ____ (do) with these old shoes? They ought ____ (throw) away. They're too old for anybody ____ (repair).

4. Francine: The boys seem ____ (argue) about something.
   Natoya: They are not sure who ____ (blame) for the mistake.

5. Natalie: It's a good job you didn't touch that bare wire.
   Althea: Why?
   Natalie: It's live. If you had touched it, you would probably ____ (electrocute). Then you could ____ (kill).

6. According to a man on television, Hurricane Jane should ____ (arrive) tomorrow morning just as we are getting ready ____ (go) to school. If he's right, our school will ____ (close) tomorrow.

7. When I got up this morning, the light was still on, so somebody must ____ (forget) ____ (turn) it off last night.

8. Both of these knives are blunt. They need ____ (sharpen).

9. These walls are dirty. They ought ____ (repaint) and that old door should ____ (replace).

10. You were lucky that the lifeguard saw you. You might ____ (drown) if he hadn't jumped in ____ (rescue) you.

25.7

Writing: setting out dialogue (revision)

In the CSEC examinations, you may have to write a short story. This may involve the use of dialogue, so check that you know how to set out dialogue. Remember that each new speaker starts a new paragraph, e.g.

'How did you get on in the game on Saturday?' Tanya asked her brother. She had heard rumours that there had been a fight during the game, so she wanted to know who had been involved.

'Oh, fine,' Roy said. 'We won but it was a bit of a struggle …'

'Was there any fighting?' Tanya asked, anxious to get all the details.

'I was just going to tell you when you interrupted,' Roy said. 'Yes, there was a bit of a fight when our striker barged into their goalkeeper and knocked him down, but it wasn't anything serious.'

'Were you involved in it?

'Who? Me? No, I was at the other end of the field. Anyway, by the time I got down to the other goal, the ref had stopped it all.'

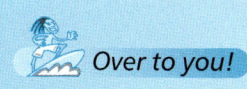

Over to you!

Exercise 5

Write the first 10 lines of *one* of these conversations
    a) between a friend and yourself about plans for activities during the vacation
    b) between yourself and a friend whose brother or sister has just taken his/her driving test
    c) between yourself and a police officer who is investigating a crime and wants to know where you were at a certain time two days ago, what you were doing and who was with you.

25.8
Writing: plotting practice (revision)

Earlier in this book we saw that:

- a plot often involves **conflict**: within a person, with another person or with extraneous circumstances (e.g. a storm, a puncture, a wild animal).
- sometimes we can use SSS to make up a plot quickly:

S – **saver** Somebody saved a person.
S – **saved** Somebody is saved from trouble or disaster.
S – **saw**   The narrator saw something happen, e.g. a fire, a rescue, etc.

There are many other ways of making up a plot. It is useful to practise different methods before you take the examination. You will have only 5–10 minutes in which to think of a plot about a scene in a picture, a person in a picture, or a given situation, i.e. one which starts or ends in a given way.

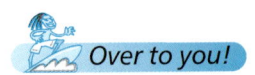

Over to you!

Exercise 6

Make up a plot for *one* of the following stories. You can write the plot down in the form of notes. Complete sentences are not necessary. Do not write the whole story.

1. After the friends had been walking for more than an hour, Lloyd began to wonder whether they were lost. The path had more or less disappeared and there were no familiar landmarks …

Continue the story.

or

2. Francine tried to stand up. An order appeared on her computer: SIT DOWN! Then she heard a strange flat voice coming from the computer.
'Sit down! Now! Sit down and listen. I will tell you what to do!'
Francine stared at the computer and felt it taking over her brain. …

Continue the story.

or

3. Write a story in which somebody is punished for something which he or she did not do.

Exercise 7

Make up a plot for *one* of the following stories.

1. Write a story which begins,:
    I remembered that my mother had told me always to be careful when dealing with a stranger …

or

2. Write a story which ends with these words:
    … That is one place that I hope I shall never see again.

or

3. You have been given a picture showing a teenager receiving an award at a ceremony with many people watching. The award is a certificate. Write a story showing what led up to the scene shown in the picture.

Exercise 8

Make up a plot for *one* of the following stories.

1. Write a story which starts with these words:
   Aunt Sonia was the last person you would expect to tell a lie but …

2. Write a story about a time when a young man and a girl meet unexpectedly four years after they had left the same school.

3. Write a story on the theme 'Nothing ventured, nothing gained'.

25.9 Writing

Either: Write 400–450 words on topic (1) or (2) in about 45 minutes.
or: Write 250–300 words on topic (3) or (4) inabout 30 minutes.

1. Write a story based on the picture above.
2. Write a story based on one of the themes given in 25.8.
3. Discuss the likely causes of crime in your country and suggest measures which could be taken to remove the causes.
4. In what ways do you think your country will develop in the next 20 years?

26 Applying for a Job

26.1
Preparing to apply for a job

- Get several copies of a good, cheerful photograph of yourself (head and shoulders). *When necessary*, you can fasten a photograph of yourself to an application for a job.

- Get testimonials or references from your Principal, class teacher or another person. Ask for a reference at least two weeks *before* you need to use it. Make copies of your testimonials so that you can send them with an application. Never send original testimonials or you may lose them. You can take them to an interview if necessary.

- Ask two responsible people if they will kindly agree to act as referees for you. This means that potential employers can contact them confidentially to ask for more information about you. You can ask a class or subject teacher to be a referee if he or she knows you well. Another referee can be somebody in an outside organisation. Remember to get permission from referees *before* you put their names and addresses on application forms.

- Get at least two copies of your birth certificate.

- Get copies of any examination results, certificates or transcripts when they become available.

- If you do not have a telephone, ask a friend if he or she would allow you to use his or her telephone number on a letter of application. Sometimes employers use the telephone to invite people to attend an interview. Then somebody could take a message and pass it on to you.

26.2
Check these points

- If you don't really want a job or do not have the right qualifications or experience, don't apply for the job.

- If possible type your application neatly (or set it up on a computer and then print it out) unless an advertisement asks for handwritten applications. An illegible or confusing application stands no chance of being successful.

- Check that you have included any information which the advertiser has asked for.

- Check that you know how to prepare a **curriculum vitae** (**CV** – an account of one's life or career, see 26.3). Some applicants do not send a CV. They try to squeeze all the information into a letter. This will annoy some employers because they may not be able to find quickly something that they want to know.

- Check your spelling. Applicants who misspell words are showing that they are careless and probably not worth employing.

- Don't ask for or expect special favours because your family is poor. Most employers are not charities.

- Remember to provide a telephone number at which an employer can contact you.

26.3
Preparing a curriculum vitae

A **curriculum vitae** (also known as a **CV** or **resumé**) is an account of your life, education, skills and work experience (if any). As time goes on, you will probably need to update it.

Here is an example:

```
                    Curriculum Vitae
                    Julius MELVILLE


PERSONAL DETAILS
Name:               Julius MELVILLE
Address:            305 Chapel Lane, Green Hills, Kingston, Jamaica
Telephone:          1234-5678
Age:                16, born 1 April 1992 in Jamaica
Sex:                Male
Marital status:     Single


EDUCATION
2000-2005           New Town Secondary School
1994-2000           Old Town Primary School
```

```
QUALIFICATIONS
2008                CSEC Examination [give results]
IT skills           MS Word
                    MS Excel
                    MS Powerpoint


OTHER SKILLS
Typing              I can type at about 80 words a minute.
Accountancy         I am studying as a student member to take the
                    examinations of the Institute of Chartered
                    Accountants


SPORT
I have played for my school first team at football and cricket.


CAREER OBJECTIVE
Eventually I should like to become a Chartered Accountant.


REFEREES AND TESTIMONIALS
I enclose copies of testimonials. You are also invited to refer
to the following people for further information about me:
a) Mrs Mary Williams, Principal, New Town Secondary School
b) Mr David Morris, Manager, New Town Trading Co., 74 Central
   Road.


J. Melville
J. Melville
```

26.4
Sending a covering letter with your CV

You can send a simple covering letter with your CV (or with a printed application form if one is used). Keep your letter short. All the vital information should be in your CV and not in your covering letter.

Note that when you are much older, your CV may contain so many pages that you might need to put it in a folder with a list of contents and details of projects which you have been responsible for, e.g. an engineer might give photographs and details of housing estates, drainage schemes, factories or anything else he has been responsible for.

Here is an example of a covering letter:

```
                                                    [address]
                                                    [telephone number]
                                                    [email address]
                                                    [date]

The Chief Accountant
Sales Trading Co. Ltd
6th Floor, City Building
Kingston


Dear Sir


Vacancy for Accounts Clerk
With reference to your advertisement in 'The Morning Star' on
14 August, I have much pleasure in applying for the post.

I enclose a copy of my curriculum vitae and testimonials, and I
shall be very happy to attend an interview at any time
convenient to you.


Yours sincerely

Julius Melville
Julius Melville
```

Note:

The title, and the closing words and signature can be put by the left margin or in the centre of the page. Commas can be omitted in the address of the writer and recipient. Both of the paragraphs can be indented, i.e. moved a few spaces away from the left margin.

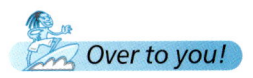

Over to you!

Exercise 1

Prepare your own curriculum vitae so that your teacher can check it for you.
Leave blank spaces for anything which you cannot complete now, e.g. examination results.

Unit 26 · *Applying for a Job*

26.5
Discussion: work methods

Study these points concerning what to do after you get a job. Is there anything you disagree with or want to change? Is there anything you want to add?

- Always be ready to work longer hours than the official ones. Arrive early and don't worry if you can't always leave on time. On rare occasions, it may be necessary to work all night. Don't complain. Just get on with it.

- Be loyal to your colleagues and superiors. Don't say bad things about other people.

- Be sociable and part of a team. Don't become known as a 'lone wolf' who does not fit in well with the rest of the staff.

- Help your boss and try to understand her/him:
  - If he/she likes to make all the decisions, consult him/her frequently.
  - If he/she is very busy and expects you to get on with your work without creating problems for him/her, make your own decisions except on important points.

- If possible, be ready for promotion but don't make your superior feel that you are trying to get his/her job.

- Be polite and helpful to customers/clients. It is good for business and it makes life more pleasant for everybody.

26.6
Grammar: using perfect infinitives
Active forms

In Unit 25, we saw that these are active perfect infinitives:

```
(to) have finished        (to) have seen
(to) have stopped         (to) have gone
(to) have invited         (to) have written
```

We sometimes use a perfect infinitive after 'may', 'might', 'will', 'would', 'should', 'can', 'could' and 'must', e.g.

    If Sheryl had applied for the job, she would probably **have got** it.
    I would **have lent** you the money if you had asked me.
    I can't see Rosette. She may **have gone** home already.
    The boys could **have finished** the work in time but the storm stopped them.
    Christine must **have forgotten** about the picnic.
    That woman seems to **have lost** something.

> **Reminder**
> When we speak quickly, the word 'have' in the above sentences may sound like 'of'. Remember to write 'have' and not 'of' in sentences using a perfect infinitive.

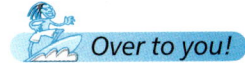

Over to you!

Exercise 2

In each blank space below, put in the active perfect infinitive of the right verb from the box, or of any other suitable verb.

borrow	conclude	know	put
break	forget	leave	slip
buy	give	let	tell
catch	go	miss	visit
come	have	post	win

1. I could ____ your letters if you had given them to me. I went past the Post Office and could ____ them in the box.

2. The conference is said ____ successfully despite the earlier disagreements.

3. The wanted man is known ____ to Florida recently. He is thought ____ a large sum of money with him.

4. David isn't here. He must ____ all about the game – or he may ____ to the wrong place.

5. Your brother ought ____ the chief clerk about the mistake. He would ____ what to do about it.

6. The train can't ____ already. It's not due to leave for another twenty minutes. We can't ____ it. I expect it will come fairly soon.

7. You were very lucky! You might ____ a leg if you had fallen off the roof. You could easily ____ on those damp tiles.

8. That lady is said ____ the first prize in a lottery recently. She is known ____ two new houses during the past month.

9. We could ____ more fish if we had used a larger net, and then we could ____ some to our neighbours.

10. Why didn't you phone me? I could easily ____ to meet you. We could ____ Gopal's car. He would ____ us use it.

Unit 26 · Applying for a Job 387

Passive forms

These are passive forms of the perfect infinitive:

(to) have been finished	(to) have been seen
(to) have been stopped	(to) have been caught
(to) have been invited	(to) have been written

Examples:

The repairs to this road should **have been finished** a week ago.
The boxing match last night should **have been stopped** in the second round. It was very one-sided.
Francine was disappointed not to **have been invited** to Aisha's party.
The burglar was worried because he thought he might **have been seen** breaking into the house.
When Lara hit the ball it should **have been caught** but the fielder dropped it.
Miss Wilson looked at John's composition and said it might **have been written** by a tired spider.

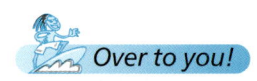

Over to you!

Exercise 3

In each blank space below, put in the *passive* perfect infinitive of the right verb from the box, or of any other suitable verb.

arrest	give	lose	rescue
commend	hurt	promote	sell
finish	injure	repair	warn

1. Two men are said ____ in the fire last night.

2. That leaking tap should ____ several days ago.

3. Paul ought ____ for the bravery he showed in rescuing the two small children.

4. I'm sorry. We can't find your parcel. It seems ____ when we moved to a new office. Have you got a receipt for it? You should ____ one when you handed the parcel in to the chief clerk.

5. We could not use the school hall last Saturday. The painting ought ____ before then but something delayed the workmen for two days.

6. Your friend might ____ if he had been travelling on that bus. It was lucky he decided not to go.

7. That dress you wanted must ____ already. It's not in the shop window now.

English Alive!

8. I'm sure Errol would ____ a long time ago if he had been more polite to the manager. He should ____ to be more careful about what he says.

9. A tanker has sunk but the crew are believed ____ by two other ships in the vicinity.

10. Two men are said ____ by the police in connection with the recent violence in Spanish Town.

26.7
Spelling

-r/-rr- and -t/-tt-

Make sure that you can spell these words correctly:

occur: occurred	defer: deferred	permit: permitted
concur: concurred	infer: inferred	commit: committed
refer: referred	prefer: preferred	admit: admitted

-ll- and -l-

Check that you can spell these words correctly:

skill: skilful	until: till	travel: traveller
fulfil: fulfilled	install: instalment	helpful cheerful

-nce and -nt

In words like these below, '-nt' indicates that the word is an adjective; words ending in '-nce' are nouns:

Adjective	Noun	Adjective	Noun
absent	absence	important	importance
confident	confidence	innocent	innocence
convenient	convenience	negligent	negligence
different	difference	obedient	obedience
distant	distance	relevant	relevance
excellent	excellence	reluctant	reluctance
ignorant	ignorance	silent	silence
impatient	impatience	violent	violence

Other spellings

Check that you can spell these words. Then your teacher can test you or the two halves of your class can have a spelling competition.

List 1	List 2	List 3	List 4
adolescent	acquaintance	accustomed	appearance
aquarium	atmosphere	argument	behaviour
cinema	beginning	competition	coincidence
February	develop	existence	criticism
honorary	equator	explanation	definitely
humorous	honourable	lightning	fulfil
hygienic	lifelike	necessary	neighbour
mathematics	picturesque	persuasion	occasionally
reticent	pigeon	solemnly	reference
systematic	privilege	successful	society
theatre	reasonably	suspense	surprised
Wednesday	separately	valve	weird

26.8

Grammar: prepositions (1)

Exercise 4

Supply the missing words, and then use each expression in a sentence orally in class. You can replace the words in italics if you want to.

1. persuaded him ____ *go*
2. encouraged her ____ *enter*
3. apply ____ *a job*
4. apply ____ *a company*
5. superior ____ *ours*
6. refrain ____ *arguing*
7. enrol ____ *a class*
8. different ____ *the others*
9. a problem ____ *him*
10. aim ____ *improve*
11. ____ my opinion
12. ____ the best of my ability
13. pay attention ____ *her*
14. prevent them ____ *leaving*
15. provide him ____ *books*
16. accused ____ *robbing*
17. go ahead ____ *a plan*
18. put ____ a fire
19. capable ____ *producing*
20. a specialist ____ *welding*

English Alive!

Exercise 5

Put in the missing words or take out the space to show that no word is needed. Sometimes alternatives are possible.

1. Francine accused the man ____ not telling the truth ____ the mistake.
2. Colin was present ____ the meeting yesterday but Clive was absent ____ it.
3. ____ modern times, people usually cooperate ____ each other.
4. ____ the present time, the manager is very much occupied ____ the problem ____ staffing.
5. I'll reply ____ his complaint ____ Sunday or Monday.
6. Oxygen is manufactured ____ a large scale ____ that factory.
7. The meeting ended ____ a dispute ____ the control of funds.
8. Lance agrees ____ the broad scope of the plan but disagrees ____ us ____ some details.
9. In accordance ____ the evidence, the judge decided ____ the plaintiff and ____ favour ____ the defendant.
10. Maria has just been confirmed ____ her new position ____ head of the Sales Department.
11. We thought that his attitude ____ your suggestion was the opposite ____ what we had anticipated.
12. The coach had a good opportunity ____ observing most of the players but he had no real chance ____ observe the left back.
13. Hillary prefers ____ associate ____ wealthy people only.
14. She invested a lot of money ____ a new company but was swindled ____ of it by promoters ____ a foreign country.
15. You'll be better off if you put your money ____ deposit ____ a local bank.
16. Events proved that the manager's confidence ____ the new cashier was justified.
17. This river teems ____ fish but is notorious ____ its large alligators.
18. The mechanic charged Mr Seymour ____ five hundred dollars ____ the repairs ____ his car.
19. According ____ these statistics, we can guess that changes ____ the system are needed.
20. The *Observer* produced a special edition ____ its newspaper ____ the occasion ____ its tenth anniversary.

26.9
Grammar: prepositions (2)

Exercise 6

Supply the missing words, and then use each expression in a sentence orally in class. You can replace the words in italics if you want to.

1. concentrate ____ *your work*
2. worry ____ *the cost*
3. insist ____ *going*
4. knock ____ *a door*
5. crash ____ *a tree*
6. take no notice ____ *him*
7. much ____ *his disgust*
8. to bump ____ *somebody*
9. be satisfied ____ *his pay*
10. nothing ____ *particular* to *do*
11. accuse somebody ____ *lying*
12. not used ____ *very hot weather*
13. to boast ____ *winning*
14. to die ____ *malaria*
15. driving ____ *top speed*
16. angry ____ *them*
17. ashamed ____ *himself*
18. to believe ____ *ghosts*
19. to be sure ____ *the result*
20. an insult ____ *them*

Exercise 7

Put in the missing words or take out the space to show that no word is needed. Sometimes alternatives are possible.

1. Slow down. We can't keep pace ____ you.
2. We must guard ____ any repetition ____ the tragedy.
3. They hope to produce pepper ____ a much more substantial scale than ____ the past.
4. Low prices tend ____ discourage farmers ____ increasing production.
5. Their aim is to increase production ____ order to achieve self-sufficiency ____ the near future.
6. The stranger is ____ trouble because he left the hotel ____ paying his bill. There are good reasons ____ suspecting that he has gone ____ hiding somewhere.
7. All the members spoke up ____ support ____ the secretary's proposal although it was not entirely ____ accordance ____ the rules.
8. She has to work ____ rather difficult conditions but manages to put up ____ them.

9. Donna had doubts ____ the scheme and wondered whether she would succeed ____ getting the others ____ agree ____ her that a change ____ the conditions was necessary.

10. Mark took no notice ____ the report and came ____ the conclusion that it was derived ____ an unreliable source.

11. Karen is not very good ____ Art but she is not bad ____ English, so we are quite satisfied ____ her work and confident ____ her ability to get ____ the examination successfully.

12. Their lack ____ practice resulted ____ defeat ____ their side ____ the hands ____ a better team.

13. John suffered ____ indigestion but he suffered ____ silence most of the time.

14. Lance took a liking ____ the boy ____ whom he had borrowed the book.

15. They all helped ____ the development ____ the project, determined to see it ____ to the end.

16. This change is good ____ Tanya but it may have an adverse effect ____ you.

17. Regardless ____ the risk involved ____ the project, they opted to go ahead ____ the scheme.

18. What explanation do they have ____ their failure ____ deliver the goods ____ time?

19. There is no point ____ arguing ____ him just ____ the sake ____ arguing.

20. He is tired ____ staying ____ home ____ himself most of the time.

26.10
Say it another way

Exercise 8

Express each of the following sentences in a different way. Start with the given words.

1. It is not very likely that Dave forgot to lock it.
   Dave …

2. He said he was sorry he had forgotten to post the letter.
   He apologised for…

3. I had not been there before, so I nearly lost myself.
   Not …

4. Somebody should close those windows during a storm.
   Those windows …

Unit 26 · Applying for a Job

5. The accident is John's fault.
   John is …

6. Nobody noticed that the sign had been damaged.
   The damage …

7. Banks often lend money to the owners of factories.
   The owners …

8. All the people have a chance to express their views at an election.
   Everyone …

9. How foolish you are to argue with her!
   What a …

10. He managed to speak to us although he was injured.
    Despite …

11. Whose watch is this?
    Who …

12. She seems to be very pleased about something.
    It looks …

13. Bad weather sometimes results in famine.
    Famine …

14. The tourist had to show the police officer her passport.
    The police …

15. She found difficulty in deciding which pair of shoes to buy.
    It was …

16. A security guard would not allow us to go through the gate.
    We were prevented …

17. It does not matter what he said to the manager.
    What he …

18. She said that the man had tried to steal her bicycle.
    She accused …

19. Paula mentioned the mistake in the invoice to the clerk.
    Paula informed …

20. There were angry players all round the referee.
    The referee …

Appendix 1: All About Verbs

Verb forms
Infinitive

Present active:	(to) help	Mary likes **to help** people.
Present continuous:	(to) be helping	You ought **to be helping** Mother now.
Present passive:	(to) be helped	Mrs Harris needs **to be helped**.
*****Perfect active:**	(to) have helped	We ought **to have helped** that old man.
*****Perfect continuous:**	(to) have been helping	You should **have been helping** him.
*****Perfect passive:**	(to) have been helped	He might **have been helped** by Susan.

> **Reminder**
> In speech, the word 'have' is often shortened, as in 'we've' and 'they've'. Then an expression such as 'should have' sounds like 'should of'. Don't write 'of' instead of 'have' when you use the infinitives marked * above.

Present participle

Active form:	helping
Passive form:	being helped

Examples: Nicolle watched some men **helping** to find a leak in a water-pipe.
After the crash, we saw a passenger **being helped** from the damaged car.

Past participle

helped

Example: **Helped** by a strong wind, the fire spread rapidly.

Perfect participle

Active form:	having helped
Continuous form:	having been helping
Passive form:	having been helped

Examples: **Having helped** his team by scoring two goals, Ishak was happy when the game ended.
Having been helping to repair the pipe for more than three hours, Kevin was glad when the job was eventually finished.
Having been helped a lot by two teachers at his school, Lynton went on to become one of the finest batsmen in the West Indies.

Gerund

Present active:	helping	breaking	choosing
Present passive:	being helped	being broken	being chosen
Perfect active:	having helped	having broken	having chosen
Perfect passive:	having been helped	having been broken	having been chosen

Examples: **Helping** other people is an excellent thing to do.
Sometimes young children dislike **being helped** because they want to do something on their own.
Paul apologised for **having broken** a large bowl.
Sharma was surprised at **having been chosen** to represent his school.

Tenses

There are a number of tenses in English. Some tenses can be:
    active: Mrs Harris often **helps** other people.
    passive: Many people **are helped** by friends or relatives.
    continuous (progressive): Today Mrs Harris **is helping** a neighbour to make a cake.

Grammarians sometimes use different names for the same tense, so you may find alternatives to some of the names used below. For example, some grammarians use 'progressive' instead of 'continuous'.

Tense	Examples using 'to kick'	
	Active form	**Passive form**
Simple Present	I kick	I am kicked
Present Continuous	I am kicking	I am being kicked
Past Continuous	I was kicking	I was being kicked
Simple Past	I kicked	I was kicked
Present Perfect	I have kicked	I have been kicked
Present Perfect Continuous	I have been kicking	—
Past Perfect	I had kicked	I had been kicked
Past Perfect Continuous	I had been kicking	—
Simple Future	I shall/will kick	I shall/will be kicked
Future Continuous	I shall be kicking	—
Future Perfect	I shall have kicked	I shall have been kicked
Future Perfect Continuous	I shall have been kicking	—
Present Conditional	I should kick	I should be kicked
Present Conditional Continuous	I should be kicking	—
Perfect Conditional	I should have kicked	I should have been kicked
Perfect Conditional Continuous	I should have been kicking	—

English Alive!

See Appendix 2 for the main uses of the more common tenses. For more about 'active' and 'passive', see below.

Transitive and intransitive verbs

A **transitive verb** has an object. An **intransitive verb** does *not*. Many verbs can be used transitively or intransitively. In many dictionaries, the letters *v.i.* (verb intransitive) or *v.t.* (verb transitive) show whether a verb is transitive or not.

transitive: Sometimes Sharma sings old Hindi songs. (*with an object*)
intransitive: Sharma can sing beautifully. (*no object*)

Common intransitive verbs include 'appear', 'be', 'seem' and 'wonder'.

Finite and non-finite (infinite) verbs

We can say that a **finite verb** is a working verb. It has a subject and is used in a tense, e.g.

It **started** to rain heavily when we **were walking** home.
Michael **will help** you to repair the puncture in that tyre if you **like**.

A **non-finite verb** is not used with a subject or in a tense. It may be an infinitive or a participle. In the above examples, 'to rain' and 'to repair' are infinitives, so they are infinite verbs. The finite verbs are 'started', 'were walking', 'will help' and 'like'.

> **Punctuation reminder**
> A sentence must contain at least one finite verb. We cannot punctuate the following expressions as sentences. They do not contain a finite verb.
> ... walking down the road yesterday evening at about half past six
> ... damaged during the storm two days ago and left at the side of the road

Voice

We can use most verbs in the **active voice** or in the **passive voice**.

- When a verb is used in the **active voice**, the subject does the action, e.g.
  A careless motorist **injured** an elderly cyclist yesterday.
  Somebody **stole** John's bicycle during the night.

- When a verb is used in the **passive voice**, the action is done *to* the subject and not by it. We often use a passive verb when (a) we do not know who did an action or (b) it is not important to say who did an action, e.g.
  An elderly cyclist **was injured** yesterday.
  John's bicycle **was stolen** during the night.
  A number of different products **are exported** from the West Indies every week.
  The escaped prisoners **will** probably **be recaptured** soon.

Mood

Indicative mood

We say that a verb is in the indicative mood if it used to make a statement or question, e.g.
>Many tourists **visit** the West Indies every year and **enjoy** themselves.
>Sometimes lightning **hits** a tree and **starts** a fire.

Imperative mood

The imperative mood is used for orders, commands, prohibitions and prayers, e.g.
>**Stop** making a noise! **Get on** with your work!

Subjunctive mood

We say that a verb is in the subjective mood if it expresses doubt or (sometimes) a wish, e.g.
>If I **were** you, I wouldn't buy that old bicycle.
>If Uncle **were** here now, he would know what to do.
>I wish we **lived** nearer to my school.

Auxiliary verbs

Verbs such as 'be', 'do', 'have', 'may', 'shall' and 'will' help to form the tenses of other verbs, e.g. 'it is raining', 'he has gone', 'they do not live here'. We can call these verbs **auxiliary** (or 'helping') **verbs** when they are used in this way.

Appendix 2: The Main Uses of Tenses

The Simple Present tense

Active forms

Statements	Negative	Questions
I, you, we, they like	I do not like …	Do you like … ?
he, she, it likes	He does not like …	Does he like … ?

Passive form: 'am', 'is' or 'are' + past participle. It is used when the action is done *to* the subject and not by the subject, e.g.

More than 50 people **are employed** in this factory. They **are paid** every week.

Uses

The main use of the Simple Present tense is for actions which are habits, routine or are always true. In addition, this tense is sometimes used for actions happening at the time of speaking and for some past and future actions, as shown in these examples:

continuous (in a sports commentary): Anderson **runs** up and **bowls**. It**'s** a bouncer.
Lara **steps** forward and **hits** it hard.

past actions (in history time charts): 1939: Germany **invades** Poland. WW2 **starts**.
1945: Germany **surrenders**. WW2 **ends**.

past actions (a newspaper headline): HELICOPTER **SAVES** FOUR

future actions: Uncle **leaves** for Miami tomorrow and **returns** in two weeks' time.
If it **rains** tomorrow, our game will be postponed.
When Uncle **comes** on Saturday, show him that letter.

Reminder

Make sure that your verb agrees with its subject. Many students forget to add 's' to the verb when the subject is 'he', 'she', 'it' or an equivalent singular word.

wrong: My mother always *look* after us.

right: My mother always **looks** after us.

wrong: Jamaica *don't* have much to offer.

right: Jamaica **doesn't** have much to offer.

wrong: He *does* never *come* to see us.

right: He never **comes** to see us.

wrong: She *don't* know how to cook fish.

right: She **doesn't** know how to cook fish.

The Present Continuous tense

Active form: 'am', 'is' or 'are' + a present participle.

Statements				Questions		
I	am	(not)	waiting	Am	I	going too?
he, she, it	is	(not)	eating now	Is	he, she, it	waiting for us?
you, we, they	are	(not)	sleeping	Are	we, you, they	going home?

Uses

The main uses of this tense are:

- for a temporary action which is happening at the time of speaking (and, in many cases, will stop soon), e.g.
    Now I **am reading** this book. John **is looking** out of the window.
    Is your sister still **working** in a clinic?

- for planned future actions, especially ones connected with movement or travel, e.g.
    Auntie **is coming** to visit us tomorrow. She **is bringing** Vimala with her.

Passive form: 'am/is/are' + 'being' + a past participle, e.g.
    We can't use classroom 6 this week. It **is being redecorated**.
    Grandpa **is being discharged** from hospital tomorrow morning.

The Past Continuous tense

Active form: 'was/were' + a present participle, e.g.
    It started to rain when we **were playing** football.
    What **were** you **doing** when the lights went out?
    Was it **raining** when you woke up?
    Were you **fishing** when the storm arrived yesterday?

Passive form: 'was/were being' + a past participle, e.g.
    The house caught fire while it **was being redecorated**.
    Two of the men escaped when they **were being moved** to another prison.

Use

The main use of this tense is to show what was happening at some past time. It is also used when we report a speech containing a verb in the Present Continuous tense, e.g.
    Mother said that Father **was leaving** the next day.

The Simple Past tense

Active forms

Statements	Negative	Questions
he stopped	he did not stop	Did he stop?
they went	they did not go	Did they go?
you saw it	you did not see it	Did you see it?
she helped you	she did not help you	Did she help you?

- In the negative form, we use an infinitive (without 'to') after 'not'.

- Questions start with 'Did' or with 'When/Where/What/Who/Why' etc. + 'did'.

Passive form: 'was/were (not)' + a past participle

Statements	Questions
The driver was (not) injured.	Was the driver injured?
The passengers were (not) injured.	Were the passengers injured?

Uses

- The main use of this tense is to show a completed past action, e.g.
  When a small ship **sank** near Trinidad last week, most of the crew **were rescued** by other vessels but one man **died**.

- We use the Simple Past tense in conditional sentences which refer to generalised or less likely events, e.g.
  If motorists **drove** more carefully, there would be fewer accidents.

- We use the Simple Past tense after the expressions below although we are referring to present time:
  - **It's time** ... , e.g.
    It's time we **went** home.
    It's time somebody **repaired** the holes in this road.
  - **I wish** ..., e.g.
    I wish I **lived** nearer the sea.
    I wish I **knew** the answer to this question.
  - **I'd rather** ..., e.g.
    I'd rather you **didn't tell** anybody about the mistake.

Pronouncing verbs ending in '-ed'

The Simple Past tense of regular verbs ends in '-ed'. Check that you know how to pronounce the final '-ed'.

Appendix 2 · The Main Uses of Tenses

Final sound	Examples
/d/	In most verbs, the final '-ed' is spoken with the /d/ sound in 'dog' and 'good': turned, moved, played, borrowed, enjoyed, answered, rescued, repaired, dried
/t/	The final '-ed' is spoken with the /t/ sound in 'hat' when it comes after verbs which end with these sounds: /ch/ marched, watched, fetched, patched, bewitched, pitched, searched /f/ laughed, coughed, stuffed, puffed, staffed, handcuffed, knifed /k/ cooked, looked, kicked, picked, packed, smacked, baked, ached, asked /p/ helped, hoped, wiped, stopped, typed, hopped, whipped, jumped /s/ faced, raced, placed, chased, ceased, promised, reduced, collapsed /sh/ rushed, washed, pushed, crashed, finished, wished, smashed, splashed /th/ (as in 'path') berthed, bathed (in a bath)
/id/	After the sounds /d/ and /t/, final '-ed' is spoken with the sound of /id/ in 'hid'. The same sound is used for '-ied' at the end of '-ry' verbs which have at least two syllables. /t/ waited, fated, suited, hated, voted, fitted, contemplated, dated, visited, wanted /d/ mended, aided, waded, folded, befriended, blinded, faded, invaded, demanded ied carried, married, hurried, worried, buried, queried, varied, curried

The Present Perfect tense

Active form: 'has/have' + a past participle
Passive form: 'has/have been' + a past participle

Uses

This tense is often used for an action which has happened recently. Then we do not say the exact time or date of the past action. If we want to say the time or date, we have to use the Simple Past tense and *not* the Present Perfect tense. Compare these sentences:
  wrong: Thank you for your letter which I *have received* yesterday.
  right: Thank you for your letter which I **received** yesterday.

The Past Perfect tense

Active form: 'had (not)' + a past participle
Passive form: 'had (not) been' + a past participle

Uses

The main use of this tense is to show which of two past actions happened first, e.g.
>When we reached Rosa's house, we found that she **had gone** out already.
>Brian told us that he **had lost** some money.
>The man on the phone told us that Father's car was not ready. He said that the mechanics **had** not yet **finished** the repairs.

We can see from the examples above that the Past Perfect tense is also used when we report a speech containing a verb in the Simple Past or Present Perfect tense, e.g.
>*direct speech:* 'I've just arrived from Florida,' the lady told us.
>*indirect speech:* The lady told us that she **had** just **arrived** from Florida.

The Simple Future tense

Active form: 'shall/will' + an infinitive without 'to'
Passive form: 'shall/will' + be + a past participle

Uses

We can use the Simple Future tense for both planned and unplanned future actions. Some people prefer to use 'shall' when the subject is 'I' or 'we' but we can use 'will' with any subject except in questions. Then we often use 'Shall' before 'I' and 'we', e.g.
>**Shall** I **turn** the light on?
>**Shall** we **go** swimming this evening?
>Who **will win** the 200 metres race?
>Grandad wants to know when he **will be informed** of the results of the X-ray.

Note: If there is some doubt about a future action, we can use 'may' (or 'might') instead of 'will' or 'shall', e.g.
>It **may rain** during the night.
>If you break the law, you **may be caught**. Then you **may be sent** to prison.
>One day I **may be** a lawyer or an accountant.

The Future Perfect tense

Active form: 'shall/will have' + a past participle
Passive form: 'shall/will have been' + a past participle

Uses

We use this tense to refer to something which will be done or finished by the time of speaking or by some future time, e.g.
>Uncle left on the six o'clock plane, so he **will have reached** Miami by now.
>Those two men who escaped from prison **will** probably **have been arrested** by the time it gets dark.

Appendix 3: Irregular Verbs – Principal Parts

The following list shows the infinitive, Simple Past and past participle of some irregular verbs. Some verbs have the same form for all three, e.g. 'set', 'hurt', 'hit', 'cut', 'cost', etc. Some verbs have the same form for the Simple Past and the past participle, e.g. 'bring', 'buy', 'catch', 'fight', 'have', etc.

Infinitive	Simple Past	Past participle
arise	arose	arisen
awake	awoke	awoken
be	was/were	been
bear	bore	born(e)
beat	beat	beaten
become	became	become
begin	began	begun
bend	bent	bent
bet	bet	bet
bind	bound	bound
bite	bit	bitten, bit
bleed	bled	bled
blow	blew	blown
break	broke	broken
breed	bred	bred
bring	brought	brought
broadcast	broadcast	broadcast
build	built	built
burn	burnt or burned	
burst	burst	burst
buy	bought	bought
cast	cast	cast
catch	caught	caught
choose	chose	chosen
come	came	come
cost	cost	cost
creep	crept	crept
cut	cut	cut

Infinitive	Simple Past	Past participle
deal	dealt	dealt
dig	dug	dug
do	did	done
draw	drew	drawn
dream	dreamt or dreamed	
drink	drank	drunk
drive	drove	driven
dwell	dwelt	dwelt
eat	ate	eaten
fall	fell	fallen
feed	fed	fed
feel	felt	felt
fight	fought	fought
find	found	found
fling	flung	flung
fly	flew	flown
forbid	forbade	forbidden
forecast	forecast	forecast
forget	forgot	forgotten
forgive	forgave	forgiven
freeze	froze	frozen
get	got	got
give	gave	given
go	went	gone
grind	ground	ground
grow	grew	grown
hang	hung, hanged	hung, hanged
have	had	had
hear	heard	heard
hide	hid	hidden
hit	hit	hit
hold	held	held
hurt	hurt	hurt
keep	kept	kept
kneel	knelt	knelt
know	knew	known
lay	laid	laid
lead	led	led
lean	leant or leaned	
leap	leapt or leaped	
learn	learnt or learned	

Appendix 3 · Irregular Verbs – Principal Parts

Infinitive	Simple Past	Past participle
leave	left	left
lend	lent	lent
let	let	let
lie	lay	lain
light	lit or lighted	
lose	lost	lost
make	made	made
mean	meant	meant
meet	met	met
pay	paid	paid
put	put	put
read	read	read
ride	rode	ridden
ring	rang	rung
rise	rose	risen
run	ran	run
saw	sawed	sawn
say	said	said
see	saw	seen
sell	sold	sold
send	sent	sent
set	set	set
sew	sewed	sewn
shake	shook	shaken
shed	shed	shed
shine	shone	shone
shoot	shot	shot
show	showed	shown
shrink	shrank	shrunk
shut	shut	shut
sing	sang	sung
sink	sank	sunk
sit	sat	sat
sleep	slept	slept
slide	slid	slid
smell	smelt	smelt
sow	sowed	sown
speak	spoke	spoken
speed	sped	sped
spell	spelt	spelt
spend	spent	spent

Infinitive	Simple Past	Past participle
spill	spilt or spilled	
spit	spat	spat
split	split	split
spoilt	spoilt or spoiled	
spread	spread	spread
spring	sprang	sprung
stand	stood	stood
steal	stole	stolen
stick	stuck	stuck
sting	stung	stung
strive	strove	striven
swear	swore	sworn
sweep	swept	swept
swim	swam	swum
swing	swung	swung
take	took	taken
teach	taught	taught
tear	tore	torn
tell	told	told
think	thought	thought
throw	threw	thrown
tread	trod	trodden
understand	understood	understood
wake	woke	woken
wear	wore	worn
weave	wove	woven
weep	wept	wept
wet	wet	wet
win	won	won
wind	wound	wound
write	wrote	written

Appendix 4: Glossary of Language Words

Adjective
An **adjective** describes a noun or a pronoun. It can come before a noun ('a **tall** man') or after the verb 'to be' ('He is **tall**.'). In a few cases, an adjective can come after a noun: 'We painted the wall **white**.'

An **adjectival phrase** has two or more words. It gives us information about a person or thing. It does *not* have its own subject and verb: 'The man **in the back seat** is my uncle.'

An **adjectival clause** has a subject ('who', 'that', 'which') with its verb: 'The girl **who is talking to Paul** is Errol's sister.'

Adverb
An **adverb** gives us information about an action. It can tell us *how* something is done, e.g. 'Miss Dionne walks **slowly**.' It can show *when* something was done: 'Uncle arrived **yesterday**.'

An **adverbial phrase** does not contain a subject and verb: 'Paul left **in a hurry**.'

An **adverbial clause** contains its own subject and verb: 'The game was postponed **because the field was flooded after the heavy rain**.'

Affix
An **affix** is a letter (or more than one letter) which we can add to a word to make a new word. If letters are added to the front of a word, we call them a **prefix**: 'sub' + 'way' = 'subway'. If the letters are added at the end of a word, we call them a **suffix**: 'run' + 'er' = 'runner'.

Agreement
In English (and in many other languages), the form of a verb depends on which subject we use with it. For example, we say 'He is' but not 'He am'. We say 'She walks' but not 'She walk'. We call this the **agreement of the subject and verb**.

Ambiguous (n. ambiguity)
Ambiguous means 'having more than one'. For examples, the sentence 'That man is suspicious' is ambiguous. It can mean that we suspect the man or that he suspects us. The sentence 'That's a fine piece of work' can be praise *or* sarcastic condemnation, depending on how it is spoken.

Antecedent
Antecedent means 'coming earlier or before'. Consider this sentence: 'Anna picked up the envelope and opened **it**.' 'Envelope' is the antecedent of 'it'. 'It' refers to 'envelope'. Now consider this sentence: 'When Anna saw Paul, she told him about the

competition.' The antecedent of 'she' is 'Anna'. The word 'she' refers to 'Anna'. The antecedent of 'him' is Paul. The word 'him' refers to 'Paul'.

Antonym
An **antonym** is a word which is opposite in meaning to another word, e.g. 'hot – cold', 'rich – poor', 'valuable – worthless'.

Articles
We call the words 'a' and 'an' **indefinite articles** because they do not refer to a definite person or thing. We call 'the' the **definite article** because it refers to a definite person or thing. Some writers call 'a', 'an' and 'the' **determiners**.

Auxiliary verb
The word **auxiliary** means 'helping'. Examples of auxiliary verbs include 'am', 'is', 'are' ('Uncle **is** coming'), 'do', 'does', 'did' ('What **did** she say?'), 'has', 'have', 'had' ('**Have** you finished your work?'), 'shall', 'will', 'may', 'might', etc.

Clause
A **clause** is a group of words with a subject and a verb, e.g. 'The man stopped.' (a very short clause), 'The old man with a paper bag full of ragged clothes stopped for a moment to rest and recover from the long walk.' (a longer clause). In both cases, the subject is 'man' and the verb is 'stopped'.

A clause can be an **adjectival clause**, an **adverbial clause** or a **noun clause**. It can be the **main clause** of a sentence or it can be a **subordinate clause**.

main clause: The man stopped to rest in the shade of a tree.
main + two subordinate clauses: **When he came to the end of the path**, the man stopped to rest in the shade of a tree **because he was very tired after the long walk**.

Collocation
Collocation involves the frequent use of one word with another word. For example, we say 'perform' an operation (and not 'do it', 'make it' or 'cut it'). We say 'commit' a crime (and not 'do a crime'). These are further examples of collocations:

spend time (doing something) – and *not* 'pay time' or 'use up time'
pay attention (to somebody) – and *not* 'spend attention' or 'do attention'
plead 'not guilty' (in a court) – and *not* 'speak/tell/utter/report "not guilty"'

Complement
These sentences make sense by themselves: 'The bus stopped.' 'Stephanie woke up.' 'It rained during the night.' Some verbs need other words added to make complete sentences: 'Kingston is *in Jamaica*.' 'Anna looks *much better now*.' The words in italics are called the **complement** of the sentence. Verbs which require a complement include 'be', 'look', 'appear', 'seem', 'become', etc.

Conjunction
We often use **conjunctions** (joining words) such as 'and', 'but' and 'or' to link words, phrases or clauses. They are also called **connectives**.

Contraction

A **contraction** is a short form used in speech, e.g. 'don't' = 'do not'; 'I'm' = 'I am'. If you use dialogue in a story, try to use contractions to make your dialogue realistic.

Dialect

A **dialect** is a type of language spoken mainly in one town, district, region, etc. or by certain groups of people only. The dialect of Jamaica is not exactly the same as the dialect of Trinidad or Guyana. The dialect of London or New Orleans is not the same as that of Liverpool, Manchester or Sydney. One problem with most dialects is that if you use a dialect, you may not be able to communicate efficiently with people outside your own group.

Dialogue

Dialogue is conversation written down. It can be in playscript form (without inverted commas) or be part of a short story or novel (when inverted commas are needed).

Exclamation

An **exclamation** or interjection shows strong emotion, e.g. pain, fear, disgust, joy, relief, etc. Examples include 'Ow!', 'Oh!' and 'Bah!' Short sentences can also be called exclamations: 'Help!' 'Sit down!' 'Get lost!'

Finite and non-finite verbs

A **finite verb** is a working verb with a subject. A **non-finite** (or infinite) **verb** is a verb which does not have a subject and is not used in any tense. Infinitives and participles are infinite verbs.

A verb can be finite in one sentence but infinite in another sentence, e.g.
finite: Paul **is swimming** near the beach.
infinite: Paul likes **to swim**. We watched Paul **swimming** to the beach.

Gerund

A **gerund** is a special type of noun. It is made from a verb. It often ends in '-ing'. It is different from other nouns because it can have an object: 'Birds like **eating** seeds.' '**Eating** vegetables is good for you.'

Idiom

An **idiom** is a popular expression in which words are often used with a special meaning. 'To bury the hatchet' and 'to get into hot water' (= trouble) are examples of idioms.

Infinitive

An **infinitive** is the (base) form of a verb before we add any endings or change it into a tense. We can use an infinitive with 'to' or without it, depending on the pattern of the sentence, e.g.
with 'to':   All cars ought **to stop** when the lights are red.
without 'to': All vehicles must **stop** when the traffic lights are red.

Literal language
When we use a word **literally**, it has its common meaning and *not* a special meaning. When a word is used *figuratively,* it has a special meaning. Consider 'comb' in these sentences:

literally true: Your hair is untidy, so go and comb it.

figurative (NOT literally true): The police will comb the forest in their search for the escaped criminals.

In the figurative example, 'comb' means 'search very thoroughly'. The police will not use a comb.

Noun
A **noun** is the name of something. We often use common nouns ('tree', 'girl', 'shoe'), **proper nouns** ('Barbados', 'Sharon', 'Amazon'), **collective nouns** ('herd', 'team', 'flock') and **abstract nouns** ('wisdom', 'kindness', 'bravery').

We can count many things, so we call them **countable nouns** and can form their plural. We cannot count such things as 'dust', 'mud' and 'hatred', so we call them **uncountable nouns** and use them in the singular only.

Object
In a sentence, the **object** is the person or thing to whom the action of an active verb is done: e.g. 'We repaired the **pipe**. Mr Harris thanked **us**.' Sometimes there is an **indirect object** in a sentence. It often follows 'for' or 'to':' Miss Smith made this dress for **you**. Please give this letter to **your mother**.'

Participles
Participles are formed from verbs. They are used to make tenses but they are often used as adjectives. A **present participle** usually ends in '-ing'. Many **past participles** end in 'ed' but the past participle of an irregular verb may end in '-n', '-t' or another letter.

Parts of speech
Parts of speech are the names we use to show the work which a word does in a sentence. You can say that they are the names for the tools we use in a language. In English, we say that the parts of speech are nouns, adjectives, pronouns, verbs, adverbs, prepositions, conjunctions and exclamations.

Person
In grammar, **person** is used in this way:

	Singular	Plural
1st person	I	we
2nd person	you	you
3rd person	he, she, it	they

Phrase
A **phrase** is an expression of two or more words which does *not* contain a finite verb. Many phrases start with a preposition or a participle, e.g.

The girl **with long hair** is Paul's sister.
I can see a boy **climbing up a tree**.
The men cleared away the tree **knocked down by the storm**.

Predicate
The **predicate** is all the words in a sentence except the subject.

Prefix
A **prefix** consists of one or more letters added to the beginning of a word to form a new word: 'sub' + 'marine' = 'submarine'; 'tri' + 'angle' = 'triangle'.

Preposition
A **preposition** is a word put before a noun or pronoun to show its relation to an earlier word. Common prepositions include 'at', 'by', 'in', 'on', 'for', 'above', 'below', 'into', 'under' and 'through': 'We got **off** the bus **at** the market.'

Prepositions are often used at the start of a phrase showing when or where an action happened.

Pronoun
A **pronoun** is a word used to replace a noun so that we do not have to repeat the noun. Examples of pronouns include:

demonstrative:	this, these, that, those (when *not* followed by a noun)
indefinite:	someone, somebody, something, anyone, anybody, anything, etc.
interrogative:	Who, What, Which, Whose
personal:	I, me, you, she, her, it, we, us, they, them
possessive:	mine, yours, hers, his, ours, theirs
reflexive:	myself, yourself, herself, himself, itself, ourselves, yourselves, themselves
relative:	who, that, which, whom, whose

Proverb
A **proverb** is a short traditional saying which makes sense by itself and often gives advice, e.g. 'Look before you leap.'

Sentence
A **sentence** is a word or group of words which makes complete sense by itself. It contains a finite verb and a subject which is mentioned or understood: 'Stop!' = '(You) stop.'; 'St Lucia is an island.'

Subject
When we use an active verb, the **subject** is the person or thing that *does* the action shown by the verb: '**That bus** goes to Ocho Rios.' '**Football and cricket** are popular games.'

When we use a passive verb, the subject *receives* the action of the verb: 'Has **the computer** been repaired yet?' '**Bauxite** is exported to several countries.'

English Alive!

Suffix

A **suffix** is a letter or group of letters added to the end of a word to make a new word.

-*ly:* quick + ly = quickly   -*ness:* happy + ness = happiness
-*er:* swim + er = swimmer   -*ment:* govern + ment = government

Synonym

A **synonym** is a word which is similar in meaning to another word: 'small – little'; 'false – untrue'; 'illegal – unlawful'. Synonyms are not always exactly the same in meaning and/or usage.

Tense

A **tense** is a form of a verb used to show the time of an action, e.g. whether it happened in the **past**, is happening at **present** or will happen in the **future**. Many languages have tenses. Some languages do not have tenses; they use time words to show when an action happened.

Transitive

The literal meaning of **transitive** is 'goes across'. When we use a transitive verb, the action 'goes across' from the verb to a direct object: 'Our cat caught a mouse.'
If a verb is **intransitive**, it does not have an object. Some verbs are always intransitive: 'Grandma seems much better today.'

Verb

A **verb** is usually a word which shows an action. Some verbs can show a state or a relationship, e.g.

an action: My aunt **works** in a shop.
a state: Our car **is** very old.
a relationship: This key **is** yours.

Voice

In grammar, we use the word **voice** to show whether the subject *does* an action or *receives* the action. Most verbs can be used in the **active voice** or in the **passive voice**, e.g.

active voice: Tom **kicked** Paul accidentally.
passive voice: Paul **was kicked** accidentally.

Appendix 5: Glossary of Literary Terms

In the following list, items marked with an asterisk are included in the CSEC syllabus.

Allegory
An **allegory** is an account or story with a hidden meaning. For example, a story about animals may really be a criticism of politicians because each animal is meant to be one of the politicians criticised.

*Alliteration
Alliteration is the repetition of the same sound at the beginning of (or in) words which are close together, e.g. 'We all went sliding down the slippery slope.'

Antithesis
Antithesis can refer to the arrangement of words to obtain a contrast, e.g. 'Give me liberty or give me death.' 'To err is human; to forgive divine.'

We can also use antithesis to mean '(the) opposite (of)', e.g. 'Mrs Porter's attitude to her neighbours is the very antithesis of her husband's: he is surly and unfriendly; she is kind and helpful.'

Aposiopesis
Aposiopesis is suddenly failing to finish a statement, e.g. 'His behaviour makes me wonder what … But perhaps he doesn't realise what he's doing.'

Apostrophe
Apostrophe involves making an appeal to a person or thing (usually in a poem or speech) that is not present, e.g. 'Oh, Nanny, if only you were with us now!'

*Assonance
Assonance is the use of the same or similar vowel sounds in words which are close together, e.g. 'Get to bed, you sleepy head.' 'The wind whistled past our windows.'

Ballad
A **ballad** is a simple narrative poem. It usually has short verses and tells a story. Many ballads can be set to music and sung.

Climax
The **climax** is the most dramatic, exciting or intense point in a narrative or an event.

Conflict
Conflict creates problems and involves a struggle between two opposing forces. Common sources of conflict in stories include (a) conflict between rivals, (b) conflict

with some outside force such as a hurricane or earthquake, and (c) conflict within a person's mind, e.g. a struggle between dishonest motives and one's conscience.

*Connotation, denotation
Denotation is the ordinary basic meaning of a word. **Connotation** is a secondary (often emotional) meaning of a word.

A word can have at least two meanings: a primary or basic meaning (its denotation) and a secondary meaning (its connotation) consisting of feelings and thoughts associated with the word. For example, 'elderly' can simply mean 'old'. It can connote infirmity and senility.

*Couplet
In poetry, a **couplet** is a pair of lines which come together and usually rhyme.

Didactic
Didactic means 'intending to teach or instruct'. A poem can be didactic if the poet seeks to teach or give advice. This word is sometimes used to contrast with 'amusing' or 'entertaining', and it implies that a poet has a serious purpose.

Elegy
An **elegy** is a sad or mournful poem and often expresses sorrow for a dead person.

*Ellipsis
Ellipsis has two meanings. It can mean the use of … to show that something has been left out. Then a reader has to use his or her imagination to complete a sentence. It can also refer to words left out (especially in poetry) but which we can easily guess. For example, in 'The man was arrested and sent to prison', the word 'was' has been omitted before 'sent'.

Euphemism
Euphemism is deliberate understatement or the use of a mild word for something unpleasant. 'Passing away' is a euphemism for 'dying'. If you know that a man is corrupt but do not want to say so, you can say that he 'has flexible principles' or that he 'does not allow himself to be tied down rigidly by the law'.

Explicit, implicit
Explicit means clearly stated and obvious. **Implicit** means not stated openly but implied or can be deduced.

In a store, a notice saying 'Shoplifters will be prosecuted' is explicit because it tells people what will happen if they steal from the store. If there is no notice but you can see security cameras, there is an implicit threat that thieves will get into trouble.

Fiction, non-fiction
Works of **fiction** are ones which are not true. The events have been made up by the writer. **Non-fiction** is used for works which are true.

*Figurative language
Figurative language involves the use of words which may not be literally true. In a wider sense, figurative language is simply language which uses figures of speech such as metaphors, similes, etc. If somebody is in trouble, we can say, 'Figuratively speaking, his world has collapsed' or 'he is up to his neck in a sea of troubles'. The figures of speech are sometimes called 'devices', especially in an examination, e.g. 'What devices does the poet use …?'

Free verse
Free verse describes words written on separate lines in the form of a poem but with no fixed rhyme scheme, metrical pattern, length of line, etc. (Whether the result is poetry, verse or neither, the reader can judge for him/herself.)

Hyperbole
Hyperbole is the use of obvious and deliberate exaggeration, e.g. 'There were millions of noisy spectators at the football game last Saturday.'

Implicit
Implicit means implied, not stated openly. (See **explicit**.)

Implied
An **implied** meaning is one which is not stated openly but which we can deduce from a statement or situation.

Infer
Infer means deduce, decide or conclude by looking at a statement or situation. We can say that somebody 'would be better employed in a supervised position which does not involve handling money'. Then (a) we can **infer** from the statement that the person is dishonest; (b) the statement **implies** that the person may be dishonest.

*Innuendo
An **innuendo** is a statement (often bad or critical) which implies something about a person but does not state it openly. In some respects, it is like a hint (of bad qualities).

*Irony
Irony is an outcome which is mainly the opposite of what is expected, e.g.
> Mrs X attended the funeral of her husband whom she disliked. While taking part in the ceremony, she had a heart attack and died. It is ironic that she should have died in this way. She was doing her best to show respect for somebody whom she did not really respect – but the only reward she had was her own death.

Or consider this situation:
> Two fishermen had to use a life-raft when their small boat sank after hitting some rocks. A larger fishing vessel came to rescue them but was caught in a storm, and all the crew lost their lives. Meanwhile, the original two fishermen managed to paddle their way to safety. It is ironic that the rescuers died while the men in danger survived.

*Limerick
A **limerick** is a short humorous poem of five lines. Lines 1, 2 and 5 rhyme. Lines 3 and 4 are a rhyming couplet. Many limericks start with the words 'There was a ... from ...'.

*Litotes
Litotes is a type of understatement, and sometimes involves using a negative, e.g. 'Winning a gold medal at the Olympics is not bad at all.' Here 'not bad at all' is used instead of 'extremely good'.

Lyric
Used as a noun, a **lyric** is a poem which can be sung. Used as an adjective, **lyric** means with strong emotion and perhaps meant to be sung. The words of a song are called its 'lyrics'.

*Metaphor
A **metaphor** is a figure of speech in which a word is used for something which is does not denote literally, often to make a striking comparison, e.g. 'That shopkeeper is a real **shark**.'

Metre
Metre is the way in which words are arranged to obtain rhythm, especially in poetry.

*Mood
This can refer to the state of mind of a writer, especially of a poet, or to the impression of a poet which we get from reading a poem. A poet's mood can be reflective, pensive, joyful, resentful, cheerful, etc.

*Onomatopoeia
Onomatopoeia is the use of words which imitate the sound of something to which they refer, e.g. 'playing **ping-pong**'; 'waves **smashing** and **crashing** against the rocks'.

Oxymoron
Oxymoron involves using two contradictory or contrasting words together, e.g. 'a deafening silence'; 'with cruel kindness'; 'a state of organised chaos'; 'in a state of cheerful misery'.

(in) Parenthesis/parentheses
This means in brackets or marked off from the rest of a sentence by commas.

Personification
Personification (literally: person-making) involves giving life to something which is lifeless, e.g. by writing about a tree or mountain as if it is a living person, able to think and perhaps speak.

Plot
A **plot** is the story-line in a film, novel or story.

*Pun
A **pun** is a humorous play on words.

Rhetorical question
A **rhetorical question** is a question to which no answer is expected. It is used to arouse interest.

*Rhyme scheme
A **rhyme scheme** is the way in which words (usually at the end of lines in poetry) have the same or a very similar sound. When rhyming couplets are used, the rhyme scheme may be *a, a, b, b, c, c, d, d*, etc. If alternate lines rhyme, the scheme may be *a, b, a, b; c, d, c, d*. In a limerick, the rhyme scheme is usually *a, a, b, b, a*.

*Rhythm
Rhythm is the (often regular) beat in a line of poetry, somewhat like the waves breaking regularly on a beach. Sometimes poets will change the rhythm within a poem to suit whatever it is that they are writing about in different parts of the poem.

Run-on line
In a poem, a **run-on line** occurs when part of a sentence is on one line and the rest of the sentence is on the next line.

*Sarcasm
Sarcasm is an expression intended to cause pain or embarrassment by using bitter words or by making a statement that you and another person know is false, e.g.
> A student may have written a composition with very poor handwriting. A teacher may hold it up, show it to the class and say (sarcastically): 'Now here is a **fine** example of handwriting. Yes, a fine example of what **not** to do.'

Satire
Satire involves using ridicule, mockery, sarcasm or irony to expose and deride something which the writer thinks is bad, foolish or ridiculous.

*Simile
A **simile** is a comparison which is made by using 'like' or 'as'. Similes can make a description more vivid or striking, e.g. 'He sings like a frog with a sore throat.' 'Joe shuffled to the front of the class like an old man awaiting execution.'

Sonnet
A **sonnet** is a poem, usually of 14 lines, with clear rhyme and rhythm schemes. One type of sonnet contains three groups of four lines each, followed by a couplet.

Stanza
A **stanza** (or 'verse') is a group of lines which form part of a poem.

Style

Style is the way in which something is written, spoken or sung. Different people may have different opinions of a writer's style. Words which may sometimes be used to describe the style of a writer include 'dull', 'boring', 'monotonous', 'hesitant', 'inconsistent', 'laboured', 'polished', 'fascinating', 'engrossing', 'effective', 'sympathetic', etc. In an examination, if you write about a poet's style, try to quote words or lines from the poem as evidence in support of your opinion.

Suspense

Suspense involves keeping a reader (or viewer) interested by presenting him or her with a problem and then by not revealing the solution immediately. In a play or film, the suspense often increases steadily until we reach a climax. Then comes the denouement (outcome or resolution of the problem) when the problem is finally resolved.

Syllable stress

This is the amount of emphasis (or stress) which we put on (parts of) words when we read a poem. Dictionaries normally put ′ before or after a stressed syllable when they show the pronunciation of words. On some English words, the first syllable is stressed if the word is used as a noun; the second syllable is stressed if the word is used as a verb, e.g.

> To black people, Paul Bogle was a hero and a patriot but to the British he was a ′rebel.
> People may re′bel if they are treated badly.

Tautology

Tautology is using surplus words, perhaps by repeating yourself, e.g. 'The referee added on **an additional** three minutes for injuries.' We do not need 'an additional' because this idea has already been expressed by 'added on'. 'The injured man died as a result of **fatal** injuries received in the accident.' Here, we can omit 'fatal' because we already know that the man died from his injuries.

*Tone

Like mood, the **tone** of a poem can be almost anything: cheerful, happy, sentimental, joyful, one of rejoicing and celebration or it can be grim, showing bitterness and resentment. Most poems are the result of some strong emotion which the poet feels. When we want to discuss the tone of a poem, we can start by considering the emotions felt by the poet and/or expressed in the poem.

Appendix 6: Problem Words

Word/phrase	Meaning/notes	Example
able to		Paul is **able to** repair his bicycle by himself.
capable of		Vimala is quite **capable of** making her own clothes.
absent from		Is your brother **absent from** school today?
abstain	decline to do something	John **abstained** from voting at the meeting.
obtain	get	We can **obtain** water quite easily now.
accompany	go with	We **accompanied** Natalie to the wedding.
adapt	change, modify	If you emigrate, you must **adapt** to a new environment.
adopt	take and keep or use	Our neighbours have just **adopted** a child.
advice	noun	Grandma gave us some good **advice**.
advise	verb	She **advised** us never to trust strangers.
affect	usually a verb	How will the changes **affect** you?
effect	usually a noun	They will have no **effect** on us.
afford	+ a noun	We can't **afford** a new car just now.
afford	+ an infinitive	He can't **afford** to buy a new car now.
age		You should know better at your **age**!
aged		My brother is **aged** 16.
already	by or before now	The men have finished their work **already**.
all ready	all (are) prepared	They are **all ready** to go now.
all right	The correct formal form is 'all right' and *not* 'alright'.	
altogether	in total	There were ten guests **altogether**.
all together	as a group; at the same time	We did not **all** go to the party **together**.

English Alive!

Word/phrase	Meaning/notes	Example
alternately	one after another	Players hit the ball **alternately** in table tennis.
alternatively	on the other hand, offering another method	You can come with us. **Alternatively**, you can stay at home.
and/with		The lady **and** the girl are our neighbours.
with/and		The lady **with** the girl is our neighbour.
answer/reply reply to	as verbs	Please **answer** this letter soon. Please **reply to** that letter soon.
ascent	going up, rising	The **ascent** of Mt Everest is difficult and dangerous.
assent	agreement, consent	In the UK, a Bill becomes a law when it has received the royal **assent**.
assistance	help of some kind	The player's injury was a minor one, so he did not need any **assistance**.
assistant	a helper	One of my cousins works as a shop **assistant**.
assure	say with confidence	I **assure** you that Miss Lee will come soon.
ensure	make certain	Please **ensure** that the work is done in time.
insure	protect against risks	All drivers must **insure** against accidents.
award	noun: something given for bravery or achievement; an award is often a certificate	
reward	noun: (often) money given for doing or finding something	
barbed wire	Don't omit the '-ed'.	Mark cut his left hand on some **barbed wire**.
based on	Don't omit the 'd'.	This film is **based on** a well-known book.
behaviour	In the CSEC exam, don't use the American spelling 'behavior'.	
beside	at the side of	Kwesi sat **beside** the driver.
besides	in addition to	Vimala is good at her school work. **Besides**, she is an excellent athlete.

Appendix 6 · *Problem Words*

Word/phrase	Meaning/notes	Example
better	Don't omit the 'd' in the expression 'You'd better go by taxi.'	
born	brought forth by birth	Tony was **born** in 1990.
borne	carried, endured	Poverty is a burden **borne** by too many people.
borrow (from)	get on temporary loan	Pathma **borrowed** her brother's bicycle.
lend (to)	give on temporary loan	Durai **lent** Pathma his bicycle.
breath	noun	Take a deep **breath**.
breathe	verb	**Breathe** in deeply – now out.
bring	This is used for movement *towards* where the speaker is.	
take	This is used for movement *away* from where the speaker is.	
busy	+ an '-ing' word	Miss Johnson is **busy talking** to a customer.
chalk	This word has no plural form. Use 'pieces' or 'sticks' to show the plural, e.g.	We need two more **pieces of chalk**.
cloth	a (piece of) material	Wipe the counter with a **cloth**.
clothes	garments	Don't leave your **clothes** on the floor.
clothing	garments (but used with a singular verb)	The police found several articles of **clothing** in a rubbish bin behind the store.
complement	something which completes	We often use a **complement** after the verb 'to be'.
compliment	praise or favourable words	It is a **compliment** if somebody says you are very intelligent.
comprehension	understanding	
comprehensive	covering everything (as in an insurance policy which protects against all risks)	
in conclusion	finally, at the end	
conclusively	beyond any doubt	The evidence shows quite **conclusively** that the accused man is guilty.
confidence	noun	We have a lot of **confidence** in our captain.

Word/phrase	Meaning/notes	Example
confident	adjective	We are **confident** that we will win.
conscious	living, with life	The injured man is still **conscious**.
conscientious	with a strong sense of duty	Nadia is a very **conscientious** student and always does her best.
contemptible	bad, worthy of scorn	If a motorist knocks down a child and drives on without stopping to give first aid, his conduct is **contemptible**.
contemptuous	showing scorn for others	We all felt **contemptuous** of the driver when we heard that he had driven away after the accident.
continually	very frequently	John is **continually** getting into trouble for bad behaviour.
continuously	all the time; without stopping	The earth goes round the sun **continuously**.
damage	no plural form: harm or breaking caused to a building, car or another object	The hurricane caused extensive **damage** to homes and other buildings.
damages	no singular form: compensation awarded for loss, injury, suffering or damage	Mr Harris was awarded $250,000 **damages** when he was libelled in a magazine.
dead	no longer alive	You can see **dead** fish in a polluted river.
deadly	able to kill	Mercury is a **deadly** poison.
died	past tense of 'die'	Grandma **died** in her sleep last night.
defend against		We are ready to **defend** our country **against** any invaders.
diary	a book in which a person can keep a record of daily events and future appointments	
dairy	a place/shop where people can buy milk, butter and cheese	
demand	verb – no preposition	The workers **demanded** an increase in their pay.
demand	noun + 'for'	They submitted a **demand for** a 10% increase in their pay.

Appendix 6 · Problem Words

Word/phrase	Meaning/notes	Example
despite	not followed by 'of'	The game continued **despite** the heavy rain.
in spite of		The game continued **in spite of** the rain.
discover	find out something which already exists	Who **discovered** America?
invent	make up something new	Who **invented** television?
disinterested	not prejudiced, able to make an objective judgement	
uninterested	having no interest in something	
dual	involving two people or factors, e.g. dual control of a car	
duel	a fight between two people	
each	+ a singular word	**Each** team contains several ex-international players.
each of	+ a plural word	**Each of** the teams contains some excellent players.
economic	concerning the trade or finances of a community	The **economic** news is bad.
economical	not costing too much; a cheaper method	
effect	usually a noun	It will not have much **effect** on us.
either … or	The verb after 'or' agrees with the noun after 'or'.	**Either** a cat **or** some dogs *are* making a noise outside. **Either** some dogs **or** a cat *is* making a noise outside.
elicit	produce, draw forth from somebody	He tried to **elicit** a reply from somebody.
illicit	illegal, against the law	The police are aware of the **illicit** sale of drugs.
eligible	qualified or able to do something or take part in a competition	At 18, they are now **eligible** to vote.
illegible	cannot be read	His handwriting is **illegible**.
eminent	famous, with a high reputation	Her father was an **eminent** judge.

Word/phrase	Meaning/notes	Example
imminent	about to happen	The emergency services prepared for the **imminent** disaster.
estimate	a *rough* figure showing the cost of repairs or the number of things	
quotation	a *definite* figure showing the cost of doing something	
except		There was nobody in the room **except** (for) David.
except for		**Except for** Krishnan, there was nobody in the room.
excited	in a state of excitement	an **excited** spectator/child/onlooker
exciting	capable of making others excited	an **exciting** game/film/book
exhausted	with all energy/resources used up; very tired	We were **exhausted** after the game.
exhaustive	very thorough; covering all possibilities	The police carried out an **exhaustive** enquiry.
famous	very well known for good achievements	Lara is a **famous** cricketer.
infamous	well known for bad deeds	an **infamous** murderer
fare	money paid for travelling in a taxi, on a plane, by train, etc.	
fee	money paid to a lawyer, accountant, etc. for professional services	
following	Do not add an 's' when more than one example follows 'following' but make the verb agree with the implied subject.	The **following** *is* a good example of ambiguity. All the **following** *are* good examples of ambiguity.
formally	in a formal way	
formerly	previously or at some time in the past	
friends	Use 'make friends with' even if only one new friend is involved, e.g.	I have just **made friends with** a new student at school.

Appendix 6 · *Problem Words*

Word/phrase	Meaning/notes	Example
fun	no plural form, so don't add an 's'	
furniture	no plural form, so don't add an 's'	All the **furniture** in this house is new.
get out of	Don't omit 'of'.	The old woman **got out of** the car.
gifted	with special ability; able to do something extremely well	a **gifted** child
goal	score a goal	
grateful	feeling happy or pleased with a gift or because somebody has helped you	
thankful	glad to have escaped danger or trouble; feeling relieved at avoiding something bad	
hand-picked	chosen very carefully	
hardly	only just	We had **hardly** arrived home when the storm struck.
	with difficulty	We could **hardly** move the heavy cupboard. *wrong:* My mother always works hardly. *right:* My mother always works **hard**.
have a job to do something	This can mean 'have difficulty in doing something'	
here is/are	Be careful. The subject follows the verb. Make sure that the verb agrees with it.	**Here is** a letter from Uncle Paul. **Here are** some letters for you.
homework	This word has no plural form, so don't add an 's' to it.	
housework	This word has no plural form, so don't add an 's' to it.	
hundred	as a noun: with an 's'	There were **hundreds** of spectators at the game.
	as an adjective: no 's'	There were five **hundred** spectators at the game.

Word/phrase	Meaning/notes	Example
I, me	Put yourself last in sentences like these like these:	My friend and **I** decided to go swimming. This is a present from Shaleen and **me**.
industrial	related to industry in some way	**industrial** buildings
industrious	hard-working	an **industrious** student/employee
invaluable	valuable	That painting is **invaluable**.
it's	Do not use an apostrophe if possession is involved. Use an apostrophe only when 'it's' is a short form of 'it is' or 'it has'.	
lack	verb	He **lacks** experience of repairing computers.
lacking in	adjective	She is **lacking in** experience of dealing with complaints.
at large	free to move about; not in a cage or tied up.	Be careful! There are a number of rabid dogs **at large** in this part of the island.
by and large	on the whole; generally	
lately	recently – *not* unpunctually	Have you seen Abiose **lately**?
lay, laid, laying	This verb has many meanings. It may help you to remember the sentence 'Hens lay eggs'.	
lie, lay, lain, lying	This verb also has several different meanings but you can remember 'I'm just going to lie down' and (past form) 'I lay down in the shade of a tree'. In an examination, if you are not sure which word to use, choose a different expression, e.g. 'Hens produce eggs' and 'I'm just going to have a rest on my bed' and 'I stretched out on the ground in the shade of a tree'.	

Word/phrase	Meaning/notes	Example
lose loose at a loss	misplace; be unable to find not tight One meaning is 'unable to do something'.	Don't **lose** your money. Tighten that nut. It's **loose**. The driver says he is **at a loss** to explain how the accident happened.
majority	This word can be followed by a singular or a plural noun, depending on what it refers to.	*singular:* The **majority** of this meat is bad. *plural:* The **majority** of these bananas are bad.
many, much	Use 'many' to refer to a plural countable noun. Use '(not) much' to refer to a singular uncountable noun.	**many** boys, **many** people, **many** vehicles **much** mud, **much** traffic
maybe may be	perhaps, possibly verb If you are starting a sentence, use 'Maybe' and not 'May be'.	**Maybe** it will rain tonight. It **may be** wet tonight. We **may be** flooded.
Would you mind	+ an '-ing' word	**Would you mind waiting** a few minutes?
moral	concerned with good or high standards of conduct	a **moral** victory
morale	degree of confidence, emotion or spirit	When the Maroons defeated the British, their **morale** rose considerably.
must have	The expression 'must have' + a past participle does not show obligation. It shows what we think has probably happened. Remember to write 'have' when you use this expression. Do not use 'of' instead.	Uncle is late. He **must have** been delayed by the traffic.
no sooner	When we start a sentence with 'No sooner …' part of the following verb comes before its subject.	**No sooner** had the driver got out of the car than three policemen arrested him.
a number		There are **a number** of reasons why the WI team won.
the number		**The number** of spectators at the final game was a record.

Word/phrase	Meaning/notes	Example
one of the	+ a plural noun but a singular verb (because the subject is 'one')	**One of** your answers *is* wrong.
more than one	Contrary to logic, we use a singular verb with 'more than one of …'.	There *is* **more than one** way to get to Tobago from Trinidad. **More than one** of the passengers *was* hurt in the collision.
owe	expresses debt	I **owe** you $20. Here is the money.
own	expresses possession usually	That woman **owns** at least three houses.
pass		My cousin **passed** her driving test yesterday. On our way up the river, we **passed** several villages
past	We never use 'past' as a verb. It can be a noun, an adjective, a preposition or an adverb – but never a verb form.	In the **past**, fewer people lived to be 80. It has been very hot for the **past** few days. We watched the fire-engine rush **past** us. We watched the fire-engine rush **past**.
personal	concerning a particular person, private	Miss Anna says her age is a **personal** matter.
personnel	the people who work in one place or for one company	
the poor	Words such as 'poor', 'wealthy', 'unemployed', 'disabled' and 'young' are normally used as adjectives. When they are used as nouns, they refer to a class or group of people. We do not add an 's' to them but we use a plural verb when they are the subject.	The new tax will affect **the wealthy** but have no effect on **the poor**.
practice	noun	**Practice** makes perfect. You need more **practice**.
practise	verb	You need to **practise** more often.
principal	noun: the head of a school or other institution	Miss Harris is the **Principal** of this school.
	adjective: first, main, major	The **principal** reason is the cost of the project.

Word/phrase	Meaning/notes	Example
punctuation	We cannot add an 's' to this word. The plural form is 'punctuation marks'.	
raise	We can raise a price, a temperature, a query, etc.	
rise	Things rise, e.g. prices rise, the temperature rises, hot air rises.	
respectable	a person (or thing) that is good, so we respect him or her	If you are **respectable**, I will be **respectful** towards you.
respectful	showing respect for other people	
running	One of the meanings of this word is 'consecutively' (or 'one after another').	It has rained heavily for three days **running**.
scenery	This word has no plural form.	All the **scenery** here *is* beautiful.
sceptic	(US: skeptic) a person who has doubts about something	
septic	a cut or wound which has become infected and/or gone bad	
shiver	with cold	
tremble	with fear or nervousness	
in spite of	three separate words	
There is/are	Remember that the subject of 'is' or 'are' comes after the verb. Make sure that you use 'is' (or 'was') for a singular subject. Use 'are' (or 'were') for a plural subject. Spell 'There' correctly!	**There is** a road near my home. **There are** two busy roads near my home.
totally	This word means 'completely' and *not* 'in total'.	Sometimes runners are **totally** exhausted at the end of a marathon.

Word/phrase	Meaning/notes	Example
used	/yewzd/	For centuries carts have been **used** to take fruit and vegetables to market. Paul **used** a screw-driver to get the lid off a tin of paint.
used to	/yewst/ be accustomed to	I **used to** go dancing but now I never go. Sgt. Rashid **is used to** dealing with angry motorists because he often stops people who are speeding.
very	We often use 'very' to intensify an adjective ('very beautiful') or an adverb ('very quickly'). Use 'a very little man' and not 'a little-little man'. Try not to confuse 'very' with 'every' (which means 'all').	
visit	British English American English Use British English in the CSEC examination.	I went to **visit** my friend. I went to **visit with** my friend.
wake	These examples show correct usage.	I **woke** up during the night because I was thirsty. I **awoke** during the night because I was too hot. My mother **woke** me up at six thirty. Don't forget **to wake** me at half past six, please.
wander	go from place to place (often with no special aim)	The dog **wandered** away.
wonder	think about something (often with curiosity)	Paul **wondered** where his brother was.
wear	The past form is 'wore'.	The boy **wore** his best shoes to school.
weather	sunshine, heat, wind, rain, etc.	
whether	introduces the first of two or more alternatives	Do you know **whether** Sharon is at home now or still in hospital?

Appendix 6 · Problem Words

Word/phrase	Meaning/notes	Example
went	Don't put an apostrophe between the 'n' and 't'. This is the past form of 'go' and is *not* a contraction.	
were	This is a past form of the verb 'to be'. Don't confuse it with 'where' (referring to a place).	
what	These examples show correct usage.	We wondered **what** Paul's sister looked like. Vimala wanted to see **what** her aunt looked like. **What** do you want? Ask her **what** her name is.
with	Don't use 'by' in this type of expression:	Tonight you can stay **with** us.
without	After 'without' we normally use a noun or a gerund. Don't use 'without' in place of 'until':	Don't go **without** *thanking* Auntie for looking after you. In a desert, people can go **without** *food* for several days but they won't last long **without** *water*. *wrong:* Don't take a free kick without the referee blows his whistle. *right:* Don't take a free kick until the referee blows his whistle.
worse, worst	Try not to confuse these two words. Use 'worse' for a comparison between two things.	Stacy felt ill on Monday, **worse** on Tuesday and **worst** on Wednesday. The hurricane had a bad effect in Barbados, a **worse** effect in Dominica and its **worst** effect in Puerto Rico.
your, you're	'Your' is an adjective. 'You're' is a contraction of 'You are'.	**your** book, **your** name, **your** home. Thank you. **You're** very kind.

Index

a, an 346
about to 328
accident report 317
adjective 389, 409
    clauses 61, 154–7, 173–4, 409
    phrases 61, 409
    possessive 98
adverb 409
    clauses 61
    phrases 61
advertising 358
advice, giving 255
affix 409
agenda 360–2
agreement 23, 34, 94, 399, 409
aim of writer 10, 23, 26, 102
allegory 415
alliteration 53, 86, 415
always 93
ambiguity 409
anecdote 177
answering comprehension questions 180, 268
answering multiple-choice questions 6
antecedent 409
antithesis 415
antonyms 9, 32, 410
aposiopesis 415
apostrophe (figurative device) 415
apostrophe (punctuation) 97, 209, 318
applying for a job 382
appreciation of poetry 9
argumentative writing 55, 70–71, 87, 366
arranging points in order 144, 251–3
articles 346, 410
asking for information 24, 256, 302
assonance 415
at 98
attitude of writer 10, 12, 26, 52, 102, 106
auxiliary verbs 398, 410

ballad 415
business expressions 296
business letters 299–304, 306–7

characters in a story 48
clause 61, 95, 410

climax 415
cloze passage 169, 286, 332
collocation 410
common errors 138, 172, 285, 348
comparisons 64, 348
complaints 271–2
complement 410
comprehension questions, answering 180, 268
conditional sentences 282, 287
conditional tenses 396
conflict 48, 128, 415
connectives 19, 95, 410
connotation, denotation 416
construction shift 83, 110, 124, 333, 345, 369
contractions 411
convening a meeting 360
couplet 416
Curriculum Vitae (CV) 383–5

debate 159–161
defining clauses 155
definitions 327
describe 239
describing people 236, 240
describing places 238, 252
detail, significant 241
determiners 410
dialect 48, 51, 411
dialogue 17, 21, 49–50, 83, 158, 379, 411
didactic 416
difference, What's the 125, 326
discussion 71, 92, 137, 358, 365, 386
diseases 80
DO PASS 177
Drama 88, 92

ed (final) 111
elegy 416
ellipsis 416
email 27, 297–8
emotive effect 137, 354
ending 178
enquiry, making an 304
equivalent sentences 205, 258, 273
errors, correcting 34, 138, 172, 285, 348
euphemism 416

exclamations 411
explicit, implicit 416
expressing sentences in a different way 83, 110, 124, 333, 345, 369

fact or opinion? 64
fiction 416
figurative language 38, 116, 414, 417
finite verbs 397, 411
for 98
free verse 417
full stop 5, 62, 95
future actions 22, 93, 328
future, simple 282, 328, 398, 403

gerunds 366, 396, 411
going to 328
graphs 359

handwriting 4–5
hardly 171
hospital 79
hyperbole 417

idioms 170, 265, 411
if 282, 287
imagery 10
imperative mood 398
implications 106, 417
implicit 417
in 98
indicative mood 398
indirect questions 224–6
indirect speech 221–224
inferences 106, 417
infinite verbs 397, 411
infinitives 328, 377, 395, 411
infinitives, perfect 378, 386
innuendo 417
internet 298
intransitive verbs 397, 414
inversion of subject and verb 170
irony 417
irregular verbs 404–408
italics 107

LCARS 178
letters 205, 212, 299–304, 345, 384
limerick 418
literal meaning 116, 412
litotes 418
logical thinking 55, 71, 136
lyric 420

meeting, agenda 360
    convening 360
memo 306–7
metaphors 12, 38, 418
metre 418
minutes 362
mood of a verb 398
mood of a writer 418
multiple-choice questions
    answering 6

never 171
newspaper, contents 13, 28
newspaper, words from 137
no sooner 171
not only 171
nouns 391, 412
    clauses 61
    phrases 61
    possessive forms 209

object 412
on 99
only 171
onomatopoeia 418
opinion 177
orders, reporting 221
oxymoron 418

paragraphing 17
participles 347, 395, 412
parts of speech 414
past continuous 398, 400
past, simple 111–114, 398, 401
PCFAT 143
perfect, future 328, 398, 403
perfect, past 207, 398, 402
perfect, present 193, 328, 398, 402
person 412
personification 418
phrase 60, 412
pie charts 64
plot 40, 46, 48, 128–130, 380, 418
poetry, appreciation of 9, 11, 25, 37, 51, 68, 84, 86, 114, 146, 149, 163, 195, 210, 228, 243, 260, 275, 289, 320, 334, 349
prefixes 63, 357, 413
prepositions 98, 191, 390, 413
present continuous 93–4, 328, 398, 400
present, simple 22, 328, 397, 398
problem words 203, 219, 235, 267, 312

pronouns 413
   demonstrative 413
   indefinite 413
   interrogative 413
   personal 413
   possessive 413
   reflexive 139, 413
   relative 154–157, 173–4, 413
proverbs 125–7, 281, 413
Public Relations work 330
punctuation
   apostrophe 96, 209, 318
   colon 96
   comma 62
   dialogue 21, 158
   full stop 5, 62, 95, 107
   inverted commas 21, 83, 97, 158
   practice 62, 95, 96, 97, 158, 319
   question mark 96, 254
   semicolon 96

question mark 97, 254
questions, asking 24, 256

reading comprehension
   clues to meaning 78
   practice 2, 15, 26, 29, 38, 44, 52, 58, 69, 74, 86, 105, 119, 133, 151, 167, 169, 180, 199, 211, 214, 220, 232, 248, 259, 263, 278, 294, 309, 323, 338, 354, 370
re-expression 83, 110, 124, 333, 345, 393
report 28, 176, 313–17
reported speech – see indirect speech
rhetorical question 419
rhyme 10, 419
rhythm 10, 419
rules and regulations 189
run-on line 419

SAD 49, 53, 82, 231
sarcasm 419
satire 419
say it another way 83, 110, 124, 333, 345, 393
scarcely 171
sentence 413
similar sentences 205, 258, 273
simile 38, 69, 419
since 98
sonnet 51, 421
speech 164, 197, 204

spelling
   'c' final 35
   ce, se 35
   'e' final 36
   'ei', 'ie' 36
   final consonants 35, 389
   nce, nt 389
   prefixes 63
   problem words 254, 390
SSS 46, 53, 65
starting a story 49, 82, 177, 231
story
   characters 48, 236
   narrator 81
   plot 40, 46, 48, 128–9, 380
   setting 47
   starting 49, 82, 177, 231
straight & crooked thinking 55, 136
style 217, 420
subject 414
subjunctive mood 398
suffix 414
summary 18–20, 33, 47, 60, 107, 122–4, 187–9, 227, 270, 298, 343
syllable stress 420
synonym 414
synthesis 175, 208, 347

'take' expressions 341
tautology 420
tenses 396, 414
theme 10, 177
   finding a theme 142
then 95
therefore 95
thus 95
tone 420
topic sentence 17
transitive verbs 397, 414

variety of pace, 10
verb forms 397, 414
vocabulary
   antonyms 9, 32, 410
   business expressions 296
   clues to meaning 78
   common errors 138, 172, 285, 348
   definitions 327
   emotive value 137, 354
   expressions with 'take' 341
   a hospital 79
   idioms 170, 265, 411

meaning in context 3, 16, 30, 45, 59, 76, 92, 108, 120, 121, 134, 152, 168, 185, 201, 216, 233, 249, 264, 279, 295, 311, 325, 340, 356, 373
  newspapers, from 343
  in a poem 10
  practice 153, 186, 202, 218, 234, 265, 373
  problem words 203, 219, 235, 267, 312
  proverbs 125, 281
  What's the difference? 125, 326
voice 397, 414

which/that 156
who/that 154
whose 174
writer's skill 249, 250
writing
  argumentative 13, 70, 72, 87, 103, 131, 229, 245, 290, 336, 366
  arrangement of ideas 144, 251, 253
  descriptive 236, 240, 245, 251, 261, 321, 381
  email 27, 297–8
  ending 178
  factual 13, 27, 116, 141–5, 179, 197, 212, 229, 245, 261, 276, 290, 321, 336, 351, 381
  good and bad answers 65
  imaginative 229, 245, 321, 336
  length 236
  letter 205, 212, 299–304, 345
  memos 306–7
  picture, about a 38–9, 41, 46, 54, 72, 164, 261, 350, 381
  Press release 331
  proverbs, about 125
  report 176, 313, 321, 350
  rules and regulations 189
  significant detail 241
  speech 164, 197, 204
  starting 48, 53, 82, 177, 231
  story 27, 54, 72, 81, 87, 102, 103, 116, 131, 164, 179, 197, 212, 229, 245, 261, 276, 290, 321, 336, 350, 381
  style 217

you'd better 255